WARSAW

WARSAW

A NOVEL OF RESISTANCE

by
Albert Litewka

SHERIDAN SQUARE PRESS · NEW YORK

This is a work of fiction, and the characters in it are the products of the author's imagination. It is, however, based on extensive factual research and inspired by historical events.

LIBRARY OF CONGRESS CATALOGING-IN-PUBLICATION DATA

Litewka, Albert.
    Warsaw : a novel of resistance / by Albert Litewka.
      p.   cm.
    ISBN 0-941781-03-8 : $21.95
    1. World War, 1939-1945—Fiction.   2. Holocaust, Jewish (1939-1945)—Fiction.   3. Warsaw (Poland)—History—Uprising of 1943—Fiction.   4. Jews—Poland—Warsaw—Persecutions—Fiction.
I. Title.
PS3562.I7823W37   1989
813'.54—dc20   89-10697
                                                            CIP

Published in the United States by
Sheridan Square Press
A division of the
Institute for Media Analysis, Inc.
145 West 4th Street
New York, NY 10012

10 9 8 7 6 5 4 3 2 1

Distributed to the trade by
Kampmann National Book Network

*Dedicated to my mother, Leah, and
my father, Julko.*

CONTENTS

DRAMATIS PERSONAE

THE JEWS:

Abrahm Bankart, former slaughterhouse worker, labor organizer, ghetto resistance leader, wanted by the SS and the Gestapo, the father of Leah Bloodstein and Sonya Gutterman.

Crazy Isaac, formerly Rabbi Isaac Bloodstein, tortured and blinded by the Nazis and reduced to living on the by-products of his imaginary cow, Zirka.

Menachem Bloodstein, Isaac's brother, a cobbler and clandestine resistance printer.

Leah Bloodstein, Menachem's wife, daughter of Abrahm Bankart.

Amy Bloodstein, daughter of Menachem and Leah.

Joseph Bloodstein, son of Menachem and Leah.

Eleazer Gutterman, the father of Heykel and Olek Gutterman.

Heykel Gutterman, Eleazer's son, a resistance fighter.

Sonya Gutterman, Heykel's wife, daughter of Abrahm Bankart.

Leora Gutterman, daughter of Heykel and Sonya.

Olek Gutterman, Eleazer's son and Heykel's brother, a member of the Jewish resistance posing as Olek Vaczek, a Polish black marketeer and SS informant.

Victor Lombiewski, a lifelong friend of Abrahm Bankart and a leader of the resistance, living undercover in the Aryan section of Warsaw.

Dr. Emil Adler, a physician who runs an underground hospital in the ghetto.

Esther Adler, Emil's wife.

Ruth Adler, daughter of Emil and Esther, Dr. Adler's nurse.

Julius Nussbaum, a member of the resistance.

Gittel Nussbaum, Julius' wife.

Gideon Zadok, a military leader of the resistance.

Sampson, another resistance fighter.

THE NAZIS:

Eugen Glueck, an SS lieutenant ordered to enter the Warsaw Ghetto, disguised as a Jew, to hunt down Abrahm Bankart.

Hans Thierbach, Glueck's superior.

Dieter, Theirbach's adjutant.

Hermann, Theirbach's assistant, the torturer of Crazy Isaac.

THE POLES:

Stefan Mierck, Polish socialist, explosives expert and supplier of weapons to the Jewish underground.

Philip Krecji, an associate of Mierck's, arrested running guns for the Jews.

Christiana Krecji, Philip's wife.

Marc Krecji, son of Philip and Christiana.

Sister Theresa, a nun who shelters Leora Gutterman on the Aryan side.

Felix Erdmann, a document forger, one of Eugen Glueck's informants, technically a *Volksdeutscher,* or German Pole, but in fact, part Jewish.

Yanina Erdmann, Felix's wife.

Anna Voytek, the daughter of Felix and Yanina.

Ivan Voytek, Anna's husband, a black marketeer.

Nicholas Kondousky, keeper of the underground bunker, a dog breeder, former slaughterhouse worker, indebted to Bankart.

Katerina, Nicholas' housekeeper and mistress.

Jan Stracho, an anti-Semitic bully, formerly a slaughterhouse worker, now a black marketeer, the uncle of Stefan Mierck.

Szander, a crony of Stracho's.

Heinrich Lutzki, another crony.

T H E
WARSAW
GHETTO

Crazy Isaac wound through the spectral crowd, crying "Please . . . a piece of bread . . . a little water."

He picked his way carefully, allowing passage for Zirka, his imaginary cow. He led her on a slack rope, trailing several feet behind him, its frayed end knotted in an enormous loop. Around his neck a small metal pan hung on a cotton strip strung through its handle. As he walked along, his gaunt frame trembling, his lower jaw bobbing seemingly unhinged, the pan tapped softly against his chest, marking cadence.

"Please . . . a piece of bread for a pan of milk."

It was past curfew. The unlit street was full of Jews awaiting deportation. Families sat huddled together, singing quietly or whispering. The more resourceful made last minute preparations, sewing money into their clothing or devising ingenious concealments for their children. Some boiled tea or scraps of food over an open fire. A few discussed the morning, voicing hope or utter pessimism. Others prayed.

Occasionally someone looked up as Crazy Isaac went by, searching his face for a glimmer of the person they had known before the war. But there was no sign in his eyes—once so lucent and expressive, now lying shrunken and recessed like burnt coals in a ground pit—of a life beyond Zirka.

In the oppressive air of resignation, muted sounds of busywork made the night shorter, dulling the terror.

Among those gathered in the night, Joseph Bloodstein, fourteen, son of Menachem and Leah Bloodstein and brother of nine year old Amy, did not need a sign of what had been. He still remembered Uncle Isaac as the handsome, jovial man who told them enchanting stories and spun the Channukah top on its thin stem with fingers that could crush the hardest walnuts. On Passover he gave them each an extra glass of wine and saved them from bed with his sonorous rendition of the Exodus. It was longer than it need have been, and not entirely accurate, but he was teaching them history and their parents could not protest. After all, Uncle Isaac was also a rabbi.

This was not to say that he was an ordinary rabbi. Sometimes he played lively songs on the harmonica, then drew forth a handkerchief and blew his nose as loudly as a trumpet. The children imitated him, shouting "Gabriel's horn!" and honking like a gaggle of geese. This was Isaac's cue to bring the barnyard to life. He made animal sounds and comic faces and rolled his eyes around and around like marbles. Naturally, his performance always delighted the children. As far as they were concerned, Uncle Isaac could do anything, and they loved him for it.

Menachem was considerably less enamored of his brother Isaac's antics.

"For God's sake, stop making an ass of yourself," he would plead.

But Isaac could not be discouraged.

"On the contrary, my brother," Isaac would say in an easy tone, "it is you who are being the ass. The children and I are enjoying ourselves."

Menachem wondered why he allowed Isaac to make a fool of him. Aside from being an atheist, he was unable to reconcile his own image as Menachem the cobbler with that of his brother, Rabbi Isaac Bloodstein. He had a lifelong apprehension that Isaac was mocking him. Their father, their friends, the community all favored Isaac. And when Menachem finally married and raised a family, Isaac was so good with his children that Menachem often feared they preferred their uncle to their father. Yet he could imagine no remedy that would insure him proper respect.

None of these thoughts crossed Menachem's mind as he sat in the street, in a circle with Leah, Joseph, and Amy, etching an identification tag for Amy on a small square of worn yellow leather. With extreme concentration he carved Amy's name and age with a penknife. Beside him Joseph carved his own tag:

> *Joseph Bloodstein 14*
> *references in America*
> *Itzchok Meyer/New York*
> *Schmuel Katzin/New York*

Amy's references were also in New York. Menachem instructed Joseph to memorize them. He reasoned that if he and Leah were separated from the children, the tags would insure their wellbeing. Other possibilities were shunted aside as so improbable as to be unworthy of his consideration. Of one thing he was certain: America was the best place to send them.

Thus it was with some satisfaction that Menachem punched a hole in the tag, looped a string through it twice, and tied it around Amy's neck. He slipped the tag under the throat of her blouse and let it drop. Joseph was almost finished lettering his tag. Menachem readied a string for him.

Leah did not share her husband's workmanlike absorption in final precautions. Her immediate task was to secrete items of greater value within items of lesser value. She did this quietly, deftly, with an intimate knowledge of the clothing they wore and the dunnage that lay within their circle. There was no fire to work by because Menachem, trusting no one, embraced the cover of night.

Leah had heard reports of gruesome experiences befalling those who had been "relocated" before them. Menachem refused to discuss them with her. But she believed them. There had been almost half a million Jews sealed behind the ghetto walls three years ago. Now there were less, many less, dead of hunger or illness or beaten or shot to death or dragged from their rooms during wild raids and shoved into trucks and trains chartered for unannounced terminals. Once gone, there was no word from them.

The first raids had been unpredictable, but recently the madness had taken a calculated turn. People were given a time and place to report for "selection" and a reason to believe, if they wished, that they were being "relocated" for constructive purposes. What a fool Menachem was, preparing them so meticulously for death.

Even if Leah's suspicions were false, they were vivid enough to arrest her concern for anything beyond separation from her children. As for Menachem, she had parted from him spiritually the morning Joseph had found Isaac on the stairs, insensible and sickeningly disfigured as the result of a Nazi "interrogation." It burned her to recall how Menachem, the man with whom she had chosen to spend her life, had refused to allow his brother Isaac's body into the house, stubbornly insisting that to do so would mark them all for similar treatment.

Having no other choice, Leah and Joseph had carried

Isaac to Dr. Adler's house. Every day they went there to help care for him. But no amount of effort could restore him. First his synagogue had been closed down, the building ransacked and the congregation dispersed, then the Nazis had tortured him, and finally his own brother had barred his door to him. It was more than any man could bear.

And so it was, Leah thought, cursing her white-livered husband, that Rabbi Isaac Bloodstein became a ghetto legend—living on the by-products of an imaginary cow.

Joseph strung the tag and tied it around his neck. Hanging inertly under his shirt, it gave him no feeling of additional security. He knew his references by heart. He could not conceive not being able to recite them. Unless he were dead or injured. In either case, America might as well be the moon.

His father took back the pocket knife and handed him a knife with a stubby wooden handle and a trimming blade hooked like the claw of a lobster. What did he want him to do now? As he awaited his next direction, a distant sound caused a stillness in his head.

"Please . . . a piece of bread for a little milk."

His mind had not yet discerned the words, but immediately Joseph knew that Uncle Isaac was in the vicinity. He had developed a special sense for his presence. His father had tried to force him to ignore Isaac, to deny his existence altogether. He had even stopped Joseph from going over to Isaac when they encountered him on the street. More than once, Joseph has sneaked out, with his mother's blessing, to bring Isaac food or clothing and returned to be greeted by a manic trouncing.

"You have to stay away from him," Menachem would scream, "or you'll be the death of us all."

Menachem was possessed of a devil that could only express itself through the force of his hand. The more urgently Leah and Joseph implored him to be reasonable, the more

intransigent he grew. In desperation, Leah abandoned pride
and enlisted her father Abrahm's help. Abrahm was a highly
respected member of the Jewish community, a dedicated socialist, a labor organizer, and since the beginning of the Warsaw ghetto occupation, a leader of the Jewish underground
resistance. But it was useless. The longer Isaac wandered the
streets, the more Menachem became like an animal. He could
not help himself. Finally, he would listen to no one. Not even
Abrahm.

For Menachem, one feverish thought came and went. If
only he, Menachem, had been home the afternoon the Gestapo had called. He might have been taken away and murdered. At the least, he would have been tortured. But what
had happened instead, what he was suffering now, would not
have followed, and in retrospect he would have given anything
for that.

In a way Joseph shared his father's guilt. The Gestapo had
come for Menachem on the suspicion that he was an agent of
an underground resistance publication. When they arrived
they found only Leah, the children, and Isaac. Menachem, as
it happened, was out delivering papers. The officer in charge
demanded to know where he was. No one could tell him.

"All right," the officer said brusquely. "The boy comes
with us. He will not be harmed. But Menachem Bloodstein,
37, must present himself at headquarters before sundown
tomorrow. There will be no extensions."

One of the officer's henchmen grabbed Joseph by
the scruff of the neck and began shoving him out the door. It
was a horrible moment. The paper could not be betrayed. But
in a few seconds Joseph's life might be foregone. Leah
rushed forward, throwing herself at the man who held Joseph.
"You can't . . ." she shrieked, and found herself slammed
to the floor. The Jewish policeman who had been forced to
accompany the Germans pulled a short truncheon and
with several rapid twacks to the head beat her into uncon-
sciousness.

Joseph was being pushed down the stairs.

"Wait," Isaac implored. "You are making a mistake."

His calm rabbinical manner detained the chief officer, who was still at the door. He eyed Isaac quizzically.

"What is it, *rabbi?*" he asked sardonically. "Have you just remembered where your brother is?"

"No," said Isaac. "But the boy is innocent. You mustn't take him."

"I said no harm would come to him," the officer said. "Do you doubt my word?"

"No."

"Then what is it?" the officer insisted, righting himself to leave. "I have no more time to waste with you."

"There is something I should tell you," Isaac said. "Something about my brother."

"You're not as religious as I thought," the officer sneered.

Isaac looked down at the floor where Leah lay, her hair matted with blood. Amy sat beside her, whimpering.

"Well?" said the officer.

"Not here," said Isaac.

He dampened a rag and gave it to Amy to hold to Leah's scalp.

"Bring the boy back and take me instead," he said. "Then I'll tell you what I can."

Joseph would never forget the love and fright in Isaac's gaze as they passed each other on the stairs.

"Please . . . a piece of bread . . . a little water."

The words were clear now. The Bloodstein circle was transfixed by the tension that emanated from Menachem. Joseph exchanged a sympathetic glance with his mother. Amy began to cry.

"Shut up!" Menachem whispered hoarsely.

Instantly he felt remorse and extended his hand to caress Amy's head. She shrank from his touch. His eyes darted to

Leah's, then to Joseph's. Neither responded. He buried his head in his hands.

Isaac had stopped at a fire thirty or forty feet away. Around it were seated three young couples without children.

"Good evening," said Isaac. "It's a nice night for sitting in the street."

"Yes," said one of the men.

His voice lacked hostility.

"Thank you," said Isaac. "Very kind of you . . ."

He asked one of the women to hold his rope and leaned gingerly toward the fire.

"It feels good," he said, rubbing his hands together over the flame and warming his face with his palms. "Ah," he purred, his frail bony hands trembling with pleasure, "very good."

When Isaac had comforted himself sufficiently, he removed the pan from his neck, nudged Zirka into position for milking, hunkered down beside her flank, and in an elaborate pantomime, filled the pan to the brim.

"A little milk?" he said, offering the pan to the man who had spoken to him.

"Thanks, no," said the man. "We've eaten."

The man signaled to his wife, who dug into a sack and handed him a piece of potato. He skewered it with a run of wire and singed it in the fire.

"Here," he said, pointing the heated potato toward Isaac.

"Won't anyone have some milk?" Isaac entreated.

He turned the circle, offering the pan. No one took it.

"Come on," said the man, waving the potato. "It's getting cold."

Gratefully, Isaac put the pan down and pulled the potato off the wire. Squatting close to the fire, he gripped the potato in both hands and attacked it with mottled gums.

*   *   *

A strange emotion surged through Joseph. He was thinking of Leora—how much he loved her, and how he ached with the feeling that he might never see her again.

Leora, the daughter of Heykel and Sonya, the treasured granddaughter of Abrahm, had been sent out of the ghetto for safekeeping. First she had lived clandestinely on the Aryan side of Warsaw with the Erdmanns, a Polish socialist family who had been imposed upon to take her in. Then, when things had gotten too hot, she had been transferred out of the city to a convent in the countryside for safekeeping.

There had been a debate amongst Joseph's and Leora's families about whether or not to send Leora out of the ghetto. Abrahm, Leora's maternal grandfather, had opposed it. So had her paternal grandfather, Eleazer, and Joseph's Uncle Isaac. Everyone had opposed it except Sonya, Leora's mother, who feared the thought of her suffering, and Joseph's father, Menachem. Leora was her daughter, Menachem had advised Sonya, and she had the right to do what her heart counseled. Menachem seemed to take perverse satisfaction in urging Sonya to act against the will of the others.

"It's as it should be," Menachem had consoled Joseph after Leora had been sent away. "When the war is over, you'll be together again."

Joseph had been unrelieved. Leora was a person, not a box of jewelry to be secreted for safekeeping. The shame and disrespect that had recently arisen turned to anger. What right had Menachem to affect Leora's fate? Joseph's aggravation grew until his mother was forced to intervene. She understood his anguish, she confided, but he was still a member of a family. If love was not enough to keep them united, they were bound more then ever by the struggle for survival. They needed one another, she said, and that included his father, despite his faults.

His mother may have been right, Joseph thought, as long as they remained in the ghetto and Leora was in the country- side. But now they were in the street, destined for an unknown place, while Sonya had begun to regret her decision. She had spoken to Heykel of bringing Leora back.

Wistfully, Joseph envisioned himself lying with Leora in a field of thick grass beneath a soft wool blanket. He felt the late afternoon sun licking their blush faces, and the heat of her bare legs against his. Gently, he squeezed her breast, raising the nipple through her blouse. She shivered and snuggled sideways, molding herself to him, and he kissed her impulsively, taking her face in both his hands.

"Leora," he whispered, softly kissing her eyes.

It was not entirely a fantasy. So many unlikely events had transpired in his young life. Isaac had known their secret, just as he had been aware of Menachem's involvement with the paper. Yet he had accepted torture until pain itself was painless. *For our sake*, Joseph quivered, *and see what remains of him.*

Joseph's mind was aflame. As he turned to catch a glimpse of Isaac, he felt irrevocably alienated from Menachem, who sat beside him, chafing in a private hell. It was a strange feeling. One minute he had a father. The next he did not.

When Menachem had come home the day of the Gestapo visit and Joseph told him what had occurred, all bedlam had broken loose.

"Leah, start packing immediately," Menachem ordered. "We've got to get out of here before the night is out. Amy, help your mother. Joseph, do what I tell you."

Menachem began running around the apartment like a madman, throwing everything into the front room for Leah to pack, pulling things out of nooks and crannies, retrieving papers, personal effects, and various tools. Leah watched him with consternation.

"Surely you've lost your senses, Menachem," she said resolutely.

"What do you mean?" Menachem said nervously, burrowing through a pile of junk in the closet.

"I mean that we're not going anywhere," Leah explained. "But you're going to the station to exchange yourself for Isaac."

"Am I to believe my ears?" Menachem asked. "You expect me to turn myself in to the Gestapo?"

The unendurable conflict of conscience spurred him to quickly lose his temper.

"I suppose you want me to take Joseph and Amy with me," Menachem yelled. "Yes, why don't we all go. We can pack a dinner and have a picnic. A splendid idea!"

He looked alarmedly at Leah, who returned his stare unblinking. Her tears egged him on.

"Good evening, Herr Klotzkopf," he whined in a self-mocking tone. "My name is Menachem Bloodstein, perhaps you know of me, and this is my family. We've come to retrieve my brother, Rabbi Isaac Bloodstein. Then we're going to have a picnic. You're most welcome to join us . . ."

"Stop it!" Leah cried out.

Her heart was bursting.

"Isaac went for Joseph," she said, gasping for voice, "and now he's there as hostage for you. You must take your own place, Menachem. For everyone concerned."

Joseph had an odious memory of his father thrashing about in search of an argument to justify not presenting himself.

"I'm afraid," Menachem finally had admitted. "Isn't that what you want to hear? I'M AFRAID!"

It was the only time that Joseph had ever seen his father cry. There were no tears, just a low agonized moaning, almost a chant, his head rocking, his body heaving uncontrollably.

"I'm frightened too," Leah had said, "but if anything happens to Isaac, I'll never be able to forgive you."

Without prelude Joseph was suffused by a deep, soothing warmth. Uncle Isaac, crouched by the fire, was playing his harmonica. The street grew quieter as people, drawn to the music, curtailed their bustling. Isaac played slowly, mournfully, the notes quavering from his unsteady hands and lips through the late night stillness.

The song was of a poor shoemaker working through the night to finish the shoes of a rich woman's daughter. Some who knew the words softly sang or mouthed them, and Joseph noticed his father pressing his hands as hard as he could against his ears.

> *Oh strike, little hammer, oh strike,*
> *Keep driving in nail after nail,*
> *There's no piece of bread in the house,*
> *Just hunger and endless travail.*
>
> *Oh strike, little hammer, oh strike,*
> *The clock will be soon sounding twelve,*
> *My eyes are beginning to close,*
> *Give me your strength, God, please help . . .*

Joseph yanked his father's arm, trying to gain his attention. Menachem resisted, without acknowledging him, pulling more tightly into his shell. Not to be denied, Joseph sprang to his feet and stood over him.

"Look at me," he said. "Menachem!"

His urgency startled his mother.

"Please Joseph," she said, alarmed by the determination that was hardening his face.

"Menachem," Joseph persisted, *"listen to me.* We can't desert Isaac. We have to take him with us."

"But he's better off here, my love," Leah said. "We're facing the unknown. Here at least he has a way of fending for himself. People will help him."

Her voice trailed off without conviction.

"Menachem," Joseph entreated. "I won't go without Isaac. Do you hear me?"

He shook Menachem forcefully.

"Please, if you hear me answer: Will you take him? *Will you?* Father . . ."

Menachem had withdrawn beyond recall. He was oblivious to Isaac's harmonica professing the weariness of the shoemaker toiling through the long night. Menachem's body, stiff as a fossil shape, rocked to and fro, to and fro, and jerked spasmodically.

Joseph was running blindly, away from the fires, at full speed his arms flailing, his legs pumping, his feet, a separate part of him, dodging people, baggage, all of tomorrow's cargo, his mind, also a separate part of him, groping beyond the final image of his mother and sister for direction, purging itself, warding off the formidable urge to keep running aimlessly until he collapsed of exhaustion, progressively clearing itself as the first great waves of energy broke and were spent, draining him, weighting his legs, crystallizing his thoughts.

There was only one place where he could be certain of finding refuge at this late hour. He hastened there through absolutely dead streets, dead houses, devoid of light, without sound, past locked doors and shuttered windows shielding those who had escaped today's quota and were safe for another twenty-four hours.

When he reached the proper yard he stopped, slipped off his shoes, and carrying them dashed into the building. The hall was pitch black. He found the staircase and tiptoed up to the second landing. The rear apartment was just off the stairs. Covering his mouth to muffle his wheezing, he knocked faintly on the door. A few seconds passed. He knocked again and waited.

T H E
METROPOLE

A few blocks away, but still in the ghetto, Heykel stood behind a gatepost watching the entrance to the Metropole. He had been waiting there since curfew had fallen several hours ago. So far there had been no sign of his brother Olek.

As it grew cooler Heykel shifted slightly to relieve the tension that was moving upward through his body and setting in around his eyes. They were accustomed to night duty, but it was a strain to keep them on the door. To resist the temptation of closing them even for an instant, he drew his pistol from an inside pocket and pressed it first against the side of his face, then against his forehead. The touch of steel helped to clear his vision. He returned the gun to its pocket and continued staring at the door.

It was not long before he heard someone approaching from the left. That could be Olek, he thought, placing the steps at a distance of two to three blocks. His ears were honed to the long, still ghetto nights. Several more steps changed his mind. The strides were too long, too heavy, and the repercussion was of military boots. His hand moved to his gun as the German drew nearer.

From the street, the door to the Metropole was indistinguishable from those around it. But as Officer Eugen Glueck opened it and let himself in, a stream of light danced onto the sidewalk and Heykel heard coarse peals of laughter. Then the door slammed shut and the street was once again forlorn.

The brief intimation of life inside roused Heykel to imagine the Metropole as Olek had described it—a noisy, congested room stinking of roasted meats and cheap perfume. At first his mind had balked at the thought of such a *nightclub* flourishing in the ghetto. How was it possible? Yet it was not the only one. There were sundry others—all catering to the SS underworld of Gestapo agents, black marketeers, corrupt wealthy Jews, pimps, informers, policemen, schmalzovniks, male and female whores, hired killers, and the rest of the parasites, persecutors, and sycophants flushed up by the war. It was as if the sewers of Hell had backed up and emptied into the ghetto.

Heykel shook his head in the darkness. How Olek had come to have blonde hair and blue eyes was a genetic mystery. Heykel had dark brown hair and dark brown eyes, as did their father, Eleazer. But when the war broke out and the Germans occupied Warsaw, the usefulness of Olek's Aryan appearance finally manifested itself. As the underground resistance organized up, Olek was designated to play the role of a Polish black marketeer. This would enable him to pass back and forth from the ghetto to the Aryan side to help smuggle people outside, to have contact with Poles and Germans, to gather intelligence, and when necessary to disseminate disinformation.

Tonight Olek was scheduled for one of his periodic meetings with a German officer who had been assigned to track down Abrahm. Their relationship was based on intelligence and some minor black marketeering. Also, according to Olek, on something else he could not quite put his finger on.

A while had passed since the German had arrived.

Heykel knew there must be a good reason for Olek's delay.
Still, he wished that he would hurry.

A painful knot bound Heykel's stomach. It was unlike
Olek to be late. He had always been precise about everything—time, appearance, opinions. And he had always been
courageous. Even though, despite being the older brother, he
had grown up to be shorter in stature than Heykel, he was
always physically brave, taking his inspiration from Abrahm.
Olek had never backed down from anyone or anything.

In the meanwhile, Heykel was left to contemplate the
Metropole. No matter how he viewed it, he could not bring
himself to understand the people inside, especially the Jews
among them. Certainly they were not oblivious to the suffering in the ghetto. On the contrary, they thrived on it. What
was it then? Fear? The will to live? No, Heykel had thought it
through enough times to feel that it was neither. But here his
inquiry always faltered, at the threshold of an uncertain
boundary that separated human beings from hyenas.

Human Beings. Heykel repeated the words to himself.
What did they mean, when men had become Nazis? He
thought them again. *Human Beings.* Then his narrow face
assumed a twisted smile as he remembered the game in which
words were rapidly reiterated until they lost their meaning.
He shrugged his shoulders. The war was three years old, and
still it made no sense.

The Metropole was in a tizzy over a new singer. She wore
black mesh stockings held by crimson garters, a lewd petticoat
that barely reached her thighs, and a skimpy blouse beneath
which her loose breasts jiggled as she moved. Working from a
small, round platform fixed by a harsh spotlight, she recited
her numbers mechanically in a rough throaty voice.

The room on which she looked down with glint-eyed
coquettish detachment was more gross then Heykel imagined. The tables, bedecked with white cloths, were resplendent with food and liquor. Obsequious waiters paraded the

floor bearing trays heavily laden with fish, roasted game, beef, steaming vegetables, and fruit. The diners, faces flushed and sweating, stuffed themselves and laughed at the singer and called for more refreshments. Hostesses plied the trade, delivering drinks, arranging for girls, and making themselves available to special clients at special prices.

At one table a dark portly man with skittish eyes stared feverishly at the singer while his companion, the German officer whom Heykel had earlier seen entering, engaged in ironic cordiality.

"Drink up, Herr Erdmann," Officer Glueck was saying. "The bottle will not remain full forever."

Felix Erdmann poured himself another glass of wine.

"No, not like that," Officer Glueck admonished, snatching the bottle from Erdmann's hand and taking a long draft. "Life is too short. Too uncertain."

The singer was winding up her set. Dismounting the platform, she sauntered unyieldingly among the tables, ignoring the hands that reached to touch her.

"What do you say, Herr Erdmann?" Officer Glueck teased.

"We're not such a bad race, are we?"

As Officer Glueck spoke the woman passed their table. He patted her disdainfully on the buttocks.

"As succulent as a Jewess, my friend," he assured Erdmann. "And cleaner. Much cleaner and safer."

Erdmann was aroused at the same time that Officer Glueck had made him uncomfortable. The sonofabitch has a cruel knack for generating ambivalence, Erdmann thought, feigning a smile. Soon he was drinking from the bottle and laughing fitfully.

"That's the idea," Officer Glueck goaded. "Enjoy yourself while you can."

With Erdmann well under control, the officer turned his attention to the black curtain that hung just in front of the door. His ears were turned back like a dog's straining for traces of suspicion.

A pox on the bastard, he muttered inwardly, unable to account for Olek's absence. Thierbach, his commanding officer, would be displeased, but he would tell him the truth: the girl was out of Erdmann's hands and he knew nothing more about her.

Olek could help him out, Officer Glueck thought, staring at the curtain. One piece of hard news would do it. One fact. But it was folly to count on anyone who had the nerve to keep him waiting half the night.

"Be wary of informers," Thierbach was fond of saying. "If they can expose another, they can undermine you."

And yet they were a necessary evil.

"Informers are to be cultivated," Thierbach would declaim, "as one cultivates poisonous snakes—purposefully, and with great care. The resultant anti-serum will prove invaluable in eradicating the Jewish disease."

Although it was difficult to combat, the sources of the disease were relatively easy to identify. Anyone who was not *echt Deutsch* was either a Jew or an informer. Erdmann was both. Technically he was classified as a Volksdeutscher, but he was strongly suspected of having Jewish blood in his veins. Thus he was not truly a Polish German but rather a Jewish Pole, which was not much better than being a Polish Jew. Were it not for his value as an intelligence source, he would have been thrown right into the ghetto. It was an atypical situation.

Vaczek, in contrast, was simply a Polish informer. Yes, and he has less to lose, Officer Glueck thought. I must be more careful with him.

He checked his watch. It was well after midnight. Something was definitely wrong.

Time was crawling over Officer Glueck's shirt, across his face, into his ears. He had forgotten about Erdmann, who was

by now entirely tipsy, and had become obsessed with Olek.
Where the hell was he?

He stared at the curtain until he almost brought it to life.
For the first time since he had begun frequenting it, the
Metropole was getting under his skin. The thick air was suffocating, and the noise aborted every thought. He tried to
review the approach he would take with Olek, but all he could
muster was the name Abrahm Bankart. It turned over and
over in his mind until his head was throbbing.

He was on the verge of exploding when the door opened,
the curtain moved aside, and Olek entered. Despite his hostile ruminations, Officer Glueck was glad to see him. If only
the bastard wasn't so cold, he thought.

Wordlessly, Olek took a chair and nodded to Erdmann,
who half-rose from the table, bowed, and slumped back into
his seat.

"Good morning, Herr Vaczek," Glueck greeted Olek.
"You're just in time for early mass."

He watched Olek's face for a reaction to Erdmann, but
there was none.

"An explanation is in order," he continued.

"I got lost," Olek said.

He returned Officer Glueck's scrutiny with the enam-
eled, kaleidoscopic eyes of a cat.

"Fortunately, I had Herr Erdmann to keep me company,"
Officer Glueck said.

"Fortunately."

"You needn't worry about him," said Officer Glueck. "A
little too much wine, perhaps. No harm will come of it."

"Of course not," said Olek, freezing Officer Glueck with
his eyes.

Erdmann was a cautious man, It was not like him to
drink.

"Well," said Officer Glueck, "what have you found out?"

"Nothing," Olek said.

"Come now," Officer Glueck said. "Surely, you haven't
been sleeping the time away."

"Sleeping?" Olek said in his compact, even voice. "How can anyone sleep with your kind roaming the streets?"

"Enough!" Officer Glueck hissed, recovering from his relief at Olek's arrival.

He continued in a lower, surlier tone.

"Your sensitivity is touching, my friend, but you cannot address me this way. Certainly not after keeping us waiting inexcusably. Any further disrespect will weigh seriously on your future, whatever remains of it . . ."

Just then Erdmann finished the last of a bottle in one long slurp and dashed it violently against the floor.

"Waiter!" he shouted with a flourish. "Another bottle of wine for the gentlemen."

A waiter rushed in to brush up the splintered glass.

"Excuse my frankness," Officer Glueck continued, ignoring Erdmann, "but the truth is often salutary. You cannot afford to forget your place in the scheme of things."

"Is that so?" Olek said indifferently. His attention had turned to Erdmann. "You've had enough to drink," he told him, motioning the waiter not to bring another bottle. Then he addressed the German. "Why don't you let him go home? He's done for the night."

"Don't be mistaken," Officer Glueck replied. "He can leave whenever he wishes. But I think he is enchanted by the lady. Aren't you, Herr Erdmann?"

Erdmann's head bolted.

"My wife would be mortally insulted," he said.

His wounded eyes swelled with shame and lust.

"Lay off him," Olek insisted.

"Easily done," said Officer Glueck. "Just give me a few tidbits on our friend Bankart and I assure you Herr Erdmann will be well taken care of."

"That's what I suspect," said Olek.

"There's no reason to be jealous," said Officer Glueck. "You'll be well taken care of too."

"How thoughtful," Olek said.

"All right," said Officer Glueck. "Stop playing this miserable game and tell me what you've uncovered."

"For the second time," Olek said, "nothing."

"You have the gall to come late and then tell me nothing?" Officer Glueck demanded. "Next you'll be asking me the questions."

"He's still in the ghetto," Olek said, "but no one knows where."

"So," Officer Glueck exclaimed. "You know more than nothing."

"Very little," Olek said.

"But you know that he's still in the ghetto," said Officer Glueck. "Exactly how do you know?"

"He was spotted in a press of workers near the Tebbens factory."

"By whom?"

"I don't know."

"Then how did you come by the information?"

"Through the grapevine," Olek said.

"Please be more precise," Officer Glueck ordered. "With whom have you been in contact?"

"That's my business," Olek said. "Your concern is information leading to Bankart. That's what you want of me, isn't it?"

"Naturally, you idiot," said Officer Glueck. "Why else would I spare your life? You're annoying, you're repulsive, you look like a mouse, have the skin of a snake, and reek of sauerkraut. But we must have that Jew. He's spreading an insidious disease."

"As long as you need my help," Olek said, "you're best off keeping your tongue in your mouth. If not," he warned, bringing his hand to his waist and patting the hard bulge in his jacket, "you might find yourself speechless. After all, while you're sparing my life, I'm sparing yours. Isn't that true, Herr Glueck? I could do you in this second. What have I to lose?"

Left to himself, Erdmann had become absorbed in watching the singer, who was perched on the edge of the platform, smoking a cigarette. A chain of spittle had formed on his lips and was dribbling into his tie.

"A night with her would be worth a few morsels of information, wouldn't you say?" Officer Glueck started.

Erdmann looked up impotently, wiping his mouth.

"You're not too old, are you, Herr Erdmann?" the German taunted.

Olek rose abruptly.

"Our business is finished," he said to the German, "and our friend here needs to get home."

"Is that what you need, Herr Erdmann?" the German continued needling.

"Save it," said Olek, helping Erdmann to his feet.

The singer ground out her cigarette and climbed back on the platform. A few cheers went up. Olek stood supporting Erdmann. Officer Glueck remained seated long enough to emphasize his rising.

"Next time, perhaps," he said vaguely, straightening himself. "One can never be sure."

Roughly, he grabbed Erdmann's free arm, as much pushing as upholding him, and together the three men passed through the black curtain and out the door from the Metropole into the ghetto street.

MANY VOICES

Heykel was surprised to see Olek, who made a strict practice of coming and going alone, emerge together with Erdmann and the German. They had gone only a short way when Erdmann doubled over and began retching on the sidewalk. Olek and the German pulled him over to the curb and he finished vomiting beside a naked corpse that had been laid out, neatly covered with paper, to be picked up by the black wagon in the morning. When he had relieved himself, the threesome continued on its way, with Erdmann unsteadily in the middle.

A cold wave of fatigue washed over Heykel. It was almost morning. The street was quiet. Surveying it a last time, he stepped into the open and set out for home. He walked swiftly, almost soundlessly, on the balls of his feet. Sonya, his wife, would still be asleep. He saw himself sliding into bed beside her, stroking her hair, nuzzling as close to her sleep-warmed body as he could without waking her.

Only a few minutes, he told himself. But as he quickened his pace the illusion of warmth and solace vanished and he felt clammy. How long was it since they had transferred their daughter Leora out of the ghetto onto the Aryan side and from there to a convent outside Warsaw where she would be safe until the conclusion of the war? It seemed at once weeks and aeons ago. How peculiarly tragedy developed. When he and Sonya made the decision they did not imagine they could ever adjust to being without her. And yet, while their hearts ached, life went on.

The sky was assuming the bluishness that presaged dawn. Heykel passed the area where lines were already forming in anticipation of the morning's deportation. How many nights remained, he wondered, before they were ordered to take their places? Or would it end with the clatter of hobnailed boots on the stairs and the harsh command "Heraus!"

As he slipped through the yard into the house, his body yearned for Sonya's comfort.

In the dim pale of pre-sunrise that filtered into the sparsely furnished, otherwise unlit room, Sonya, Eleazer, Joseph, and Abrahm presented a tableau of incalculable sadness and despair.

In the darkest corner of the room, Eleazer, the father of Olek and Heykel, dressed in his traditional Chassidic street clothes—high black shoes, long black coat, black hat—sat in his ancient rocking chair, as he did day and night, living in it, sleeping in it, even worshipping in it since Rabbi Isaac's misfortune. From the rapid rising and falling of his beard, Heykel could tell that he was praying.

On the floor beside him Joseph lay curled in the curve of a scythe. His shoes were tucked under his head to serve as a pillow and his feet were bare. His face was puffy from crying, and his eyes shone with hatred.

Abrahm and Sonya, father and daughter, were on the cot, their backs propped against the wall, their legs stretched limply before them. They resembled disarranged mannequins. Abrahm had grown a beard, accentuating the contrast between his war-thinned face and body and his still powerful arms and hands, their strength derived from years in the slaughterhouse.

Heykel closed the door behind him and stood rooted to the floor. He was so shocked to find four people awaiting him that the presence of Joseph and Abrahm registered physically but without immediate cognition. Intuitively he understood that something catastrophic had happened. Beyond this his mind would not untrack.

As his eyes became accustomed to the light, he focused on Sonya. Her face was veiled by a cloud of gloom and he could not make contact with her. Any second now she would rise to greet him, touch him, say something. But she remained passive and motionless, unable to help, hypnotized, as were the others, by a specter that he could not see.

"What is it?" he finally whispered.

He heard his own words as if they had been uttered by someone else. Sonya, Eleazer, Joseph, and Abrahm remained fixed in their poses. As his eyes passed from one to the next, he suddenly realized that the form on the floor was Joseph, and that Joseph should not have been there. Not twelve hours earlier Leah had come by to bid them farewell. At this moment the lines were forming. Menachem would be one of the earliest to fall in. Could he have changed his mind? It was unlikely. They had tried to convince him not to go, but he was unshakable in his conviction that relocation was his family's passport to survival. Then what was young Joseph, Leora's true love, doing on his floor?

Abrahm would explain. One could always rely on him for an answer. Abrahm, their leader. The man whose life meant more than anything to them. *Abrahm?* A shiver ran through Heykel. Abrahm was no longer in the ghetto. It was a fact. Abrahm was safely underground on the Aryan side. Joseph. Abrahm. Was someone playing a diabolical trick on him?

He jumped back against the door. Without a word the figure of Abrahm had risen from the cot and was moving like an apparition toward him. Stop, he wanted to shout. Stop and explain.

"What are you doing here?" Heykel heard himself say. "What's going on?"

Abrahm enveloped him in his strong arms.

"Heykel," he said painfully, "how good to see you. How good to touch you."

Heykel was bewildered. He returned the embrace.

"Abrahm," he said reverently, "how can it be?"

He stepped back and held Abrahm at arm's length. Here he stood, sentenced to death in absentia by the Gestapo, risking his life *for what*? It had to be one of two things. Either the cellar where Abrahm had been hiding had been discovered or . . . Heykel's mind boggled . . . he did not even want to entertain the second alternative . . . the cellar must have been . . . no, he would have known about it . . . but the other was unthinkable . . . there must be a third possibility . . .

"Leora is dead," Abrahm said.

Heykel braced himself. The words hovered before him. He wanted to reject them, to wave them away, to open the shutters and let the morning sun dispel the darkness that confined him in the presence of dark figures and dark thoughts. He tightened his grip on Abrahm.

"How . . . ?" he asked, losing his voice.

The spell was broken. Sonya got up and, stepping in front of Abrahm, threw herself into Heykel's arms. Her face was wet and swollen.

"Oh," she cried, clutching Heykel. "Oh, oh . . ."

Her fingers dug into his back and she clung to him with uncanny force. From behind them Eleazer's prayer became more audible. Joseph sat up and somberly put on his shoes. The first rays of sunlight slanted into the room.

"It happened suddenly," Heykel heard Abrahm saying. "She was taken violently ill the night before last, after a perfectly normal day. The morning found her worse. Sister Theresa rushed her into the city. She died in the hospital yesterday afternoon. The cause was unknown. She's to be buried tomorrow . . ."

Heykel's ears were on fire. Only four days ago Mrs.

Erdmann had visited the convent and reported that everything was fine. Leora had adjusted so well, according to Sister
Theresa, that she actually appeared to be enjoying herself
under the circumstances. One day brought such encouraging
news. The following day his daughter was dead. Next, Heykel
thought, the sun would rise in the West.

MANY GODS

At eleven the chapel bell rang and two wardens emerged bearing a small coffin. As they approached, the mourners bowed their heads. The coffin was set on the ground and one of the wardens drew a bottle of whiskey from his coat. "Aah," he groaned, uncapping it and taking a long draft. He handed the bottle to his partner, who was sitting on the coffin, and they took turns stoking themselves until a sallow priest entered the yard.

The priest made the sign of the cross and ordered the lid pried. Inside lay a young girl clothed in a blue linen dress. Her brown hair, neatly combed, framed a slender face that was innocent save for deep lines set beneath her eyes. One by one, the mourners stepped up to view her.

She will not be anyone's bride, Sonya thought, standing over her daughter. Numbly her mind skimmed a lifetime of expectations that the war had finally managed to crush. In the beginning it had been very difficult to believe in the possibility of such a holocaust. Then, as it materialized, Leora became their only hope. They expected to die, but she would survive and marry and raise children in their memory. She would . . . NO! . . . it was useless to look back. She would rot in a Christian grave.

The priest was eyeing Sonya impatiently.

"Good bye, my love," Sonya breathed, kneeling to kiss Leora's face. She stood to walk away but her legs would not respond. Her head began spinning. In her dizziness she felt the terrible urge to lie down in the coffin and be taken to the grave along with Leora. They would try to stop her, but she would resist. "I'm going with my daughter!" she heard herself scream. Let them kill her. There remained nothing for which to live.

"Please, madam," the priest said, "let the others come forward."

Heykel caught her before she fell and guided her back to the nun and the Polish woman who comprised the remainder of their small party.

"Have strength," said Sister Theresa, receiving Sonya.

Mrs. Erdmann removed her coat and placed it around Sonya's shoulders.

It was a bright, sunny day. Standing over the coffin, Heykel marveled at the sense of peacefulness that prevailed on the Aryan side. In the ghetto the street quavered with harrowing wails and the shrill cracking of pistols. But here there was scarcely a sign of war. The air was tranquil and refreshing and the trees that surrounded the yard smelled of the forest. Has it come to two worlds, he mused?

He could not help thinking that Leora would have made a priceless bride. What pride he would have taken in leading her to the altar. And how glad he was that she had chosen Joseph as her betrothed. He had laughed when Sonya told him. They were still children. Why, at Joseph's age Eleazer had spent his days studying the Talmud, not courting. At least that was what he had told his sons. "You'll learn all you need to know about women in the Scriptures," he promised. But Olek expressed a stubborn preference for first-hand experience and Heykel, being the younger brother, naturally followed his example. They were of another generation, they said, and had no use for praying on horseback. "Perhaps not," Eleazer granted, "but your children may want to know things you will not be able to tell them."

When the time came, the Talmud had nothing to do with it. Leora asked endless questions about the war. How had it started? When would it end? Where was God in the meanwhile? The epitome of her religiosity was the desire to be married on the night of the First Feast of Passover.

"A youthful eccentricity," Eleazer would say. "But do not worry. Love will teach her the proper time for everything."

Now the guilt that had moved in like slow hunger struck at the pit of Heykel's stomach. Eleazer had been right! They should have never sent her out of the ghetto.

"*She must remain with us,*" *Eleazer had insisted. "It is God's will.*"

"*God's will is madness,*" *Heykel had argued, standing up for Sonya. "There is only the will to live, the will to continue. If Leora stays, she dies. For what?*"

"*Perhaps you are right that she will not survive here,*" *Eleazer had conceded, "but at least she will die as one of us. Let her be buried in an open pit rather than lie disguised as a Christian corpse.*"

Behind him, Heykel heard Sister Theresa consoling Sonya. For the first time in their life together a powerful force was working to separate them. Piece by piece, it was hacking away at all that had been worthwhile, demoniacally reducing their world to a senseless daily struggle for existence.

There was no longer a meaningful basis for making the impossible decisions with which they were being faced. Menachem had chosen deportation. Where would it get him? Leah had wanted desperately to remain in the ghetto. Sonya advised her to keep the children and let Menachem decide, for himself, whether to stay or go. But Leah was unwilling to risk depriving her children of their father, so she went—and lost Joseph.

What would have been, Heykel wondered, if he had not given in to Sonya? There was no way of knowing. He was powerless to revive Leora, he was powerless to guarantee Sonya's safety, he was powerless to undo what had been done or to control what was to be, and for this he felt sharp anger and hot shame.

"Good morning," said the priest. "May I help you?"

Heykel whirled about. In his absorption he had not noticed a strange man enter the yard through the hospital.

"Yes," said the man. "I have come to pay my last respects to the daughter of a cherished friend . . ."

As he went on, apologizing for his interruption and begging the priest to continue, Heykel glanced quickly at Sonya, Mrs. Erdmann, Sister Theresa. There was no recognition of the stranger in their eyes. A fierce stabbing rushed to his head. Had they been discovered?

Out of the corner of his eye he saw Sister Theresa digging her fingers into Sonya's arm to combat her faintness. Sonya was on the verge of collapse. Don't, Heykel prayed. Hold on. He tried to sort his thoughts. Where was Olek? Had he seen the stranger enter the hospital? Who was he? What did he want? As he racked his brain for a key, Heykel felt himself panicking. *My God, what did he want?*

"Surely, I have come to the right place," the stranger said, disrupting the silence that followed his introduction.

"Of course," said Sister Theresa, leaving Sonya and alertly stepping in front of the priest. "But you have come early. We are burying several children today."

The color had drained completely from Sonya's face. Calm! Heykel urged himself. Reflexively, his hand slid into his jacket. Calm, he repeated, easing it back to his side. Sonya was straining to master herself. There was no choice but to remain dumb and trust to Olek.

"On the contrary," said the stranger. "I was told to come precisely at eleven."

It's the Devil's work, Heykel thought, smarting from the fresh memory of the wardens drinking over Leora's body. He was helpless to stop them, helpless to mitigate Sonya's grief, helpless to ward off the stranger. Too much was being demanded of him. Too much of him had been compromised. He was not a saint. He could not take any more abuse. He was ready to confront the stranger.

Then why was he holding himself in tow, struggling with the impulse to lash out? What was there to hide? What more to lose?

In a flash of horror he saw the Nazis crowing over the exposure of a pair of ghetto Jews who had sneaked onto the Aryan side, disguised as Catholics, to bury their daughter in a Christian cemetery. There remained a great deal to be lost. There were his life and Sonya's. There were the lives and integrity of the Jews still in the ghetto. And there was revenge. *Revenge.* How could there ever be revenge?

"Clearly there has been an error," Sister Theresa was saying. "If you will only wait inside, I'll have someone check the records for you."

"Thank you," the stranger said with polite finality, "but I insist on waiting here. It is my obligation."

"Very well, then," said Sister Theresa, seeing that he would not be budged. "Wait here if you must. But please be respectful of the occasion."

Nodding curtly, the stranger walked some distance to the other side of the coffin, where he stopped and stood facing Heykel. He had one eye that was darkly intense and one that seemed to have no inner light.

"We have but a few minutes," warned the priest, suddenly coming to life.

Avoiding the pointed stare of the stranger, who would not avert his eyes, Heykel looked down for the last time at Leora.

His body trembled with rage and anguish. Here lay his own flesh, his love, his hope, cold and unfulfilled. And even now he could not preserve the dignity of her being. First life, then death, had been degraded beyond imagination.

"Forgive us," he said inaudibly. "We had no way of knowing . . ."

He moved away, resisting tears, his thought unended. Mrs. Erdmann and Sister Theresa approached the coffin in turn. When they had finished, the priest sprinkled holy water and recited a prayer. Then the wardens replaced the lid.

The stranger watched impassively as the priest led the small procession toward the cemetery. When it had passed out of sight, he walked briskly through the yard and the hospital and disappeared in the midday traffic.

THE ARYAN SIDE

From his vantage point, Olek had seen the stranger enter the hospital. Having no reason to suspect him, he dismissed him from mind, only to have him appear several minutes later in the yard. Immediately he sensed danger.

He watched patiently as the stranger forced his presence upon the group. He observed Heykel struggling to control himself and Sonya, supported by Sister Theresa, growing weaker. Time elongated, rendering the scene in slow motion, but he knew that it could break in an instant. He was prepared to move when Sister Theresa stepped in.

Heedfully, Olek studied the stranger as he took a position opposite the coffin. His bearing was stiff, almost formal, he wore a good suit of clothing, he seemed highly self-assured, and he was obviously trying to unnerve Heykel. But it was peculiar that once he established his position, he made no further attempt to interfere with the service.

Baffled, Olek watched Sister Theresa follow Mrs. Erdmann to the coffin. The stranger ignored them completely, concentrating instead on Heykel.

As the procession advanced toward the cemetery, Olek saw him scan the yard nervously and enter the hospital. With trained precision, he abandoned his lookout and hurried up the block in the direction from which the stranger had come.

In a minute the stranger exited from the hospital, glancing right and left, and turned toward the corner where Olek stood feigning interest in a shop window. As he approached, Olek ducked into the shop, letting him pass, then picked him up, following at a distance.

Away from the hospital the Warsaw streets were lively, teeming with pedestrians, noisy with trolleys and church bells, bustling with store activity. "Life goes on as before," Olek often said in describing the Aryan side to those in the ghetto, "but only for some."

He had inherited both his sense of humor and his fatalism from his father Eleazer, who loved to tell the old joke about the rabbi who prayed in the midst of a pogrom—"Dear God, if it is not yet time to redeem the Jews, please, at least redeem the Gentiles." He had never taken to religion, but he admired his father's stubborn courage. As old-fashioned and dogmatic as he was, he had the strength of his convictions. He didn't give a damn whether the Nazis knocked on his door and ordered him downstairs or sent him a hand-engraved invitation to report to the *umschlagplatz*: he was staying in his chair, true to himself, until he was face to face with God.

As Olek threaded his way through traffic, staying safely behind the stranger, he was careful not to display the least sign of anxiety. One didn't have to be a Chassid's son these days in order to be set upon and roughed up. The *schmalzovniks* had grown bolder recently, pouncing on fellow Poles as well as on Jews. He could not afford to be stopped for sport or profit. At one point, thinking that two young hooligans were sizing him up as a shakedown prospect, he halted in front of them and calmly lit a cigarette. Their hunch deflated, they turned and set out in search of another victim.

He closed the widening gap between himself and the stranger, changing the rhythm of his step to keep pace. Something about the stranger was nagging at him. He had made a mental note in the shop . . . there was something odd about his attire. His suit was conventional, but his shoes had curiously thick heels and soles. And another thing . . .

Moving along, the stranger acted entirely unaware of being followed. His gait was steady, he never looked back, he bode his time at intersections, and he seemed to be taking the most direct route to wherever he was going.

Soon Olek found himself in a familiar neighborhood of wide, tree-lined streets and well-kept houses. Ticking off street names in his head, he began to have an idea of where the stranger might be leading him. Holy shit! he thought. Had everything the mind could imagine become possible?

He aborted his speculation but became more cautious, switching to the opposite side of the street and following at a greater distance. Within several blocks the stranger's stride slackened perceptibly. He's nearing home, Olek concluded, certain now of his destination.

Satisfied, he stopped short and headed for the river.

ARMS

The poor worker's district smelled of cooked cabbage and kolbasse. Tattered urchins ran the sooty streets and the houses, each more wretched than the next, sat like mildewing plants beneath the dense smoke and roar of heavy machinery. It was a depressed neighborhood and yet, Olek thought, it was Edenic in comparison with the ghetto.

He passed between two flaky buildings into a yard that was not visible from the street. In the yard, which was strewn with fragments of furniture, crates, barrels, and scrap metal, stood a small dilapidated shack, its door ajar.

Olek saw a shabby room cluttered with broken objects. The floor was littered with dusty rags and moth-eaten clothing. In one corner a limp-legged table stood framed by two low stools propped atop large gray cinder blocks. Opposite it stood an iron cot with protruding springs. Against the far wall there was a large, antiquated family bed in which an old, pale, yellowing woman lay groaning.

The crone was attended by a short, blonde, chunky Polish

man of twenty-eight or so who jumped up from the edge of the bed when he heard someone at the door.

"Comrade Olek!" he said enthusiastically, sweeping his long hair out of his eyes. "Please come in. I was expecting you."

"Stefan Mierck?" Olek inquired, remaining in the doorway.

"Naturally," Stefan laughed. "You don't think I'm Adolf Hitler."

He broke into a Chaplinesque imitation of the Fuehrer. Olek frowned. With ten zlotys for every false identity in Warsaw he could buy enough arms to show the Nazis some fight. But it was a passing thought. Stefan had clear eyes, an honest face.

"Well, come in already," Stefan said, offering him a stool. "This is my mother, may she rest in peace."

"How do you do?" Olek said, coming over to the bed.

Without looking up at him, the woman pulled the stringy blankets over her chin and took up her groaning, more loudly then before.

"It's nothing serious," Stefan smiled. "She's 'dying' because my uncle said she looked Jewish."

"She does at that," Olek agreed, studying the room.

"Oh," Stefan exclaimed, emitting a high whinny, "if only my father could hear you." His face twinkled roguishly. "You see, Comrade Olek, since my father was killed my mother is not supposed to go out alone—a simple precautionary measure. Last week, as it happens, I go out for a few hours and when I return she's nowhere to be found. My first thought is that the Germans are on my trail. But I have no choice. I wait. Six, seven, eight o'clock, no mother. I don't know what to think. Finally, around nine o'clock, she shows up with my uncle, fit to be tied. It turns out that she's been sneaking out regularly in my absence to barter at the gate. As fate would have it, a *schmalzovnik* stops her and demands her money. She refuses to give him a cent, he calls a policeman, she's taken in on the suspicion of being Jewish. At the station they bring on a priest who asks her to recite certain prayers. She tells him to go to hell in a skillet. When they go to lock her up, she mentions my uncle's name. Fortunately, he's a smuggler, very friendly with the police, and in no time she's released in his custody. On the way home he scolds her for having gone out. And to bury the fright in her he tells her that the *schmalzovnik* was right, she looks as Jewish as a rabbi's wife. The next time she pulls this stunt, he tells her, he'll let her sit in the jail. Now tell me Comrade Olek," he concluded, "can you imagine those pinheads keeping my mother? She would drive them crazy."

At this the woman produced an extended, highly theatrical moan. Stefan burst into laughter.

The words "on suspicion of being Jewish" snaked through Olek's mind. He wavered momentarily over whether or not to broach the subject of his visit with his flighty host.

"You know why I came?"

"But of course," Stefan answered. "And I must say, it's an honor to meet a member of your underground." He extended his hand to Olek. "I'll do everything I can to help you."

"We need guns and explosives," Olek said. "Especially rifles. A machine gun would be a godsend. But we'll take revolvers, grenades . . . anything with fire power."

"I know," Stefan bubbled with amiable cleverness. "That's why they sent you to me. I have a friend who's a conductor on the Warsaw-Radom line. The rest is very simple. Where are there guns? In Radom. And what part of a train is most likely to be overlooked in an inspection? The locomotive."

"And if they checked the locomotive?" Olek asked.

"Then I've lost a friend," said Stefan.

Olek smiled at his light-heartedness.

"You make it sound so easy."

"It is," Stefan said.

"I assure you it isn't," Olek said.

"You'll see," Stefan said. "I may even round up a tank."

"If you don't," Olek said, "and if the train scheme fails, have you any alternatives?"

"I have some contacts," Stefan said. "I can come and go freely, and I can concoct bombs the likes of which no man has ever seen."

"How soon can you reach your friend?" Olek asked.

"Tomorrow," Stefan said.

"All right," Olek said, "find out what's available, when, at what price. Then we'll lay a plan."

"Agreed," Stefan said exuberantly.

Olek rose to leave.

"Not yet," Stefan said, blocking his path. "This calls for a celebration."

"There's nothing to celebrate," Olek said.

"Make yourself at home," said Stefan, not to be denied.

He ran out, promising to return in five minutes.

Olek stretched out on the cot. He was ennervated by endless days and nights of tension and sleeplessness. Often, when he did have a chance to doze off, he would be jarred back to consciousness by a premonition that he would not awaken. Frequently he felt more tired after a dream-filled sleep than before. Whether awake or asleep, his mind was preoccupied with one thing: *Resistance*. He had no illusions about the imminence of death. But he would not submit his life for terminal processing. They would have to take it from him.

The old woman groaned, bringing Olek to his feet.

"Grrr," he muttered, clearing his head. "I almost fell asleep."

"It wouldn't have hurt you," said Stefan, who had returned with a bottle of whiskey. "Here, this will help dissolve the cobwebs."

He poured Olek a full glass and retained the bottle for himself.

"Cheers," he said, saluting Olek.

"To life," Olek rejoined.

Stefan put the bottle to his lips and tipped his head to swill.

"You know," he said, smacking his chest after the long

swallow, "as long as you keep your pants on, no one would ever guess you're a Jew."

"That's very Christian of you," Olek said.

"It's a fact," Stefan allowed.

He took warmly to the whisky, guzzling with abandon, and was soon rambling on about the lifelong feud between his deceased father and his uncle. As Olek followed the story and watched two red spots bloom like love apples on Stefan's cheeks, he was suddenly filled with dark foreboding.

GESTAPO

The streets were slurred by lamplight. Walking steadily, almost arrogantly through the elegant neighborhood into which he had previously trailed the stranger, Olek approached the gate to a stolid, forbidding edifice which had been commandeered by the Gestapo. Several armed guards stood duty in front. Without breaking stride, Olek bade them good evening as he passed. They returned his greeting politely. It was a nice night.

On the ground floor of a smaller building down the street, guttural voices drilled into the hallway from a partially opened door beside the staircase. As Olek mounted the stairs, the door swung open, throwing light on his ascending form.

"Too many failures, and far too many excuses," said a blunt voice, emerging into the hall.

Concentrating on the stairs, Olek continued evenly, unhesitatingly, until he reached the fourth floor.

"Lombiewski?" he said in a normal tone, knocking at the rearmost door.

He could hear his heart pumping blood.

"Who is it?" a voice asked from inside.

"Vaczek," Olek replied.

The door opened, presenting a tiny man of aristocratic bearing with long white hair and a handsomely clipped silver-white mustache and goatee.

"Good evening," he said rather formally. "Won't you come in?"

He locked the door behind Olek and ushered him into a small, well-furnished study which served, in the middle of a Nazi neighborhood, as a strategic command post for the Jewish underground.

"You surprised me," he said, embracing Olek. "I wasn't expecting anyone."

"Neither was I," said Olek, sitting down at a square teak table the top of which was inlaid with an ivory and jade chessboard.

"What do you mean," asked his host, whose real name was Victor.

Olek watched with pained affection as Victor took a tin of tobacco and a packet of cigarette paper off a shelf and sat down opposite him. He had known Victor all his life, first as a student, then as a political disciple, and now as an agent of the resistance.

"Victor, answer carefully," Olek said. "Who knew about the funeral?"

Victor began fussing with the cigarette paper, laying six oblong sheets down at the edge of the table, prying open the tin, taking pinches of dark brown tobacco between his thumb and forefinger and sprinkling the brown sheets. Olek had dispensed with amenities, he thought, rolling the first cigarette and licking the seam. He braced himself.

"Heykel . . . ?" he said reluctantly, "Sonya . . . ?"

"Everyone's safe," Olek said. "But it could have been a disaster. Now tell me, who would have known?"

"You and I," Victor started, handing Olek a cigarette and taking one for himself. "Heykel . . . Sonya . . . Abrahm . . . Eleazer . . . little Joseph . . . the Erdmanns . . . Anna and

Ivan, I suppose . . . Sister Theresa . . . I think that's everyone . . ."

"You've omitted someone very important."

Victor took a deep drag on his cigarette and then held it in
front of him, watching the fire burn its way up the paper.

"Who?"

"A stranger," Olek said.

"What stranger?"

"I don't know," Olek said. "But he was kind enough to
attend."

Victor eyes screwed up in disbelief. He listened intently
as Olek recounted the funeral. Occasionally his tongue flicked
over his nicotine-stained teeth and beard, seeking loose tobacco. Otherwise he was impassive, absorbing every detail
into the festering mass of information that was his burden.

"Taking everything into account," Olek concluded, "I
think he might well be a neighbor of yours. Or a friend of a
neighbor. What do you make of it?"

"He was after Abrahm," Victor asserted, curling smoke.
"The rumor that he's out of the ghetto is a hydra. The Germans
reasoned that if he ever showed himself, other than for a fight,
it would be for something like this. So they sent an 'envoy,'
knowing that he couldn't be turned away, and when he didn't
find Abrahm, he left peacefully."

"It may still end badly," Olek said. "Too many things don't
add up."

"Such as how they knew about the funeral?" Victor said.

"For starters," Olek said. "Also, did they think Abrahm
was going to show up alone? Unarmed? They sent one man."

"There may have been others," Victor said.

"An amusing thought," Olek said.

"Quite," Victor said, "beside the question of how they
knew."

"It had to be Erdmann," Olek said, recalling the inauspi-
cious night at the Metropole. "He's a compromised man."

"The indications are there!" Victor said, "but I'm not
convinced.

"Erdmann could have given Leora away earlier. Why would he have waited, kept her in his house, helped her out of the city, and then betrayed her?"

"Maybe he didn't have the heart as long as he was face to face with her," Olek suggested.

"Then why afterward?" Victor asked.

"As you said," Olek supposed, "in connection with Abrahm."

"The only way Erdmann would know anything about Abrahm is from the Germans," Victor said. "But since they presumably knew nothing of Leora, they wouldn't have any reason to raise the subject of Abrahm with Erdmann. The argument is circular."

Wearily, Olek closed his eyes and massaged them with his fingertips. Victor might be right. Anna had even told them how loving Erdmann had become toward Leora, playing with her after dinner when he wasn't in a foul mood, helping his wife Yanina teach her to recite prayers in Polish.

"I don't know what to think," Olek said.

Just then several cars whooshed by and screeched to a halt up the street. The nocturnal peace was broken by an echoing punctuation of rapid footsteps, followed by the metallic slam of doors. A pack of motors roared off into the night.

"My neighbors are going hunting," Victor announced.

"It's a fine night for it," Olek said.

The cars droned out of earshot, leaving a deeper silence.

"There are other possibilities," Victor said, getting back to Leora.

"For example?" said Olek.

"The convent . . . " said Victor.

"You don't think Sister Theresa . . . ," Olek interrupted.

"No," Victor said. "But there are quite a few people in the place besides Theresa. The mother Superior, the other Sisters, whatever help they have, the girls, visiting parents . . . almost anything could have developed."

"Certain things are straightforward," Olek said. "Leora *did* take ill. Sister Theresa personally took her into the city and remained in the hospital until she died. Unless Erdmann betrayed us, communications from then until the funeral should have been airtight."

"Not really," Victor objected. "Any number of hospital personnel would have been aware of her presence and death."

"You're right," Olek said, fingering his thinning blonde hair. "The pigeon could be someone we don't even know exists."

"Correct," Victor affirmed.

Pensively, he pinched the fiery head off the cigarette and shredded the butt with his middle and index fingers, which years of smoking had dyed a medicinal orange. Of all their brave comrades, he thought, Olek had the best temperament for relentlessly dangerous work.

"The fundamental question," Victor said, "is why did Leora die?"

"As to the physical cause," Olek said, "the diagnosis was food poisoning. As to why it had to happen that way, ask Eleazer."

"Let's stay with the food poisoning," Victor said, leaning forward. "As far as we know, no one else in the convent contracted a similar ailment. What would she have eaten that none of the others ate? The doctor in charge of her case was unable to identify the source of contamination. When she died, the body was removed and was not seen again by Theresa until it was brought into the chapel yard."

A low whistle escaped Olek's lips.

"For all we know," Victor continued, "she may have died from something altogether different."

"An unknown pigeon and unknown poison," Olek said.

"Correct," said Victor.

Olek glanced at the burnished wall clock. It had been risky to come in the first place and there were so many things to discuss. Victor outlined a scheme for investigating Leora's death and the stranger's intrusion at the funeral. When a plan was agreed upon, they turned to other business.

Tersely, they reviewed the difficulties besetting the resistance. The ghetto population was dropping rapidly with each succeeding day of deportations. There were probably less than half the original five hundred thousand Jews remaining. Of these, some had not reported as assigned and were therefore "illegals." The rest were waiting to be called. The current population could be broken down into three segments: those who would be deported; those who would go into hiding on the Aryan side; and those who would make their last stand in the ghetto. There was a desperate urgency for quarters for those crossing over and weapons for those staying behind.

Smelling the demise of the ghetto, and with it increased danger to themselves, the majority of Poles were becoming less tolerant than ever of that small group among them which felt active compassion for the Jews. This substantially worsened the environment in which the Polish underground had to operate. The Nazis were exacerbating the situation with their genius for inducing self-destruction. Consequently, members of the Polish underground were becoming increasingly reluctant to risk Polish lives for the Jewish cause when the Jewish cause was all but lost and the real fight for Polish survival was still to take place.

"Maybe the ghetto should field a team in the next Olympics," Olek said as their discussion drew to a close. "That would put us in the public eye."

"It wouldn't do any good," Victor said. "The world only loves a winner."

"We could register a moral victory," Olek said.

He rose heavily from the table and stretched his arms above his head.

"You're exhausted," Victor said empathically.

"Nothing new," Olek said.

Victor remained seated.

"One last thing," he said.

Olek shook his head vigorously, like a wet dog shedding water.

"We must get Abrahm back out of the ghetto," Victor said.

"It's no use," Olek said philosophically.

"There is no alternative," Victor said.

"Leora's death has been very hard on him," Olek said. "If he goes at all, he'll go when he's ready, not before."

"He has to go now," Victor argued. "The funeral incident only emphasizes this. They'll stop at nothing to get him."

"Where will we put him?" Olek asked. "He can't return to the same place."

"It will be worked out within forty-eight hours," Victor said.

"Don't bet on his cooperation," Olek said.

Victor looked up at him sternly, his eyes aflame with fierce determination.

"The day is coming, Olek," he said, thrusting his tiny fist in the air. "*Our* day is coming. But whatever else happens, *Abrahm must not die!*"

JESSE OWENS

"T hen I order you, as of midnight tomorrow . . ."

Officer Eugen Glueck removed his jacket, draped it over a chair, eased off his shoes, and reclined on his bed. Would it have made any difference, he wondered, if he had somehow known to wear his uniform? Without it he resembled less an officer of the German Reich than a plump stool-pigeon. He was short and stocky, had dark curly hair, and was bitterly sensitive about his long, flared nose, which had been an object of ridicule since his early school days. On another person it might have gone unmentioned. But in his case it accentuated his non-Aryan appearance and in the eyes of some made him seem distinctly Jewish.

His gun belt lay beside him on the bed. He patted the holster reassuringly. It was solid—durable leather encasing hard steel—and dependable. He liked the feeling of it strapped across his waist. Even lying down, it gave him basic security. No one could barge into his room against his will. He could rest easily. A gun made all the difference in the world.

As he tried to unwind, the mounting tension that he had

been forced to control during the day rose swiftly on him. In the privacy of his room he could no longer contain it. A devitalizing energy rushed through his body, making him feel weak. He was deeply afraid.

It had not happened in any of the ways that he had secretly grappled with over the years. Yet he had not been trapped unaware. No one had outfoxed him. Nothing had taken place that he could not have anticipated. A series of events had occurred that should have been prevented, or avoided, or handled differently. Inexplicably, he had let them develop, knowing half-consciously that he should not. At times he had the perception that he, rather than an external force, was spinning the web that was closing in on him. But his compulsion bore a mechanism that anesthetized his anxiety whenever it threatened to force him back onto the narrowest course of self-preservation.

So, finally, one part of him had allowed Thierbach to get the best of another part. Or was there a better explanation?

The angry black smear on the ceiling seemed to be hanging over him like a giant spider. In the beginning it had made him uncomfortable, constantly reminding him that a family had been forced out to make room for him, that the lumpy bed was theirs. Then he became used to it, as he became inured to many things, living and dead. It was just an eyesore. Until this evening.

He turned from his back onto his side, facing the wall. His gun lay behind him. He planned to take it with him and stash it somewhere, for use at the crucial time, but he would have to learn to do without it day to day.

Thierbach was mad, Eugen thought. No question about that. He had taken such farfetched measures to snare Bankart, going to the extent of staging the girl's funeral without Eugen's knowledge, and then he was wildly indignant when he came up empty.

"What kind of animal is he?" Thierbach had snarled. "Even a dog would come to his granddaughter's burial."

Eugen had remained silent, watching Thierbach gesticulate and plumbing the significance of having been bypassed in the macabre plot that was just being revealed to him.

"Speak up, Glueck," he demanded, "He's your man. What went wrong?"

"I was under the impression that he was one of mine," Eugen answered, "but apparently that has been changed. I cannot answer for a situation that is out of my hands."

"Is that so?" Thierbach sneered.

"I can pick it up again, or forget it," Eugen said, "as you wish. The other cases are progressing."

"You'll do whatever I say, will you?" Thierbach said. "That's very generous of you. Especially considering that you have no choice. You have no choice, have you, Glueck?"

"Of course not," Eugen said.

"Then I order you, as of midnight tomorrow, to transform yourself into a Jew, go into the ghetto, and remain there until you have apprehended Bankart. If at all possible, bring him back alive. Do not bother to return without him or I'll have you shot. Is everything clear?"

Eugen struggled to retain his consciousness. The room turned black, then white. Thierbach loomed like a cartoon villain, the words floating out of his mouth in bold type.

"Not entirely," Eugen said aghast. "What about a cover? Contacts?"

"We've prepared an identity for you," Thierbach said. "Otherwise you'll be on your own. We've gone as far as we can by the book. It's gotten us nowhere. Now our best chance of ferreting him out is for you to become one of them."

Eugen shuddered.

"How will I get out once I have apprehended Bankart?" he asked.

"It will depend on the circumstances," Thierbach said. "You will know how when the time comes."

"I would appreciate your being somewhat more specific," Eugen said.

"I am being as specific as you have been," Thierbach said, "in locating Bankart."

"And the other investigations?" Eugen asked.

"I'm relieving you of all responsibilities but this one," said Thierbach, stiffening. "Heil Hitler!"

"Heil Hitler," Eugen saluted.

He rolled away from the wall, onto his other side, his stomach pressed against his gun. On his dresser sat a neat bundle that had been handed to him by Dieter, Thierbach's adjutant. He rose and brought it back to the bed.

The brown paper wrapping and rough twine reminded him of the parcel his mother had prepared when Franz—his older brother and, like his father, a printer—had arranged for Eugen to go to Berlin in 1936. There had been a sturdy old wood-frame valise in the family that his father had packed two years before, but it had disappeared along with him. His father was to have gone to Berlin for a reason he would not divulge. When several weeks passed without his return, Franz set out in search of him. He came back without having found any clue to his whereabouts. Reluctantly, because his father had taught him never to trust them, Franz had reported his father missing to the Dresden police. But they were not able to help. He had vanished into thin air. In the meanwhile Franz's employer, who had originally given him an apprenticeship at his father's insistence, but who had never liked either of them, fired him on the pretext that he had been absent too long from the shop. Franz protested that it had been an emergency, but to no avail. Then he was unable to find another job. He began to drift and finally joined the SS.

Eugen undid the string and opened the bundle. It smelled like a tin of Spanish sardines. On top was a pair of dark, grimy pants. Wrapped inside the legs was a pair of crinkled black cardboard shoes with wooden heels. Beneath the pants lay a deeply soiled work shirt with a bloodstained collar. Next came a wool cap with a short, hard visor. Inside the cap were nested a goldplated wristwatch and a pair of severe, wire-framed glasses. Then there was a threadbare undershirt and, at the bottom of the pile, a pair of rancid undershorts.

Between the shirt and the shorts was sandwiched a white arm band bearing a blue Star of David.

This is some kind of bad joke, he said to himself, knowing full well that it was not. Thierbach didn't have even a morbid sense of humor. And Dieter, at his best, had the mentality of a flatworm.

He left the things on the bed and sat down in the chair in front of his dressing table. When he first moved in he had noticed traces of perfume, powder, rouge, and had tried to visualize the woman to whom they belonged. Was she attractive or plain? Intelligent? Warm? As for her husband and child, they had left no tracks, and for him they did not exist.

Now, viewing himself sullenly in the mirror, he wondered whether Thierbach or Dieter had selected that particular bundle. If it was Thierbach, the man had probably been picked to specifications. Dieter would have taken something from inventory.

Whoever handled the clothing, it was unquestionably Thierbach's brainstorm to commit him to the ghetto. Eugen had never experienced such a shock. It was as if he had been plugged into an electric socket. The order had bypassed his logical faculties and directly tapped an emotional nerve. He could not think, only obey. In retrospect, he realized that if Thierbach's sole motivation had been to punish him, he could have accomplished it much more simply. But there was more to it than that. The man was obsessed with Bankart.

There had been plenty of signs along the way that of all Eugen's cases, Thierbach cared most about this one. He was always looking over Eugen's shoulder, fiendishly making suggestions and flying into a black rage when still another ploy proved for nought. But until learning of the funeral, Eugen had not discerned anything deeper. Abrahm Bankart was a murderer and an agitator and had to be eliminated. In this light, Thierbach's splenetic antics were half-understandable.

Eugen frowned in the mirror. There was a thick file on Bankart, but he had never developed a satisfactory mental picture of him. Something was always missing. The forehead. The legs. A facial expression. Pursuing him was like stalking a ghost. People were aware of him, but no one could pin him down. He appeared and disappeared seemingly at will, leaving his influence behind, but not a trail.

Officially, there were six counts against him—five on murder, and one on conspiring to publish an illegal newspaper. For all he had seen, it nauseated Eugen to recall how that poor rabbi had kept silence through the most brutal interrogation he could remember witnessing. He would not be beaten, burned, or shocked into acknowledging the newspaper or renouncing his dignity—and when Hermann gouged his eyes out, his vacant face took on a strange, supernatural expression that alarmed Thierbach's goons so powerfully they tried to kick it out of his unconscious head.

Later Eugen questioned his own judgment in pleading for the rabbi's life. His rationale to Thierbach was that if they returned him alive, it might convey the impression that he had broken. But he had acted emotionally. He had never intervened on anyone's behalf. And of all the victims he had dealt with, this one should perhaps most appropriately have been granted final release. Had cruelty and compassion, then, exchanged places in his psyche?

Too, Eugen thought, he was all the more moved by the rabbi because he had believed he was ignorant of the newspaper and had sacrificed himself to spare the boy. Now he was not so sure. There seemed to be a curious pattern. The better-founded the presumption that a prisoner had a connection with Bankart, the less susceptible he was to torture. They had pulled many Jews off the street, and some Poles, on the off-chance that they could gain serendipitously what they could not achieve systematically. Usually those who knew nothing broke down the quickest.

Thank God he would have a respite from that aspect of his work, Eugen reflected. He was painfully cognizant of those who, while they may not have practiced torture before becoming instruments of the SS apparatus, now craved its sensation as they craved women, cigarettes, whiskey, narcotics, and in many instances each other. But he was simply not made for it.

Eugen watched his face darken. He had not been able to apprehend Bankart with all the Gestapo machinery at his disposal. How in the world was he going to do it alone?

Four persons thought certain to be in contact with Bankart had died recently during or as a result of interrogation. In each case, one of Thierbach's informers had turned up dead shortly thereafter. The murders were so cleverly designed that to the unsuspecting eye several of them appeared to be natural deaths. Despite a painstaking investigation, there were no clues to the identity of the killers. But for circumstantial reasons, and because Thierbach had anything but an unsuspecting eye, Bankart was charged with all four murders.

To this day, Eugen had been unable to substantiate the charges to his own satisfaction. Publicly, of course, this made no difference. But privately he could not ignore the ramifications of the indictment. If Bankart was innocent, there was not much of a problem. He had unquestionably committed the fifth murder and would be brought to justice for it. But if he was truly responsible for the others, there was cause for grave personal concern—because whoever had engineered them was not only a cold-blooded murderer, but also knew far too much.

Since the murders, Eugen had found himself increasingly nervous about whom he could or could not trust. He became nightly more reluctant to frequent the Metropole and the other clubs. They were infested with informers, including his own, and he had learned well enough the basic lesson that pigeons were always a threat to come home to roost. Even the fairly decent ones were threatening. Vaczek, for example, had several times hinted at killing him. What was to stop him?

There it was. He could be as superior as he wished. Behind the pomp and the pomposity there was flesh that would yield to bullets, a knife, devouring fire. The cloak of Nazism was not inviolable. Nevertheless, it had stood him in

good stead. While hundreds of thousands had died, it had
preserved him. And in a day and a night he would be without it.

Eugen swallowed, feeling his Adam's apple rise and fall.
The fifth murder, the one that Bankart had indisputably committed, had occurred first. They had been lucky enough to
extract an eyewitness report from a man arrested at the scene.
According to his story, a young woman who had just finished
trading near the gate was walking back, basket in hand, when
two boys as thin as spindles ran smack into her, knocking her
over and escaping with the basket. She scrambled to her feet
and gave chase, yelling after them, but they slipped through
the passive crowd, weaving in and out, and escaped. Hearing
her scream, a Jewish policeman came over to see what was the
matter. She told him. Abruptly, he reached out and grabbed
the front of her blouse, ripping it open. A half-dozen potatoes
and onions tumbled out and landed on the stones. The policeman tore the blouse completely off her back. When she tried
to tug free he grabbed one of her breasts and squeezed a cry of
pain out of her. There were quite a few people in the street,
but they shuffled by, heads down, acknowledging nothing.
Holding a breast in one hand, the policeman lifted the
woman's skirt with the other, raising it almost to her waist and
lowering his head as if searching for something. When she
asked him to unhand her, he began clawing at her underpants
and grunting obscenities. She started to fight her way out of
his grasp. Enraged, the policeman dug his hand forcefully into
her crotch and yanked her to the ground. Just then, out of
nowhere, Bankart appeared. He shouted at the policeman to
leave the woman alone. The policeman rose, pulling the
woman up by the hair, and told Bankart to get lost or he would
have to arrest him. Bankart insisted that he apologize to the
woman and let her go. By now a small crowd had gathered.
The policeman warned Bankart again and drew a cudgel from
his pocket. Loudly, so that everyone could hear, Bankart said
that there was no more disgusting sight in Hitler's world than a
Jew who had turned policeman to save his skin abusing an-

other Jew. The policeman responded by letting fly a wild blow that glanced off Bankart's shoulder. Bankart stood his ground, once more demanding an apology. Indignantly, the policeman struck again, with greater force, catching Bankart sharply across the nose. Before he could launch a third blow, Bankart lunged at him, wrenched the cudgel out of his hand, knocked him down, and began smashing his head against the stones. At the sight of blood spraying through the policeman's hair, a voice called out to Bankart to run. The crowd panicked, and as it dispersed, Bankart sprang to his feet and fled. The policeman died that night.

The eyewitness was an innocent bystander who ran with the crowd and had the misfortune of being cornered by a gendarme arriving to check out the commotion. He was brought into headquarters and charged with murder. That was enough to elicit a full account from him. To insure its veracity, Thierbach had Hermann give him a light working over. Then it occurred to Thierbach that the man, who worked in a bakery, was an excellent prospect as an informer.

"I'm sorry we had to cause you some slight discomfort," Thierbach told him when Hermann brought him back, "but you understand the importance of a case involving a policeman's death. You are going to be released, but under stringent conditions. While we would like to believe your story, we cannot drop the charges against you until the man you claim is guilty is in our hands. We expect your unlimited cooperation towards this end."

The man uneasily agreed to serve them and developed into an excellent source. Then one day he was found dead, apparently of asphyxiation. His demise was one of the four undocumented charges against Bankart.

Eugen glanced over at the bed. How would he bring himself to wear those filthy pants? That reeking shirt? And those shoes—how could anyone walk in them? Anyway, they would never last through the rainy season. What would he do when they dissolved?

Would never last through the rainy season . . . Jesus

Christ! He banged the heel of his hand against his temple to jar himself off the track. What a black thought. He would have to erase from memory that look of damnation on Thierbach's face. There had been no warmth in his eyes. Not even the warmth of anger.

How ironic, Eugen mused, that he was frightened to step into the ghetto for reasons that had little to do with why he was being sent there. He was afraid for his life. How could he expect to survive in another man's jungle, especially when that man was a murderer? But Thierbach didn't give a damn about murder. Slaying a Jew was not a crime. Thierbach cared about business. Intelligence. Control. Facilitating the deportations. Bankart's crime was resisting the deportations, fighting with reptilian stubbornness for every life, every building, every worthless stone. Fortunately for Thierbach, there were not many like him. They would never stop the flow of history. But they were tenacious enough to slow it down and make it expensive.

It had probably never crossed Thierbach's mind that Eugen might need warmer clothes.

"Then I order you, as of midnight tomorrow . . ."

It had required all Eugen's self-discipline just to stand there. He experienced a moment of *déjà vu*. Thierbach had always been contemptuous of him. He had often felt the sarcastic lash of his tongue on the underbelly of their relationship. And the familiar biting edge was in his voice as he recounted how Felix Erdmann had admitted sheltering not only the girl but also her mother. Why, it intimated, had Eugen not found this out? Or had he neglected to report it? What else might he have overlooked, or suppressed? He was concentrating on these insinuations—trying to determine what the strange turn to them was while reminding himself that unflinching forbearance was still the best response— when Thierbach's words hit him.

Eugen could feel the night shifting through him, tickling his skin ever so lightly, raising gooseflesh. He rose, removed his clothes, and stood naked in the mirror. Fully dressed he appeared taller and slimmer than he was. From his knees to his chest he was one squat hairy chunk.

He cupped his balls in his hands. His penis, too, even when aroused, was short and fat. He had never been self-conscious about it, though, or about any part of his body, until he had gone to Berlin. Then he had seen the panther-like black men the Americans trotted out and could not believe his eyes. They had the most beautiful bodies—supple, lithe, powerful—and such majestic bearing. And as taken as he was with their physiques, he was even more affected by their deportment. He had heard how the Americans kept their Negroes in captivity, breeding for manual labor, entertainment, and sexual gratification. He had expected them to be somewhat like circus animals trained to imitate a few of the cruder actions of men. But he was in for a great surprise. From the opening day parade through the closing, they had incarnated the highest standards of the Olympic Games.

It was such a blasphemous thought that he had to beware the whole while he was in Berlin lest he have a beer too many and blurt his mind. His brother Franz had warned him to be careful at every turn. The days when a man could afford to slip had passed. Signs forbidding Jews and other indications of the "revolution" had been taken in for the duration of the Games, but they would come right out again as soon as the world had turned its attention elsewhere. In the meantime, Hitler was treating it to a spectacle unprecedented in modern times— and God help anyone who got in the way of his triumph.

How clearly Eugen still remembered Jesse Owens churning his way through 200 meters, his powerful stride gobbling up the track, his dark finely muscled arms pumping wind, his black head held proudly, as if he was competing only with himself. The crowd had reacted explosively, thundering its appreciation. It was an uplifting moment, filling Eugen with such rising exultation that he hoped it would not subside. When it did, he had the queer wish that the crowd would remain silent after the next event. But it continued to roar as it had before.

That was what would finally make him a Nazi. No matter what went on down on the field, there was no denying the will of the Fuehrer. Owens could have won eight medals instead of four and it would not have changed anything. Hitler's image was reflected on the streets of Berlin by the throngs, the pageantry, the flags, the uniforms, every swastika, every goose-step, every salute. It was even projected in the applause for Owens, because it was resounding in Hitler's stadium—his grand theater—for the edification of his citizens and the diversion of his guests.

Eugen began to have an inkling of this in the beer halls. He heard the Americans denounced for having brought a mixed team when everyone knew that in America whites and blacks were not even permitted to travel together. There were rumors of scientists injecting the blacks with potions before every race that would leave them debilitated within a year, by which time nothing could be proven and no one would care anyway.

He did not take everything he heard seriously, but as the games progressed he grew confused.

"You know what, my friend?" said a half-drunk worker who sat down next to him in a noisy cellar. "We should make a deal with the Americans—their Negroes for our Jews. Then they could forget about the Civil War and all their ghosts and we would have an inferior class that did all our dirty work, didn't talk back like the Jews, and won the Olympics for us every four years."

Was he kidding or not, Eugen had wondered? In a few days the distinctions between mirth and malevolence had so blurred that he was no longer sure who was being cynical, who was simply ignorant, and who was drunk. And where did the philosophy that Franz had been trying to sell him for the last year fit into all this?

It was disconcerting to recall the picture the American relay team had inspired in him of thoroughbreds romping in a green meadow, their giant unsheathed cocks stiff with joy.

There was a whorehouse in Berlin which Franz had recommended where Eugen came to like a girl named Ellen. She
had made him feel welcome by talking for a few minutes
before they fucked and letting him tarry afterward. She never
rushed him, and twice she sucked him back in the middle of a
conversation and stuck it in her ass.

"Have you ever been with a black?" he had asked her one
night.

"Yes."

"How was it?"

"A man's a man," she said.

"They're said to have enormous pricks," Eugen said diffi-
dently.

"Don't work yourself into a fret," she said. "You're perfectly well equipped. Besides, there are other things to worry
about."

So there were, Eugen thought. Franz had been implor-
ing him to wake up before it was too late. But wake up from
what? For reasons that partly eluded him, it took the games to
bring Franz's message home. The tide of Nazism was rising. It
was not just another political movement. It was a revolution.
Anyone who could not find a way to swim with it would
literally be swept off the face of the earth. They were especially in danger, Franz warned, because of a certain skeleton in
the family closet. If Eugen did not get himself quickly into a
uniform, he might become the object of someone's suspicion—and that, however ill-founded, could result in both
their demise.

His penis had risen in his hand. Ellen was as real in his
mind as if she were there with him. She had turned to pros-
titution when her father was thrown into a concentration
camp. There was a soft, brown quality about her and she was
exceptionally intelligent for a whore. She had never said that
she was Jewish, but Eugen surmised that she was. Nevertheless, he was very fond of her. She had lustrous brown eyes and
hair, and warm, pliant thighs. He had a surging desire for a

mouth, a cunt, an asshole, any orifice in which to relieve himself. But Ellen was probably in a ditch, crushed between other corpses.

With his blood-filled penis standing out from his fat hairy-loins, the disgusting sight of himself in the mirror reminded him of a zoo baboon standing in a mire of excrement, peanut shells, banana peels, and vomit, earning food for his family by jerking off to the delight of Sunday strollers. Appalled, he removed his jacket from the chair and draped it over the mirror to put an end to his masochism.

There were no socks among the articles on the bed. He took a black pair from the dresser and pulled them on. The underpants were too vile to even look at. Picking them up with the neck of a hanger, he dropped them into the wastepaper basket. Deliberating briefly over the undershirt, he dumped it in too. There were limits to the requirements for authenticity. Let Thierbach wear his victims' shit-covered shorts. He would use his own.

Having donned fresh underwear, he decided to try the trousers on before the shirt so that he could find out whether or not the shoes fit. This was what worried him the most, for he had always had trouble with his feet. Shutting his eyes, he pulled on first the right leg, then the left. They were stiff in spots, as was the seat, but slipped on easily. As he drew them up, however, they began to bind him. The waist was so tight he had to suck up his gut to loop the top buttons. There was also pinch in the crotch. But overall it was better than he had expected. He opened his eyes. The man had been about his height.

Optimistically, he sat down on the edge of the bed and set the shoes before him on the floor. Please fit, he said to himself. He heard that he had spoken the words out loud. Please fit, he repeated. He was not in the habit of self-conversation, but it felt good.

The right foot was sorely cramped. He removed the shoe, worked the cardboard heel out a little, and put it on again. Comfort was out of the question, but it would do. The left foot, slightly longer than the right, did not fit at all. His anxiety climbed. He tried to think the problem through, but a cloud of ambiguity rose like a covey of bats and drove him off. Instead, he settled for slicing a notch in the heel of the left shoe, enabling him to ease his foot in. A short walk to the door and back convinced him that he was going to suffer.

It was small consolation that the shirt fit well. The armpits were starched with sweat and body grease and stank. Whoever had worn it must have been rotting. It was clear now that Thierbach had chosen someone for his size-likeness to Eugen. Poor fellow, Eugen said.

He removed the watch and glasses from the cap. As he picked the cap up, he heard a rustling. He probed the cloth between his fingers. There was something inside. The cap was unlined. He brought it very near his eye, looking for signs of a double layer. There it is, he said, spotting a thin thread. It was woven into the perimeter of the crown. Fetching a penknife from his good pants, he pulled the thread carefully, so as not to damage the cap. Then he peeled back a round ply of material, unveiling a paper nest.

On top was a small brown photograph of a young boy in a camp shirt with an open collar, his tousled hair hanging onto his forehead, his face alive with a shy smile. Scrawled on the back were the words: "Noah/Age 12/in the forest."

Beneath the snapshot was a birth certificate in the name of Noah Silver, born March 11, 1911. Father—Ezra Silver. Mother—Myra (Bronstein) Silver. Jewish.

Last there was a work permit made out to an Ephraim Schloss. Eugen examined it expertly. It was spurious. He could not identify the source of the forgery, but it had obviously been done by a relative novice. The deportations had set off a ripple of poor workmanship. He felt sorry for Noah Silver. The wretch had been reduced to carting his hope in his hat.

He got a needle and, using the original thread, began to sew the papers back into their nest. He was surprised that no money had been included. For himself, Eugen chose to include a note for 1000 zlotys. He would have preferred smaller notes to make up the sum, but more than one note would change the feel of the cloth. The rest of his money would have to be carried in his pants. When that ran out, he doubted if it would matter exactly how much remained in the cap.

He put the cap on. The fit was snug over his thick head of hair. Then he removed the cap, went over to the sink, took a scissors that he sometimes used to trim his nostrils, and began snipping off his locks in curly tufts. Soon the sink and floor around him were strewn with hair. He ran his hand over his head. It felt like a scouring brush that had lost most of its bristles.

Not satisfied, he picked up his razor and without wetting it scraped off his sideburns up to the tops of his ears. He felt the sting of the dry blade catching his skin. He knew he was bleeding but it made no difference. The blood would cake and add to his disguise.

Now he retrieved the cap and put it on again. It felt looser than before, but rougher where the lining met his stubble. Taking off his watch, which he had kept on out of habit when he stripped, he replaced it with Silver's. It was stopped at 5:26. His own watch showed 1:38. Midnight had come and gone. Less than twenty-four hours remained.

Standing, he tried on the glasses and almost fell over. Silver had been terribly shortsighted. Once they took his glasses away, he must have been helpless. Poor fellow, Eugen said again. The words gave him a brandywine feeling.

He was curious to see himself. For years he had paraded in front of the mirror in his resplendent uniform or with his balls hanging. Now he would take a look at Noah Silver. He put the glasses in his pocket and shambled over to the dresser. The shoes made him walk as if he had aged drastically. Removing his jacket from the mirror, he flung it across at the bed. It missed and landed on the floor.

Standing before the mirror, he averted his eyes, then looked again. It was startling. All that was left of Eugen Glueck was the nose.

Moving slowly, he went back over to the bed. He had

purposely left the arm band there, planning not to profane himself until the moment before he crossed into the ghetto. As a servant of the black swastika, gravely locked in a white circle on a field of red, he had learned to despise the white band with the blue six-pointed star branded upon it. But it was no use being squeamish. There was a job to do.

He slipped the band over his wrist and pulled it up until its lower edge was just above his elbow. How thoughtful of Thierbach to provide him with all the appurtenances of his role, he reflected morbidly. Returning to the mirror, he settled in front of the image that Bankart would see. *Bankart.* He would never allow himself to be taken alive.

What a sight, Eugen heard himself say. For a few minutes he sat looking into a world beyond the glass. Then he rose, picked his jacket up off the floor, and put it on over his filthy shirt. Curling up on the bed, he closed his eyes and made a wish that sleep would come swiftly. This was his last night as a German. Tomorrow he became a Jew.

HEYKEL'S DREAM

Heykel and Sonya are naked on a bed in an otherwise empty room. He reclines, propped on an elbow. She nests against him, the tips of her breasts to his chest, their wet loins grazing. They are engrossed in one another's eyes.

Nearby, Ivan and Anna Voytek can be heard arguing strenuously with Anna's father, Felix. Mrs. Erdmann is attempting to mediate, but without success.

The argument is bitter.

In the background a rubber ball is bouncing, bouncing, bouncing against a brick wall. Leora talks to it as she hits it, asking it how it feels, whether it has many friends, and other personal questions.

The bouncing has a constant rhythm that aggravates Erdmann.

"Doesn't she ever get tired?" he screams in exasperation. "Just wait and see. She'll get us all put away on account of that ball of hers."

Sonya passes her fingertips over Heykel's hair, his face,

his lips. He kisses her hand. She draws his head back and fixes his gaze. He places his free hand between her moist thighs and pulls her toward him. Their faces are flushed and intense.

The mood quickens. Ivan is calling his father-in-law a swine. The hard, distinct sound of Leora's ball becomes a sodden thudding. It is Spring in the forest.

A soccer ball slams into a tree. A scuffed shoe boots it solidly on the rebound. It soars beyond an alcove where six or seven people are seated around the remains of a picnic lunch. Sonya and Leah are gossiping and watching their men cavort. Abrahm, clean-shaven and muscular, in his early forties, is playing both sides of a chess match. Eleazer, engrossed in a book on ancient Egypt, is stretched out a few feet away, his long black coat luxuriant on the new grass.

"You'd better get over here," Abrahm says, good-naturedly trying to lure Eleazer into a match. "I'm trouncing your ass."

"Then stop cheating," Eleazer says. "I have better things to do than play with a shark."

"You prefer to lose?" asks Abrahm.

"No," replies Eleazer. "I prefer that you beat yourself fairly and squarely."

"Go back to your pyramids and mummies," Abrahm says.

Footsteps pursue the ball. Olek retrieves it, lets out a war cry, and drop-kicks it into the alcove. As it skids past Eleazer, Heykel, coming from the other direction, dives for it, tucks and rolls, and comes up beside the women, ball in hand, laughing.

The scene is unnaturally limpid. The sun is translucent, the leaves and branches are sharply defined, and Heykel's vibrant laughter dies perfectly framed by silence.

Time passes.

Visions of words and faces vie for consciousness. Blood flows naturally in the abattoir. Carcasses are butchered into rational parts. Stones have long, secret lives. People die.

Time passes and people die.

Later, the sun throws shadows into the alcove. The light is cooler, but the clarity remains.

"Check!" Abrahm calls out.

No one pays him mind.

"Check again!" he exclaims. "Hey, Eleazer, take a look. You're making a devil of a comeback."

Eleazer looks up with an expression of mock seriousness.

"I am that I am," he proclaims.

Some distance away, Heykel and Sonya are lying in the trees. Their playful, rustling voices intimate the earth rejoicing. In the pure twilight, their bare flesh gleams against the bark.

ELEAZER

The room was dark. Abrahm slept across the foot of the narrow cot, his head tucked into a corner, his knees jammed almost to his chest, dreaming fitfully, starting up in a cold sweat, seeing nothing, falling asleep again. His dreams were youthful and strangely innocent of dread.

Beside him, on the body of the cot, Heykel and Sonya lay nestled together, his front snug against her back, his knees tucked into the crook of hers, one hand around her waist, under her skirt, on her stomach.

On the floor, Joseph awoke feeling chilly, curled himself into a more compact shape, and pulled his blanket around him like a cocoon.

Sitting in his chair, his head aslant as if he were asleep, Eleazer kept vigil. He had lost track of the months since he had slept at night, remembering only that it was before the Gestapo had chewed Isaac up and spit him out on the stairs. The news so upset him that he thought he had suffered a heart attack. Thunderbolts of pain shot through his chest, piercing him to the quick, paralyzing his body. For five days and nights he had sat tied into his chair with blankets, refusing to let himself be put to bed for fear that he would never rise.

How had such a thing happened, he asked himself? How *could* it happen? Every few minutes, until Heykel and Sonya could hardly stand it, he had asked about Isaac. How was he? What does he say? When would he be able to resume his duties as the head of what remained of their congregation?

His burning desire was to see Isaac, to be with him. On the sixth day Leah had sent word with Joseph that it would be possible to visit the following day. Eleazer perked up. It was a sign from God. The feeling began returning to his limbs. There was a painful heaviness, followed by tingling, then numbness pricked by myriad pins and needles, then a lightness, a giddiness, as if his arms were about to fly away from his body.

The night sped. Overjoyed at the prospect of visiting Isaac, Eleazer had reminisced about incidents that went back thirty, forty years, preceding Warsaw, to the village where he and Isaac had been born. The floodgate opened and scenes poured forth. Such as the night he and Isaac, to repay Herschel Silver for divulging that they had whispered to one another while taking an examination, stole out before dawn, milked Herschel's father's cow dry, and went from house to house depositing unexplained liters. And their transgressions with Ziva, the Village Educator, as she was called. He had introduced Isaac to her, and it almost caused Isaac to be disqualified from pursuit of the rabbinate.

In the darkness, dark himself in his black shoes, black coat, black hat, an invisible grin traversed Eleazer's face, tugging at the corners of his half closed eyes. What a rascal he had been.

In the morning Sonya found him a new man.

"Are you sure you should go?" she had asked him, handing him a glass of tea.

"Positive," he said.

He could hardly wait to see her face when he stood up without help. The tea felt good, scalding his throat, warming his insides. He liked to drink it piping hot. It was the custom of a man who rose habitually before the sun to read the Scriptures.

"Tell Uncle Isaac he must get well before Passover," Leora had said. "We can't have a seder without him."

"Hush," Sonya admonished.

Eleazer shifted in his chair. A chill ran through him. *Leora.* Was Leora still with them then? Their golden child. *Dead. Dead. Dead.* It was not quite onomatopoeic. *Dead.* How inadequate. Like God. But God had an infinite capacity for assuming meaning. Dead was just the opposite. It negated meaning. They loved her. She was not dead. She was something else. Something for which there had never been a word.

"You can be sure I'll tell him," Eleazer had said.

It was snowing outside when Joseph arrived for him. His clothes were frosted and his nose was stinging red.

Leora's face came to life.

"Good morning, Eleazer," Joseph said, wiping his nose. "Good morning, Mrs. Gutterman."

Heykel had already left for the day.

"Will you have some tea?" Sonya asked Joseph. "You look chilled through and through."

"I'm all right," Joseph said, chafing his hands. "And the snow's getting worse. The sooner we go the better."

Sonya walked them downstairs and watched them go out through the yard into the street. They were an odd pair: young Joseph in ill-fitting winter clothes, taller than Eleazer, arm in arm with him, taking small, slow steps to match his, and Eleazer, in his black regalia, like a shadow searching the white street, leaving white spoor.

"It's not so bad," Eleazer said, feeling spry.

His breath made four pearl clouds.

"Don't talk," Joseph said, holding him firmly. "Your beard will freeze."

"There's a divine spark within each of us," Eleazer said. "It keeps my beard warm enough."

At the Adler's the living room couch had been converted

into a bed for Isaac. He lay closely bundled in several layers of
sheets and a down quilt. There were bandages around his
head and his eyes were bandaged and the bandages covered
by a dark fold of cloth. The window shades were drawn and the
room was somber.

"So this is the Adler Dispensary," Eleazer said, greeting
Mrs. Adler and Leah. "Ah, and you are Nurse Bloodstein. I've
heard wondrous . . ."

"Shhh," Leah whispered, placing a finger on her lips.

She held Eleazer back as he started for the couch. Mrs.
Adler disappeared with Joseph into another room. Eleazer
was struck by the paramedical atmosphere, the darkness, the
gloom, and above all the silence. Isaac had not yet reacted to
his presence, had not spoken, had not moved.

"Isaac . . . " Eleazer said to break the spell.

Leah clamped her hand over his mouth and leaned her
lips to his ear.

"It's very serious," she breathed. "You must be completely quiet and do as I show you."

The impact of her words sent pain directly into Eleazer's
chest. He reached for her arm and leaned heavily on her. As
quickly as he could compose himself he searched her eyes and
found himself involuntarily in her jurisdiction. He followed
weakly as she led him to the couch. Holding dearly to her, he
lowered himself onto the chair that she set for him near Isaac's
head.

Pointing at Isaac, Leah passed her hand in front of her
eyes, left, right, like a metronome, staring straight ahead,
unblinking, unseeing. Then she looked at Eleazer. Did he
understand? Eleazer nodded that he did.

Leah was bending over Isaac, moving her lips so near his
ear that there was no space between them. Eleazer moved his
hands in front of his face, as Leah had done. His eyes were
open but he could not see. He had not really understood.
Beneath the black cloth Isaac's head was bound like an oblong
spool. They had blinded him. Crushed his skull. Set him on
fire. Eleazer's body ached and burned and he could not re-

member what he had learned then and what he learned subsequently.

"He knows you're here now," Leah had whispered. "You can sit a few minutes. But don't talk."

He could not talk and he could not touch him, neither the tortured body under the sheets nor the dear blind face. Nor could he bring himself to pray, for he knew of no prayer for such an occasion. He had not been prepared, and all he could do was sit in the glum room, blindly, until Leah called Joseph in to escort him home.

Eleazer had only a vague recollection of the trip back. Joseph had turned him over to Sonya and left and the thunderbolts shot through his chest again, turning his arms and legs to lead. As before, he refused to be put to bed and had to be tied into his chair. He never slept through another night.

How had Eleazer finally learned the details of Isaac's torture? Had Joseph told him on the way home? Would he have been able to relate how they had gouged Isaac's eyes out? Who had described his hands and feet, beaten until they were swollen, shapeless stumps? And the deep blistered holes in his flesh? What had Heykel told him? He could not remember. Was it Sonya who had recounted how Menachem had refused to take Isaac in? Or was it Leah? One detail was inseparable from the next. There had been shock, depression, the Adlers' apartment, deeper shock, seizure.

He had really been in pain now, not in his arms and legs, which were heavy and dull, but in his stomach, his bowels, and somewhere deeper inside him. White paroxysms gripped him—explosive painquakes such as Isaac must have felt. Isaac had not told them a thing. It was remarkable. A miracle. He had not opened his mouth, the instrument of prayer, and God had witnessed his silence.

As he sat in his chair, hardly eating or sleeping, Eleazer had begun to undergo a transformation. During the day he occupied himself with his prayer book, appearing to be deeply absorbed in it, refusing to respond to things around him. But his mind was removed, away from the meaningless words, away from God, closing in on a reality that was closing in on him. At night, when everyone else was asleep, it enveloped him completely. And in the darkness, a shadow among shadows, he thought dark thoughts.

"Good morning," he had heard Heykel say.

"What?" Eleazer mumbled.

"I said the bear is coming out of hibernation," Heykel said.

It seemed to be early evening. Heykel, Sonya, and Leora were eating. Eleazer felt woozy.

"What happened?" he said, trying to shake the fluff out of his head.

"An act of God," Heykel joshed. "You fell asleep."

"Leora, fix Grandpa tea," Sonya said.

"Never mind," Eleazer grumbled.

While he waited for the tea, he fought to recover his dream. He was under the influence of a powerful force, a mood that could not be captured. Not fluff. Dirt. Dry earth. Too old for grass, worms, insects. Without roots or pits or any living thing. Pure earth. *And the desert shall rejoice and blossom as a rose.* It was not the desert. There were no flowers, no rejoicing. But it evoked the desert. Brown tones. Brown earth. Brown clothing. Brown bodies.

Leora handed him a steaming glass of tea and kissed him on the cheek.

"Thanks, dear girl," Eleazer had said. "You're a good daughter and granddaughter, and you'll be a good wife and mother."

Eleazer held the glass between his palms. It radiated a soothing heat that travelled through his hands to his body. The dream pulled him back.

The hills were sand brown and the tribe was a darker brown, nut brown, and its tunics were the brown of its animals. And the dead were wrapped in coarse brown sacks that would shrink around the skeletons as the bodies shrank, leaving neat bags of bones planted in the earth to be found at another time by gardeners of another tribe. He did not know what he was doing there among these people. Certainly his black garb was out of place. His shoes were uncomfortable for walking in the hills and his coat was too heavy under the stark sun. It was furiously hot, though the dead seemed not to mind. Only his hat was useful to shield him from the sun as he dug up their bodies, one after the next. When he had all the sacks spread out on the brown ground at the base of a sand brown hill, he opened the first sack and sitting down beside it in the sun he contemplated the bones, beginning with the skull.

Imagining the face, and the life that it had led, he wondered why the flesh and skin were necessary. He studied the bare spine, the trunk of the tree, and the arms and legs, its branches, and he could see that it was not like a tree, and that it could not be otherwise, any more than a tree could be otherwise or will to be. But the face could be otherwise. The skull could be the beginning or the end of life. The first skull, the second skull, each skull in the row preceded the dream and would survive it. Into the contours of the skull he could breathe an ancient life, the life of a tribesman as brown as the earth and the animals and the seeds that dropped from the trees when the fruit ripened or the wind blew. Or he could breathe into it a modern man, tribeless, not the color of the earth but of his clothes, his house, his uniform, his blood. This skull could be Heykel's. It was long and narrow and the eyes were Heykel's eyes. And this could be Olek's, smaller, thicker. And he breathed the life of everyone he knew into a skull until the sacks were full of bodies—not of skeletons but of the bodies of everyone he knew. Yes, there was Isaac's body, the eyes empty. And there was Leora's, so lifelike that he could not tell whether it had just expired or was still alive. One by one, the brown men who had been watching him from a ridge just above the foot of the hill as he resurrected them disappeared without a trace. Until there remained but one brown man, and on the ground one skeleton, and beside it Eleazer, leaning over, placing his mouth on the skeleton's mouth and breathing into it . . .

"Here," Leora had said, tugging his sleeves. "Your tea is already cold."

She took the half-empty glass from his grasp and replaced it with a full, steaming one.

"You fell asleep again," Heykel said. "With your eyes wide open."

"It's to be expected," Sonya said. "He hasn't slept in so long."

"I wasn't sleeping," Eleazer said.

"Of course not, father," Heykel said. "You were addressing the British Parliament on behalf of the Jewish Orthodox Contingent of the Polish Army Command."

"I was dreaming," Eleazer said.

"So was the Polish Army Command," Heykel said.

"Previously I was sleeping," Eleazer explained. "Now I was only dreaming."

"I see," said Heykel, eyeing him comically.

Eleazer shook his head.

"You don't," he said. "Everything has changed."

He was not sure what he meant until the words came out of him.

"For example?" Heykel said.

"The hall," said Eleazer.

"What about it?" Heykel asked.

"I want to build a broom closet in the hallway," Eleazer said.

He felt inexplicably exhilarated.

"You what?" Heykel said in disbelief.

"I want to build a broom closet in the hallway," Eleazer repeated.

"For our magnificent collection of one used broom?" Heykel said.

"No," said Eleazer. "For us."

"Our humble room no longer suits you?"

"Not in the event of a raid," Eleazer said.

"But we're well provided for," Heykel said.

His hand swept toward the sink and the floor cabinets,

behind which he had constructed an intricately engineered and camouflaged set of chambers, each large enough for one person. He had worked on them night after night, often until morning, providing each chamber with a ventilation system and a supply of dried food.

"Half the apartments in the ghetto have kitchen shelters," Eleazer said.

"I suppose you made a survey in your sleep," said Heykel.

"In a manner of speaking," Eleazer replied.

"And you came away impressed with the idea of a broom closet?" Heykel asked.

"Yes," Eleazer said.

"I think you're still dreaming," Heykel said.

Initially he did not believe that Eleazer could have become interested in such a crazy thing, but it turned out that he was deadly serious. The subject became a running debate that lasted a full week.

Heykel reminded Eleazer that he had opposed building the kitchen shelter, or any shelter at all, insisting that it was foolish to seek salvation in four cubicles behind a sink. Only God could be of material assistance against the German machine. Heykel had countered that if God had any interest in their case, he would have intervened long before. Not necessarily, Eleazer had maintained. It was not for them to question God's ways. Heykel had contended that he was not questioning His ways, he was merely building the shelter in case He should suffer a lapse during a raid. Eleazer had ended the discussion then by advising Heykel not to bother building a hole for him because he would not crawl into it under any circumstances. He was not a cockroach, God had not created him to hide behind sinks, he was not afraid of the Germans or anyone else, and if they came for him they would have to take him as he was.

Now, Heykel discovered, Eleazer's attitude had changed. He could not determine precisely why, but his logic in the matter was uncharacteristically pragmatic and free of religious assumptions. Finally Heykel was forced to admit that Eleazer was right. The kitchen shelter did not afford the security it may have promised when it was built. The Germans had probably come across too many by now. A second idea was needed.

To Heykel's complete astonishment, Eleazer had not only proposed the broom closet but worked out all the details. Their door was just to the right of the landing, making a corner with the wall facing the stairs. Behind this wall, which was blank, was an extension of their room containing their bathroom and a clothes closet. A broom closet could be built into the blank wall facing the stairs so that anyone reaching the landing would be standing directly in front of it. The closet door would have a normal waist-level knob and also a chest-level latch and lock. The closet would be stocked with utility items. It would have double walls, with the entrance to the false front space being through the bathroom. In an advanced emergency, the closet itself could be entered through one of the false walls and the closet door, which appeared permanently locked from the outside, could then be opened from within, allowing egress to the stairs.

Though he had never shown a proclivity for handiwork, Eleazer assumed complete responsibility for the project. With occasional help from Heykel at night, he worked methodically, managing everything with an architect's perspective of the whole, while performing each small detail with a jeweler's precision.

He became so involved in what he was doing that it fell to Sonya to keep clean around him, lest someone drop in unexpectedly, and to get him to eat now and then. He toiled in his black clothes and not only slept during the day but usually right in the bathroom, taking catnaps between sustained periods of exertion.

To conceal the project until is was a *fait accompli*, the shelter was designed so that everything could be accomplished working from the inside out. On the night of completion, Heykel joined Eleazer in effecting the ultimate step:

removing the last remaining layer of the outer strip of wall and replacing it with the laboriously perfected wooden door. They achieved this shortlybefore dawn. Then the system was tested and retested and found faultless. All that remained to be done were the finishing touches on the bathroom facade.

In the prime bluish-gray, Eleazer and Heykel had joined in a silent glass of tea. Unspoken but sensible between them was a melancholy reflection about Olek. Where was he this very moment? Exposed to what hazards?

Gray gave way to blue. Heykel rose to go to the bathroom. It was time to leave for work.

"You can get some sleep now," he had said on his way out, stopping to rest a hand on Eleazer's shoulder.

Eleazer folded his hand over Heykel's, pressing it warmly, and for a few long seconds felt their blood flowing together.

Then Heykel had left and Eleazer had settled into his chair. He was exhausted, the project was all but finished, and a mysterious weight had been removed from his shoulders. Still, the sweet relief of sleep would not descend. Instead, he sat with his eyes closed, seeing himself in the transparent dream light that borders day, his mind repeating what his body had performed and seeking its significance.

After so many years with God alone, he had been possessed by another spirit—a phantom force that had driven him to build the shelter and that he had thereby expelled. He could not identify it by name, nor could he visualize it. It had entered him so forcefully, and done its work so well, that its effect did not become wholly apparent until after it had vacated his soul. Or rather, until he found himself without God. For the demon had secularized him and left him a stranger within his own body.

He saw now that for him the war had been terrible not only for the reasons that were destroying others but also because he had been forced to accept it. To question it had been contrary to his most fundamental dedication. "I am that I am." God was that God was. Some things were comprehensible in light of His words. Some were not. That which was not intelligible to man was still a product of His will. It was to be accepted no less than that which was apparent to a child.

He had lived through the First World War and found it horrifying. But it had only strengthened his faith. So when this war began he was secure in the knowledge that it would travel its course and that in the long run the damage and suffering incurred would be justified by a proportionately greater good. It might happen sooner or later. It might happen here or in another world. But it *would* happen.

God was that God was. But there had never been a war like this one. One day he was making a living as a bookseller on what was now the Aryan side. The next day he was not. In the same day he lost his apartment and whatever rights he had as a Polish citizen. Overnight his fate was taken completely out of his hands. It was unexpected, but if God willed it, there was nothing he could do. He adjusted to it.

That was still near the beginning. He could not yet imagine the endless chain of cruel, unfathomable events and circumstances to which he would be forced to reconcile himself. As they unfolded, it became progressively more difficult to close his mind to them. Olek and Heykel did not attack him personally, but he saw them fighting tooth and nail against the secular consequences of his position. Of course, it had been this way even twenty years prior to the war. From boyhood on they had neither accepted his religion nor honored his passivity. Their way was Abrahm's—to militate for the rights of Jews to live publicly as fully franchised Polish citizens and privately as Jews. They would not be deterred in this fight, nor would they compromise now. Eleazer's sons would die defending his integrity.

It became an ugly irony. His integrity had been reduced to prayer while all around him people—his people—were being shot, burned, beaten, starved, degraded, humiliated. He was contributing to the effectiveness of their worst enemy—delusion. And he could not plead ignorance. He had heard his sons discuss it so many times with Abrahm and others. The Nazis' firepower, however devastating, was not as difficult to combat or ultimately as defeating as their Satanic power to keep a population at bay by spreading fear through terror, then creating artificial hopes, and playing the one against the other.

Olek and Heykel were right, Eleazer knew. Perhaps he should not have, but he had finally thought it through himself. Their resistance was daily undermined by the very people for whom they were willing to give their lives. That included him. He looked to God, as though it were still peacetime. Others looked to rumors of relocation, dreams of a new life in America or elsewhere, and in the case of many of the imported German Jews, resuming their lives in Germany. They would all die blindfolded. Only a few would tear the black cloth from their faces and confront the hangman with open eyes.

God was that God was. But Eleazer's guilt was growing. He had reached a point of paralysis. Virtually everything in which he believed was being destroyed or discredited. Only God, whom he could not judge, remained intact. So he prayed with Isaac and the others, and then he prayed alone. The rest of his time was frozen. He could not take himself outside; he hated even to hear what was going on out there, though often he could not avoid it. He could not envision the beginning or project the end. Heykel's apartment became his world, and with blind faith he sat in his chair and waited.

Until the dream. He had prayed and carried on like the Devil's fool. But he could not be accused of vacillation. One day he still accepted the war. The next day he did not. He had been faithful to the end. Now God was the darkness in Isaac's eyes.

In the darkness Eleazer watched Abrahm raise up, mumble a few incoherent words, look around with blank eyes, and drop his head back onto the cot. What could he be dreaming, this strong man with German blood on his hands who slept like a jack-in-the-box? It was a wonder he could sleep at all. He knew how badly the Nazis wanted him, and he had no illusions that they would spare him with a bullet. If they could they would tear him from limb from limb.

Heykel stirred momentarily, adjusting his position. Then he and Sonya were again a perfect still life.

Tightly wrapped in his blanket, Joseph was in deep sleep. He had not so much as twitched for several hours. Eleazer felt paternal towards him. He was an orphan now, and it was far into the night.

Suddenly there was an uproar, engines, screaking brakes, the squeal of rubber on stone, voice commands, followed by a brief silence. Eleazer's heart skipped. A burst of adrenalin virtually catapulted him out of his chair.

"Abrahm," he whispered excitedly. "It's a raid!"

Abrahm looked up groggily.

"Hurry!" Eleazer implored, shaking him strongly.

The room stirred into waking. From downstairs the familiar sounds of impending death were already in the air and rising—the wild hellish shouting, the cries, the clatter of hobnailed boots. There was no time to think. Heykel jumped up, pulling Sonya with him, and ran into the bathroom. Eleazer pushed Joseph in after them. Just as they had practiced, Heykel and Eleazer removed the wall facade.

In the seconds that had transpired Abrahm was carrying out his own plan—hastily making an escape ladder by knotting the cot bedding and Joseph's blanket end to end. He could not risk the shelter. Before the others realized what he was doing, he had opened the windows, which faced the back, and was tying one end of the makeshift rope to the framepost.

The noise was rising, the uproar mounting, the boots climbing the stairs.

"Heraus!" came the shout. "Jeder heraus!"

Sonya and Joseph had already disappeared into the bathroom wall. Heykel tried to push Eleazer in, but he would not be moved.

"Where's Abrahm?" Heykel asked as he struggled with Eleazer.

"Get in!" Eleazer ordered.

He forced Heykel into the shelter with almost superhuman strength. Then he turned back to the room. It was empty. He dashed over to the open windows. The ladder had snapped half way down, but there was no sign of Abrahm three stories below.

There were a few seconds left.

"Close it up!" Eleazer hissed into the bathroom.

Then he pushed the chair in front of the kitchen sink and ran into the hallway. There was mayhem on the first landing. He reached into his pocket for the key to the outside lock on the broom closet door. At last the time had come for the maneuver he had clandestinely practiced, without Heykel's knowledge, in the darkest hours of the night, repeating it until he could do it with his eyes closed. He opened the lock and freed the latch. They were coming up the stairs. Deliberately leaving the lock hanging open on the latch hook, he let himself into the closet and shut the door behind him, holding his breath.

The stairs creaked and trembled.

"Out!" said a voice. "Everybody down to the street."

"Dogs, pigs, Jews," said a second voice. "Everybody!"

"There are only dogs and pigs here," said a third voice.

The voices broke into laughter.

"Down the hall, you pretzel," ordered the first voice.

"All right, let's go," barked the third voice.

Lermer's door opened.

"Where's your family, you turd?" asked the third voice.

"I live alone," Lermer said.

The first and second voices had entered Heykel's apartment.

"There's no one here," said the second voice.

"Don't be a fool," said the first voice.

"See for yourself," said the second voice. "They went out the window. There must have been more than one. The last one fell. Someone had to help him away."

"Is that so?" the first voice asked from across the room.

A chair slammed against the floor.

"I'll give you three to come out of there," the first voice said. "One . . . two . . . three."

An automatic broke into staccato cackling. Bullets smashed into the sink and cabinets, puncturing everything in their path.

"Pull it apart," said the first voice. "We'll see if there's no one there."

"If there was, there won't be now," the second voice said.

A cabinet door swung open. Another. Contents went flying. The sink was fractured with a gun butt. There was a respite. Then other volley of bullets.

"Well I'll be damned," said the first voice.

The voices were back in the hall.

"Please," Lermer whined. "I'll give you a thousand zlotys. Two thousand."

He was being shoved towards the landing.

"Move on before I crack your skull," the third voice threatened.

"No," Lermer screamed.

He rushed forward and threw himself at the broom closet door.

"Let me hide in here," he begged. "Tomorrow I'll give you two thousand zlotys. More if I can get it. Just let me stay."

"What do you think you are, a broom?" the third voice wheedled. "Get on or I'll wipe the stairs with you."

"No one will know," Lermer said. "I'll . . ."

Before he could be stopped he ripped the door open, revealing Eleazer.

"My God," Lermer gasped, staggering backward.

The soldier out of whose grasp Lermer had broken pounced on him and threw him down the stairs, shooting and kicking him as he descended.

"Well, well, well," said the first voice, ignoring the shooting and studying Eleazer. "What have we here?"

"A little black Jew," said the second voice, "with a long . . ."

Before he could finish his sentence, Eleazer sprang out of the closet and drove a chisel into the soldier's eye, plunging it deep into the socket. The soldier let out an agonized scream. His partner caught Eleazer in the side of the head with his gun. Eleazer swung around and gouged an ugly hole through his cheek. Boots stormed up the stairs. Shots fired.

THE
DEATH
WAGON

A mournful harmonica conjured up the sun. At the gate the sentries who had stood watch since the evening curfew prepared for the changing of the guard. It had been an uneventful night.

"Hey, Crazy Isaac," one of them said, straightening his tunic, "can't you play something a little more cheerful? It's morning and the war is almost over."

"Leave him alone," said another sharply.

He turned to Isaac, who had tied Zirka to the gate and was squatting on the sidewalk.

"Just ignore him, my good friend," he said amiably. "The lout has no appreciation of the finer things in life."

"Right," said a third sympathetically. "He's loonier than you are."

"I'm just tired of the same thing every morning," said the first. "It's too fucking sad."

Isaac broke off his playing and rose facing the direction from which came the familiar clip-clop, clip-clop, clip-clopping of hooves on stone. A rickety black wagon drawn by a bony gray horse pulled up to the gate.

"Whoa!" said the hoary, stout old man holding the reins.

The horse stopped before the man had finished his tongue-clucking. Beside him sat his new assistant, a slim, chestnut-haired young boy whose well-cut suit had once been of quality. The man himself had a shock of white hair and wore heavy duty boots and pants and a red-checked shirt of thick wool. His sleeves were rolled up to his elbows, displaying massive forearms.

"Good morning, old-timer," said the second soldier.

"G'mornin'," the old man responded.

"Who's your new friend?" asked the soldier.

"Name is Peter," the old man said.

The boy sat shyly with his eyes downcast.

"Where's Gregor?" asked the first soldier.

"Dead," said the old man.

"Overnight?" asked the soldier.

"Overnight."

The soldier shrugged. Gregor sometimes brought him a home-baked sweet roll so fresh it steamed when he broke it open.

"He looked all right yesterday," the soldier said.

"His stomach burst," said the old man. "Some kind of infection. He turned green and blue and then it was over."

"It's a shame," said the soldier.

"Are the kid's papers in order?" the second soldier interjected.

"In order," said the old man, poking the boy in the ribs.

The boy reached into his jacket for his papers.

"That's all right," said the first soldier. "He's harmless enough."

"He looks downright weak, if you ask me," said the fourth soldier. "Throwing bodies around is hard work."

"I'm not weak," said the boy.

His first words were spoken quietly in a thin, high-pitched voice.

"Never mind," said the old man.

Isaac had untied Zirka and approached the wagon.

"Good morning," he said, lifting this face toward the old man's voice, "Perhaps your friend would like some milk?"

The boy viewed Isaac curiously.

"They call him Crazy Isaac," the old man explained. "He was once a rabbi."

"What happened to him?" asked the boy.

"He fell in love with a cow," the third soldier jumped in.

The first soldier abruptly smacked him across the mouth with the back of his fist. The third soldier reeled sideways.

"What's gotten into you?" he said, rubbing his mouth.

"I told you to lay off him," the first soldier said.

"A little milk for a piece of bread?" Isaac asked.

He touched the wagon and reached up blindly for the seat. His hand caught the boy's shin. Involuntarily, the boy shrank away, pulling his leg free. The third soldier wanted to say something, but the first soldier eyed him menacingly.

"Can I give you a ride?" the old man offered.

"That would be very kind of you," Isaac said, extending his hand.

"Help him up," the old man told the boy.

The boy reached down awkwardly, grabbing Isaac's wrists.

"Here, let me help," said the third soldier, coming over to the wagon.

He took the rope from Isaac and lifted him up to the boy.

"He sits between us," said the old man.

When Isaac was seated the third soldier handed up the rope.

"Thank you," said Isaac.

The old man was ready to go.

"To the bakery?" he asked Isaac.

"If you please," Isaac said.

"Hee-a," the old man said to the horse as he yanked the rein.

"You can take your time today," the second soldier called after the wagon. "It was a slow night."

The horse pulled away from the gate and worked into a slow, rhythmic step. Clip-clop, clip-clop, clip-clop. The wagon swayed from side to side, its wooden wheels creaking and groaning over the cobblestones.

"Bend your knees when you lift them," the old man said to the boy. "You'll feel good in the morning, but by the end of the day you'll be sore. We'll take turns throwing and catching . . ."

As he talked, the horse turned once, then again. It knew the route by heart. The sidewalks along the way were punctuated by dead bodies, many of them naked—stripped by relatives or ghouls—or with just their faces neatly covered with a sheet of newspaper. Those emaciated from hunger resembled skeletons dug out of the earth rather than the remains of persons who only yesterday had been alive.

"Throwing used to be murder," the old man continued. "But the longer the war's been going on, the lighter they've been getting. This horse used to be bigger than the first one. A real worker. Lately she's been getting to look like her passengers. But unless she gets sick, she ought to make it all the way now. There aren't that many left to carry."

"What about him?" the boy asked about Isaac, who sat impassively between them.

"He'll be getting off a couple of blocks down," said the old man. "There's a fellow at the bakery who gives him breakfast."

"Does he understand things?" asked the boy.

"Sometimes," said the old man.

The horse pulled up at a corner secured by a narrow, yellowish building with gaping holes where once there were windows and a front door. Its frame was cankered with water-thin children whose heads seemed too large for their scarecrow bodies.

"Scavengers," said the old man, dismounting the wagon.

On the sidewalk lay the nude bodies of two women and a man. There were no visible wounds to account for their deaths. From their twisted positions it was apparent that they had been searched from head to toe for any valuables that may have been overlooked by whoever had set them out for collection.

The old man motioned for the boy to climb onto the wagon platform. Then he straightened out the smaller of the two women, scooped her off the sidewalk with a shovel movement of his arms, and tossed her up to the boy as easily as if she were a doll. The boy tried to catch her gracefully, but her torso slipped through his hands and her head landed with a thud against the platform. Before he could recover, the second woman came flying up and she too wound up half in his arms, half on the floor.

"Just a minute," the boy called down, trying not to get flustered.

"Don't grab for them," the old man advised. "Let them fall into your arms."

He threw the man up and the boy caught him somewhat more fluently.

"You'll get the hang of it," said the old man.

He came around to the back of the wagon and hopped up nimbly. The boy was laying the man down beside the woman, whose bodies were sprawled uneconomically.

"No," said the old man. "You stack them like shoes in a box—head to foot, foot to head. Keep a separate pile for children."

He helped the boy line up the corpses.

"What did they die from?" the boy asked.

"Nothing in particular," said the old man. "Gradual hunger. Natural causes."

He leaned over the bench and grabbed the reins. A short whistle pointed the horse's ears. The wagon was moving, slowly, clip-clop, clip-clop, stopping for a body, moving again. The soldier was right. It had been an uneventful night. Only eight bodies so far—five woman, two men, and one horribly mutilated little boy of seven or eight. The side of his head was blown open and he had been castrated. The old man picked him up gingerly and handed rather than flung him to the boy.

"My God," said the boy, averting his eyes as he took the body. "What happened?"

"Caught smuggling," said the old man.

The wagon moved on. The boy prepared to take his turn at throwing. It amazed him how deftly the old man handled the bodies. They might as well have been empty suitcases.

"Whoa," said the old man. "What have we here?"

The boy jumped down from the wagon. Before him lay a diminutive, fully clothed Jew with a striking pepper-and-salt beard. In contrast to the usual naked corpses, his black shoes, long black coat, and black hat made him appear almost supernatural.

Although it was his turn to catch, the old man came down off the wagon too. Of the thousands of bodies he had harvested, never had he come across one so composed and lifelike that it would not have surprised him entirely if it had suddenly picked itself up off the sidewalk and ambled away. It was riddled with bullet holes, especially about the head and chest, but the blood appeared to have been washed off its face and neck. The front of the coat was stiff and crimson, like a bullfighter's muleta.

"They poured an arsenal into him," said the old man, bending over the body.

"It's strange," said the boy. "He looks like he's dreaming so peacefully."

He slid his hands under the corpse, as the old man had shown him, and lifted it off the ground. It seemed almost weightless. Rather than throw it he carried it around onto the wagon, being careful not to let the hat fall off.

"Put him with the child," the old man said, climbing back onto the bench beside Isaac.

CRYSTAL
NIGHT

The sky deepened, flickered, and exploded in a long,
silent flash of cold white light. Then it was dark. The next
flash was brighter, leaping closer to the earth.

Eugen Glueck raised his arm to shield his eyes. He had
just begun to make himself comfortable at the fire of a family
that had been kind enough to invite him into their circle when
the lightning glowered. It was too bad. He was lonely and he
had been looking forward to spending the night in the proximity of other, friendly human beings.

The street was suddenly busy with people making diverse efforts to protect their belongings. Some took off their
coats and jackets and swathed them in newspaper or packed
them within other possessions. Others constructed stopgap
awnings. One woman removed all her clothing, made her
daughter do the same, and stuffed everything into an already
crammed suitcase. In view of the journey ahead, having dry
clothing was more important than modesty.

The fires scattered along the street illuminated the scene
through a dim orange haze. With each blaze of lightning the

soft nude forms of the women flared up like matches, then faded. Between flashes, the pregnant sky loomed darker.

Silence.

Eugen felt a few pricks of moisture on the back of his neck. He picked himself up off the street. The family that had adopted him all too briefly was crowded together under the father's raincoat. Using their arms as tent poles, they held the canvas over their heads and waited.

The flashing abated.

Eugen turned and walked away. Should he have expressed thanks, he wondered? After the father invited him in, not a word had passed between them. He was still deciding what to say, how to present himself, when the lightning had started.

Bchrrr. Khrooom. Khrrbchooom. Bchrrroom.

Now the thunder had caught up and was pounding its rhythmic toll . . . BCHOOOM . . . BCHKHRCHOOOM . . . and the clouds were releasing sheets of rain.

Eugen broke into a sprint, but was shortly forced to slow down. His shoes were cutting into his heels, and his feet were so cramped across their breadth that he was afraid the cardboard would burst like the skin of an overripe tomato.

The rain was quickly so heavy that the sheets appeared greenish-white against the black screen of night and lit the street when they fell.

Eugen veered left at the corner, running haltingly, stepping away from the pain in his feet, and soon came to a building with broad eaves overhanging the front. There were no lights on. He skipped across the yard and up three steps.

Safe.

Standing with his back to the door, the angle of the rain was in his favor, falling aslant over his shoulder and being deflected by the eaves. A fine mist sprayed his face as he watched the waterfall rush of the sheets, gushing down . . . swoosh . . . and crashing onto the stones.

He patted himself. Except for his socks, his clothes were

damp but not wet. Even his shoes had not fared too badly. But his ankles were soaked, and his toes felt cold. He would investigate them later.

His thoughts turned to passing time. What would he do until the downpour stopped? He could venture inside the house, but he preferred not to. Once away from the street and the open air, it would be difficult to come out again. That would defeat the whole point of camping out. He would wait an hour. If it was still raining, he would reconsider entering the house. If not, well . . . he would wait an hour.

He reminded himself not to look at his wrist. Even though Silver's watch had been broken from the moment he put it on, he had found himself referring to it constantly. No matter what time it was, it read 5:26. But it was better than having no watch at all. Compulsively, he turned his wrist. Where the watch had been, a band of pallor contrasted with his dark, matted hair.

At the time he could not understand what anyone would want with a broken watch. He had just begun to bargain with an old Polish woman for some vegetables when the soldier had stepped in.

"I couldn't help noticing your watch," the soldier said. "It catches the sun."

Eugen was dumbfounded.

"What do you want for it?"

"It's broken," Eugen said.

"Then it's not worth very much, is it?" the soldier said.

"I guess not," Eugen said.

"Where are you from?" the soldier asked.

"Dresden."

"I thought so," the soldier said. "I'm from Dresden myself."

Eugen squirmed.

"Seen better times, huh?" the soldier added.

"Yes," Eugen replied.

"Don't worry," the soldier said. "We'll work out a deal."

He turned to the crone.

"What do you have there?" he asked, pointing to her skirts.

She seemed to be wearing everything she owned, one outlandish dress above the next, the overlapping hems hanging lopsided at disparate lengths. Near the ground her thick flesh-colored stockings were stuffed like sausages into faintly pink slippers. A garish gypsy kerchief clashed with her yellow face.

"Potatoes, onion, garlic," she said tonelessly.

"What else?"

"A girdle."

"What else, what else," the soldier said impatiently.

"Stockings, pants, a brassiere . . ."

"I'm not interested in your underwear," the soldier said. "Let's see what else is in your trousseau."

He grabbed a fistful of hems and began thrusting his hand up between the layers.

"Be careful," the old woman screeched. "You'll break the eggs."

"What kind of egg do you call this?" the soldier asked, triumphantly disengaging the end of a salami from the string by which it hung between two skirts.

"A butcher's egg," said the old woman.

"Put everything in here," the soldier exploded, ripping the kerchief off her head and flinging it at her. "Everything."

Resignedly, the old woman began drawing things out of her clothing, plucking her blouses, sorting her skirts, her hands moving expertly through the traps and pockets of her barter landscape.

"Do you have any money?" the soldier had pressed on with Eugen.

"Very little," Eugen said.

"How much?"

"A few hundred zlotys," Eugen lied.

"Let's see it," the soldier said.

Eugen dug into his pocket and picked two or three notes out with his fingertips.

"Two thousand!" the soldier exclaimed. "You said a few hundred."

"I was mistaken," Eugen said.

"Obviously," said the soldier.

Without formality he plunged his hand rudely into Eugen's pocket, his fist driving to corner the remaining notes.

"Four, five, six, eight, ten," he counted victoriously.

"What's in there?" the soldier asked, pointing to the white pillowcase looped at the open end through Eugen's belt.

"Underwear," Eugen said. "Personal effects."

The old woman had spread her wares on the kerchief.

"That looks like ten thousand zlotys worth," said the soldier.

He reached into his pocket for some change.

"Wrap it up," he said to the old woman, handing her several coins.

The old woman tied a four-cornered knot and surrendered her bundle to Eugen.

"Now scram," said the soldier, dismissing her with a flick of his wrist.

Eugen was dazed.

"How much do you want for the watch?" the soldier said.

"I told you, it's broken," Eugen said.

"Never mind, I'll give you a thousand zlotys for it," the soldier had said.

He pulled a note from the wad he had taken from Eugen and urged it upon him.

"Here, it's a deal," he said, hooking the gold-plated band with his index finger.

Eugen removed the watch and gave it to him.

That was several days ago.

Eugen decided to sit down. His legs ached, whether from running in those shoes or from the humidity. He lowered himself onto the doorstep. Aah, he said, that feels better. The rain had not let up. He reviewed his options. If it continued he could sleep in the house. But if it stopped he would definitely go back to the street. Under no circumstances would he spend another night in the Bloodsteins' apartment.

He had gone there by way of running down one of his few leads to Bankart. When there was no response to his knocking, he had turned the knob and found the door unlocked. Inside, the apartment was apparently uninhabited, but strangely intact. He searched through it. Everything had been cleaned out—the closets, the drawers, the cabinets. But the furniture had remained, perfectly arranged, and one bed had even been left made up with clean sheets and a quilt.

Was someone planning to return, Eugen had wondered? He renewed his scrutiny, probing the walls and floor for a false surface. What was this? The floor in the large closet had indentations in it such as would have been made by the legs of a desk. Someone had tried to fill them in with putty, but the compound had contracted, exposing slivers of lighter wood. Still, he would not have noticed them had he not been on his hands and knees. He examined the floor more closely. There were many nicks around the depressions. Suddenly, he realized that the dark flecks he had taken to be leather dye stains might be something else. Ink, for example. Shoes could not grind holes in the floor. There had been some sort of machine in the closet. A mimeograph machine, perhaps, or . . . his thought snapped. The little rabbi had known after all!

The discovery had affected him unpleasantly. He was excited by it, but he could not get out of the building quickly enough. As he walked away, looking nervously around him, he determined to drop in periodically to see whether the bed had been used. Yet when night fell, and he had no place to stay, he found himself irresistibly drawn back. He would sleep in the bed himself. If anyone else showed up to use it, well . . . he would see what developed.

Tonight would have been the fourth night there, Eugen thought. The first three had been uneventful enough. Too uneventful. No one had appeared. No one had bothered him. The only noteworthy thing had been the condition of the sheets. He had smoothed them out perfunctorily the morning after the first night. But when he returned that evening, the bed looked as if it had not been slept in. There was not a wrinkle anywhere. It was spooky. That night he slept with the bed across the door.

In the morning he had tarried in the apartment. There was a legitimate excuse for not going outside: whoever may have come yesterday might come again today. Finally he went out, but not without carefully placing folds in the sheets. They were still there at the end of the day. He slept more easily knowing that no one was shadowing him, but he also felt more isolated. There had been undeniable comfort, if also concern, in thinking that he might not be alone.

The next day he hardly ventured out, and today he virtually had to force himself downstairs. In the building at least there was a woman on the ground floor at whom he could direct an occasional thought. And there remained the possibility that someone would appear to use the bed. But the street was ugly, disheartening, without hope.

Eugen was not making any headway in his search for Bankhart. On the contrary. He was finding it increasingly difficult to work up the energy for pursuit. It was as though the Bloodsteins' bed were sapping his determination.

The rain was easing up. Instead of falling in sheets, the thinner drops were coming down like shards of glass, sparkling, almost like frozen snowflakes.

Eugen had seen glass showering like that upon the sidewalks once, bursting out of windows and cascading down for seven days and nights. It was so long ago that he remembered it only as a dream. A seventeen year old German refugee had walked into the German Embassy in Paris and fatally shot Ernst vom Rath. Because the boy was Jewish, every Jew in Germany was made to suffer for it. Buildings were pillaged, shops destroyed, houses ruined, synagogues burned to the ground. Jews were killed and beaten and humiliated.

Upon reflection, it was not so long ago—four years, no more. Someone had come by Eugen's house on a motorcycle and announced that at last the Jews were open game. Before he knew it Eugen was downtown, smashing windows, pulling people out of buildings, cracking them over the head with his club.

At one point a mean crowd trapped a young Jewish boy who had been dragged from his house and was being forced by a stern, corpulent man in evening clothes to write "Jew" across the front door with a crayon. A frail old man with a white beard emerged from the building and confronted the fat German.

"Don't do it," he said to the boy, drawing him away from the door.

The fat German kicked the old Jew in the back of the legs, staggering him. In the bedlam of the street, Eugen had found himself on the scene, his adrenalin surging.

"What's going on here?" he had asked assertively.

"This eggless chicken is interfering with justice," said the fat German.

"Is it true?" Eugen demanded.

"No," said the Jew. "It is he who is breaking the law."

"I'll break you apart like a wishbone," the fat German growled, reaching for the old Jew.

"Wait," Eugen said, stepping in his way. "First we'll see how the chicken cooks."

He produced a book of matches and struck a light to the old Jew's beard. There was a singeing sound, and then the searing odor of burning hair. The old Jew made no attempt to save himself. He stood looking up at Eugen, his eyes praying, his face wreathed by a ring of fire.

This vision had more than once awakened Eugen in the middle of the night. Before then he had done what was necessary to get by—attended meetings, fraternized with Franz's consorts, uttered slogans. But that night he committed himself beyond his intention.

In the week the madness raged, feeding on itself, everything Jewish had turned to flames or rubble or blood. Thousands of Jews were rounded up and shipped off to concentration camps. And not an unbroken window remained in a synagogue anywhere.

The images had stayed with him: The old Jew's face, crowned by fire, and the broken glass falling like crystal rain.

Eugen inhaled. Water was still trickling down from the eaves, but the rain had ceased and the purged air was refreshing.

He raised his eyes to see whether there were still any large clouds overhead. The sky seemed clear. Where before it had been dark, there was now a gold moon crescent on the horizon. He inhaled again. It would feel good to sleep in the cool, buoyant air with a fire burning and the comfort of people near.

The street had resettled for the night. Eugen picked his way among the enclaves, walking on his toes to prevent his wooden heels from rapping on the stones. He did not want to wake anyone.

"Where did you go?" a voice said in the night.

Eugen stopped in mid-step and looked down. There was his family—the children sleeping, the mother resting beside them with her eyes open, the father rubbing a pair of socks over the fire.

"I went for shelter," Eugen said.

His heart skipped. Another two steps and he would have been by them.

The father finished drying the socks, put them down, and held up another pair. Behind him his raincoat was stretched out to dry like an animal skin.

"Your feet look pretty wet," the father said. "You'd best bake them out."

"I don't want to disturb anyone," Eugen said, fighting himself.

"Sit down," said the father. "A little heat will do you good."

He moved a few things aside, clearing a space between himself and the youngest of his three children. His wife lay on

the other side of the fire. Eugen sat down cross-legged, holding the pillowcase against his flank.

"Thanks," he said quietly.

He began to take off his shoes.

"Be careful," the father said. "They're liable to shrivel up
on you."

Eugen withdrew his hands. How foolish of him, he
thought. Held empty to the fire, the wet cardboard shoes
would have puckered up in the shape of potato skins. He
extended his legs toward the flames, crossing them at the
ankles for maximum exposure.

"Where'd you get the shoes?" the father asked.

"I found them," Eugen said.

"Well you'd better find another pair," the father said. "A
few more showers and they'll have had it."

Watching the father drying a small pair of boy's pants,
Eugen felt discouraged. He had packed enough underwear for
two. Why had he not brought a decent pair of shoes?

"Do you have any extra socks?" asked the father.

"Yes," Eugen said. "Several pairs."

"If you want," said the father, "I could devise something
to make your shoes more comfortable and keep them drier."

"It sounds like a good idea," Eugen said.

He pulled the pillowcase out of his belt, delved in, and
brought out five or six pairs of socks.

"Two pairs would be fine," the father said. "And something for insulation. Do you have anything that's fairly thin and
waterproof?"

"I don't think so," Eugen said, "but I'll look."

He struck his hand in the pillowcase and felt around.
Then it occurred to him. He brought forth the old woman's
bundle, set it on the street, and unknotted it.

"How about this?" he asked, embarrassedly holding up a
salmon girdle.

"Perfect," said the father.

The food rested on the flattened kerchief as on a tablecloth. Potatoes. Onions. Salami. Garlic. Eggs. Greens.

"Can I offer you something to eat?" Eugen said.

"You'd best save it," said the father.

He motioned to his wife for a needle and thread.

"I'll do it," she said, still looking into the fire.

The father handed her the socks and the girdle.

"Please take something," Eugen said.

"No thanks," said the father. "There are five of us and one of you. It wouldn't make any sense."

The mother had taken out a sewing kit and was cutting up the girdle.

"Are you from Berlin?" the father asked, resuming his drying chores.

"Dresden," Eugen answered.

"What does a Jew do in Dresden?"

"I'm only half-Jewish," Eugen said, hoping the father would stop.

"It used to matter which half," the father said.

He smiled, self-amused.

Eugen lifted the eggs from the kerchief and set them down atop a pair of warm pants that the father had just folded.

"For the children," he said. "I insist."

At that instant he felt a heatspot on his leg. He turned around. The child nearest him, the little girl, had raised her hand in her sleep and it had fallen on his thigh.

"You may need them along the way," said the father.

"Eggs don't travel well," Eugen said.

"Why don't you cook them now and keep them hard?"

"I'm not going tomorrow," Eugen confessed.

The father looked at him oddly.

"These should do," said the mother, handing Eugen what looked like knit slippers.

"So quickly?" Eugen said, admiring her handiwork.

She had sewn one pair of socks into the other, with swatches of the girdle inserted between them for insulation.

"It's a simple thing," she said.

"I'll always appreciate it," Eugen said.

He tried to offer her something, but she ignored his gesture.

"Good night," she said, reposing again before the fire, her eyes still open.

Apparently dreaming, the little girl pulled herself toward Eugen and nestled her head against his leg. Timidly, Eugen let his hand slide onto her head. The back of her neck was feverish, and her lips were pursed with the peculiar innocence of sleep.

The father reclined on his side and squirmed about for a comfortable position.

"Good night," he said.

"Good night," said Eugen.

He resisted the urge to follow the father's example for fear that if he moved to lie down he might lose the wonderful feeling of warmth, almost of fusion, that existed at the point where the little girl's head was touching his leg.

He stroked her hair. His fingers found her forehead hot and damp. It occurred to him that somewhere on the street there might be the very family whose apartment he had usurped on the Aryan side. If they were not there tonight, they had either passed this way, or would soon. He would recognize her perfume if he smelled it.

As the rain's moisture evaporated, a coolness was rising from the ground. The little girl parted her lips like a fish gulping for air. Eugen had a horrible thought. He could just pick her up by the legs and dash her head against the pavement. Human life was so durable, and yet so frail.

The father had worked himself into a compact shape and was breathing heavily, but Eugen sensed that he was not asleep. There was an inequillibrium about him, like a buoy gradually sinking. Across the fire, the mother kept her doe-eyed vigil.

Were they thinking similar thoughts about tomorrow, Eugen reflected, or dwelling in private realms?

Immersed in a suspenseful dream, the little girl wiped her mouth unconsciously and dropped her head back onto

Eugen's leg. A reservoir of feeling welled up in him.

Above them, the rain-washed sky was full of brilliant stars. Eugen glanced at the dull star on his sleeve. It was obscure in the darkness. But the sky stars were sparkling like facets of a vast, priceless crown.

When he was a child his father had tried to teach him the constellations, but he could not understand him. Lions lived in the jungle, not in the sky.

"This knowledge is precious," his father said. "It has inspired and guided men throughout the ages. Some day you will be happy that you acquired it while you were young."

He would have to do without it, Eugen thought. The sky was a moving sight: deep blue patterned with white lights. But if instead of being in the ghetto he were lost in a field or in the woods, he would not know which way to turn. Rude, sadistic Thierbach was his beacon.

A twisting thought forced itself into Eugen's consciousness. What difference would it make if Bankart were never found? There had been twice as many Jews in Warsaw as there were now. And there were twice as many now as there would be several weeks hence. Bankart could not prevent the ghetto from being emptied. He could only make a nuisance of himself. Left unprovoked, he was less likely to do even that. But if Thierbach was determined to provoke him, Eugen pondered, why was he compelled to obey?

Suddenly, Eugen had the sensation of heat thawing ice. Someone was playing the harmonica.

Turning, he saw a gnarled figure crouched by the fire of the women who had earlier disrobed to save their clothing. They were still naked. The music conveyed the simple, open sadness of a child.

The mother's eyes had risen from the fire and were set on Eugen. How long had she been watching him? He looked down at the little girl warmly asleep on his lap. With one bullet he could spare her the agony of waking.

"What's her name?" he asked the mother.

"Tzipora."

JUDAS

"'**S**he'll get us all put away on account of that ball of
hers.'" shouted Ivan Voytek, who was Felix Erdmann's son-in-law. "Is that all you had to worry about,
Felix? Well, you can be happy now that she's dead."

"You're jumping the gun," said Olek.

The Erdmann's living room was hot. Erdmann sat on the
window side of the couch like an overstuffed bolster. He was
still wearing the eye shade he used for work. Beneath it his
grey sweating face was tinged with green.

"Look at you," Ivan went on. "Thousands of people starve
every day and you're growing fatter. What turns a human
being into a dribbling pig, Felix? What?"

"Please," said Mrs. Erdmann. "Can't you see he's not
well."

Sitting across the room from her husband, Yanina
Erdmann was no longer even sure she pitied him. Nevertheless, her betrothal was for better or for worse. It had to be so if
life was to have meaning.

"This isn't a hospital, Yanina," Ivan said. "It's a morgue."

"Ivan!" Anna said.

Although she had taken her place beside her father on the couch out of habit, Anna's compassion for Erdmann, as with her mother, was dwindling.

"We all know he's sick," Ivan said. "The question is whether he's sick enough to be guilty of two heinous crimes. Tell us, Felix. Are you or are you not a murderer?"

"Not," Erdmann said in a barely audible grunt.

The word was disconnected from the body, which remained immobile, head downcast.

"Did you say something Felix?" Ivan twitted.

"Leave me be," Erdmann said lamely.

He pulled himself up and shifted to face the door.

"His guilt is not proven," Olek intervened.

"It'll be certain when we're all fit for worms," said Ivan. "I'd like to know beforehand."

"What does he want from me?" cried Erdmann, appealing to Olek.

"Ask him why he comes home at night draped in vomit?" said Ivan.

"A murderer?" squealed Erdmann. "And two crimes! Who's the drunkard, when he sees double?"

"Tell him," Ivan said.

"Not yet," said Olek, motioning for Ivan, who had been pacing back and forth, to sit down.

"Then I'll tell him," said Ivan, bouncing forward.

"Simmer down," urged Olek, intercepting Ivan's line toward Erdmann.

Ivan recoiled. Mrs. Erdmann let slip a gasp, but quickly regained her composure. Her lips were tightly set. First with one hand, then the other, she twisted a claret napkin around her fingers like a tourniquet.

"Tell me what?" asked Erdmann.

"Never mind," said Olek.

"Yanina, what is it?" Erdmann asked his wife.

She looked at him without answering.

"All right, your honor, let's get on with it," said Ivan.

He reached for Anna's hand on the arm of the couch. She withdrew from his touch.

"Felix," Olek began, "you know there were peculiar circumstances surrounding Leora's death . . ."

"And the funeral," Ivan interjected.

" . . . and the funeral," Olek said.

A dark red flush rising up from his neck muddied Erdmann's complexion.

"You've been cooperating with the authorities from the first . . ."

"What would you do in my place?" Erdmann mumbled.

"Hold on," Olek said. "We've known what you're doing and yet Leora was put in your hands. Obviously we trusted you. Even now you have every benefit of the doubt."

"Speak for yourself," said Ivan.

"I'm speaking for everyone but you," Olek replied, continuing. "There are some things that have to be cleared up, Felix. If you're innocent, there's nothing to hide."

"I loved her as my own flesh," Erdmann said. "Anna's man has not yet given her a child. You know how I loved her. I used to play with her. I helped Yanina teach her the prayers. It's true, sometimes she made me nervous, but is that a crime?"

"What eloquence," Ivan said bitterly. "I haven't given him a child for burning."

Erdmann jumped as if an electric shock had passed through his cushion.

"You're impotent," he said, his voice rising with excitement. "You've tried everything, but you can't do it."

"Impotent and sterile," Ivan said, "as my father was before me."

"Deny it!" Erdmann said. "Anna is still our daughter."

"You have ink on the brain," said Ivan. "Nazi ink."

Anna was crying to herself.

"Enough," said Olek.

He paused to let the air clear.

"Now, Felix, let's start from the beginning," he said. "Did you ever divulge Leora's presence to anyone?"

"They knew," Erdmann said uneasily.

"Who?" asked Olek.

"The neighbors," said Erdmann.

"Anyone else?" asked Olek.

"No."

"Did any of them question her identity?" asked Olek.

"Not to my knowledge," said Erdmann.

"What about your contacts?" asked Olek.

"I said nothing," Erdmann stated.

"It never came up?" asked Olek.

"I said nothing."

"You said nothing to Officer Glueck?" asked Olek.

He watched Erdmann's eyes scud willy-nilly.

"What does Glueck have to do with it?" said Erdmann.

"That's what I'm asking you," said Olek.

"We discussed documents," said Erdmann. "Nothing else."

"Leora was never raised between you?" asked Olek.

"What is this, an inquisition?" Erdmann erupted. "You come to my house and ask me questions so that you can call me a liar?"

"No one has called you a liar," Olek said. "No one wants to and if you tell the truth no one will."

"I've told the truth," Erdmann said.

His face had become saturated with blood and was changing colors like a chameleon.

"Did you tell Glueck?" asked Olek.

"He already knew," Erdmann replied.

Olek felt a surge of adrenalin rush through his body.

"Knew what?"

"That Leora was staying with us," said Erdmann.

"How did he know?"

"Ask him," said Erdmann.

"How was it mentioned?" asked Olek.

"He wanted to know who she was," said Erdmann.

"Did you tell him?" asked Olek.

"Of course not," said Erdmann.

"What did you say?" asked Olek.

"I gave him the cover story," said Erdmann.

"And he accepted it?"

The clock above the table struck ten. As if heeding the carved pastoral figure whose staff pointed the hour, the neighborhood church bells pealed ten gongs.

"Tick-tock, bing-bong, tick-tock, bing-bong," said Erdmann, oscillating like a pendulum. "This house is cuckoo. The city's cuckoo. Everything's gone cuckoo."

"How remarkable," said Ivan.

"Did he believe you?" asked Olek.

"You asked me that," said Erdmann.

"You didn't answer."

"I don't have an answer."

"Was that the end of it?" asked Olek.

"Not quite," said Erdmann.

"He brought it up again?"

"Yes."

"What happened?"

"He wanted to know what had become of her?" said Erdmann.

"How did he know she was gone?"

"I don't know."

"What did you say?" asked Olek.

"I told him I didn't know."

"If, as it appears, he didn't believe you the first time," Olek said, "he certainly wouldn't believe that."

Erdmann shrugged resignedly.

"It's obvious he's lying," Ivan said.

"You must have said something," Olek said.

"I had no choice," said Erdmann. "If it was just a matter of personal safety I would have choked on my tongue. But he threatened all of us. How could I let him harm Yanina?"

"What did you tell him?" asked Olek.

"That Leora had been sent to a convent," Erdmann said. His words cast a momentary spell.

"There!" said Ivan crowingly. "He's admitted it."

Mrs. Erdmann dabbed her eyes with the napkin.

"Don't feel badly, Yanina," Ivan added. "He did it for you."

"Control yourself!" Anna said.

She was visibly troubled by the vitriolic stranger emerging in Ivan's outbursts. He began to say something more but checked himself.

"Felix," said Olek, resuming the lead, "did he ask about me?"

"No," said Erdmann.

"Did he ask about anyone else?"

"Only Leora," said Erdmann.

"Did he say anything about her?" asked Olek. "Who she was? Why he was interested in her?"

Leaning forward, Erdmann dug a rumpled handkerchief out of his back pocket and nervously patted the perspiration that had broken over his features.

"I can't remember," he said after deliberation.

"Is that why you're sweating like a slab of bacon?" Ivan said.

"It's hot in here," said Erdmann, wiping his mouth.

"Not nearly as hot as it is where you're going to wind up," said Ivan.

"Don't worry so much about him that you forget about yourself," said Olek.

"What are you insinuating?" demanded Ivan.

"Whatever you think," said Olek.

"I was thinking of the Metropole," said Ivan.

Erdmann's head swiveled around like a puppet's.

"That's very sporting of you," said Olek.

His tone straightened Ivan in his chair.

"Ask him why he's been coming home stewed in his own juices," Ivan countered.

"In due time," said Olek. "But first let me ask him whether Glueck referred to Sister Theresa?"

"No," said Erdmann quickly.

"Did you mention her in connection with the convent?" asked Olek.

"Naturally not," said Erdmann.

"I thought you couldn't remember," said Ivan.

"That regarded Leora," said Erdmann.

"But you're sure about Theresa?" asked Olek.

"Absolutely," said Erdmann.

"And you know she's dead?" said Olek.

Instinctively, Erdmann looked to his wife. Her visage was a cameo of grief. Bewildered, he turned to Anna. Her mind was elsewhere. He felt himself flickering hot and cold.

"That's impossible," he said, groping.

"It's a reality," said Olek.

"But there was nothing wrong with her," Erdmann said. "Yanina would have told me."

Again he bestowed her an asking glance.

"There was nothing wrong with her," Olek said. "She was executed."

"Yanina!" Erdmann said desperately. "What is he saying?"

Mrs. Erdmann gathered her lips to form a word, but it would not come forth. Her head began shaking softly and she could not regulate its motion.

"It seems she never returned to the convent after the funeral," said Olek. "Someone . . ."

He stopped short. Laboriously, Mrs. Erdmann gained her feet. As if responding to an inner signal, Anna rose instantly and helped her mother into the bedroom.

"The head was severed from the body," Olek continued. "Two of the sisters found it lying on the road near the gate on their early morning walk."

"It must have b . . ." Erdmann began, but failed to finish.

He clamped a hand over his mouth and plunged off the couch toward the sink, where he stood convulsively puking.

"It's pathetic," Ivan said to Olek. "He did it out of weakness."

Ivan's voice, which a few minutes ago had been forceful, sounded as if it were coming from his head instead of his chest.

"He didn't do it," said Olek.

Ivan shrank.

"He may not have done the physical killing," he said. "But he might as well have."

"You'd like him to think so, wouldn't you?" said Olek.

Ivan flew out of his chair and rushed over to the sink. Erdmann was coughing up the last recalcitrant drops of food and slime. Grabbing him from behind, Ivan dragged him across the room and threw him roughly onto the couch.

"A picture of innocence," he said sarcastically. "As fine a man as would ever betray a child."

"Back off," said Olek.

"I've seen enough of your coddling," said Ivan. "Look at him cringe. The truth has to be beaten out of him."

He bore down on Erdmann, striking him high on the chest with his fist.

"Confess, you Jewfish!" he said, uncorking a hail of blows.

Erdmann made no effort to defend himself. A trickle of blood smudged his mouth, fanning Ivan's fury.

FLOWERS
ON   A
BATTLEFIELD

Stretched prone on the attic floor, his eye pressed to a crack in the shutter, Joseph beheld the passage of night to day.

"Keep one eye on the darkness and one on the light," Uncle Isaac had told him, "and when both share the same vision, you will have seen a miracle."

In the interlude between the fading of darkness and the first splintered kindling of the sun, the sky was a lead-blue umbra faintly whitened by cold starlight. Against it, the silhouette of the factory, crowned by black smoke-stacks, was neutral beneath the cold-eyed moon.

With the patience of a glass blower, Joseph watched for the precise cosmic moment when night ceased to exist and day became. His throat was dry from having slept on the dust-cached floor. How good a glass of tea would feel scalding his gullet.

A slow tap plashed and filled his mind with afterthoughts of sleep. The stranger had stopped coming to the apartment as mysteriously as he had started. Could someone have known that his mother had left a bed for Isaac?

His father had tried to obstruct her, pulling out the sheets as she folded them under, but she continued around the bed until he gave up. Amy had helped her, following behind her father.

"Why don't you make one up for the cow?" Menachem had said.

Joseph forced himself to concentrate on the sky. A glimmer of pink appeared. Then yellow hues. The sun was not yet visible, but the leaden pall had risen and the air was turning watercolor blue. Pastel bulbs sprouted jonquil, orange, and periwinkle blades. A high rack of white-rind clouds swooped off with the moon. It was light. The moment was gone forever.

It was too early to venture out. He would visit Abrahm after he had warmed his insides at the bakery.

The dream lingered. Joseph had been sleeping with Leora on a bed of leaves in the forest. When he awakened she was gone. Her form was perfectly impressed upon the leaves beside his, but there was no trace of her flight.

"Leora!" he called out, using his hands as a megaphone. "Where are you?"

His skin tingled with goose pimples. The earth was damp and the chill autumn air stung his nipples.

"Leora . . . Leora . . . Leora . . . Leora . . . Leora . . ."

The first rays of morning were praying through the treetops. In summer they were green and lush and vibrant with chirping and cricking. Now they were not yet bare, but they were thinning and the birds were going elsewhere. The seasons of hope and life had passed, leaving the ground russet and orange and gold.

"Leora . . . Leora . . . Leora . . . Leora . . . Leora . . . Leora . . . Leora . . . Leora . . . Leora . . . Leora . . ."

The wet leaves squelched underfoot and clung to his shoes as he followed his voice deeper into the forest. The surrounding quietude was unmarred by response or echo.

"Le-o-ra . . . Le-o-ra . . . Le-ora . . . Leora . . . Le-ora!"

In his absorption he did not notice the figure that had materialized from among the trees and was coming upon him with long, soundless strides.

Although he was actually not much bigger than Joseph, he seemed twelve feet tall. He was clothed in black riding boots, black jodhpurs, black tunic, black hood—accentuated by the bright crimson band on his left arm, on which a black swastika was implanted upon a white circle. His face was chalk white.

Across his chest he wore a dark leather cartridge belt. Gleaming with bullets, it attached to a revolver that rested on his right hip. A submachine gun was slung over his right shoulder. Over his left shoulder was looped a thick rope that ended in a hangman's noose. In his left hand he gripped a coiled bullwhip. From a silver girdle around his middle, an ornate sword hung almost to the ground.

Joseph turned to run, but the ground slid back under him. His feet threshed the leaves in futile motion. At his back he heard a voice.

"Are you ready?"

He stopped running and spun around. The man was where he had been, but his face had become incandescent. There was something else strange about it, suggesting a Halloween pumpkin sitting on a window sill, its vacant candle-lit smile flickering into the night. It had no nose.

"Well, are you ready?"

The man's lips had not moved. Joseph studied his paraffin-featured face, but saw nothing in it.

"For the last time," said the voice, "are you ready?"

At that moment the face shone so brightly that Joseph thought the hood was going to burst into flames. The white-hot eyes were pulsing with an intense energy, compelling him to respond.

"I don't think so," he said.

"You have your choice of weapons," said the voice.

Joseph was speechless. Although it was morning, the forest abruptly grew dark, as if a shroud had been draped over the trees. The only light came from the cowled face, which glowed fierily.

"The time has come," said the voice.

The man, who had been standing stock-still, moved forward. He put his hand to his sheath, as if to draw his sword. But when he pulled the jeweled handle from its scabbard, it bore no blade. Instead, a string of constellations began to issue forth—an endless chain, one following the other, of all the stars and asteroids, floating out and standing in the air before them, each in its assigned configuration.

"Which do you choose, Joseph Bloodstein?" said the voice.

The whip was uncoiling itself and turning into a snake. It slid through the man's hand like a heavily weighted rope and slithered over the ground, rustling the leaves.

"Which?" said the voice.

The noose rose from the man's shoulder and hovered overhead.

"Choose," said the voice.

The bullets popped out of their belt like shooting stars and sailed into the constellations.

"Orion," Joseph heard himself say.

"Good, very good," said the voice.

The man unbuckled his silver girdle and let it drop from his hips. When the scabbard hit the ground, the stream of stars that was still discharging became a torrent of scorpions, thousands upon thousands of them scuttling the leaves, their venomous stinger-tails dragging the earth for victims. Then a river of crabs began to pour out of the scabbard and creep sidelong among the scorpions and the leaves, and the snake, attacked on all sides, divided into two snakes, and the two halved into four, and the four into eight, until soon there was a swarming profusion of snakes among the scorpions and the leaves and the forest floor was writhing.

Flames were nibbling at the edges of the man's cowl, charring and curling his face like a piece of parchment. Behind the face the cowl was dark and empty.

A sharp point pierced Joseph's calf. Almost instantly he was nauseated. A second prick, more painful than the first, was promptly followed by myriad others. His legs began to spasm. Cramps invaded his pelvis. His chest constricted, shortening his breath, and his heart palpitated wildly. Over-powering changes were taking place in his body. His jaws ached bitingly. He felt himself losing consciousness and then, yelping and snarling like a rabid dog, he bucked free of the mangle of poisonous creatures about his feet and bounded into the shadowy core of the forest.

The attic was taking shape under two narrow shafts of light that slanted in from the roof. Outside, in the factory yard, men padded about like patients under the after-effects of ether.

Joseph scratched his crotch. He had not changed or washed his clothes since the day his mother prepared them for deportation. Beneath the cloth of his trousers the erection with which he had arisen was residually pleasant and warm. He lay his hand over it, pressuring it gently. Had he really spent the night with Leora, or was her disappearance a dream within a dream?

Menachem's face intruded. Joseph recognized the features, but the person was not his father. Uncle Isaac had taught him about the heavens, the planets, the vast imagined forms of constellations. If there was another part to the dream, it had not survived. Yet it was not entirely a fantasy, even if he had not dreamed it. God knows what Menachem would have done had he found out.

Once he had caught Joseph trying to masturbate in the bathroom.

"What the hell are you doing?" he asked, looming in the doorway.

"Nothing," said Joseph.

"Some nothing," Menachem said. "What's that in your hand?"

As he asked the question, he ripped a small, stapled booklet away from Joseph. The page was turned to a crude pencil sketch of a fat woman, on her knees with her hairy underside facing the reader, sucking the penis of a man seated on the toilet.

"Where'd you get this?" Menachem asked.

"On the street," Joseph said.

"You bought it?" Menachem asked.

"The boys were passing it around," Joseph said.

Menachem flipped to another drawing.

"Which boys?" Menachem asked.

Joseph fixed his eyes on the bottom door hinge.

"David?" Menachem asked, his voice rising angrily. "Meier? Chaim? Laib?"

Joseph kept his eyes averted.

"Who had it just before you?" Menachem growled, cocking his hand as if to strike him.

Joseph raised himself to pull his pants up, but Menachem pushed him down. The clang of the white metal wash pan being kicked against the tub brought Leah in.

"Is everything all right?" she asked.

"If you don't mind your son being a sex pervert," Menachem snapped.

He thrust the booklet into her hand. Joseph took advantage of the moment to hide his shame. Leah thumbed through the pictures.

"Imagine," Menachem said. "We're in the middle of a war, the walls are closing in on us, and he's sitting here raising warts on his hands. Whoever's responsible for this is going to suffer."

"Fine," Leah said. "In the meanwhile, please stop roaring and let him out of here. He's not a prisoner of war."

"A few days in jail might do him some good," Menachem said. "He's barely a man and his mind is already depraved."

He reached for the booklet, but Leah would not relinquish it.

"Are you planning to donate it to the library?" Menachem asked.

"I want to show it to Isaac," Leah said.

"How did he get into this?" Menachem asked.

"By default," said Leah.

"What kind of shit is that?" Menachem erupted. "I work my hands raw to keep us alive and your son sits in the bathroom like a pornographic prince on his throne and plays with himself."

"Humiliation won't accomplish a thing," said Leah.

"Neither will Isaac," Menachem said. "It's none of his business that we have a goddamn deviate in the family."

With his mother's help, Joseph finally escaped the bathroom unharmed, though not without a stern warning against a repeat performance. She remained incarcerated with Menachem. Their argument dragged on. Several times the tub resounded from the impact of the pan. Joseph cringed. His mother was standing up for him, but he was not sure he deserved it. He wondered whether she knew that the drawings were his.

A few days later, while Menachem was out of the house, Uncle Isaac had invited Joseph into the bedroom for a talk.

"Close the door," Isaac said intimately. "This doesn't concern anyone but us."

He plunked onto the bed and stretched out, whacking the space beside him with the flat of his hand.

"Come sit over here," he said. "That's it, make yourself comfortable."

When they were settled side by side, Isaac reached into his long black robe and produced the booklet of sketches.

"Do you recognize this?" he asked.

Joseph was mortified.

"Your mother gave it to me," Isaac said.

He riffled the pages without looking at them. The obscene poses flitted by like still frames in a movie.

"You know that Leora may be sent out of the ghetto," Isaac said.

"Yes," Joseph said.

"Have you ever given thought to consummating your relationship?" Isaac said softly.

"Some day," Joseph replied.

"I mean now," Isaac said. "Tomorrow. The next day."

Joseph felt the heat of blood splotching his face and neck.

"I don't understand," he said in embarrassment.

"Then listen carefully," Isaac said, putting an arm around him. "I'm going to be very direct with you, though your father would hate me for it. We all know the end is in sight. The ghetto is beyond hope. To comply with deportation is suicide. To resist is certain death. There is only the choice of how to die. Heykel and Sonya accept this for themselves but not for Leora. Eleazer has tried to persuade them that it is too late to salvage individual claims—that we are best off sharing what has become our common fate. What sense will it make for Leora to live on without us? Her days would be like nights, and her nights would be empty.

"This is what I want to talk to you about, Joseph. It's a ticklish subject. I may be overstepping my bounds. But each man sees according to his light, and the light is growing dim.

"You have no say in the decision that would separate you from Leora, yet in a way it affects you as much as it does Heykel and Sonya. For while she is their flesh and blood, she was to have become yours. As it is written in the Song of Solomon, she is your beloved, and you are hers. You are young and fairly innocent. Yet you have witnessed things in your time that men five times your years have never seen. So if you are not a man, neither are you a child. And if it is your destiny to be denied the typical progression to adulthood and the chance to be a husband in due course and then a father, it would not be entirely unrighteous or profane for you to take a bride while you still could."

Joseph seemed mesmerized by a vision that had tran- quilized his face and illumined his eyes.

"Well, what do you think?" Isaac asked, tapping him on the ribs.

"I don't know," Joseph said.

"You don't know what?" asked Isaac.

"I don't know if I understand you," said Joseph.

"If you didn't, you wouldn't be the first," said Isaac. "Now hear me: I propose that I, Rabbi Isaac Bloodstein, perform a marriage ceremony uniting Joseph Bloodstein and Leora Gut- terman in the eyes of God and man for all eternity."

"Do you mean it?" asked Joseph.

"I'm not practicing for the afterworld," said Isaac.

"What about father?" asked Joseph.

"We'll have to do without him," said Isaac.

"And Sonya?" asked Joseph.

"You worry about Leora," said Isaac. "Leave the rest to me."

Joseph rubbed his perspiring palms against the knees of his pants. There was a corky taste in his mouth and his head felt light.

"When would it be?" he asked.

"As soon as possible," said Isaac. "When else?"

"Where?" asked Joseph, intoxicated with Isaac's spirit.

"In the best of places," said Isaac. "Right here."

"It's a little scary," said Joseph.

"Balderdash," said Isaac. "Just take a deep breath and ask me anything you want to know. That is, if you don't already know more than I do."

With that he held up the booklet which was the osten- sible reason for their conversation.

"I was waiting for you to come back to that," said Joseph.

"You have artistic talent," Isaac said.

His large brown eyes twinkled in amusement.

"Father doesn't think so," Joseph said.

"That's to be expected," Isaac said with upturned hands, "It's his parental duty to go berserk over every inconsequentiality. And sex is always the touchiest business. Think a minute. What would your reaction be if you discovered your son making love to a filthy book?"

Joseph shrugged sheepishly.

"I'll tell you what your grandfather would have done, may he rest in peace." Isaac said. "He would have strapped your father's ass bloody. Your father has a few scars to prove it."

"You mean those thin white lines . . ."

And God said, let there be lights in the firmament of heaven to divide the day from night; and let them be for signs, and for seasons, and for days and for years.

Joseph's thoughts returned to his dream. He knew from Isaac's lectures that Scorpius had been on the horizon this morning. But why had it occupied his sleep?

While they were sitting on the street awaiting deportation, Joseph remembered, he had pointed the fishhook shape of the scorpion out to Amy.

"Can you catch a fish with it?" Amy asked.

"No," said Joseph. "It only looks like a fishhook."

"Why doesn't it look like a scorpion?" Amy asked.

Joseph had once asked the same questions of Isaac.

"Different constellations were named in different ways," Isaac explained. "Some in honor of gods. Some to memorialize myths. Some to explain their presence. Some to correspond to what the astronomers thought they saw."

Isaac had imbued him with a surpassing fascination for the sky. It was real, with precise details, yet it was as infinite as the imagination.

Menachem had railed against Isaac's instruction.

"Erase it from memory," Menachem had once said to Joseph, referring to the myth Isaac was recounting about the blinding of Orion by the King of Chios for attempting to elope with his daughter Merope. "Stand on your head until everything he's ever told you falls out."

"While you concern yourself with the structure of shoes," said Isaac, "someone has to worry about the tectonics of heaven."

The tectonics of heaven. Joseph loved the phrase. He put his hand to his chest and swallowed the plug that was forming in his throat. He pictured Amy crouched on the floor beside her mother, damping her split scalp with a bloodstained rag. What more could he have said to her in those last minutes on the street?

And what of Menachem?

In the stark refuge of the attic, second thoughts took root. Isaac had striven to show him that everyone belonged to a larger, incomprehensible whole. And he had learned in the ghetto that fear could have the force of nature. Perhaps his father could no more help himself than a boy who stood on a hill screaming his name at the top of his lungs just because it was spring.

But Amy was gone, and Joseph was secreted in a dusty attic, hoarding his life and dreaming strange dreams.

The details were fading, destroying the narrative, leaving elemental impressions.

Sunrise. The forest. Leaves. Coolness. Leora. Stillness. Leora. Stillness. The Stranger. Blackness. Bullets. Guns. Bullwhip. Noose. Jeweled sword. Whiteness. Stars. Constellations. Orion. Scorpions. Crabs. Fire. Snakes. Dizziness. Ashes. Swarming. Biting. Stinging. Leora. Blackness. Leora. Madness. Leora. Forest. Stillness. Leora. Darkness.

Joseph scraped his teeth over his lips. Once Isaac might have been able to make sense out of it. He knew that dreams had to be dealt with instantly.

The leather tag still hung from his neck: Joseph Bloodstein/14/references in America/Itzchok Meyer/New York/Schmuel Katzin/New York.

* * *

Leora smiled radiantly. She had worn a light blue dress with short sleeves and a white garland in her hair. Her arms were white and slender, and her dark brown hair lay softly on her shoulders.

Joseph had worn a neatly patched white shirt and a black silk skull cap.

They were standing side by side, facing Isaac. On the dressing table were two crystal wine glasses filled with water.

"Join hands," Isaac had said.

Their hands moved together and interlocked.

"My beloved spoke and said unto me, rise up, my love, my fair one, and come away.

"For, lo, the winter is past, the rain is over and gone;

"The flowers appear on the earth; the time of the singing of birds has come; and the voice of the turtle is heard in our land;

"The fig tree puts forth her green figs, and the vines with the tender grape give a good smell.

"Arise, my love, my fair one, and come away."

On the street Joseph had forgotten many things: how Isaac's hands had danced in the air as he went on in his melodic voice, stirring the north wind to blow south into the garden, tasting honey and milk and wine, smelling the orchard with its pleasant fruits and camphire, spikenard, saffron, calamus, cinnamon, frankincense, myrrh, aloes, and all the chief spices.

"I am my beloved's, and his desire is towards me.

"Come, my beloved, let us go forth into the fields; let us lodge in the villages.

"Let us get up early to the vineyards; let us see if the vines flourish, whether the tender grape appears, and the pomegranates bud forth; and there I will give you my love."

The door had closed behind them. A hush descended. Isaac was gone, and they were together.

Awkwardly, Joseph took Leora's thin face between his hands and kissed her forehead. Keeping her arms shyly at her sides, she pressed her head against his lips. He touched her brows, and her eyes, and lingered on each warm spot he kissed.

He kissed her smooth eyelids, her cheekbones, her soft cheeks, and then her lips. Her eyelids were like the inside of a velvet flower, and her cheeks were like the outside. Softly, softly, he kissed her everywhere on the face, and then he kissed her in the hollow of her throat, which was warmer than her face. Her throat blushed, and her cheeks, and he could feel her body trembling.

He kissed the side of her neck, and her ear, and placed one hand high on her chest, above her breasts. Her neck strained to exact the fever of his touch. He kissed her again on the throat, and the neck, and she tipped her head toward him, rubbing her ear against his rustling mouth.

He trailed his fingers lightly across her chest, back and forth, tracing her collarbone. She raised her head and kissed his ear, his cheek, the corner of his mouth. Their lips brushed once, and again, softly. Her lips parted, releasing her tongue, and she licked his lips, wetting and parting them. Then she thrust the tip of her tongue between his teeth, and their mouths opened, and his tongue rose against hers.

Their kisses were hot and sweet: his breath like a zephyr, and hers like dew.

He ran his fingers through her hair, and underneath, and over her nape, and down to the top button of her dress. She pressed herself against him, her arms dangling at her sides, and drew her breath. One by one, he opened the buttons of her dress.

Her smooth back tingled, and she shivered each time his fingers touched her skin.

When he had opened all the buttons, she helped him remove the dress by shrugging her shoulders, then raising her arms and easing them out of the sleeves. He held the dress by the shoulders and slipped it over her waist, and her hips, and down her legs to the floor.

She watched him stoop at her feet, and stepped out of the dress, her eyes enchanted.

Beneath the dress she wore a delicate peach chemise. The fluent material clung to the form of her breasts, and her nipples protruded like rosette buds. She extended her arms and they embraced. Then she moved back, crossed her arms, grabbed a pinch of hem in each hand, and pulled the chemise over her head.

Joseph's pulse quickened and his arms and legs tightened along their length. Leora stood before him artlessly, her bony shoulders sloped, her arms slack. Her chest was lean, but her breasts had remained fairly full. They were as white as if they had been washed in milk, tapering to pointed wine-filled nipples. Her ribs were taut against her skin, and beneath her rib cage her stomach was nearly concave before it curved into her underpants. Through the skimpy white cotton, her dark brown pubic hair spread like a shadow.

Looking unashamedly at him, neither timid now or bold, she had pulled down her underpants, so that she was absolutely naked.

Joseph's penis had swollen and grown erect and was throbbing under his clothing. Uncertain of the moment, he advanced anxiously, encircling her in his arms. She molded herself easily against him. Her body was warm and smooth and yielding.

They kissed passionately, their kisses being stronger than before, and following more quickly. He caressed her back, and her flanks, and brought one hand around to feel her breast. She shifted to facilitate his fondling. Eagerly, he cupped and squeezed her breast, and stroked her nipple, and plied it with his fingers.

She swept her hand over his chest, and began unbuttoning his shirt. When she had finished, and the shirt was free, she undid his trousers, and felt his penis spring into her hand.

"Behold, you are fair, my beloved, yea, pleasant: also our bed is green.

"The beams of our house are cedar, and our rafters of fir."

They were lying naked among the trees, his left hand under her head as a pillow. Above, the superb reticulation of leaves and branches formed a natural canopy.

He reached down and inserted his right hand between

her thighs, sifting her hair with his fingers. Responsively, she made a ring with her thumb and forefinger and worked it up and down his penis, increasing the friction until it quivered with each pass like a kite twitching on the wind.

As Joseph remembered making love to Leora, other memories and dreams filtered in.

There was a peaceful silence in the alcove. The late afternoon sun sparkled through the trees, strewing the ground with dancing wildflowers of light.

A soccer ball lay idly beside a motionless foot. As if anesthetized, a group of people sat lifelessly around a picnic lunch. Hordes of ants foraged noiselessly for food. One phalanx traversed an intense, muscular figure frozen over a chess board. Out of the path of the insects, a small man with a flecked white beard was slumped over a book, his long black coat riddled with bullet holes.

Off among the shimmering trees, the naked lovers shuddered and were still.

"Set me as a seal upon your heart, as a seal upon your arm; for love is as strong as death."

THE
BREAD
LINE

A queue had formed some time before the bakery was due to open.

It was going to be a sultry day. Already, dark puffs of factory smoke gushed out of the stacks like billows of thick black paint. The street was wet, although it had not rained, and a foul odor hung in the dampness, as if a large quantity of garbage had been steamed.

In one sweep, Eugen glanced at his wrist and then at the back of the man in front of him. He no longer expected to find a watch on his wrist, but vestiges of the time habit persisted. Now he looked upward, into the haze. Both the sun and the moon were in place.

"Five twenty-six," he said to himself.

The man in front of him turned sideways in response to Eugen's voice. His face was caved in, as if the glue holding his features together had been boiled off and what remained was a plastic tangle of bones at the bottom of the pot. Gathering that Eugen had not been addressing him, he turned his head forward again. The back of his skull and his thin neck suggested an ostrich.

Five twenty-six, Eugen thought. Somehow the time on Noah Silver's watch, which the soldier at the gate had taken from him in exchange for the crone's wares, had become a point of reference. Little by little he was getting better at guessing when it was five twenty-six in the morning, when it was five twenty-six in the evening, when it had been five twenty-six, and when it would be five twenty-six again.

Eugen was seventeenth in line. In front of him he counted four men, ten women, and two bodies of indeterminate gender. There were twice as many people behind him.

He was, by all indications, the healthiest person on queue. His posture was weakening, but he remained fairly upright and had not yet lost all his fat. As he let his beard grow out, though, and dropped weight, his nose was becoming more prominent and his general appearance increasing in likeness to those around him.

His stomach gurgled and contracted. He worked up a ball of saliva and swallowed it. His hunger pangs were coming earlier each day.

Potatoes. Garlic. Eggs. Greens. Onions. Salami.

He had thought he appreciated them properly when they were in his possession, but now he saw that it was not so. After the food on the Aryan side, potatoes and onions were nothing special. He considered them interim staples. So he had not conserved them, and they had run out all too quickly.

Each word was a picture. The deep red salami, speckled with white veins of fat and gelatinous pits of gristle, the round end casing tied in a knot, the sliced end smooth and oily, with a spicy odor. The potatoes, brown skinned, with dark mud-brown eyes and a crisp, vinegary beige finish. And the eggs, lovely white enamel shells faintly tinged with pink, each oval pearly white and bright warm yellow inside and capable of reproducing the miracle of life.

"There are five of us and one of you."

In the morning, Tzipora's father had tried to return the

eggs, but Eugen would not take them. Finally, the mother had
boiled them over the fire and the father had cut off the tops
one third of the way down. Tzipora and her youngest brother
received bottoms. The oldest boy and the mother got tops.
Eugen was offered a bottom, then a top, refusing both.

"You need energy for the trip," he had said. "I have
enough else to tide me over."

He watched Tzipora cupping the warm egg shell in her
palm and scooping out the insides.

"Do you want some?" she asked, extending her spoon
after dipping it into the egg.

"No thanks," he said. "I'm not hungry."

It was the first time he had heard her speak. Her voice
was soft and had a burr in it. A sensation of skin brushing
napped velvet spread over his body.

When she had finished, she licked the spoon clean and
handed it to her mother. The edges of her lips were stained
yellow.

"Wipe your mouth," her mother said.

She flicked her tongue over her lips, moistening them
like a cat, and finished the job with the back of her hand.

"All gone?" she asked Eugen.

He nodded. Her mouth was so fine. He imagined her soft
wet tongue lapping his face.

Although it was not yet day, the street was growing active. Some people had already set out for the *umschlagplatz*.
Others made their final preparations.

It was time to go. Eugen's family stood packed and ready
beside their extinguished fire. The father reached out and
clasped Eugen's hand.

"God be with you," he said.

His voice expressed a determined kindness. Eugen was
unable to reply. He tried to indicate with a gesture of his head
that he appreciated the father's words. Then he bent over and
kissed Tzipora on the cheek. Goodbye, my love, he thought.
He wanted to kiss her again, to lift her to his chest and smother
her with his kisses, but he did not.

The father had started toward the *umschlagplatz*. He carried a heavy valise in one hand and a large canvas-wrapped bundle in the other. Behind him walked Tzipora and the older boy, hand in hand, and behind them, also hand in hand, followed the younger boy and his mother.

Eugen watched them move away. His stomach clenched. He could not remember when he had felt as warm inside as he had sitting by their fire. He had a notion to run after them.

The street was gradually being abandoned. Indecisively, Eugen took a few steps in the direction of the flow. He did not want to lose sight of his family. As they moved further away, they began to merge with other families, all straggling toward the *umschlagplatz*.

They were almost out of view when they turned the corner: Tzipora keeping pace with the crowd, taking small, quick steps, like a spring wound doll.

Salami. Onions. Potatoes. Garlic. Greens.

The bakery had still not opened. As the line grew longer, Eugen's hunger advanced. If only he had those provisions back, he could make do for a month on what he had eaten in a few days. But he had not come to the bakery to think about food.

"Excuse me," he said to the back of the ostrich head of the man in front of him.

The head did not move.

"Excuse me," Eugen repeated.

Again there was no response. He tapped the man on the shoulder, weakly, then more firmly. Finally the head moved, ever so slightly, tightening the cicatrixed skin on the neck.

"Could I ask you something?" Eugen said, leaning toward the man's ear and tapping him.

With exaggerated slowness, the man turned sideways, sliding his feet in tiny increments, without lifting them off the ground, until he was facing Eugen. His collapsed profile was even less pleasant head-on. He seemed to be regarding Eugen with his entire face rather than just with his eyes.

"I'm looking for someone," Eugen said. "Perhaps you know him. His name is Abrahm Bankart."

Eugen's voice came out louder than he intended. The man held his impassive pose for a moment, as if trying to digest what Eugen had said. Then his body began to move, almost imperceptibly, rotating in his slow, incremental motion, leaving Eugen once more viewing the back of his ostrich neck.

Eugen angled to catch a glimpse of the man behind him. As he did so, he felt that he was being watched. He turned to face the man fully.

"I don't mean to bother you," he said, "but I'm looking for someone. Bankart. Abrahm Bankart."

The man, who was younger, and whose face was still a face, looked at Eugen as if he would bore holes in his forehead.

"Excuse me," Eugen said, turning around.

Wherever he had been, he had gotten the same blank stare. No one had heard of Abrahm Bankart.

Eugen's stomach gurgled loudly. He pulled in his abdominal muscles to cut off the noise, but the gnawing persisted and built into another long, involuted grumble.

It was, for the hungry moment, a happy coincidence that his search had brought him to a bakery. Finkel, Thierbach's stoolie, had worked there before he came up dead. Actually, it was not this very bakery, but several shops had been consolidated since then. As far as Eugen had been able to determine, at least some of Finkel's co-workers had come here. There might be no one left, the turnover was so rapid, but he could not leave any stone unturned.

"Open up," someone shouted from the back of the queue. His voice sent a wave of complaint through the line.

"Open up," said another voice, weakly echoing the first.

"It's torture standing in one place."

"We've been waiting since dark."

"Please."

"It's almost supper time."

"My wife is dying."

The voices were low and indistinct, as if each were addressed to itself.

"I'm hungry," Eugen heard himself say.

He could feel the stones pushing unyieldingly against the arches of his feet.

At last the door opened. The queue came to life, tightening up and surging forward. A table was placed in front of the door and a large cauldron of piping hot soup was placed upon it. A woman brought out a stack of soup plates, and a man followed with an armload of cups.

The man, who had a long, narrow face, said something that Eugen could not hear. The line began to move. Eugen watched him ladle the steaming soup into the first bowl and hand it to the person at the front of the queue, who took it and stepped aside. The second person received his bowl. He too, moved to the side of the table, but did not walk away.

"There's no bread," Eugen heard someone say.

The words did not register.

Instead of remaining straight and growing shorter, the queue was forming a knob around the table.

"No more bread."

"No bread."

"Nothing to eat."

The message had passed Eugen and was making its way to the back of the line before he grasped the situation. The bakery had been late to open because of a problem. They were not serving any bread. Just soup.

Swallowing their disappointment, the first people in line finally moved away from the table and found spots to drink their soup, leaning against the building or sitting down on the ground. The tempo of the queue accelerated.

Three places in front of him, a woman slumped and toppled onto the street. The woman behind her walked over her, as did the man in front of Eugen. No one as much as looked down. Eugen hesitated and considered kneeling to see

what was the matter, but stepped over her feet. He did not
want to call attention to himself, and his stomach was becoming spastic.

When the man who was serving the soup saw that the
fallen woman was not moving, he called inside for help. A
large, muscular man appeared. Eugen recognized him as having helped bring out the table and the cauldron. He had dark,
closely cropped hair, a broad forehead, wide cheekbones, a
thick neck, square shoulders, and strong hands which, like his
neck, were prominently veined. Peripherally, Eugen saw him
turn the woman over on her back, feel her pulse, and press his
ear against her chest. Then he lifted her off the street and
carried her up onto the sidewalk.

"I need a piece of paper," he said, laying her body parallel
to the curb.

The woman who had set out the plates brought some
paper and the man laid it over the dead woman's face.

Eugen's nostril's twitched. The soup had a light yellow
color, like sunlight streaming into an attic. He could see right
through it as the man with the narrow face filled the bowl of
the man with the ostrich neck.

"There'll be seconds today, because of the bread," Heykel
said to the old man.

His hands were so unsteady that the soup splashed out of
his bowl as he walked away. He won't have anything left by the
time he finds a place to drink it, Eugen thought.

"Excuse me," Eugen said, clearing his throat as his soup
was being poured, "but perhaps you could help me. I'm looking for an old friend. Abrahm Bankart. I thought someone
here might know of him."

Heykel handed Eugen his bowl.

"Step aside," he said, plunging the ladle into the cauldron
and filling a bowl for the man behind Eugen.

Eugen moved to one side of the table. A few drops of soup
jumped out of his bowl and scalded his thumb. His hands had
been perfectly steady before, but holding the soup they were

trembling almost as much as the old man's. He leaned against the wall to steady himself.

The dead woman lay unceremoniously under a sheet of paper. Eugen wondered what the strong man who had tended to her was doing inside the bakery. Something about him struck a curious chord.

"Now who is it you're after?" Heykel said over his shoulder.

"A man named Bankart," Eugen said. "Abrahm Bankart."

"It doesn't ring a bell," said Heykel.

"Before the war he worked in a slaughterhouse," Eugen said. "Someone who was leaving the ghetto entrusted me with something to give him. I promised I would."

"What is it?" asked Heykel.

"It's personal," Eugen said.

"Can you describe him?" Heykel said.

"I understand he was very muscular," Eugen said. "Middle-aged. Dark hair. Strong features."

"You said he was an old friend," Heykel said.

"I never knew him personally," Eugen said. "He was close with my uncle."

"I'm afraid I can't help you," Heykel said. "I'll remember the name though. You can check back if you want."

"Much obliged," Eugen said.

His hands had grown accustomed to the heat of his bowl. Holding it as steadily as he could, he moved away from the table and found a spot on the sidewalk facing away from the serving table.

The soup was disappointingly tasteless. It had no fat content, no bubbles, no film, no trace of skin or marrow, no carrots, no hint of salt or pepper or paprika. He wondered how long it would have sustained the dead woman, had she been able to reach the table.

Thirstily, he polished off his bowl and assumed a new place at the back of the queue.

*   *   *

No one seemed to pay attention as the black wagon approached. The queue moved forward slowly, steadily, the steaming yellow water filling bowl after bowl.

Clip-clop, clip-clop.

Eugen watched the skinny horse that was drawing the wagon come to a halt without any signal from the old man who was holding the reins. Beside him sat an unsightly beggar, and next to him, a young boy with brown hair and a smooth, earnest face.

"Hello there," the old man called down from the wagon.

"Hello," Heykel said.

The large muscular man emerged from the bakery and took over the ladle.

"If it isn't Samson," the old man said.

"Then who is it?" said Samson.

"Miserable day," the old man said, mopping his brow with his shirt sleeve.

"It could be worse," said Heykel, coming over to the wagon.

"Not for her," the old man said, referring to the woman on the sidewalk.

"She fell out of line when she heard there was no bread," Heykel said.

"Can't blame her," the old man said.

"Good morning," Isaac said. "A fine day, isn't it?"

"Good morning," Heykel said.

"Ready to come down?" the old man said, climbing off the wagon.

"If you please," said Isaac.

Holding the boy's hand, Isaac stood and edged over to the side of the bench well. The old man reached up and grabbed him under the armpits.

"Down we go," he said, lifting him up and swinging him onto the ground.

The boy handed the old man Isaac's rope.

"Here," the old man said, placing the rope in Isaac's palm.

"Thank you," Isaac said.

He turned toward the looped end of the rope and groped in the air for Zirka's head.

"We're at the bakery, my love," he said, stroking her mane.

The end of the rope was very near the dead woman's feet.

"Come," Heykel said, taking Isaac by the elbow and leading him over to where Eugen had downed his bowl of soup.

The old driver stooped over the dead woman, scooped her off the sidewalk, and flung her up to the boy, who had gone over the bench onto the platform.

"Sorry there's nothing for you today," Heykel said to the old man.

"We'll survive," the old man said, climbing back onto the bench.

"You'd better," Heykel said. "Someone has to keep the streets clean."

"The horse knows the route as well as I do," the old man said. "She could do it alone if only the passengers would get on without help."

"If they could, they wouldn't want to," Heykel said.

The old man smiled.

"Hee-a," he said, picking up the rein.

The wagon pulled away, clip-clop, clip-clopping.

The beggar squatted on his haunches, laid his rope flat on the sidewalk, inched over until he was halfway between the looped end and the straight end, removed a dingy pan from around his neck, set it on the ground, and raising his hands a foot above it, began a pumping, squeezing motion, as if he were milking a cow.

Simultaneously, he seemed to be talking, although there was no one near him. The man with the narrow face had gone inside, leaving the man called Samson to dish up the soup. Was that really his name, Eugen pondered, or had he detected an undertone in his brief exchange with the driver? Eugen was twelfth in line. He hoped the other man would be back at the ladle by the time he reached the front.

As he watched the beggar move his hands through the air in a repetitive series of jerky motions, Eugen suddenly realized why he had been perched so stiffly between the old man and the boy on the wagon bench, why they had let him down so carefully, and why the man with the narrow face had steered him clear of the dead woman's body. He was blind.

Eugen frowned in self-rebuke. How could he not have noticed?

The man with the narrow face and the woman brought out a large pot of fresh soup and dumped it into the cauldron. This time the liquid had long noodles in it.

"Please . . . a little milk for a piece of bread."

The beggar had picked his pan off the sidewalk and was carrying it in one hand, carefully, so as not to spill its contents. In the other hand he held his rope, the oversized loop trailing the ground. He made his way toward the table, sniffing the air.

"Ah, that smells good," Isaac said, stopping short of the table.

Eugen was close enough to see the dark holes of his eyes and his jaw hanging disjointedly, like a snapped branch.

"How's Zirka today?" Samson asked as he poured a bowl of soup.

"Very well, thank you," Isaac said. "I have a full pan."

"We could use some milk," Samson said, pouring another bowl.

Eugen perked up. The last few bowls had each contained several noodles.

"Yes," Isaac said. "Milk is good."

He extended the pan eagerly toward Samson.

"A piece of bread for a little milk," he said.

"We don't have any bread today," Samson said. "Just soup."

He took the pan and handed it into the bakery.

"Wait a minute," Eugen heard someone say.

The man in front of him turned around.

"We've been waiting in line."

"What's that?" Samson said.

"We've been waiting all morning."

"Go poke your eyes out," Samson said.

Eugen felt the remark as if it had been intended for him. He lowered his eyes and moved over so that the man in front of him blocked his face from Samson's view.

Shortly, the man with the narrow face came out with the beggar's pan and walked him over to the place where he had been milking his cow.

"Sit down here," he said.

Isaac squatted and Heykel set the pan down in front of him.

"It's a little hot," he warned.

Isaac gripped the pan with both hands and raised it to his chin. He paused to smell the steam, then dove through it into the soup, lapping it up like a dog and splashing it on his clothes.

"I'll be inside," Heykel said, leaving him. "There's more if you want."

Eugen's turn had come. He handed his bowl to Samson. As if he had read Eugen's mind, Samson reached deep into the cauldron and filled his bowl plentifully with noodles. Then he dipped the ladle a second time and covered the noodles with broth.

"Thank you," Eugen said, feeling a rush of gratitude.

The beggar was occupying his old spot. Eugen started in another direction, then changed his mind. He had been re-miss in resenting the beggar's privilege at the front of the line. Perhaps he could make up for it with a gesture. He walked over to where he was squatting and sat down beside him.

"It's very good," said the beggar, hearing Eugen come near.

The beggar dipped his hand into his soup, then thrust a small piece of potato into his mouth. His fingers were brown. Eugen looked into his pan. Instead of clear soup, he saw that it contained a dense liquid, almost a stew, with little bits of potato and other ingredients that were unidentifiable in the thickness. So that was why they had taken the pan inside! He stared at it until it began to simmer before his eyes. What had imparted the rich, dark color?

He tipped his own bowl and took a sip. The soup had no flavor, only a faint sweetness. He stuck his fingers into the bowl and took out a few noodles. They were hard. When he bit into one, it was like twine. He tried a few more. They were not noodles but straw.

The beggar was heartily enjoying himself: stirring his stew, sifting for particles, licking and sucking his fingers.

Eugen's bowl was so clogged with straw, there was scarcely any soup. He tilted his head and drained it off in one swallow. There was no use aggravating himself. Empty of liquid, the bowl resembled a bird's nest.

He considered getting back into line, but thought better of it. It frightened him that he had been singled out for such treatment. When Samson filled his bowl so amply, he had almost inquired again about Bankart. It was a good thing he had not.

"There's more soup if you want," he said to the beggar.

"Yes, thank you," said the beggar. "It's very good."

Eugen rose to return his bowl.

"Can I get you some more?" he asked.

"If you please," said the beggar.

He held the pan over his head. Eugen took it and went over to the table.

"Twice is the limit," Samson said.

"It's not for me," Eugen said, holding both his bowl and the pan out in front of him.

Samson turned toward him and snatched the pan, catching Eugen by surprise. He was pulled forward before he could release it and bumped into the table. Shaken, he set his bowl down and moved aside to wait for the pan to be refilled.

Observing Samson from behind, Eugen was doubly glad that he had not asked any more questions. In fact, he wished

he had never come in the first place. He could have anticipated that no one here would have heard of Bankart. No one
had anywhere. And what was the point of a bread line without
bread?

Eugen glanced queasily at some of the people on queue.
Why were they letting them starve? The woman who had
been picked up by the wagon came to mind. They would not
get any work out of her. If it had already come to serving straw,
he would not be amazed if one day soon they were forced to
start chopping up corpses as they fell out of line and throwing
an arm or a leg into the cauldron.

His mind began to wander in a dark, barbaric region, but
he was swiftly brought back to his senses by the sound of a
harmonica. Instantly, he saw Tzipora, beautiful Tzipora, her
head resting on his thigh, the light of the fire shining on her
face.

The music seemed to be everywhere. Eugen held still.
Was he dreaming? The queue moved forward and Samson
poured a bowl of soup the color of Tzipora's hair.

It was coming from the side. Eugen turned his head.
There, set in a wide, crouching stance, was the swaying figure
who had played at the naked women's fire. With his feet barely
touching the ground, and his frail hands fluttering about
his mouth, the beggar appeared to be on the verge of flying
away.

"It's ready," Samson said.

Eugen could not break the spell of the beggar's music.

"Here, take it," he heard Samson grumble.

Something burned Eugen's hand. He was holding the
pan. It had been replenished with a fresh, hot portion of stew.
He was tempted to put a finger in it, but dared not, for fear
that Samson would see him.

The beggar stopped as Eugen came toward him and
moved his head from side to side in silence. Then he fumbled
with his clothing and squatted down.

"Here," Eugen said, placing the pan in front of him.

"Yes, thank you," said the beggar.

He rubbed his hands together and raised the pan, sniffing it and murmuring satisfaction.

Eugen began to leave, but gave in to an impulse to stay a moment. His head was still coping with the music. He looked closely at the beggar's face. It was the same mask that had just played the harmonica, but it was not the same person.

SHADOWS

The sun set brilliantly, spreading a magnificent run of colors over the city. Stiffening his neck against the breeze, Olek stood near Kazimierz Square waiting for a trolley. With the poignancy of dusk, he felt a twinge of unrequited love for the Warsaw that had produced him, nurtured him, inspired him, and then outraged him.

The countless open shops and stalls of the great market swarmed with buyers and sellers, raising a hubbub that was oblivious to the twilight. As a boy, Olek had been fascinated by the overabundance of shapes, colors, odors, textures. There were as many kinds of fruits and vegetables as there were animals and people. It was exciting to see them, to be aware of them, and to imagine the possible reasons for their existence. Now he experienced the market with the same detachment that it exhibited toward the death of his father. He did not care if it were blown to smithereens that very instant. Life would stop for some and go on for others.

As he boarded the trolley, Olek's blood turned to ice water. Sitting near the front of the car, a man with a hard face and a glass eye was staring straight at him. It gave him the sensation of having been taken out of a warm bed in his sleep and thrown into the cold river.

The trolley was moving. It was too late to jump off without engendering suspicion. Several seconds passed. Olek had to take a seat quickly, without faltering. Bracing himself, he walked directly toward the man, returning his stare. Who was he? Unnervingly, the man was not searching his face for anything, but was simply confronting it with his own, as if this in itself had some significance. Keeping cool, Olek took the bench immediately adjacent to his. Their eyes remained locked. Two could play the same game.

It seemed that time was freezing en route to the next stop. Olek weighed his alternatives. He could get off and see whether or not the man followed. Or he could stay on for a while and try to force his hand. One thing he could not do was ride to the end of the line, where lay the suburb that was his destination.

As Olek studied the man's face the feeling grew compulsive within him that this was someone he should know. How could he be so certain of recognizing a person and yet be unable to place him? But the war had a funny way of distorting things. Fatigue deadened reflexes. Fear suspended judgment. Tension could heighten perception or warp it. Perhaps he was mistaken, had never seen this man before, and had no reason to know him. The city was cursed with a cornucopia of deranged people. Was it not possible, among the lunatics of every description, for there to be a humorless man whose obsession was staring at people? It was no more unlikely than that the person he had chosen to bother this time was a blond, Aryan-looking Jew masquerading as a Polish civil servant.

It was an intriguing line of thought. Before Olek could pursue it further the man, who had still not disengaged his eyes, rose from his seat, strode unhesitatingly to the door, and without waiting for the trolley to reach the next stop, leapt off.

The trance was broken. As Olek rushed to the door, the images, if not yet the words, swam to mind. The man was crossing the tracks and walking back in the direction of the square. He did not know why it had eluded him at close range, but at a distance he was almost sure of it—he had been sitting face to face with the intruder at Leora's funeral!

He returned to his seat. There were not many passengers on the car. He scrutinized them to determine whether anyone had noticed the byplay between himself and the stranger. Negative. In the twilight they sat fixed like wax dummies.

The temperature was dropping rapidly and points of white light were dotting the city. Could it really have been coincidental, Olek wondered? If so, why such odd behavior? And if it had been intentional? Impossible. No one could have known that he was going to be on that trolley.

He turned the puzzle over and over, but the pieces would not fit. Something was missing. Finally he forced himself to lay it aside and concentrate on the job at hand. Abrahm had managed a hairbreadth escape, but they were closing in on him. There was not much time.

As the train made its way out of the city, Olek sat with his head against the window, watching the day meld into night.

T H E
SLAUGHTERHOUSE

It was a short walk to Nicholas Kundousky's house. Although he had never met him, Olek knew the way blindfolded. "Big Nick," as he was called, was a giant of a man who had fought valiantly in the service of Kaiser Wilhelm only to find himself on the losing side. In the confusion of the times, he was not even certain what nationality to consider himself. Adventurous at heart, he decided to try his luck in the newly established Independent Polish Republic. But the Russians were not so enamored as he with his new homeland, and before he knew it he was at war again. This time, with help from the French, he found himself on the winning side and a confirmed Pole.

For several years he had trouble finding satisfactory work. He was without a profession, there was an unskilled labor surplus, and whenever someone took him on it was usually for the most strenuous manual job. Frequently he damned the mysterious genetic design that had caused his mother to issue forth such a beast of burden. But the problem was not his physical prowess. It was rather the combination of his mild, introverted temperament and his huge, dumb appearance. He spoke simply when he spoke at all, and he looked stupid. Subsequent years would prove him quite resourceful, but in his late twenties, after the greatest war the world had ever seen, no one would give him a chance.

So he wandered from town to town, staying a few weeks here, a few months there, doing the farm chores he had mastered as a boy or whatever else came along. Sometimes he slept in a bed, but usually he was left to create his own accommodation in a barn, a stable, a grain shed, or some other ancillary structure. Oddly enough, this was the aspect of his situation that he minded the least. In his youth he had developed a healthy affection for animals, particularly dogs and horses, and his liking for them was buttressed during his soldiering days. On a number of occasions animals had shown themselves more dependable than men.

His transience was reinforced by the fact that he felt more comfortable sleeping in an outbuilding than in the house of someone who had hired him for dirty work and considered him less a human being than a drudge. Most employers found his independence disconcerting. They could not understand why a man, offered a bed, would choose a barn. But even in places where he was accepted as a person and treated well, he refused to stay long. Inwardly, he was driven by the conviction that there was a better place in life for him and that he had to keep moving until he found it. The trouble was that he had no idea what he was looking for.

Eventually, by the most circuitous route imaginable, Nicholas found his calling in Warsaw. For a long time he had resisted the blandishments of the large cities because, although he did not know what he wanted, he knew what he did not want. He did not want to go to work in a factory and become a machine. He did not want to live in the cramped, decrepit neighborhoods reserved for the workers. He did not want to spend his life breathing poisoned air only to die early of it. But when he turned thirty-two or thirty-three—he suspected he had lost a year along the way—and was still a nomad, unfulfilled and without favorable prospects, he had an insight. There was not a single indication that his wandering had been salutary. Maybe he had been pursuing the wrong path.

The more he thought about it, the more firmly he resolved to take a drastic step. He would go to Warsaw. If he could not find what he was seeking there, it probably did not exist in all of Poland.

Nicholas had arrived in Warsaw in the cruel white heart of winter, without money or a place to stay. After some weeks of hardship, he was fortunate enough to find employment in one of the biggest slaughterhouses in the city. His job was to clean up the blood and guts that poured out of the cattle as they were killed and butchered. It was messy work and did not pay much, but it enabled him to rent a bed in a garret and feed himself and it was preferable to standing beside a deafening machine all day in an infernal factory. What bothered him most was the sickening stench that permeated everything and clung to his nostrils when he went home at night. But in time he became accustomed to it.

When he had been there two months or so, an incident occurred that was to drastically change the course of his life. One morning, as he was standing there mopping blood, he unexpectedly heard someone down the line booming out his name.

"Kundousky!" he heard. "Which one of you bastards calls himself Nicholas Kundousky?"

Something told him not to look up immediately.

The voice was unfamiliar, and none of the workers called him by his full name. He was Big Nick even to the foreman. And he got along well with everyone. So well that he was in line for the next cutting job that opened up. The voice was growing louder.

"Kundousky! Show yourself, you chickenshit."

Before he could step out, Nicholas heard the ominous

clanking of metal hooks and blades hitting the stone floor. He
pulled his knife from his belt and let it drop.

"I'm Nicholas Kundousky," he said, turning to face the
voice.

His fellow crew members had backed away and merged
with the mob of butchers and trimmers that had gathered
around. A bald man with the body of a bull—thick neck,
bunched shoulder muscles, stocky torso—moved forward.
His eyes were bloodshot.

"You fucking Jew bastard," he said in a gravel voice laced
with whiskey.

He advanced menacingly. Nicholas had no idea who he
was.

"I'm not a Jew," he said, "and I'm not a bastard. What is it
you want from me?"

The man was so close that Nicholas could smell his
breath. Alcohol and garlic. In the background the men stood
motionless, like figures in a painting of a crowd.

"You're worse than a Jew, you kosher bloodsucker," the
man growled. "You're a goddamned motherfucking son of a
diseased whore."

As he finished the man exploded forward, ramming his
lowered head into Nicholas' gut. He felt a searing flash in his
groin. The man kneed him viciously in the crotch, once,
twice, again. He could not see his face but he could hear him
grunting with each blow. It was getting hard to breathe. He
tried to protect his midsection with his elbows but he could
not coordinate them against an attack that had taken him by
surprise and now had him completely off balance. The man
was swarming all over him, pushing him back against a wall
and punching and kicking him savagely. His nose broke with a
sharp snap. A stream of blood gushed forth. The shock of it
jolted him out of the initial paralysis of bewilderment. The son
of a bitch was trying to kill him, Nicholas realized, and he was
letting him get away with it!

In the instant the man let up to shake off the warm torrent
of Nicholas' blood that had spurted onto his forehead and was

running down into his eyes, Nicholas braced himself against the wall and threw his left shoulder forward, catching the man high on the chest. He bounced backward, losing his momentum, and before he could recover Nicholas was on the attack. A flurry of ham-fisted punches pushed the man further back and then, as suddenly as the fight had begun, a crunching forearm smash to the jaw stopped him dead in his tracks. Nicholas saw that his eyes were glazed and stepped back. The man lurched forward, still intent on injuring him, but his arms would not obey the command to rise and his legs had lost all coordination. He dropped to the floor like a felled ox.

A lusty cheer went up from the men.

"That a way, Big Nick," voices called out. "You really showed him . . ."

"He had it coming to him, Nick."

"You shouldn't have let him off so easy."

"Two ears and a tail."

"One of these days he'll wind up in a string of blood sausage."

Someone handed Nicholas a rag with which to stanch the flow of blood from his nose. It throbbed sharply, as though his nostrils had been stuffed with fractured glass. The men were buzzing about his victory, but there was not a word about the reason for the fight. He was so engrossed in trying to comprehend what had befallen that he was unaware that his attacker had come to, picked up one of the knives that were still on the floor, and was stealing toward him.

"Look out!"

The words did not register until, a split-second later, a hair-raising scream turned Nicholas' head. A knife clattered against the floor. Not six feet from him, his attacker was being strangled by an intense, wiry Jew who had intercepted him in his rush toward Nicholas and disarmed him before anyone else had even realized what he was up to. The Jew had a hold on the man's neck from behind and his grip was so overpowering that in a few seconds his captive had ceased his dazed flailing and was going limp—his body slumping, his arms flapping in slow motion, his eyes bulging and rolling upward, the color draining from his face until he was unconscious.

The Jew dropped his carcass on the floor and ordered several men to guard it. Nicholas saw how quickly they responded to his soft-spoken command. There was implicit authority in his sinewy body and sensitive, darkly brooding face.

Nicholas had often noticed him from afar. He was widely recognized as the leader of the Jewish workers. Among the majority of Polish workers he was respected as tough but honest. But there were those who resented his influence and were constantly plotting to undermine him. So far no one had succeeded, for in addition to being politically able, he was an indomitable fighter—a vital requisite for supremacy in the slaughterhouse world.

"Consider yourself initiated," said the man, who was known as Comrade Abrahm.

There was a hypnotic quality about his face. He had high cheek bones and prominent bony ridges above his eyes, which were deeply set and the color of rich brown loam. A projection from within appeared to reflect the flames of a distant fire.

"I consider myself lucky," Nicholas replied, "and most indebted to you."

Abrahm introduced himself and extended his hand. Nicholas shook it eagerly. Abrahm's arms, like his eyes, seemed to have a life of their own. They were heavily muscled, far out of proportion to the rest of his body, and rippled with blue-green veins which swelled with exertion.

"You fought well for a newcomer," Abrahm said. "But you should never have turned your back."

"I thought it was over," Nicholas said, still baffled over why it had begun.

"With his kind it's never over," said Abrahm.

"But I don't even know him," Nicholas said. "What on earth could he want with me?"

"His name is Jan Stracho," Abrahm explained. "He used to work here. A bully and a Jew-baiter of the first order. Chronically on the bottle. He and his friends made life unbearable for the rest. We forced him out. Most of his cronies went with him. They're still causing plenty of trouble elsewhere. But a few stayed here. One of them may have fingered you."

"But for what?" Nicholas protested.

"We'll find out," Abrahm said.

Stracho had revived and was coughing to clear his windpipe. Abrahm signalled his men to bring him over. They pulled him up roughly. The rage to murder was in his red eyes.

"So we meet again," said Abrahm.

Stracho spit at Nicholas, but the saliva drooped off his lips onto his own shirt. Abrahm struck him in the mouth, knocking him down. The men hauled him up again. His lower lip was gashed and bleeding.

"What have you against this man?" Abrahm asked.

"Figure it out," Stracho answered.

"I want to know now," Abrahm demanded.

His arm tightened as if to strike again. Stracho flinched.

"Someone saw him with my wife," Stracho said, licking the blood from his lip. "I traced him here."

"Don't test my patience," Abrahm said.

"I swear it's true," said Stracho.

"He should have done us all a favor and finished you off," Abrahm said.

"But Szandor will vouch for it," said Stracho. "The bitch hasn't slept with me in months."

Nicholas was surprised to hear Szandor's name mentioned. They were in the same crew together. From the start there had been a coolness between them, but nothing troublesome.

"I'm sure he will," Abrahm said. "But understand this, Stracho. The next time you set foot in this factory you'd better have a damn good reason, because if you don't you'll wind up on a hook. Now apologize to this man and get your ass out of here."

Szandor was within earshot but did not come forward. Stracho stood his ground nervously. Abrahm raised his hand to his throat and pressed his thumb to the main nerve on the side of his neck.

"Apologize," he said, beginning to apply pressure.

"All right," Stracho conceded, unable to squirm out of his grip.

Abrahm released him. Stracho straightened himself and faced Nicholas.

"I'm sorry," Stracho said contemptuously, "that someone saw you with my wife."

Abrahm lashed out so quickly that Stracho did not feel the back of his head cracking against the floor. He eyes went blank and blood oozed out of the split in his shaved and waxed scalp. A viscous puddle formed under his head and a bloody froth seeped out of his mouth.

"Heinrich," Abrahm said, "you'd better get him to a doctor. Szandor will give you a hand."

Heinrich, who had remained inconspicuous during the fight and the confrontation with Abrahm, now emerged to take charge of Stracho's body. Several henchmen followed suit.

"Water," Heinrich said to one of them. "Kurt, run ahead and alert Dr. Schreiker. Szandor, get some rags."

The men obeyed Heinrich mechanically. He was a cut-throat butcher who had been Stracho's right hand and upon his expulsion had inherited the post of chief factory tormentor and anti-Semite. Although on the outside he remained subordinate to Stracho, there were those who surmised that he had helped drive him out. He had not only chosen to stay behind, but had purged those who would not exchange Stracho's style of flagrant violence for his own more diabolic methods of coercion. Less demonstrative than his predecessor, Heinrich was even more determined to prevail—a dedication accentuated by the sinister, unblinking expression frozen on his face by virtue of a glass left eye.

As they were carrying Stracho's body out, Heinrich turned to Nicholas.

"We know who you are," he glowered. "You'll get your due."

Ignoring Abrahm, Heinrich pivoted on his heel and marched out in wake of the others.

ANIMAL
MAN

One evening shortly after the fracas Abrahm appeared
unannounced at Nicholas' room.

"You have an explanation coming," he said.

Apparently Szandor, who had been in the factory for
years and was notoriously shiftless, resented Nicholas for having been put in line for promotion after such a short time.
Also, Szandor was aggravated by Nicholas' assertion that he
preferred most animals to most people. Therefore he passed
the word to Heinrich that the new man had confided over
schnapps that he was actually a Jew but had lied to improve his
chances of being hired.

Heinrich may or may not have believed Szandor, but out
of the blue he saw an opportunity to eliminate Stracho without
implicating himself. He knew that Stracho was itching for a
measure of revenge in the factory. But only an extreme provocation could bring him back, for he had been strongly warned
of the consequences.

The strategem was to make Stracho rush in with a
grudge. If Nicholas was as formidable as he seemed, Stracho

would find himself disgraced. If not, the act of starting an unwarrantable fight might in itself bring about his undoing.

To set the trap, Heinrich embellished Szandor's complaint by concocting the story that not only was there an unacknowledged Jew in the factory, but that the boys had seen him hanging out at the dive where Stracho's mistress sang and sold after-hours favors.

"He was telling the truth," Abrahm chortled, "when he said he hadn't slept with his wife in months."

Although they had nothing obvious in common except physical strength, Abrahm and Nicholas found a natural affinity for one another and began to spend time together.

Abrahm indoctrinated Nicholas in the history and goals of the socialist labor movement. But when he suggested introducing him to some of his Polish socialist contacts, Nicholas always balked. He was in accord with the ideals Abrahm expressed, but wanted nothing to do with any organization.

"But active solidarity is the workers' only hope," Abrahm argued.

Nicholas replied that though he understood, something in his makeup would not allow him to submit himself to the claims of a movement. He had twice been a soldier, and that was more than enough.

"You don't belong in the factory," Abrahm said to him one night. "You should pull out while you can. I'll help you get something else."

"But what?" asked Nicholas.

"One of our Polish comrades is a veterinarian," Abrahm said. "He needs an assistant. The pay is better than in the factory and you can live in."

"I must be dreaming," Nicholas said.

His eyes drew water. He was a simple soul who had never found his niche, and now someone was offering him a chance.

"Try it," Abrahm said, "and if it doesn't work out, you

won't have lost anything. We can always find another job for a Gentile."

Nicholas struggled to exercise caution against his hopes rising, then being crushed. But Abrahm's overture had set him vibrating like a tuning fork. The years of frustration were parting and he was a child again.

On the following Monday Nicholas proceeded, baggage in hand, to the home of Bronis Ganzs, who lived and worked on a large, wooded lot on the outskirts of town.

In addition to his wife and three children, Bronis' house abounded with dogs, cats, chickens, birds, and miscellaneous creatures. The animals were compartmentalized according to his system for admitting patients through the back door and discharging them through the front. Behind the house, which was two stories high, he had built a spacious barn where he could treat larger animals—horses, cows, and the like. Also, there were two storage sheds—one for animal feed and supplies, the other for tools and firewood.

Nicholas was speedily made to feel at home. Bronis greeted him cordially and showed him his room on the second floor. It was twice the size of the one Nicholas had been renting, pleasantly furnished, and had a nice window facing the trees in the back.

Mrs. Ganzs fixed some tea and sweet cakes and Bronis enthusiastically described his practice. It had flourished so, he said, that he could no longer make do with family help alone. He was delighted that Comrade Abrahm had found such a good man for him.

The first week sped by, and the second, and the third, and before he knew it Nicholas was in his second happy month on the job. He rose before the sun every morning and worked straight through to supper. Often he went out after supper and worked late in the barn or puttered around the sheds, mending a cage, rewiring a coop, doing whatever he could find to do. He enjoyed the work so much that he felt slightly guilty drawing a salary as well as room and board.

To top everything, Mrs. Ganzs was a wonderful cook and prepared plentiful meals the likes of which Nicholas had not eaten in fifteen years. Sometimes, sitting at the table in the dining room on a rainy night with the food steaming and everyone talking away, he thought of army food, long nights in dank barracks or in a ditch somewhere, days without any food at all, and the gory slabs of meat and globs of intestines in the slaughterhouse. Moved by feelings he could not express, he liked to go out in the rain on nights like that and lie on his coat in the hay and listen to the water on the roof.

Nicholas had so few expenses that Bronis opened a bank account for him and paid most of his earnings directly into it. As the months passed, Bronis began to kid him about his savings, calling him a rich man in poor man's clothing. They had good laughs over it, but he had no idea that ten years and numerous raises later, long after the account had lost its reality for him, the ledger would indeed show him to be a moderately wealthy man.

Nicholas had a particular liking for dogs. In this third year, when he had effectively become a member of the household, he approached Bronis with a proposal. They had always been burdened with a considerable number of homeless animals, either through owner desertion or when, out of compassion, strays were brought to them for attention. The majority wound up at the pound or the slaughterhouse. Instead of condemning the dogs to certain death, why not breed and train them? He volunteered to build a kennel and assume all responsibility for its operation.

Bronis jumped at the idea. Why had he not thought of it before? He authorized Nicholas to begin construction immediately.

It turned out to be a highly successful venture. Within a year Bronis had turned a slight profit. Before the second year was up he was making such handsome money that he offered

Nicholas a junior partnership. When Nicholas declined, saying that he was happy with things the way they were, Bronis assigned a percentage of the kennel's income to his savings account. A third man was hired on a part-time basis to relieve Nicholas of some of his veterinary chores so that he could concentrate on the dogs. He built a second kennel and developed training implements and techniques. By the fourth year of kennels, in his seventh year with Bronis, dogs had become his total occupation.

When he had first moved in with Bronis, Abrahm paid Nicholas several visits to see how he was getting along. Also, Bronis' house was well-suited for political meetings and Abrahm frequently participated in these. Nicholas attended two or three times, but he could not stomach the arguments that invariably followed the organizational business and reports. After that he would not go even when Abrahm was there.

No amount of persuasion could change his mind. He believed in the ideals of universal brotherhood, economic equality, religious freedom, cultural integrity, and non-persecution of the Jews—but he did not believe in fighting and arguing and carrying on like madmen.

Bronis spent hours trying to convince him that conflict, among friends as well as enemies, was an inevitable part of any serious attempt to combat the complex evils that infected the bowels of society. Nothing he said made a difference. Nicholas had seen enough to last a lifetime.

"I have a bellyful," he would say. "Can't hold any more."

Bronis prevailed upon Abrahm to try his hand. Abrahm complied in order to satisfy Bronis, but as expected, Nicholas would not budge. He appreciated Abrahm's continuing interest in him. He sympathized with the goals Abrahm espoused. He was willing to make a regular contribution to any fund Abrahm recommended. But under no condition would he subject himself to politics. He would give up his job first.

"You're right," Abrahm conceded the second time they talked. "It's not your cup of tea. As for a contribution, that's between you and Bronis. But I'm not going to let you all the way off the hook. I want you to promise me that if I ever come to you for help, you'll give it, no questions asked."

"Of course," Nicholas said humbly. "But what could I possibly do for you?"

"Whatever it is," Abrahm said.

"I promise," Nicholas pledged.

They shook hands on it and the subject was dropped. From then on, whenever Abrahm attended a gathering at Bronis' house, he came early or stayed late to have a few words with Nicholas—an event Nicholas looked forward to and always enjoyed.

Then, in the fourth year, after the first kennel had been built, Abrahm suddenly stopped coming to meetings.

In the past, Abrahm had occasionally failed to appear without giving notice, but it was understood that his schedule was peppered with crises. Thus Nicholas was less concerned than disappointed when Abrahm missed several meetings in a row. He began to have second thoughts only when three or four months went by and there was still no sign of him.

Bronis became uncustomarily edgy whenever Nicholas inquired as to the date of the next meeting. When Nicholas finally raised the subject of what might be keeping Abrahm away, Bronis turned his back on him without answering, and walked off shaking his head.

The next months without word from Abrahm made even casual conversation uncomfortable. Nicholas was plunged into gloom. Had Bronis severed their connection? Had Abrahm? Had he been arrested? Injured? Could the worst have happened? He had always felt that Abrahm was too good to spend his life in the slaughterhouse, trying to civilize a pack of jackals. He knew so many things. So many people. He even had an education, though he did not like mention of it. Nicholas had always wanted to suggest that Abrahm find a less bloody way to carry forth his idealism. But he had never quite worked up the courage. Now he lay awake at night debating the merits of taking the initiative and seeking Abrahm out. Again he reached a passive conclusion. Abrahm would not desert him. If he was alive, he was incommunicado for a good reason. He had vowed his help. The rest remained a mystery.

In time Nicholas could not refrain from broaching the subject once more with Bronis. It was that or leaving. He chose an exquisite evening in Indian summer.

"Bronis," he said when they had finished eating and were lingering at the table discussing the economic depression that was spreading from America around the globe. "I want to show you something in the kennel."

"Can't it wait?" Bronis said. "I was just beginning to relax."

"No," said Nicholas.

He led the way to the kennel, stopping at the entrance. The air was cool and soothing after a hot day and the earth exuded the sweet fragrance of grass.

"Well," Bronis said, "aren't we going inside?"

"I just wanted to be out here," Nicholas said, fidgeting with his scratched hands.

He took a deep breath to bolster his resolve.

"What is it?"

"I'm sorry, Bronis," Nicholas stammered. "I've held off as long as I can. This time you must tell me. What's happened to Abrahm?"

Bronis blanched. He turned to march back into the house. Then he changed his mind. His face showed turmoil.

"I don't know," he said at last.

"I've been with you every day for four years," Nicholas said.

He was acutely conscious of the inadequacy of his words to his emotions.

"I don't know what to tell you," Bronis said. "I wish I did, but I don't."

"You mean you can't tell me why he hasn't come to any

meetings?" Nicholas asked. "Or where he is? Or what you last heard of him?"

"I can't," Bronis said. "I swear to you."

"You haven't had any word from him?" Nicholas persisted.

"Not one," said Bronis, dropping his chin dejectedly.

"Bronis," said Nicholas in a final effort to extract the truth, "a man like Abrahm doesn't just evaporate."

"Believe me," Bronis said, "the whereabouts of Comrade Abrahm is as enigmatic to me as to you. There isn't any more I can say."

"But can't we do something?" Nicholas asked.

His voice trailed Bronis into the house, and he was left standing alone beside the kennel.

Inside the barn the air was a mixture of grain and animal odors. Nicholas stretched out on a litter of hay. Was he to believe Bronis or not? Four years in one place, the best four years of his life, were not to be renounced lightly.

Nicholas longed for an assuaging rain, one that would nourish the soil and clear the air and wash away the haziness that obscured his thoughts. He loved the startling light and thunder of a cloudburst and the fertile downpour that brought man and beast together through a magic older than Noah, rhythmically driving off accumulated pressures and leaving behind a pristine calm.

In his nostrils he carried a fragile recollection of how, on the battlefield after a rain, the morning grass smelled of freshly baked bread. Bodies were strewn as far as the eye could see, and yet there was a sweetness in the air. The stench of released flesh rotting in its own pudding of blood and urine and feces rose while the rain was falling and when it was over the ruptured corpses lay neutralized in the solace of the mud. When the field dried the bodies could be buried or heaped in a pyre and burned like tinder. Some of the men would hack up a mule and roast their portions over the flames on sticks.

Others, with more respect for the dead, kindled a separate fire for their repast. A few were suspected of cannibalism, but it was hard to censure ravenous soldiers. The rule was live and let live.

If there was not time to wait for the field to dry, the bodies were left to dissolve into the earth. Years later there would be no trace of the shell holes or the trenches or the graves or the bodies of the men and the animals that had shared a common fate. The crops would grow and a farmer would follow his ox over the furrows and when the plow unearthed a hollow cartridge or a buckle or a skull it would not be written whether the owner had been buried or left to decompose.

Or if a field remained uncultivated the grass would luxuriate in the wind and on gentle spring and summer days young lovers would spend their virgin charge in it, cows would deposit hot clumps of ordure on it, and carefree dogs would pee in their secret places.

And as always the rains would come and blend their essential fertilizer.

That night, however, there was no rain. There was not even a breeze to ventilate the barn. The atmosphere was oppressive. Nicholas took it as an augury that it was time to move on. The feeling was not new. It had carried him from place to place until he reached Warsaw. But it was the first time he had experienced it since casting his lot with Bronis. He thought he had outlived it. Yet here it was. The barn was closing in on him. His body tingled unbearably, as if his limbs had fallen asleep and were all waking up together. Frantically, he packed himself in hay and masturbated.

DOGS

A howl rose from the kennels. Nicholas rushed to the window. Someone had stopped in front of the house and was turning in. Who could it be after dark?

He threw on his shirt and went downstairs. There was a perfunctory knocking on the door. He stood to the side of it.

"Who's there?" he asked.

"Comrade Vaczek."

The name was strange to him.

"What do you want?"

"It concerns a friend of yours."

"Who?"

"Let me in."

"Are you seeking Bronis Ganzs?"

"No. I have a message for Big Nick."

"What?" said Nicholas, taken aback.

"I have a message for Big Nick."

Nicholas unlatched the door.

"Enter slowly," he said.

Olek walked into the room, knowing that Nicholas was

behind the door. When he heard it latch, he turned to face him.

"Who are you?" Nicholas asked.

He towered over Olek.

"An emissary for Comrade Abrahm," Olek said. "He needs your help."

Nicholas was jolted. Strongly on guard, he sized up the blond, sharply featured man who stood before him calling up the past. It had been seven, eight years since he last saw Abrahm.

"He's still alive?" Nicholas asked incredulously.

"Very much so," Olek replied.

"Where is he?" Nicholas asked.

"In the city," said Olek.

"How can I believe you?" asked Nicholas, weighing his excitement with skepticism.

"Hear me out," said Olek.

Nicholas led the way into the next room. When they had taken opposite seats at the table, he nodded in readiness.

"My name is Olek," he heard. "My brother is Heykel. His wife, Sonya, is Abrahm's daughter . . ."

Succinctly, Olek explained how it had once been his job to accompany Abrahm to certain meetings and that he was thereby familiar with Bronis, the house, and Nicholas. To support his story, he recounted details that would only have been known to Nicholas and Abrahm. Now, he concluded, Abrahm was in jeopardy and asking to redeem the pledge that Nicholas had given years ago.

"What am I being asked to do?" Nicholas asked.

"To keep Abrahm here," Olek replied, "and to build a shelter that will accommodate him and five more."

Nicholas peered into the swatch of table between his hands as if it were a pond of brown water.

"How bad is the leg?" he asked.

"The break from the fall was severe," Olek said, "and running on it created nasty complications. The doctor fears a protracted healing process."

"I can't imagine Abrahm staying in bed very long," Nicholas said.

"Neither can he," said Olek. "That's part of our problem."

"And the others?" said Nicholas.

"They haven't been chosen," said Olek. "Our immediate concern is for Abrahm."

Nicholas held his palms together as if he were praying, then interlaced his fingers and pressed his mouth against them contemplatively.

"How soon would you want to bring Abrahm here?" he asked.

"As soon as possible," said Olek. "He's a sitting duck where he is."

"And how frequently would you need to communicate with him?"

"It's hard to tell," said Olek.

"It's necessary to know," said Nicholas.

"I can't tell you precisely," said Olek.

"I'm entitled to some idea," said Nicholas.

"It's a one-way street," Olek said. "If you decide to help, you'll be risking your neck."

"I don't care so much about that," said Nicholas.

"Then what's bothering you," said Olek.

Nicholas drew a hesitating breath.

"I thought he was dead," he said.

"I've assured you he's not," Olek said.

"He may as well have been," Nicholas said.

"What's past is past," Olek said.

"Why did he disappear?" Nicholas asked. "And with never a word?"

"You'll have to ask him," said Olek.

There was a heavy silence. The dogs were still and there were no sounds of life from the street.

"Your expenses would be reimbursed," said Olek.

"It doesn't matter," Nicholas said. "I can absorb them."

"It would have to be done so as not to attract the slightest bit of attention," Olek said.

"Leave it to me," said Nicholas.

"Then you'll do it?" asked Olek.

"It was never in question," said Nicholas.

They set about planning the shelter. Olek specified bedding, staples, utensils, and other particulars. He marked those things which Nicholas would have to do exactly as instructed and those which would require ingenuity. A few objects would have to be constructed differently than in other bunkers because of Abrahm's condition. But on balance the needs of six people dictated design.

Once the structure was built, the most important function after security would be the provision of food. Nicholas could not simply double or quadruple his purchases. Spreading his shopping around would partially ease the pressure, but there remained the need for a plausible alibi. Here the dogs, who varied in number from week to week, were doubly valuable.

It was agreed that the bunker would be dug underground directly beneath the large kennel. The entrance would be inside the kennel, making it easier for Nicholas to bring food in. Also, this placement would preclude anyone from entering without him.

"Only a fool would try to get in there alone," said Nicholas.

"There are plenty of those around," Olek said.

"Don't worry about them," said Nicholas. "The dogs will know what to do."

"I'll have to be able to get in," said Olek.

"Why?" asked Nicholas.

"Something could happen to you," said Olek.

"Nothing will happen to me," said Nicholas.

"I'm sorry to be so morbid," said Olek, "but you're not immortal. Even if you were, I'd have to have independent access."

"If you don't trust me, you're putting Abrahm in an unnecessarily precarious situation," said Nicholas.

"It has nothing to do with that," Olek assured him.

"Then what is it?" asked Nicholas.

"Necessity," Olek said. "And sensible precaution."

"All right," said Nicholas. "I'll teach you to get through. But what if something happens to you?"

"A replacement will appear bearing the code name Malachi," said Olek.

The main disadvantage of situating the bunker below the dogs was that the ventilation system would have to outlet beyond the perimeter of the kennel. It was decided to dig the bunker three feet longer than the back wall of the kennel. The vents would then be run beyond the wall. In the same area a camouflaged hole just large enough for a person to stick his head through would be cut into the ground, allowing the bunker inhabitants to come up for a few whiffs of fresh air at night.

"Imagine the look on Bronis' face if he paid a surprise visit to his old home on a moonlit night and stumbled over a head in the grass."

"He'd faint," Nicholas said, relishing Olek's humor. "Especially now that he's accustomed to walking streets paved with gold."

"Do you envy him?" Olek asked.

"Heavens no," Nicholas said. "I still don't know why he went to America or what it's like there, but I can tell you that he was not a happy man when he left."

"And are you a happy man?" said Olek.

"I'm at peace with myself," said Nicholas.

"What about the war?" Olek said.

"I have a clear conscience," said Nicholas. "The war in which I fought was not the first, nor will this one be the last."

"Not for the clay earth," said Olek, "but certainly for many of us on it."

"War and peace are seasons," said Nicholas, "like summer and winter."

"Horseshit," said Olek.

He was about to rise when a harrowing scream pierced the house.

"Help!" a woman's voice cried out. "Oh my God, save me."

It was coming from upstairs. Olek whipped out his gun and scooted against the wall nearest the staircase. There was a quick, hysterical trill of words, then quiet.

"Take it easy," said Nicholas, who had not moved from his chair. "It's only Katrina talking in her sleep."

"Who?" Olek demanded, sticking to the wall.

"Katrina, my housekeeper," Nicholas said sheepishly.

"Your housekeeper?" said Olek, glaring at him.

"I should have told you about her," Nicholas said. "Put that gun away. I'll explain."

"I'm listening," said Olek.

He moved back to the table but kept his gun out.

"When Bronis went to America," Nicholas said, "I was so busy I started having a woman in to clean house once a week, sometimes twice. One day Katrina brought her pup in for treatment. The cleaning lady happened to be there. Katrina noticed and struck up a conversation. She was looking for a housekeeping position and thought this might be it. She was very forward, but she had a case. I needed assistance, she needed a live-in situation, and the house was big enough to make both ends meet."

"How long ago was that?" asked Olek.

"A year or so," said Nicholas.

He could see that Olek was enraged.

"And have both ends met?" Olek asked sarcastically.

"I'm very fond of her," said Nicholas.

"It's evident," said Olek.

"Men are grandfathers at my age," said Nicholas, "yet this is my first home since childhood. Is that too much?"

"No," said Olek. "But you should have told me. Abrahm's life is at issue."

"It was stupid of me," said Nicholas. "I'm sorry."

"So am I," said Olek, unable to calm down.

"Abrahm will be well cared for," said Nicholas.

"Is there anything else you should tell me?" asked Olek.

"She's half German," said Nicholas.

"Go on," said Olek.

"That's all," said Nicholas.

"How old is she?" asked Olek.

"Your age," said Nicholas.

"Does she always go to sleep this early?" asked Olek.

"She works very hard," said Nicholas.

"Is she trustworthy?" asked Olek.

A troubled look came over Nicholas. His thickset fore-arms hardened and his meaty hands sought comfort in one another.

"I don't know much about her," he admitted.

"Friends or relatives?" asked Olek.

"None to my knowledge," said Nicholas.

"Does she receive mail?"

"No."

"What was she doing before she joined you?"

"The same thing," said Nicholas. "Housework. Odd jobs."

Olek probed further. It was distasteful, but he had no choice. However reliable Nicholas might be, there was an unforeseen perplexity. He could not build the bunker without Katrina's awareness.

"Once it's finished, she'll have to forget the ground ever opened," Olek cautioned. "The identity of anyone inside must remain your secret."

"I understand," said Nicholas.

"Now," said Olek grimly, "do you have second thoughts about taking Abrahm?"

Nicholas lowered his head. When he raised it, his eyes were clear.

"My life is his," he said.

"It may come to that," said Olek.

GHOULS

Clip-clop. Clip-clop. Clip-clop. Clip-clop.

The black wagon was nearing the bakery. It was later than usual, having taken a different route, and the platform was laden almost to the top with corpses.

"All set?" the old man asked.

"Ready," said the boy.

He took his cap out of his jacket and put it on deliberately so that it would obscure his eyes and forehead.

"This is your stop, my friend," the old man said.

"If you please," said Isaac.

Wedged between the old man and the boy, his milk pan dangled from his neck with the bumpy action of the wagon over the stones.

"Remember," the old man said. "On three. And don't be clumsy."

The bony horse strained against the dead load. Rather than being evenly stacked, the bodies were piled higher on the sides of the platform, forming a concavity toward the center.

"Ah, I can smell it," Isaac said, holding a finger to the side of his nose and sniffing the air. "So sweet and fresh."

"Whoa!" said the old man.

He checked the horses so that the back of the wagon was in line with three bodies that lay on the sidewalk, their faces covered with paper.

In front of the bakery hollow-eyed Jews waited on queue, some resembling the skeletons heaped on the wagon.

Heykel, dressed in a baker's apron, appeared at the door.

"Hello there," the old man said.

"Hello," Heykel replied. "That's quite a load you have."

"There always seems to be room for another," the old man said.

He climbed off the wagon and helped Isaac to the ground.

"Good day," said Isaac, facing Heykel's voice.

"How are you, Isaac?" Heykel asked.

"Very well, thank you," Isaac said.

The boy came around and handed Isaac his rope.

"Thank you," Isaac said.

Isaac wrapped the rope around his fist and pulled Zirka to him.

"Good girl," he said, patting her on the head.

"You must have worked up an appetite," Heykel said.

"I'm not getting any younger," said the old man.

"Send the boy in when you're done," Heykel said. "We'll fix you something for the road."

The old man took Isaac by the elbow and guided him to a spot adjacent to the bodies. The paper masks screening their faces had been fastened with string to prevent them from slipping off.

"Right here, my friend," the old man said.

"Yes, thank you," said Isaac, hunkering down.

Instead of reaching for his pan, he immediately brought forth his harmonica.

Of the three bodies on the ground, the one in the middle had no shoes. Simultaneously, the boy lifted it by the shoulders and the old man by the feet. Keeping it perfectly level, they carried it steadily to the back of the wagon. Then they maneuvered it gingerly into the depression that had been created in the center of the platform and laid it on its back.

Heykel stood watchfully in the doorway.

The other two bodies were hoisted up and set crosswise over the first.

"Go," said the old man under his breath.

The boy jumped down and approached Heykel.

"All the way in the back," Heykel said, letting him pass inside.

"Make it quick," the old man called after him.

He remained on the platform, rearranging the corpses.

On the sidewalk, Isaac was playing a song.

Heykel's attention was focused on the wagon.

The old man finished his puttering and climbed down from the platform.

"That's very nice," he said to Isaac in passing behind him.

His eyes momentarily met Heykel's. Stolidly, he pulled himself up onto the bench and took the rein.

"Finished for the day?" Heykel said.

"I could go on," said the old man, "but the horse can't draw any more."

"It's just as well," said Heykel.

They stepped aside and the boy appeared carrying a small packet. His hat was drawn tightly over his eyes.

"Thanks," the old man said to Heykel as the boy mounted the bench.

"Don't mention it," said Heykel.

The boy settled into place, his hands folded across his lap, his head turned down.

"Hee-a," said the old man.

The horse bunched its shoulders and tugged forward, engaging the inertia of the wagon.

"Hee-a," the old man repeated, holding the rein slack.

The wagon staggered into motion and slowly gained momentum.

"Easy now," the old man said. "Nice and easy."

Isaac's plaintive notes grew fainter and the wooden wheels turned smoother circles.

Clip-clop. Clip-clop. Clip-clop. Clip-clop.

"Whoa!"

The horse pulled up at the gate and stood flexing its neck.

"It's pretty sore, isn't it?" the old man said, letting out the reins.

One of the guards excused himself from a bartering session and came over to the wagon. He held several pieces of jewelry in his hand.

"Can you use a ring, old timer?" he asked expansively.

"Not really," the old man said.

"How about a gold watch, then?" asked the guard.

"No thanks," the old man said.

"But you're not wearing one," said the guard. "How do you know what time it is?"

"I can tell by the sun," the old man said.

"Is that why you're so late today?" said the guard.

"There was a lot to do," said the old man.

"So I see," said the guard, scanning the neatly tiered corpses.

"Hey, what's the matter with him?" said a second guard, approaching.

In his preoccupation with the jewelry, the first guard had neglected the boy doubled over on the bench, his head cradled in his hands.

"An eighteen carat watch isn't good enough for him," said the first guard over his shoulder.

"Not the old man, you nitwit," the second guard said. "The boy."

"The boy?" said the first guard. "Why, he's asleep. Anyone can see that."

"He doesn't look as if he's sleeping to me," said the second guard.

"Well, he's not dead," said the first guard, "or he'd be

back there. The old timer's very meticulous about his corpses."

"He's sick," the old man interceded.

"I told you," said the second guard.

"What is it?" asked the first guard.

"Something in the stomach," the old man said.

"Sounds familiar," said the second guard.

"He'll be fine when we empty him out," the old man said.

"Like you emptied the other one?" the first guard said.

"That was different," the old man said.

"What was his name?" the second guard said. "Gottfried? Gustav?"

"Gregor," the old man said.

"That's it," the first guard said. "Gregor."

"The sooner I get him home, the better," said the old man, seizing the reins.

"All right, go ahead," said the second guard.

"Hee-a," said the old man.

"Let me know if you change your mind about a watch," the first guard said. "If this one's gone, I can always get you another."

The horse braced its haunches and tensed its neck.

"Hee-a."

The wagon moved through the gate and onto the Aryan side. As always, the city beyond the ghetto was of another world. There was a military presence, and fear skulked everywhere, but there were no arm bands, no starving children with pipestem arms and distended stomachs, no living skeletons inching along the pavement, sitting down to rest, and dying there.

"Unbelievable, isn't it?" the old man said.

Joseph had just raised himself and resumed an upright position with his hands on his thighs and his chin against his chest. It was the first time since early in the war that he had been out from under the shadow of the ghetto walls.

His breathing was cramped. It had not been easy to lie on the bench with his back to the guards. He pressed his elbows against his sides. The gun Heykel had given him was hard against his hip. He turned his head enough to bring the span of the platform within view.

"So far, so good," the old man said.

Joseph felt slightly relieved. The wagon was proceeding at a steady pace and the gate was well out of sight.

"I could stand a bite to eat," the old man said.

Joseph unwrapped the packet that had been fixed at the bakery. It contained the two ends of a bread and a length of sausage. The old man drew a knife out of his pocket and handed it to him.

"You should have seen that watch," he said as Joseph skived the sausage. "It was big enough to hang on a wall."

Joseph sliced one of the bread ends and inserted the disks of sausage.

"Thanks," said the old man, munching into the sandwich.

Joseph rewrapped the leftover bread and sausage.

"Aren't you hungry?" the old man asked.

"No," Joseph said.

The truth was that he had not been near sausage in so long, the mere proximity was nauseating. It had been obtained especially for the old man.

"That one with the watch is dangerous," the old man said, chewing and talking at once. "Always drunk and liable to turn mean for no reason."

The pungence of the sausage rose unsavorily on his breath.

"I used to work in the slaughterhouse," he went on, waving his sandwich. "You should see what goes into this delicacy. Rats, shit, glands, everything. But those were the days. If someone had a gripe, he could have it out. There were

lots of fights, some pretty good ones, but you didn't see any
wagon coming to pick up dead workers every night."

Joseph took in as much as he could of the environs without seeming to look around. They were passing through little
used streets with modest houses unravaged by raids or fire or
spindlefingers picking at their frames.

"How big's your family?" the old man asked.

"I'm alone," Joseph said.

"But I thought . . ."

"Everyone's gone," Joseph said, cutting him short.

"You can't be very old," the old man said.

"Fourteen," Joseph said.

"Now there's something to think about," the old man
said.

Whereupon he lapsed into silence.

The old man tightened the reins and rotated his thick
forearms to the right.

"Easy there," he said, clicking his tongue.

The horse had established a homeward rhythm and was
balking at the unfamiliar direction.

"Come on," the old man urged, maneuvering a slow,
wide turn.

It brought them onto a dead end street that tailed off into
a coppice. The curtainless windows and wildgrown grass gar-
nishing the houses suggested that they were abandoned.

The old man piloted the wagon down the street and into
the bordering woods.

"Don't let her graze," he said, handing Joseph the reins.

He alighted from the wagon and got up on the platform.
Unhurriedly, but without wasting a second, he began unpiling
the top layer of corpses, enabling access to the first of the three
bodies that had been loaded at the bakery.

The horse had not yet settled into a comfortable stance
when the low sound of a motor perked its ears.

"Steady," Joseph said.

He held the reins in his left hand, firmly gripping the pistol with his right. As Heykel had instructed, he did not turn upon hearing the noise. His eyes moved along the grass, up and down the trees, never standing still.

Behind him, a black car lumbered down the street toward the wagon and pulled up parallel with the back edge of the platform.

The driver, an elderly gentlemen, appeared to be alone, but as he looked straight ahead, the back door opened and two men scrambled out. Both were short and blond.

The old man bent over and dug his arms under the body he had uncovered. Taxing his strength to avoid any shaky movement, he raised it quickly from its bed and let it down to the two men, who stood an arm's length apart, one facing the wagon, the other perpendicular to him. The one receiving the shoulders backed into the car, and the one holding the legs followed sideways.

There was a brief hesitation. Then the door closed and the car, again apparently empty except for the driver, made a reverse turn and pulled away.

The horse picked up speed with the certainty that its route was near completion. As the road turned to dirt, and the dirt to sod, the clip-clop, clip-clopping of its hooves became a muted padding.

The wagon moved beneath a roof of trees and out into an open, grassy space that had once been a park and was now a cemetery. Checkered with large, rectangular mass graves that had been filled in with dirt, the green expanse resembled a providently tilled farm with sown fields rich beside the fallow.

The old man guided the horse to an enormous gaping pit that was feculent with decomposing bodies. Two coarse, rugged men in heavy work clothes shambled over. One carried a pitchfork, the other a shovel. They surveyed the abnormally full wagon.

"What's the idea?" said the first, scaling the platform.

He speared a woman in the neck and flung her through the air.

"The spirit must have moved him," said the second.

"One of these days it'll really move him," said the first.

The old man and Joseph sat with their backs to the drudges as they pitched and tumbled the corpses into the pit.

CHIMERA

I could just walk out of here and to hell with it, Eugen thought as he made his way along the street. His shoes had merged with the inner boots Tzipora's mother had made and were molded to his feet like moccasins. He could feel the warm nuances of the terrain, and was conscious of scraping the ground with every step.

It was a fine day for strolling. The buildings were bathed in the clear, beneficent warmth of a midsummer sun. There were more people voluntarily outdoors than at any time since Eugen had entered the ghetto. Some were so frail in the sunlight they appeared to be merely shadows of others nearby. He envisioned them hidden for weeks or months in attics and closets, under beds, in cellars, like worn clothes and old toys put away against the day when they might once more be useful.

Other sunny days had come and gone, but at the peak of the deportations, it had made no difference what the complexion of the sky was. No one went outside unless they had to.

Recently, however, things had been puzzlingly uneventful. Initially, no one took notice. There had been slowdowns before. But gradually people began to realize that a change had taken place. Its exact nature was unclear. One explanation was that as many persons had been taken as were needed to fulfill enforced labor quotas, leaving the rest indeterminately secure. Another view was that the Germans had temporarily turned their attention to the outlying towns, which they wanted to evacuate before finally emptying the ghetto. Whatever the correct rationale, hardly anyone risked unnecessary exposure the first few days. But when the sun came out so luringly, and the lull had lasted a while, many could not resist.

Eugen wondered whether Bankart was among them. He doubted it, but he could not dismiss any possibility. The rumors of Bankart's whereabouts were even more numerous and less consistent than those surrounding the deportations. It was said that he was in the ghetto, out of the ghetto, active, in hiding, sick, and in one case, dead. The last had come from a man who had overheard Eugen asking around on the street. His fireside story was that Bankart had been secretly arrested and summarily shot by the Gestapo. But he could not document his thesis, and as far as Eugen could determine, its sole basis was his belief that this was the most likely reason for Bankart's invisibility.

Nevertheless, it was conceivable that Thierbach had managed to find Bankart—although if he had, he would not have been kind enough to shoot him. Eugen did not like to think of Thierbach having accomplished this without somehow getting word to him that he could emerge from the ghetto. In darker moments he had gone so far as to consider whether Thierbach might not already have had Bankart safely in hand before giving him the assignment. Or suppose Thierbach had just found Bankart and wanted to notify him. How would he do it? No one knew him here. Could it be that right now there was someone combing the ghetto for him, even as he was sifting for Bankart?

Clip-clop. Clip-clop. Clip-clop. Clip-clop.

The sound grew louder, remaining distant, and quickly

dropped as the black wagon traversed the intersection a block ahead. Eugen saw the thin horse, the husky form of the driver, the line of the wagon, than a mirage-like wave of air. He had not seen anyone else on the bench. The angle had obscured the boy and perhaps the beggar.

The thought caused him to stop. Suddenly he felt nervous. He crossed the street and began walking back in the opposite direction. There was no point in going to the bakery this late in the day. It was too hot to stand in line, and besides, he would not find anything. He was better off taking advantage of the weather.

The sun felt good on his face. He tilted it slightly upward as he walked, letting it absorb the rays like a sponge drawing water. If he could, he thought, he would have removed his shirt, sprawled out against a wall, and taken a sun bath.

He fended off a smile. With his dark beard grown full and his bony, milkwhite body, he would look like a stray goat on the sidewalk. Where previously he had been amply larded around the rear and midriff, his ribs now protruded and his buttocks were so lean that he could not sit long in hard places. Just above his thick beard, his cheeks had sunk, his eyes deepened, and his nose had lost it fleshiness, rendering it less bulbous and more akin to a beak or a small horn.

He would try the bakery tomorrow. The last time he had gone by, neither the man with the narrow face nor Samson had been there. A woman was serving the soup. She had dark features and chestnut hair. When he inquired about Bankart, she ignored him.

It bothered him that the men were absent, although he felt intimidated by Samson. He was relieved to find the beggar holding his spot. Or so he thought until the wagon rolled up. He could not understand it. Was this the second time it had come this morning? It was doubtful. There were no bodies to collect. But if it was the first trip, how had the beggar gotten there?

*   *   *

Eugen watched a feeble old man shuffling across the street with such slow, trembling, infinitesimal steps that it seemed he would never get to the other side. He was so thin, his arm band gave the illusion of holding his arm in place. Might he possibly know something about Bankart? Eugen mused.

It was admittedly farfetched, but he had found in the ghetto the same pattern that had established itself at headquarters. The more likely it was that a person knew Bankart, the less likely it was that he would acknowledge him. The little he had learned thus far had come from random questioning.

As Eugen approached him, the old man paused in midstep and slowly, like an aging turtle grown weak in its shell, began the tedious process of turning away. Eugen hesitated, lest he cause him to topple over in his haste to pivot. Then he thought that the old man might be mistaking him for a policeman and removed his hat.

Hatless, he resumed his approach, speaking in advance of himself.

"Don't be frightened," he said. "I just want to ask you a question."

The old man wavered in his minute sidestep, then continued his motion.

"I won't come any closer," Eugen said, stopping four or five feet from him.

The old man finished one slow step and undertook the next.

"Perhaps you could help me," Eugen said in a low voice. "I'm looking for a relative. Abrahm Bankart. If you know him, it would be very helpful."

There was no indication of whether or not the old man had heard him. He was still turning. It was such a graduated procedure, Eugen thought, that if he had not seen him begin his revolution, he would have supposed that he was plodding straight ahead.

"Excuse me," he said.

He backed away and then, in order not to alarm the old

man further, he executed a wide semi-circle around his side and set off in the opposite direction. He felt a drop of regret for having so discomforted him on an impulse, but it was unavoidable. Among all the dumb, worn, frightened faces he had sounded, some knew something, even if they would not tell.

"Help! Stop him! Thief! Thief!"

Eugen turned in time to see a small boy sprinting away from the area where he had left the old man. He was clutching something in his hands—a chunk of bread, perhaps, or a large onion. The woman he had knocked down and robbed was picking herself off the street. The boy darted in and out of the sparse crowd, almost bowling over the old man, ran directly by an oncoming Jewish policeman, who made no effort to stop him, and scampered up the block from which the policeman had emerged.

"Thief! Thief!" the woman yelled at the sight of the policeman.

Instead of giving chase, the policeman pushed his hat back on his head, setting the star at a rakish slant appropriate to his swagger. The woman was being attended to by several onlookers. When they saw the policeman disregard the boy and continue toward them, they tried to lead her away. But she seemed posted to the spot, stunned at having lost her treasure.

"Wait!" the policeman shouted.

Save the old man, who could not react quickly enough, everyone veered to safety as the policeman approached. By the time he reached the woman, the samaritans—who on a less sunny day might not have stopped at all—had fled. She stood diminutively before him. They appeared to exchange remarks. The woman began to move away, but the policeman grabbed her by the hair and, pulling her head groundward, kicked her feet out from under her.

The street cleared. Only the old man stood nearby, resting. The policeman seemed unaware of his presence. Screaming, the woman struggled to repulse his weight, then submitted.

Eugen went on his way. He felt sorry for the woman, but there was nothing to be done. Her plight was a strong reminder that while the rare serenity and summer sun might conjure up daydreams of the Aryan side, he was after all still in the ghetto. He liked to think that only a wall separated the two, that he could cross over whenever he wished. But what if he were detained by a stubborn soldier or *schmalzovnik* who refused to believe his story? He was certainly a sight for sore eyes, and every morning, as regularly as the black wagon made its rounds, an Opel stopped at Orla Street and a manacled Jew who had been caught on the Aryan side without a permit was thrown into the first housefront and shot.

It was paradoxical. As bad as the ghetto was, there were worse places to be taken for a Jew. Especially on such a fair day. He amused himself with the speculation that it was Bankart who was responsible for the peacefulness, and that the sunshine was an emanation from the small but intransmutable core of resistance that remained within the ghetto. If there were not a critical weakness in the deportation machinery, Thierbach would not be so occupied with it. Apparently something was amiss. Could it be that Bankart had found the plug and wrenched it from its socket?

Regardless, Eugen thought, it might be best to keep to himself for a while. He would not go to the bakery tomorrow. And if the sun and tranquility abided, he might just pass through the gate and make his way to his room on the Aryan side and bathe and shave and take a comfortable nap, undisturbed by terror, and then go down and buy some newspapers and walk over to a nice little restaurant near the fountain and have a cold beer and a meat sandwich and a cup of good, strong coffee, syrupy with cream and sugar, and catch up on the news of the world.

BLACK MONDAY

The door dropped snugly into its frame, strangling an oblique beam of starlight.

Abrahm braced himself on one arm and reached up with the other to secure the wooden crossbolt that locked the bunker from within. It slipped firmly into place. A fierce pain ripped through his right leg. Grimacing, he eased himself down until he was resting on his elbows with his shoulders poised above the cot. The pain subsided, giving way to a moment of relief, followed by the return of a hot, steady aching.

Close by a kerosene lamp provided a dim, flickering light that reminded him of the night fires near the *unschlagplatz*. He sniffed the air. The odor of dogs that had entered when Nicholas opened the door to get out blended with the prevailing smells of illness and confinement.

He rotated his heel slightly to divert the pressure that mounted regularly. A searing edge sawed across his shin into his knee. His leg was bolstered by a large cushion made up of two eiderdown pillows wrapped in a sheet. Under the bandages, his swollen knee was the size of a melon. It burned and throbbed as if it were about to rupture and fill the bunker with boiling lava.

"It's not going to be pleasant," Dr. Adler had warned him. "You know how poorly equipped we are, and you'll probably have to be moved afterward. There are risks involved, and it will be very painful."

There had been no choices as far as Abrahm was concerned. The operation was hazardous, but if it succeeded, he would still be a useful person. Otherwise, he would be crippled.

In a negative sense he felt good. He was alone in the bunker, at least temporarily safe, able to catch his breath and regain his strength. Before the injury, he had been flagging, and Leora's death had disheartened him. Now, while a part of him suffered, the rest was able to recuperate. It was a depressing, frustrating experience, but perhaps it was also a blessing in disguise.

"Aye," he winced.

The pain traversed his leg like a fractured shock wave. His buttocks flinched, his torso spasmed, his elbows shook, and his body was again quiescent.

He groped for a pill, then changed his mind. The dosage he had taken while Nicholas was there would have to do. He poured himself a glass of water.

"Try to get by with the round ones," Dr. Adler had told him. "The oblong are for the extremest pain, and even then, preferably only at night."

Immediately after the trip Abrahm's nerves were so raw that he had swallowed the stronger pills as if they were sugar. But he found that they were slow to affect him, and although they put him briefly on a cloud, they quickly dropped him on a stomach-churning slide. Before he knew it, his tolerance for pain began eroding and he developed a sour craving. So, belatedly, he started heeding Dr. Adler's advice.

He quaffed the water and set the glass back on the crate

that served as a shelf. Actually, it was a hollow cube almost the height of the cot that could be used as a table or a chair and also for storage. There were four in the bunker and Nicholas was planning to build more. It was a wonder he had accomplished as much as he had, Abrahm thought, admiring his Herculean labor.

The bunker was in the shape of a narrow boxcar. At one end, cut into the ceiling above Abrahm's head and to his left, was the door to the kennel. At the opposite end was the ventilation system. Of the long walls, one harbored an unfinished work-counter and pantry section, including a series of shelves and partitions for stocking supplies, utensils, and food, and a corner area for bathroom functions. The other bore six cots, vertically arranged in sets. Each cot could be folded against the wall, creating day space, or with a pillow or rolled blanket, converted into a sofa. For privacy, black cloth could be unfurled and pegged around the sets. Also, the crates were designed to fit flush under the cots, like trunks, or between them, as dividers. Abrahm's corner was somewhat modified in that the cot above him was intended to stay up until he recovered, he had a more enveloping curtain, and there was a lamp shelf just over his left shoulder so that he could control his own light. But overall, the bunker was uniform, neat, compact, and thus far, sufficiently airy. How it would function with five or six people remained to be seen.

Abrahm dug his fingers into his beard and scratched his chin. The sensation was gratifying. At the infirmary they had wanted to shear him for sanitary reasons, but he would not let them. He would be too easily recognizable, he said. The argument that he was in hiding failed to sway him. Nothing could. The beard had become a part of his resistance. He would remove it when the war was over.

He was proud of the hospital. It had taken thousands of man-hours to establish a place underground to care for the sick and wounded. And he was proud of Dr. Adler, whose contribution was immeasurable. He could have bought his family

out of the ghetto. His qualifications would allow him to practice anywhere in the world. Even now they were willing to get
him out if he wanted. But he insisted on staying.

Abrahm had watched him work, commanding the situation, instructing the other doctors and nurses in low, efficient
tones, handling patients sympathetically, never breaking
down under the strain of inadequate facilities, lack of medi-
cines, and constant tragic deaths. It was not easy to preside
over the deterioration of a person, especially a young boy or
girl, who obviously would have survived under normal conditions and whom he could not help for want of a specific
prescription or piece of equipment. Sometimes, when a patient had just died, Dr. Adler would disappear for a few minutes, collect himself, and return as quiet and gentle and
determined as before.

The dogs were probably asleep, Abrahm reflected. Nevertheless, he thought he heard scratching on the roof. Even in
the daytime he was not always sure whether the rustling was
from the kennel or the noise of silence.

Daytime. Nighttime. Day . . . Night. Night . . . Day. It
was morning when Nicholas brought the first meal and evening when he brought the second. When he made his last
check and asked if everything was all right, it was night.

How time had flown. One night he saw Nicholas and the
next night he saw him was eight years later. Then, he remembered, the first kennel had just been built. Now he was beneath it. The dogs had fared better than he.

Nicholas, too, had prospered. Outwardly there was little
sign of it. His features were basically unchanged. But his eyes
were not quite as clear, and his characteristic innocence
seemed to have passed behind a cloud. It was not something
tangible. He was cooperating perfectly. Yet behind his faith-
fulness and application was a certain correctness, a disciplined
obedience, which suggested that although it was Nicholas
giving succor, it was not entirely the old Nicholas.

Still, it was remarkable that his loyalty had endured eight
years. Olek had reported the grievance attached to Abrahm's

disappearance. He expected Nicholas to press him for an explanation. It was wholly justified. Nicholas had put his trust in him and been let down. Painstakingly, Abrahm acknowledged his feeling, listening earnestly, and attempted to account for what had happened.

It was, they both recalled, 1934. Abrahm had an uncle who lived in Berlin. He had not seen him since childhood. One night he did not come home from work. His wife assumed there was a reason, but when the next day passed without his return, she reported him missing. The authorities denied any knowledge of him, but assured her that they would do their utmost to locate him. Of course, they never did. She looked everywhere for him, but without success. No one knew anything. Finally, she contacted Abrahm. When word reached him, he was having problems of his own, but he recognized his obligation and prepared to go. He had heard various stories of the growing terror in Germany. Now he was anxious only not to help, but also to see the state of affairs himself.

What he found in Berlin was worse than he had anticipated. The Nazis were officially the only party in Germany. Hitler was in his second year as Chancellor and, with the death of von Hindenburg, had made himself President as well. Thus he was at the head of both the state and the armed forces. His power had magnified rapidly.

His uncle's wife, understandably, was a frightened woman. In the sanctity of her own house, with the curtains drawn and the radio on, she spoke in a furtive whisper. Frequently she prefaced a sentence with, "You must not tell anyone." And since her husband had vanished, her neighbors, Jews and Christians alike, had taken to avoiding her as if she were a leper.

But on the streets there was nothing wrong. Daily activities continued normally while Hitler set about dismantling the entire structure of the German society and remaking it in his own image. If ten years ago people had laughed at the antics of this semi-comic wild man, they were not laughing now. Godless, he was becoming their God.

There were rumors afloat that some factories had secretly begun adapting machinery for eventual war manufacture. It was incredible. Germany was a bankrupt country. There was a nation to rebuild. How could anyone be projecting another war?

Ensconced in the bunker, Abrahm could not be sure precisely how much of what he related to Nicholas he had seen then, and how much he had come to know later. But there was no question in his mind, while he was still in Berlin, that Hitler was a force to be reckoned with.

Yet, few seemed to realize fully how dangerous he was. In the Great War, the German people had been told until the very end that they were winning. When the Army surrendered, they were shocked. Now Hitler was priming them to avenge that betrayal under the shibboleth, "Away with all illusions."

Meanwhile, Abrahm left Berlin without having found his uncle.

It was not until a year later, after Hitler promulgated the Nuremberg Laws, that Bronis finally decided to pack up and go to America.

Directed against the Jews, the first of these laws deprived Germans of Jewish blood of their citizenship. The second forbade marriage between Germans and Jews, and the employment by Jews of German servants. Bronis was a decent man, a good socialist and a humanist, so the laws were fundamentally repulsive to him. But compounding his sensitivity was the fact, not widely known, that his wife was Jewish.

Shortly after Abrahm was summoned to Germany, concern arose that there was a leak emanating from the meetings at Bronis' house. There had been a convocation of socialist labor group leaders to plan a protest against job discrimination and poor working conditions. When the demonstration took place, the crowd was attacked by a vicious mob of hooligans armed with clubs and metal pipes. Some of the assailants had crude swastikas pinned on their jackets. A number of workers were badly injured, with the worst beatings going to Jews.

Abrahm stopped coming to Bronis' house. An investigation was made to determine who had divulged the demonstration plans. Several people were suspected, Nicholas among them. There had always been comrades who were uncomfortable with his presence around the house and they sought to implicate him. It was unfounded, of course, Abrahm was quick to assure Nicholas, who was distressed by the revelation. He obviously had no knowledge of what went on at the meetings, and his name was duly cleared.

Bronis, on the other hand, had no such excuse. In fact, there had been periodic security problems ever since his house had become a meeting place, and he had himself long been under suspicion. Abrahm felt he was basically trustworthy, but he was conscious of a thorny possibility: That someone who had not known Bronis' wife was Jewish had found out and was holding it against him. This, however, could not be substantiated. Bronis pleaded innocence and was exonerated along with the other suspects. The informer was never identified.

At the same time that Abrahm continued to boycott Bronis' house upon his return from Berlin, he threw himself more committedly than ever into trying to improve the lot of the Jews, and of all workers, and to warn people of the threat that Hitler posed to a tolerable life for everyone.

In retrospect, Bronis was one of the rare cases who did not have to be convinced. The Nuremberg Laws may have been the handwriting on the wall, but the idea of going to America had not occurred to him overnight. It was hard enough to have a Jewish wife in Warsaw as things were; and he had long been fascinated with the idea of a place where rags to riches was the national dream, where social mobility was common, where freedom of religion was unrestricted, and where the worker was strongly represented. The Depression had stripped some of the gilding from the fantasy, but the basic attraction persisted.

Bronis made the decision, according to Abrahm's sources, the afternoon his oldest son came home from school bloodied and crying.

"My God, what happened to you?" Mrs. Ganzs said.

The boy bit his lip and turned away. But when Bronis took him out back, he confessed.

"They were yelling, 'Your mother's a Jew, your mother's a whore,'" he said. "I asked them to leave me alone, but they kept yelling and then they started to beat me."

Bronis had told the story with tears in his eyes, Abrahm related. Nicholas was saddened. He remembered the day very clearly, he said. He was never informed what had occurred, but it was not long thereafter that Bronis sold him his property and went off to America.

"Aye," Abrahm twinged.

The seizure in his leg closed his eyes and tightened the muscles in his buttocks and lower back. He held still until it ebbed, then poured himself another glass of water. Despite Dr. Adler's warnings of pain and exhortations of patience, the discomfort was so great he had the feeling things were not as they should be. It was nice to think he would be up and around in several weeks, but at the moment it did not seem realistic. He swallowed an oblong pill with the water and waited for it to take effect.

America.

The country was young, but the name had the aura of a Bethlehem or a Babylon.

America.

It was a strange place, Abrahm thought. He knew workers who had gone over there and become independent businessmen, earning a good income and enjoying the freedoms of permissive, flourishing society. But others had come back heartsick and broken, while the majority, remaining there, existed under terrible conditions. Bronis, it was known through comrades, was among these—residing with his family in a dismal, bathroomless room on the fourth floor or a rat-infested building without hot water, barely eking out a living hawking second-hand shirts and trousers from a sidewalk stall.

Still, the dream perpetuated itself.

If it were 1939 again or earlier, and the chance to go to America presented itself, he would not take it. He would continue to defend the right of anyone else to go. It was not sensible to advocate personal liberty and then oppose it when-ever it was convenient. But he rejected it for himself, and disapproved of it generally, because he felt it was escapist and would not accomplish anything in the long run.

There was no way for a Jew to flee the Jewish past. This was why he had devoted his life to establishing the right of a Polish national to be a Jew and a Jew to be a Polish citizen. He was neither religious nor traditional, but he took violent issue with those, whether Jewish or Catholic, who argued for seg-regation, voluntary or imposed, or for assimilation. Every person who was born or who became a Polish citizen was entitled to full and equal personal, social and economic privi-leges, and was charged with equal obligations and restrictions. And every person who fulfilled the requirements of good citizenship was inviolably entitled to complete private freedom—to do as he wished, to pursue a religion, a lan-guage, a culture, or chase butterflies.

These were the ends, beyond those of the general social-ist movements, for which the radical Jewish socialists had been fighting. And there had been some progress toward them, albeit painfully slow, until Hitler reversed the tide. Now Jews were being deprived not only of public rights and private autonomy but of the fundamental liberties and dignities of the human being and, indeed, of life itself.

This was why Abrahm objected to emigration. The move-ment in America had resulted in a weakening of the Jewish community of Europe. He had always argued that the judg-ment day would come. Wherever Jews resided, they were sooner or later made to suffer for that psychic wound with which all humanity was afflicted and for which the Christian faith blamed the Jews. Now it had come to pass in German Europe. One day it would happen in America. And there, as here, the Jews would find themselves defenseless, few in number, alone.

With deep conviction, Abrahm believed Poland was his home. Whether it was called Poland, or in worse times something else, and whether he was a Jew first and a Polish citizen second or vice versa, the only right thing to do—before the war, now, and when the war was over—was to stay and fight for those things to which all human beings were entitled.

Poland was his home as France was home to Frenchmen and China to Chinese. And Warsaw was his Paris or Peiping. He knew the language, the history, the customs, the traditions, and the myths. He knew the economics and politics, the sports, and the arts. He could pick up a newspaper and read anywhere in it with interest and understanding. He knew the politicians, the society figures, the industrialists, the athletes, and the actors. He knew the neighborhoods, the streets, the parks, the stores. He knew the tramways and the train routes and the outlying districts, and farther away he knew the towns and the cities and the lakes and precious woods. He knew the border to the East, violated by the Russians, and had known it before it was a border. And he knew the border to the West, violated by the Germans, and had known it too, before it was drawn. He knew Poland inside and out, and what was good about it and what was bad, and he was determined to make it better.

He could not reproach Bronis, or the thousands of others, for emigrating. Everyone had illusions. For some they culminated in Zion. For some in birth. For some in death. And for some in America.

Zion was an old illusion. America was new.

In the sweat of your face shall you eat bread, till you return unto the ground.

But Poland was a reality.

* * *

A tremor hitched Abrahm's neck. The pill was taking effect. His head had begun to float and the relentless pressure was easing out of his leg. America was a reverie. He would never see it. In his cot in the bunker beneath the dogs, even the ghetto, a few miles away, seemed unreachably far.

Why had he allowed himself to be transported?

When he had come back to the ghetto after Leora's death, he had sworn not to leave again. It was a mistake the first time. His place was there. So was Leora's, but Sonya had insisted on sending her out. She was wrong. There should not have been a ghetto, but once there was, everyone who found themselves in it belonged there.

His position had been constant. No one should go hostage. No one should submit to deportation. No one should cooperate with the Nazis in any way.

"You can't stay in the ghetto much longer," Victor had argued in a rendezvous after Black Monday.

"I can and I will," Abrahm had answered.

Victor was among those for whom it made sense to be on the Aryan side. Working under the nose of the Nazis, he provided invaluable contact with the Polish underground and coordinated various elements in the outside world. Olek operated more covertly, serving as a courier not only between the Aryan side and the ghetto, but also between Warsaw and other cities. But these were acts of resistance, not of compliance. They were part of the same strategy that called for Abrahm to remain in the ghetto until the showdown.

Numerous organizations and parties were striving to supply ghetto residents with food, clothing, medical care, and other services. Although they were harassed and often directly governed by the Germans—who richly enjoyed coercing Jews into denying fellow Jews succor—they did manage to achieve some of their aims. Because of fear and corruption, however, they could do but little to satisfy the emotional and spiritual needs of the people. It was to nourish these, as well as to support physical sustenance, that the underground waged its bitter struggle: to give the people strength and courage as they grew weaker and further removed from external reality; to keep them informed; to penetrate the illusion—carefully nurtured by the Germans and reinforced by the Jewish officials they controlled—that survival was possible only through docility and cooperation; to destroy the myth of relocation; and to organize the resistance.

Every day that went by, the capacity of the ghetto to resist decreased immeasurably. Every day of deportations its population and its will diminished. Every day there was less to defend. Every day there were fewer people to defend it. And every day the end grew nearer.

But there would be a resistance, even if by the time it came it were merely symbolic. There should have been one when there were five hundred thousand Jews in ghetto. There would be one even when there were but five hundred. Then, as before, it would be the only course that did not lead automatically to death.

"Finkel may be out of the way," Victor had said, "but they have numerous agents snooping around. If they look long enough, they're bound to find other weak links."

"They'll wind up annihilating the whole chain," Abrahm said. "Why should I hide myself until they do?"

"At the moment you can't show your face anywhere," Victor said. "So it's not a matter of whether to hide, but where."

"I'd rather hide among the people," Abrahm said. "I can still be effective that way."

"And if they find you?" Victor asked.

"They may, whatever I do," Abrahm said. "But if I move onto the Aryan side, I'll be playing into their hands."

"On the contrary," Victor said. "If you stay put, they're more likely to keep torturing people until they've trapped you. You must come over."

"I can't do it," Abrahm reiterated.

But finally Victor had prevailed. Abrahm would do as much as he could from the Aryan side, and when it came time to make his stand he would go back into the ghetto.

Then Leora died and there seemed to be no reason to stay out any longer. If he waited until the resistance, Sonya might be dead too, and Heykel, and all the others. It would be a hollow victory. Look, he would say to the Nazis. Despite everything your face is bloodied. And they would say, tell that to your family, your friends, your comrades. But tell them loudly, because they cannot hear.

The second time it had happened so quickly.

He hit the ground and felt a sharp snap in his leg and then a numbness set in almost instantaneously along with the pain and he started running.

When he woke after the operation, there was a surprise visitor sitting on the floor beside his mattress. Abrahm opened his eyes slowly, barely focusing, his nostrils singed with anesthetic, his leg on fire. The room smelled at once putrid and antiseptic.

"Victor," he said weakly.

He tried to raise his head, but a shaft of pain speared him to the mattress.

"You shouldn't be here," he said.

"Neither should you," said Victor.

He took Abrahm's hand off the floor and pressed it warmly between both of his. His brow was knit, but he managed a nervous smile.

"The apartment?" Abrahm asked.

Victor told him what had occurred, Abrahm's mind flickered at the margin of consciousness. Victor faded and returned. Behind him the room was dimly lit and strewn with casualties. There was little moaning. A few mattresses away he recognized Ruth Adler tending to a patient. Only a few years older than Leora, she held the lives of others in her hands.

"Dr. Adler will notify us as soon as we can move you," Victor said.

"Move me?" Abrahm asked groggily.

"We're taking you out of the ghetto," Victor said.

"No," Abrahm said.

"We must," Victor said. "It's not safe enough here, and you may be endangering the other patients. If we lodge you elsewhere in the ghetto, you'll still be too vulnerable. You have no defense in this condition."

"It won't be long," Abrahm said.

"If all goes well," Victor said. "But it's not a casual injury. It will be a while before you're running again."

"Ruth," Abrahm whispered, raising his hand to catch her attention.

"What is it?" Victor asked.

"Water," Abrahm said.

His mouth was dry and a white film was forming on his lips.

He followed Victor with his eyes as he went over to Ruth. She was taller than he. A sixteen year old girl and an old man. She might have been his granddaughter. But everything had flip-flopped.

"Here," Victor said.

He slid his hand under Abrahm's head and tilted it gently, bringing the water to his lips.

"Slowly," he said.

Abrahm took a sip and washed the film off his lips with the tip of his tongue. His mouth cooled as the light moisture evaporated.

"I'm staying," he said, laying his head back on the pillow.

He wanted to argue with Victor but he did not have the strength.

"Rest," Victor said. "Don't worry yourself."

"What will they think of my leaving?" Abrahm said.

"They don't know you're back, and they won't know you've left," Victor said. "The important thing is to uphold their morale."

"The important thing is to be with them," Abrahm said.

"When you're recovered," Victor said. "As you are, you would only demoralize them."

He took a folded handkerchief from his jacket pocket and wiped Abrahm's forehead. The he dipped a corner into the cup of water and wiped the film that was forming afresh like a dry foam on his lips.

"Better the truth than illusion," Abrahm said, feeling his consciousness recede.

"Sometimes . . ."

Abrahm felt as if he had run too far and was passing out. Time was slowing down, stretching, standing the moments before him. The bunker was without sound or movement.

His ears buzzed with silence as Black Monday flashed through this mind.

April 17, 1942. He had been sleeping, of all places, in Menachem's apartment. It was an unnervingly quiet night. He kept rolling over, nodding off, and jumping up as if a dream had poked him in the ribs. Then he awoke not to something in his sleep, but the echo of gunshots. He raced to the window.

The street was dark. Suddenly a light flared down the block, sweeping across a knot of persons backed up against a courtyard wall. The darkness swallowed them again, and a salvo of single fire shots spattered the silence. A percussion of footsteps and doors followed, and several cars rumbled away.

In the morning the only signs of what had transpired were stains on the sidewalk. The Germans sent burial wagons to gather the bodies and the police drove the victims' neighbors into the streets to scrub off the blood.

Word spread quickly that countless people throughout the ghetto had been dragged from their homes during the night and summarily executed. The assassins were SS and Gestapo men working from prepared lists. The raids were not random, and each team of Germans was accompanied by a Jewish policeman who led them directly to their quarry.

It was rumored that among the chief targets of their scourge were members of the printing trade, and that the

Germans were trying to blot out the ghetto's illegal printing plants and underground literature. Piece by piece, the hand press in Menachem's house was smuggled to another location. Abrahm himself never set foot there again.

A new phase of ghetto life was ushered in. Until Black Monday, most of the half million Jews who had been packed together were still alive and not without private gardens of hope. They had survived more than two years, there had not yet been any telling move toward liquidation, and if life had not been pleasant, it had at least been continuous and some-what predictable. Now the assumptions that had so carefully been raised, the self-deceptions that had been husbanded, all the ways and means of thriving in adversity that had been cultivated through necessity, ingenuity, courage, treachery, and fright, were brutally trampled.

Night raids became common. Regularly, hundreds of persons were dragged out of their buildings in the terror-pitched darkness and blown into lifelessness. Sometimes people were hauled into the ghetto from the Aryan side and mowed down on the street. No one knew from where they had come, or who they were.

It was no longer possible to believe that the future was reasonably hopeful, or that while a few thousand might die tragically, the rest would endure to see a better day. Any night of the week anyone in the ghetto might be kicked downstairs and brained.

And in July commenced the first great wave of deportations.

Abrahm was neither comfortable nor pained. The black wagon bumped along like a skiff on choppy water, without clip-clopping, and Leora's voice was mute.

JUSTICE

Ivan felt the blindfold being removed, but he saw nothing. His eyelids had locked over his eyes. He raised his hands, which were tightly bound at the wrists, and pried them open. Still, he could not see. Dropping his hands, he ran his fingers over his ankles, which had been tied in such a way that he was limited to stunted steps, advancing one foot at a time. Someone of considerable strength had quickly loosened them after helping him to the floor and his feet had jerked upward against the absence of constraint. Now his skin burned from the rope, but where the blindfold had circled his head, his scalp and eyelids breathed as if a cool breeze were blowing over them and his blindness gradually evaporated.

He found himself toward one end of an obscure, window-less space with opaque walls and a single lamp set in a corner. The air was stuffy and tinctured with fumes of kerosene or petrol. It did not seem to be a room in which anyone lived, but whatever its function, pains had been taken to conceal it.

"Where am I?" Ivan asked in a voice dry with disuse.

His question rose like a wisp of smoke. There were several people in the room, but the only one recognizable was Olek. He sat a short distance from Ivan. The others were behind him, in the darkness.

"What about these?" Ivan said, extending his coupled fists.

"Will you restrain yourself?" Olek asked.

"What choice have I?" Ivan said.

He peered over Olek's shoulder, trying to make out the forms behind him. One seemed much larger than the others.

"All right," Olek said, moving toward Ivan and freeing his hands. "But I warn you—don't act up."

"Thank you," Ivan said.

As he rubbed his wrists to stimulate the circulation, he continued squinting into the blackness behind Olek. Who were these apparitions? At the same time that he wondered, he was conscious of the conflicting desire not to know. The tension was partially resolved when a diminutive figure materialized out of the background, sitting down beside Olek.

"Ivan," he said, "this is a distasteful occasion. But if you cooperate, you have our word that fairness will guide our conduct."

The speaker was a man in his later years with long white hair, a clipped white beard, precise diction, and a reassuring if slightly nervous manner.

"Who are you?" Ivan said.

"Unfortunately, it is not for you to ask the questions," Victor said. "We are here to inquire into your role in the deaths of Leora Gutterman and Sister Theresa."

"Who is he?" Ivan asked Olek.

Olek did not react.

"All of a sudden you can't hear me," Ivan said.

"None of your sarcasm," Olek said.

A sickly half-smile came over Ivan's face. It would be better not to ask who was back there.

"If you'll permit me, I'll explain all you need to know," Victor said.

He slid closer to Ivan, nudging Olek to the side.

"Leora and Theresa perished at the design of deliberately nihilistic forces," Victor continued. "We believe you are not without complicity. If this is so, you will be punished accordingly."

"The law requires a courtroom to fly the Polish flag," Ivan said.

"You will have every opportunity to prove your innocence," Victor said. "It behooves me to say, however, that we assume your guilt."

"I didn't kill anyone," Ivan said. "I wouldn't know how."

"The charge against you is betrayal," Victor said, "resulting in murder."

"I'm guilty whatever you say, so I might as well admit it?" Ivan said. "Is that your game?"

"Not at all," Victor said. "Your guilt is presumed, but despite the trying circumstances in which we find ourselves, your fundamental right to establish innocence has been preserved."

Ivan pulled up his shoulders and squeezed the tight, uncertain smile from his face.

"Fire away," he said.

"You first became involved in this matter through Olek, is that correct?" Victor asked.

"Yes."

"Describe how?" Victor said.

"He approached me and said that he had a young girl who was being taken out of the ghetto and would need a place to stay. I wanted to help, of course. Felix agreed to take her, and she stayed with them until Yanina arranged with Theresa to put her in the convent."

"Didn't Olek ask you to take her personally?" Victor queried.

"I'm not sure," Ivan said. "I don't think so."

"Did you, Olek?" Victor asked.

Olek nodded.

"And what was your response?" Victor asked Ivan.

"I told you, it's not clear," Ivan answered.

"But you remember recommending that Felix take her?"

"Yes."

"Why didn't you take her?"

"I wasn't equipped to," Ivan said.

"Were you any less equipped than Felix?" Victor asked.

"Anna works," Ivan said. "She's away all day. Yanina is at home."

"Weren't you home much of the day?" Victor asked.

"Caring for a child isn't a man's job." Ivan said. "Besides, I was busy."

"What is a man's job?" Olek said.

"Don't you know?" said Ivan.

"What were you doing?" Victor said.

"Tailoring," Olek said sarcastically.

"That's right," Ivan said.

"Smuggling?" Victor said. "Black marketeering?"

"Supplying the ghetto," Ivan said.

"With what?" Victor said.

"Necessities," Ivan said.

"What sort of necessities?" Victor asked.

"Whatever people needed," Ivan said.

"Such as?" Victor said.

"Whiskey," Olek said. "Narcotics. Perfume."

"Whatever people could pay for," Ivan said.

"You could simply have said no to Olek," Victor said. "Why would you have gone to the trouble of involving Felix?"

"It was Heykel's daughter," Ivan said. "I wanted to help."

"So you said you would try to arrange for her to stay with the Erdmanns?"

"Exactly," Ivan said.

"How did you know it was Heykel's daughter?" Victor asked.

"Who else's would it have been?" Ivan said.

"Did Olek tell you whose?" Victor asked.

"He must have," Ivan said.

"Did you?" Victor asked.

Olek shook his head.

"No one's memory is perfect," Ivan said.

"How did you know?" Victor repeated.

"I don't recall the details," Ivan said. "But why would he ask me personally if it wasn't someone special?"

"Did you give any indication that you knew who it was?" Victor asked.

"The situation called for discretion," Ivan said.

"In what way?" Victor asked.

"Olek seemed uncomfortable about soliciting me," Ivan said. "He was very tense. It was my impression that he didn't want to bring her over, but that it had been decided by others and he was implementing their wish."

"And you thought the Erdmann's would be a more suitable place?"

"It was a natural," Ivan said, growing less antagonistic. "Yanina's a competent woman, and she has the confidence of her neighbors. She could do the job without botching it. And Olek could keep tabs on the situation without being associated with the girl."

"You had it very neatly reasoned," Victor said.

His direct, even manner was putting Ivan at ease.

"As I've said," Ivan acknowledged. "I wanted to help."

"Did you go to Felix yourself?" Victor asked.

"No," Ivan said. "Anna did it."

"Why?" Victor asked.

"Felix and I haven't been getting along," Ivan said. "Anna can get through to him."

"What did you tell her?" Victor asked.

"I don't keep a diary."

"You must remember something," Victor said.

"I suppose I told her that a girl was being brought across and that I thought Yanina could take care of her."

"And what was her response?"

"She agreed to approach her mother."

"Not Felix?"

"No," Ivan said. "Yanina would be caring for her, so she had to be enlisted first. Then the two of them could bring it up to Felix."

"What did Anna tell her?" Victor asked.

"I don't know," Ivan said.

"That Leora was Heykel's daughter?"

"Whatever it was stayed between them."

"And what did Yanina say?"

"She agreed to do it."

"What about Felix?"

"At first he resisted the idea," Ivan said. "He claimed it was bad enough that a man had to dig his own grave, without being asked to commit suicide in it."

"You heard him say that?" Victor asked.

"Anna heard it."

"Then what changed his mind?"

"Don't ask me," Ivan said.

"But he finally consented?" Victor said.

"Yes."

"Were you involved in this at all?"

"Not directly," Ivan said.

"You mentioned that you were not getting along with Felix," Victor said. "What was wrong?"

"It doesn't matter," Ivan said.

"It may," Victor said.

"Felix resents the fact that Anna and I haven't given him a grandchild," Ivan said.

"Why haven't you?" Olek interjected.

"Why haven't you?" Ivan said.

"I'm not his son-in-law," Olek said.

"Lucky for you," Ivan said.

"Enough," Victor said. "We'll leave it be."

"That's all right," Ivan said. "I don't mind telling someone who will listen sensibly. It's just that we didn't want a child while we were young. We wanted to be free, to enjoy each other without anything standing in the way. Our intention was to wait until three or four years ago. But the war came along, and it seemed wrong to have one then. So we held off. As things got worse, Felix became increasingly frightened. He started riding me, but really it was the war getting to him. The last six or nine months he's been unbearable. Every other word is an insult."

"It's clear that he's not well," Victor said. "How did he behave when Leora came over?"

"According to Anna, he was quite unpleasant. She would return home distraught from seeing them."

"How often was that?" Victor asked.

"As always," Ivan said, "almost daily."

"And how frequently did you call during this period?"

"Seldom," Ivan said.

"Did you ever chance to visit when Olek happened to be there?"

"No," Ivan said.

"Or anyone else?" Victor asked.

Ivan looked uncertain.

"Who?" he said.

"Never mind," Victor said. "Tell me instead, when did Felix's attitude toward Leora begin to soften?"

"Anna said she sort of grew on him. After she was gone, I couldn't get near him without hearing how fate had done a better job than I had in bringing him a grandchild."

Victor extracted a snuff box from his pocket and brought a pinch of tobacco to his nose.

"While Leora was with the Erdmanns," he said, "did you discuss her with anyone other than Anna?"

"No."

"Positively not?"

"Positively."

"Did you discuss her with anyone other than Anna from the time Yanina took her to the convent to the time Sister Theresa brought her to the hospital?"

"No," Ivan said.

"No one asked you about her?" Victor said.

"No one," Ivan said.

"And between the time she was brought to the hospital and the time she was buried?"

"The same," Ivan said.

"So, you never in any way discussed Leora with anyone other than Anna?"

"That's right," Ivan said.

"How did you know Sister Theresa was dead?" Victor asked.

Ivan flustered. His eyes scrambled to order his thoughts.

"What do you mean?" he said.

"When Olek was questioning Felix, you accused him of two crimes. Felix didn't know what you were talking about. You pressed Olek to confront him. When he finally did, Felix was so shocked he vomited. It was evident that he had no idea Theresa had been killed. But you did, Ivan. And we want to know how."

"Anna told me," Ivan said.

"I'm afraid you're lying," Victor said.

In the same gesture, Ivan seemed to straighten and collapse.

"I need a lawyer," he said. "Why should I answer all your questions. The more I tell you, the more bloodthirsty you get. Someone's dead. Can't you leave her memory alone? Thousands of people are dying. Why talk about one?"

Jumping up in a frenzy, he tried to push Victor over, then turned toward the lighter end of the room, looking for an exit. Before he could find it, Olek spurted across the floor, grabbed him by an ankle, and stopped him with a quick, vicious twist. Ivan screamed and fell writhing. He did not see several forms lunge out of the darkness and promptly retreat as Olek dragged him back to the spot where he had been.

"Stop it, you bastard," Ivan whimpered. "You've broken my leg."

"If I break anything, it'll be your neck," Olek said.

Dexterously, he unlaced Ivan's shoe and removed it. Victor appeared unperturbed. Trifling with his snuff box, he waited for Ivan to settle down.

"Whatever you've done, you can still be useful to us by answering further questions—truthfully," Victor said after a calm. "If you refuse, I can assure you quite candidly, you will be eliminated. If you cooperate, your lot will depend on your testimony."

"I won't be blackmailed," Ivan said.

The sock over his rapidly swelling ankle looked as if it had been wadded with tissue. He peeled it off agonizingly.

"You won't be anything," Olek said.

"It would be easiest for all of us if you stated what you knew of Theresa's death," Victor said.

"I've told you everything," Ivan said obstinately.

"Let me prompt you a little," Victor said.

"It's your party," Ivan said.

"It's Heinrich's party," Olek said.

"Who?" Ivan exclaimed.

"Heinrich Lutzki," Victor said.

"I've never heard of such a person," Ivan said.

He looked away disdainfully, as if the subject was hopelessly irrelevant.

"Not even at the Britannia?" Victor asked.

"It's a crowded place," Ivan said. "You brush shoulders with many strangers."

"Is that all?" Olek said.

"You must know," Ivan said.

"What about the Metropole?" Victor asked.

"What about it?"

"You referred at the Erdmann's to Felix having come home drunk from there one night . . . "

"More than once."

"How did you know he had been there?"

"I surmised it," Ivan said.

"On what basis?"

"It's a popular club."

"Do you go there?" Victor asked.

"No," Ivan said.

"He prefers the class of trade at the Britannia," Olek said.

"I attend for business reasons," Ivan said.

"That's what I mean," Olek said.

He pictured Heinrich standing opposite Heykel in the chapel yard.

"Ivan," Victor said, "don't you think it's normal for Felix to want a grandchild?"

"What are you asking?" Ivan said.

"Earlier you asserted that as the war came on and Felix's anxiety heightened, he grew increasingly offensive."

"It's true," Ivan said. "The pig wouldn't leave me alone."

"Was it characteristic of him to abuse people gratuitously?" Victor asked.

"Take my word for it," Ivan said. "He's not the weak, cautious man you think he is."

"How did he insult you?" Victor asked.

"Use your imagination," Ivan said.

"My imagination is apt to be much less accurate than your memory," Victor said.

"I doubt it," Olek said.

"That's asinine," Ivan said. "An insult is an insult."

"Was he generally uncivil," Victor asked, "or pointedly vulgar?"

"I didn't take notes," Ivan said.

"Did he insist that you were impotent?" Victor asked.

"He was crazy."

"Did he call you a noodle?" Olek said. "A limp prick? A rotten-assed queer?"

"He was going mad with the fear that he would die without having propagated his breed," Ivan said. "It didn't matter to him that the world is unfit to bring children into."

"How did you know Sister Theresa was dead?" Victor asked.

Ivan's body tightened, as though he might make another break, then slackened.

"The word was around."

"Where?" Victor asked.

"At the Britannia."

"What was said?"

"That a Sister had been found near the convent."

"And you knew it was Theresa?" Victor asked.

"I put two and two together," Ivan said.

"From whom did you hear it?" Victor asked.

"It was in the air."

"Word travels quickly," Olek said.

"Blame me," Ivan said.

"Was there any speculation as to why she was murdered?" Victor asked.

"No," Ivan said.

"Do you know why?" Victor asked.

"I don't know anything more," Ivan said.

"Then permit me to share something of what I know," Victor said.

"I'm not interested," Ivan said.

"You will be," Victor said.

He moved so close to Ivan that their legs were almost touching.

"Some weeks before Theresa's murder, Heinrich came to you with the story that Felix was under official scrutiny for abetting Jews at the same time that he was collaborating with the authorities. It had been discovered that he was part-Jewish, Heinrich said, and that he had been sheltering a Jewish girl. They wanted to question her about him, but had been unable to trace her. Wanting to conceal their interest, they assigned Heinrich to investigate. He asked you whether you knew anything about her. You said no. He suggested that even if you had nothing valuable to contribute, it would be foolish to deny what you certainly must know: that a young girl had stayed with the Erdmann's. You balked at admitting even this. Then he intimated that neither Felix nor Anna were definitely aware of your homosexuality, nor of all the ways you made money, and that your social and business privileges would be operative only as long as you gave him your full cooperation. Still you held fast. But Heinrich persisted. Why sacrifice yourself for Felix, he asked, when he was jeopardiz-

ing you, Anna, Yanina, everyone near to him. He was a Jew,
and he had harbored a Jewish girl. When she was found, her
interrogation, together with independent evidence, might result in his arrest and quite possibly that of others. If you only
told him who the girl was, however, or what had become of
her, no harm would befall you. Hating Felix for his persecu-
tion of you, and fearing exposure if not worse, you finally
broke down and told Heinrich that Leora had been taken to a
convent. You never imagined the consequences of this dis-
closure. In fact, you did not at first even divulge Leora's
identity. Heinrich promised you that your information would
be held confidential, and that all that was now required of you
was to keep an eye on Felix. You acceded. Then he startled
you by asserting that a woman had come to the Erdmann's
with the girl, stayed several weeks, and left. Who was she, he
asked? You disavowed any knowledge of her, but when he
pressed you, emphasizing the dangers in not telling him, you
did. Later on, when you became aware of Leora's death, you
did not immediately connect it with what had transpired between you and Heinrich. But when you heard the account of
the funeral, you began to wonder."

"The night after Theresa's slaying, you were at the Britannia. So was Heinrich. He apprised you that she had met an
unfortunate end and conjectured that Felix might have had
something to do with it. You were unsure what to make of this.
For all his faults, Felix was not a violent man. In the next day or
two you learned that while you had heard the news at the
Britannia in the late hours of the night, Theresa's remains had
not actually come to light until the following morning. Although it was still not clear what was going on, you realized
that Heinrich was unquestionably involved and that, whether
you liked it or not, you were to some degree his accomplice. It
was then that you seized upon the rationale he had insinuated
and began to channel whatever doubt might be cast your way
toward Felix. Now," Victor finished, "did you find that interesting?"

Ivan's face had shrunk and blanched, as if the flesh and

blood had stolen away, leaving only a layer of fat between skin and bone.

"Will you tell us the rest?" Victor asked softly.

Ivan looked around terrifiedly, like a man about to be jammed into a straight jacket. His body hardened and grew angular.

Olek prepared for another rush, but it did not come. Instead, Ivan began to raise himself slowly and collapsed with a shriek. His ankle had failed. Painfully, he pushed himself into sitting position and began unbuttoning his shirt.

"What is it?" Victor asked.

"It's cold," Ivan said.

His voice had a hollow ring.

"Do you want to lie down?" Victor asked.

Ivan started to shiver as if he were immured in a freezer. He removed his shirt and then his other shoe and sock. The injured ankle, discolored and tumid, resembled a purple and yellow mouse.

"That's all I know," Ivan said remotely.

He pulled off his undershirt and dropped it on the floor. His teeth were clacking, and his arms prickled with goose pimples. He had a flat, hairless chest and narrow shoulders.

"Cold . . . ," he chattered, unbuckling his pants.

He removed them roughly, tugging at the legs as if he were no longer attached to his ankle. Observing him, Olek, too, felt cold.

"Brr . . ." Ivan mumbled, his lips flapping.

Victor took off his jacket and draped it over Ivan's shoulders. He seemed not to notice. As Ivan removed his underpants, the jacket slipped awry, clinging to one shoulder like a cape. Mesmerically, he sloped toward the floor, reposing on his right side, his arms curled before his face, cradling his head, his right leg fully extended, his left drawn up to his chest, revealing his anus. His buttocks were scotched with welts and ridges, and lower, near his scrotum, the flesh was branded with indigo craters.

"Chhh . . ." he said, quivering.

STAR OF DAVID

Eugen wiped the sweat off his forehead with his sleeve and fanned himself with an open hand. It was a sweltering day and there was no ventilation in the little kitchen where he sat watching a young woman open the stove and take out a small loaf of bread. She brought it over to the table and set it down beside a large tin of wine herring.

"Why don't you open it," she said.

She had a full, sensuous mouth and strong, gapped teeth. As she went over to the pantry, Eugen observed her figure. She did not appear to have lost much weight as a result of the war, and in contrast to the skeletons he was accustomed to seeing, she seemed voluptuous.

"Go ahead, start," she said.

A sweet aroma wafted up from the bread, but Eugen could not tear his eyes from the back of the woman. When she opened the cupboard, he saw that it was filled with what must have been several hundred tins and jars, neatly stacked to the depth and height of the shelves. She selected a jar of dark red jam and a short, upright tin that he could not identify.

"So you're Abrahm Bankart's cousin," she said, joining him at the table.

"Distantly," Eugen replied.

Behind the woman, on the sewing commode that partitioned the kitchen from the main room, stood a framed picture of a young man, no more than twenty-two or twenty-three, with a snub nose, cropped, bumpy ears, a dimpled chin, and a cigarette slung jauntily from the corner of his mouth. An oversided beret perched on his head at a rakish angle. Across the upper left of the portrait was the inscription:

> Miriam is my love
> Miriam is my princess,
> The only thing I miss
> Are mother's blintzes.

> Her Doting Daniel

"Funny looking, wasn't he," said the woman, whose name was Miriam.

Eugene surveyed the face of the man whose head Bankart had crushed on the cobblestones.

"Not at all," he said politely. "He projects quite a sensitive impression."

"He wanted to be a poet," Miriam said.

She pushed the tin of herring toward Eugen.

"I'll cut the bread."

Hesitantly, Eugen detached the welded key from the tin and threaded it. The lid opened easily, and he began to wind a narrow strip around the perimeter.

"Do you look like him?" Miriam asked.

"Like who?" Eugen asked.

"Bankart."

The key was becoming harder to coil. Eugen rested his cramped fingers.

"I don't think so," he said.

"It's curious," Miriam said, taking a knife to the bread. "I don't imagine him too differently than you appear."

Eugen glanced at her strangely.

"You should be flattered," she added. "I understand he's a very attractive man."

A sharp stitch caused Eugen to retract his hand quickly from the tin. A fine pink line grew darker across the top of his thumb, where he had slashed it.

"Clumsy of me," he said.

Feeling the blood throb, he brought his thumb to his mouth and sucked it, running his tongue over the slit.

"It always happens with those tops," Miriam said. "I should have warned you."

She washed his thumb with alcohol and fixed him a bandage. Then she finished opening the tin. The silver scales of the herring sparkled through the plum-colored sauce. Its tart, vinegary odor tingled Eugen's nostrils. He envisioned the fish on a platter with boiled potatoes and fat slices of raw onion. The thought turned his stomach.

"Help yourself," Miriam said, shoving the tin under his nose. "Herring's the best thing for you. It's very nutritious."

"I'll have a piece of bread first," Eugen said.

Trying not to show the extent of his hunger, Eugen took a slice of the brown, rough-grained bread. Its weight surprised him. He uncapped the bottle of jam and scooped a spoonful onto the bread, spreading it in a thin, even layer. Before he could bite into it, the bread absorbed the jam's liquid, leaving a pulpy residue on the surface.

"You needn't be stingy," Miriam said. "There's more than enough."

Without asking she tipped the jar and poured three or four times as much jam over the first coating.

Eugen stared into the pool of strawberries floating on the bread. He wanted to pick out the fruit and set it aside to have with his tea, but he was too embarrassed. Instead, he nibbled into the bread as slowly as he could, savoring each bud of sweetness as it blossomed on his tongue.

For herself, Miriam folded a slice of bread in half, inserted a herring fillet, and sprinkled it with paprika.

"You're probably wondering how it could be that the pantry is so full," she said.

Averting his eyes from her sandwich, Eugen concentrated on his bread. The copiously dispensed jam swam off the edges, over his toothmarks, dripping onto his fingers, the table, his pants.

"You should have seen it when Daniel was alive," Miriam said. "We had enough food to feed an army. Not just in these cupboards, but stacked up on the floor, in the living room, under the bed. It got so I couldn't clean house."

Eugen tried to stem the flow by licking clean the borders of the bread, but the jam kept trickling.

"And then when it came time to eat, we had a terrible problem making a choice. It's true. While so many people were starving, we couldn't decide what to feast on next. When Daniel went to work in the morning, he would hide our empty cans and bottles under his jacket and dispose of them wherever he could. It would have been trouble if anyone in the building had found out, but no one did. We had almost no visitors after he joined the police force. What I have here is only what remains of what there was the day he died."

Miriam rose and brought a pot of steeping tea to the table.

"Weak or strong," she asked.

"As it is," Eugen said.

She filled his glass and then her own.

"I haven't given you a chance to say anything," she offered. "How is it that you happened to look me up?"

The steam from the tea made the hot kitchen air still more humid. Eugen swabbed his brow again and delayed a second slice of bread.

"Through Obad Finkel's wife," he said.

"She thought I would know where your cousin was?" Miriam said.

"Not necessarily," Eugen said apologetically. "It grieves me to bother you in this regard, but I cannot neglect any possibility."

"You're deeply attached to him, aren't you?" Miriam said.

"Yes," Eugen said.

"But how did you come across Sarah?"

"Accidently," Eugen said. "By way of a bakery worker who had been familiar with Obad."

"He was a good man," Miriam said, "with rotten luck."

"You knew him?" Eugen asked.

"Very well," Miriam said. "He and Daniel used to play cards before the war. Even during, until Daniel became a policeman."

"Did they see each other at all after that?" Eugen asked.

"They sometimes passed on the street," Miriam said, "but Obad refused to acknowledge him."

"Then it was pure coincidence that he was nearby when the misfortune occurred?" Eugen said.

"Absolutely," Miriam said. "Obad didn't realize it was Daniel on the ground until it was over."

"Who told you that?" Eugen asked.

"Sarah," Miriam said. "She came over to express her sympathy. Then Obad disappeared."

"What were the circumstances?" Eugen asked.

"No one's sure," Miriam said.

She prepared another sandwich and held it out toward Eugen.

"Will you have some herring now?" she asked.

"Not just yet," Eugen said.

Self-consciously, he reached for a second slice of bread and covered it liberally with jam. Then he took a modest bite and followed it with a sip of tea, creating a sweet, seed-filled soup in his mouth.

"Sarah thinks the Gestapo killed him," Miriam said.

"Why?" Eugen said.

"For refusing to tell them anything about Bankart," Miriam said.

"I don't understand," Eugen said.

"They arrested Obad after Daniel was beaten," Miriam said. "As a witness."

"Was that it?" Eugen said.

"No," Miriam said. "They let him go. He vanished later."

"Without a trace?" Eugen asked.

"There was talk of his body being seen, but Sarah was never able to find him."

"These things must have drawn you two together," Eugen said.

"Briefly," Miriam said. "But now, were it not for you, I wouldn't know whether she was dead or alive."

"Forgive my inquisitiveness," Eugen said, "but I must ask, where did you acquire the notion that Abrahm was a handsome man?"

"From Daniel," Miriam said.

Eugen set his bread down on the table.

"From Daniel?"

"Where else?" Miriam said.

"How would he have known?"

"How would he not have?" Miriam said. "Bankart was renowned among all the workers."

"Yes, of course," Eugen said, "but . . ."

"Daniel wasn't always a policeman, you know," Miriam said. "I told you that his ambition was to be a poet. While waiting for the world to discover him, he did odd jobs. He could have had a bakery post, and there were other opportunities, but he never wanted to get tied down. 'Someday,' he said, 'we'll have a house in the country and from the second floor you'll be able to see the forest and I'll sit up there and create beautiful visions while you raise our bright-eyed children.' He was a dreamer through and through."

Viewing the puckish face spiritedly confronting him out of the picture Eugen felt inexplicably buoyant.

"How did Daniel befriend Obad?" he asked.

"In the line of duty," Miriam said. "He used to deliver sacks of flour to the bakery where Obad worked."

"Did they play cards with anyone in particular?" Eugen asked.

"Who didn't get dragged into those games?" Miriam said. "They met regularly in a schoolroom. Even Bankart came."

"Did he play with them?" Eugen asked.

"Once in a while," Miriam said, "but if he won anything, it always went into the treasury for supplies for the children."

Contemplating the bread lying temptingly before him, Eugen sifted his memory for any recollection of Obad Finkel's relationship with Daniel. There was none. When he was apprehended, Finkel admitted knowledge of Bankart, but never of Daniel. Why, Eugen pondered? A disturbing notion encroached. What if Thierbach, noting that all the information Finkel had provided had failed to point the way to Bankart, had discovered that he was keeping secret his acquaintance with the person Bankart had killed?

"If he knew Abrahm," Eugen thought aloud, "why would Daniel have struck him to begin with?"

"Shame," Miriam said. "He was ashamed of being a policeman, and he was doubly ashamed of being caught in the act by Bankart, whom he admired. He suppressed his guilt about wearing the star on his hat, but I felt it in him. He couldn't stand himself for it."

"Then why did he do it?" Eugen asked.

"His nerves exploded," Miriam said.

Eugen dropped a spoonful of jam into his tea-glass. The bits of strawberry hydrated as they sank, driftily changing shape in the dark orange water.

"Everyone's nerves are overtaxed," he said.

Miriam's face, which had been responsive, seemed to congeal.

"When the call first went out for police, he didn't go," she said. "I didn't even know he was thinking about it. But being a frustrated poet is insecure enough in normal times. When we were in school, other people studied with a trade in mind, an occupation. Not Daniel. No matter what anyone said to him, he answered: 'I'm studying to lead my life.' That was it."

"When the war arrived, the last thing anyone needed was an unskilled poet. Things became impossible. Daniel looked around and saw death and became afraid. We had to eat. So when a call was issued for more police, he rushed down and got a position. He was relieved, temporarily. The work looked easy, he could do as little as he wanted, he could even help people, and it was the best available insurance against the unknown. But almost immediately it turned out to be a nightmare for him. Except for a few men who had also joined the force, and whom he couldn't stand, his friends ostracized him. He tried to tell them that it was not so bad, that he could be effective in the underground while wearing his hat, that it might be advantageous for them to have a man on the inside, so to speak. But they were unequivocally opposed to the police and unwilling to have anyone participate for any reason. To them it was tantamount to donning a Nazi uniform. Daniel struggled to make light of it, saying it was a misunderstanding, but it hurt him deeply. And the job was awful. Much worse than he expected. One unpleasant thing after another. He wanted to quit, but he was afraid for our lives, and we needed sustenance. That was how he came to be involved in contraband. He decided that the only way he would ever be able to get free and rejoin his comrades was to guarantee us enough food and other necessities so that eventually we could survive without his working.

"He began bringing home goods—mostly food, but later also jewelry and even money. I don't know what he did to get them. Every day he walked in with a little, and we fared sparingly, to save as much as we could. We were accumulating things at a moderate rate when something ghastly transformed him. To this minute I have no idea what it was. He stepped through the door one evening a shadow of himself. His hands were shaking so violently that he could hardly eat. I asked him what was wrong, but it only aggravated his trembling. All he would confide, finally, was that he wanted desperately to resign, to forget he had ever put on the star. But it was too late. The authorities would not tolerate it. To emancipate himself from his bondage, he resolved to rapidly build up a supply of provisions that would enable him to go into hiding.

"Suddenly he began producing much larger quantities of goods. Sometimes he came home now three, four, five times a day to deliver a load. He became a frantic squirrel. It wounded him profoundly that he had been so weak as to become a policeman. He needed to regain his self-respect, and the respect of his comrades. As his stockpile mounted, he began to feel better and have visions of himself out of that cursed black hat and in his beret again—as you see him in the picture, Daniel the poet, working heroically in the underground. Then he was dying."

Miriam's eyes had puffed up, but her voice remained clear.

"Did Obad know the woman?" Eugen asked.

He visualized Obad's account of how Daniel had ripped open the woman's blouse, raised her dress, and clawed at her underpants. What else had he concealed?

"I doubt it," Miriam said. "But Daniel did. She was once a schoolmate of ours."

Eugen's eyebrows rose.

"It sounds peculiar," Miriam said, "but it was probably easier for him to assault someone he knew than a complete stranger."

She raised the tea pot and refilled Eugen's glass. The strawberry remnants swirled and billowed like sponge algae.

"What became of her?" Eugen said.

"Deported," Miriam said. "If I'm not mistaken, she volunteered."

Eugen felt a startling surge of hostility toward the woman. Were it not for her, he thought, he would still be on the Aryan side, tending his cases, living well, sleeping in a clean, cozy bed. Bankart would never have encountered Daniel, Finkel would not have been caught in the middle, and whoever killed him would have had no cause. But that was insane. Bankart was not whoever. Finkel's wife could believe what she wanted. Thierbach had nothing to do with it.

"It's a pity," he said.

"What?" Miriam asked.

"The whole story," Eugen said.

"I'm sorry," Miriam said. "I got carried away."

"It was interesting," Eugen said.

"But not of much worth in locating your cousin," Miriam said.

"Nevertheless," Eugen said, "you've been most helpful."

"I don't see how," Miriam said. "I had no right to ramble on. I was concerned you would march out the moment you perceived you trip was wasted. At least you got something to eat. You were plainly hungry. You haven't finished your bread. But take your time. You can stay as long as you like."

Eugen strained the remainder of his tea through his teeth, leaving a strawberry mash in the glass.

"That's kind of you," he said, "But I'll have to be going shortly."

"It's a windfall that you are here at all," Miriam said. "I'm the last person in the world who would know about Bankart."

"I thought he might have paid you a visit," Eugen said.

"Why would he do that?" Miriam asked.

"To apologize," Eugen said.

"For what?" Miriam said.

"Killing Daniel," Eugen said.

"He deserved his end," Miriam said.

"You don't mean it," Eugen said.

"It's true."

Eugen began to get up from the table, but Miriam hurriedly circled behind him and wrapped her arms around his neck.

"The day's nearly gone," she said. "Why not hunt for Bankart in the morning?"

JEWS AND GENTILES

"It's the damndest thing," Stefan said. "For weeks my mother lay there moaning and groaning, you should have seen her, howling for all she was worth, but I knew there was nothing wrong with her so I let her carry on, took good care of her, mind you, but didn't take her too seriously, and then, as quickly as she seemed to have recovered, she died."

"Do I have enough nails?" Joseph asked.

He was holding what resembled a hollow candle without a top.

"Let's see," Stefan said.

Taking the tube from Joseph, he balanced it in the palm of his hand.

"It could stand a few more," he said. "You'll get the feel of it."

"Wouldn't it be better to count them?" Joseph asked.

"I had a teacher once who used to grade papers by weighing them. 'Master Stinski,' I asked him, 'why don't you bother to read them?' 'There are too many things to consider,' he said, 'and too little time.' When the shit hits the fan, Joseph my friend, you won't have much time either. You'll have to do this on the run, down with the worms or who knows, up a chimney. And you'll have to improvise. You won't be able to do it without the touch."

Stefan emptied the charge, which consisted of nails and a black powder speckled with metal scraps, into a makeshift corrugated pan with a pleated pour spout. Then he added a dash more of nails to the recipe from a tin can and scooped up a handful of the mixture.

"Load up on nails," he said. "You can always stuff in powder."

Joseph followed his example.

"All right," Stephan said, "let's try again. Keep your fist tight, but allow some play. That's it. Now shake your fist up and down the way you would to make a stack of pennies. You can feel the bastards falling into place. Get a good thick column, almost the width of the tube. It doesn't matter if it's a pipe or a penis. The powder will sift its way through and pack everything tight."

"How's this?" Joseph asked.

"Better," Stefan said, examining Joseph's work. "A smidge of powder, another quiver of needles, tamp it down, and I think you'll have it."

Scattered around them in the darkened room lay an assortment of ingredients for the sundry bombs that Stefan had perfected or was still in the process of devising: lengths of pipe, bottles, cans, wicks and fuses, wire, paraffin, benzine, explosive powder, caps, cartridges, sticks, nails, screw chunks, clock movements, and various tools and molds.

"I don't know who I'd rather have watching me teach a Jewish boy how to blow up Germans—my father or my mother," Stefan said. "He would love it. She would die all over again."

When he had filled the tube almost to the brim and plugged it with cotton, Joseph stood it upright in a narrow can and, dipping his finger in a jar of glue, gummed the inside rim. Then he took a simulated taper head, complete with wick, pasted its base, and slid it partially into the tube. Through a slit in the side of the head, he grasped the wick with a tweezers and drew it down, past the cotton, into the powder. Finally, he mated the tube and the head, forming a finished candle.

"Father was a good man," Stefan said. "Honest. Open-minded. Nothing against Jews or anyone else. He believed that all men were the same and wanted the same things, but that conditions corrupted them. The slaughterhouse was his world, you know. His church. His university. If not for that, you wouldn't be here now. Everything's connected to the slaughterhouse. My uncle, Stracho, my mother's brother, worked there too. He was a horse of another feather. Hated Jews. Hated Russians. Hated children. Hated himself, if you ask me. But for some reason he didn't hate my father. Or maybe he did. Anyway, he and my father became acquainted because they were both chopping meat in the same place and he introduced his sister to my father and my father married her. So far, steaks and loins. The trouble arose when the Jews started to horn in on the factory. My uncle was dead against them. He ganged up with a bunch of troublemakers to stop any more from getting in and to drive out the ones who were already there. They were taking up Christian jobs, he said, laying bare Christian cupboards, starving Christian babies. Father didn't agree. 'Blood is blood,' he said. 'A person's a person.' But my uncle wouldn't take no for an answer. He began coming over for dinner and staying far into the night, haranguing father about the impending world disaster if the Jews weren't kept from taking over. 'They'll hang us all from lamp posts,' was his war cry. Mother got so earsore she eventually came around to his point of view. The two of them teamed up against father. But father stood his ground. 'There's no more difference between a Jew and a Gentile,' he insisted, 'than between one end of the salami and the other.'"

Stefan laughed shrilly, and Joseph could not help laughing too. He enjoyed the way Stefan could work so adeptly while talking. It was as if he had two minds—one serious and precise, the other lax and jocular. The first inscribed details on a set of technical drawings, while the second continued its narration.

"It was about this time that a Jew named Bankart made himself felt. I heard so much about him from my father that he became my boyhood hero. Who else could have pushed my uncle out of the factory? We couldn't even get him out of the house. Well, Bankart managed it and my uncle, along with some of his friends, wound up in illegal trades. He was not about to work side by side with a tribe of Jews, he said. Where would that get him? After a lifetime of breaking his back he would be right where he started—side by side with Jews. He wanted to be above them, away from them. Not father. He stayed in the factory, side by side with the Jews. The only problems he had were not with them, but with fellow Catholics trying to set him straight. My uncle in the meanwhile started to make money and buy my mother expensive presents, flouting them under my father's nose. 'You could provide these for her, instead of my having to do it,' he would say. 'All you have to do is stop letting those Jews get the best of you.' By the onset of the war, he had become quite well-established in the underworld. Naturally, he cashed in on the carnage. My father was still in the factory. The Jews were out, but that didn't make it any more satisfying for him. My uncle came to him with an offer to join his smuggling operation, but father refused. He'd been decent all his life, he said, and he wasn't about to change. Not too long after that, on the way home from work, he happened to cross a band of *schmalzovniks* forcing an old man to undress on the street while hopping on one foot. Each time the man protested that he wasn't a Jew and had nothing to give them, they kicked his foot out from under him. When father went to his defense, the louts attacked him too, beating them both to a pulp. He sustained a fatal injury to his kidney. His last words were: 'Remember, Stefan, the Jews are worth dying for.'"

Stefan fished a bottle of whiskey out from among his paraphernalia. His face was suddenly sober.

"Have a tipple," he said, unscrewing the top and extending the bottle toward Joseph.

"No thank you," Joseph said.

"Don't be so proper," Stefan said. " A nip now and then oils the system."

He put his lips to the mouth of the bottle and took a swig.

"There, it doesn't do any harm," he said, wiping the bottle on his sleeve. "As a matter of fact, it's positively good for you. You'll see how your hands loosen up."

Again he offered the bottle to Joseph.

"I don't drink," Joseph said.

"Neither did I," Stefan said.

Joseph watched Stefan's Adam's apple jolt like a cork as he lubricated himself.

"They think Christmas is such an enlightened holiday," Stefan said. "Wait till they get an eyeful of Channukah."

He clamped one eye shut and opened the other especially wide, comically effecting consternation. Joseph smiled. As an offshoot of his more vital projects, Stefan was designing a "menorah" that would explode several minutes after the candles were lit. It was a frivolous invention, to be used once or twice, but the idea amused him.

"Is your mother alive?" Stefan asked.

"I don't think so," Joseph said.

"Those krautfuckers," Stefan said.

He blew aslant into the bottle, attempting a tugboat wail, but the whiskey level was too high.

"Mine's deader than a doorknob," he said. "And fittingly so. You know how she died?"

"No," Joseph said.

"Of very unnatural causes," Stefan said. "She'd been lying in bed, moaning and groaning, as I described. Then, while I was out one morning, just like the last time, she got out of bed, took all her hidden treasures, and went down to the gate to barter. When I got home she was in bed again, yapping and whining worse than ever. 'What's the matter?' I said, but I didn't mean it sincerely. She was always yelping. A regular watchdog. She kept right on dribbling and whimpering and swearing at my father for deserting her. Then she started to tremble, really badly, and I realized she might actually be ailing. 'Mother,' I asked, 'what is it?' At this historic point she confessed that she had sneaked out to do business and that— hold your pants—she'd been raped by a German soldier. To get the full impact of that you have to picture my mother. She looked like a potato that had been thrown into a drawer and forgotten. Now I ask you, who would violate such gross decay. But she demanded credence and indeed showed me where her blouse had been ripped open. 'Maybe the blouse was raped,' I said, 'but mother, not even a blind man would rape you.' That made her squeal like a bitch run over by a tram. 'I'm not saying it was always that way,' I told her. 'My reference is just to the last ten years.' 'Is that so?' she said. 'You think your mother can't be raped?' And then she told me the grisliest story of how she had been standing near the gate, venturing to sell a confused Jew a few vegetables, when a guard had come up and interjected himself into their transaction. He made her give the Jew everything she had, including some silk under- wear she had taken from a Jewish woman in exchange for half a potato. Then he dragged her into a building and raped her and made the Jew rape her and raped her again himself. When the fun was over, he pounced on the Jew and charged him every- thing he had, which turned out to be ten thousand zlotys, for the privilege of having defiled her magnificent body. Also, the Jew was wearing a beautiful gold watch. 'It sparkled like a crown,' mother portrayed it. The German offered to let the Jew have mother once more in trade for this trinket, but the Jew declined, so the German bought it from him for a thou- sand zlotys and gave mother a few cents for her trouble. 'He could at least have shared the ten thousand zlotys with me,' she said. Her shivering grew worse and all that night, no matter how warmly I bundled her up, she was freezing. But she wasn't too cold to keep jabbering on about being raped. The next day she died in the middle of praising the gold watch. Her fist had such an iron grip around the coins the

German had given her that I had to pry it open with a jimmy."

Joseph found himself receiving the bottle from Stefan and drawing a sip. The whiskey passed smoothly down, leaving behind a faint taste that was neither pleasant or unpleasant. Then his tongue began to sour, and a fire scorched his lungs, rising up into his throat. He wheezed for air. Soon the heat peaked, having burned off the aftertaste, and a pleasant feeling spread through his chest.

"My uncle gave her a royal funeral," Stefan said, retrieving the bottle. "A nice stone, a huge cross of flowers, and a sarcophagus the size of a hippopotamus. The priest didn't say anything about her having been defiled by a Jew and a German. Just that she was a fine Catholic, a good mother who carried on with her son after his father went to heaven, and a conscientious citizen who lived and died bravely in Poland's darkest hour. A man would have to eat toads and lizards to dream up such an eulogy. It was the most fantastic thing I'd ever heard."

AROUND
T H E
F I R E

"**E**xcuse me," Eugen said, stopping in front of two women. "I couldn't help noticing your difficulty in starting the fire."

The two women stared up at him. Both had closely cropped hair and plain features. There was one suitcase and one bedroll between them.

"We don't need help," said the older looking of the two.

She had a broad nose and pockmarks on her cheeks. The younger woman had a harelip.

"You have to deflect the wind," Eugen said.

"If you know so much about fires, why don't you build your own?" said the pockmarked woman.

"Your friend is shuddering," Eugen said.

The pockmarked woman glanced sideways at her companion.

"Are you a doctor?" she said.

"No," Eugen said. "I merely . . ."

"Let him try it," said the harelipped woman.

Her speech was so nasal that it was difficult to catch her

words. Hostilely, the pockmarked woman passed him the matches.

"I suppose no harm can come of it," she said.

"Could we use the suitcase as a baffle?" Eugen asked.

In a minute he had kindled a nice fire using the split board the woman had set out and some of the tinder he carried in his pillow case for just such an occasion.

"If you have a pot," Eugen said, "I could fetch water and you'd have steam."

"What are you, an arsonist?" said the pockmarked woman.

"I was in the army," Eugen said.

"Good for you," said the pockmarked woman.

"Why doesn't he bring water," said the harelipped woman, "and I'll make tea."

"Maybe he won't come back," said the pockmarked woman.

Eugen climbed the steps to the porch where he had once sought refuge in the rain. Since then he had been back several times to check on his gun. Now he was there to fetch water for the pockmarked and the harelipped women.

The night Tzipora slept in his lap, he had resolved to bury his gun as soon as the ground dried. He had delayed parting with it long enough. There was a ribbon of dirt along the front of the house and around the steps where flowers had grown. Working at night, using the gun to burrow its own way, he sunk a hole right beside the steps. It was such an obvious place, he reasoned, that it would be safe there.

The next day he felt gratifyingly unencumbered, but shortly thereafter the weight reappeared like a phantom limb. Perhaps he had been rash in disarming. Someone could assault him for his pillow case, his miserable clothes, or entirely without cause. Who would come to his rescue? And how would he defend himself if Bankart attacked?

He began to have a recurring dream that he was being set

upon in full view of faceless strangers who looked on blankly or glided by without concern. The attack took diverse forms. Sometimes he was throttled. Sometimes he was mauled. Sometimes his head was dashed against the street until his brains were orange pomace. However it happened, it was frightening but quickly painless, blanking his senses with the swiftness of a tiger dispatching its prey.

Despite the frequency of the dream, he was never able to visualize his assailant. It was unquestionably Bankart, but as always, the picture was incomplete. He tried to freeze specific features in his memory, then piece them together, so that he would be prepared for the confrontation. But the harder he tried to control his anticipation, the less manageable it became. Increasingly, as he turned a corner, sat on the street, or lay sleeping, he found himself confronted by a tawny face with fierce black markings and cold, luminous eyes.

Finally he decided to recover the gun and be ready. When he returned to the house, a portent awaited him. The earth, which had been bone dry when he excavated it, was slightly moist only a few inches from the sock in which the gun was encased. Why would that be? It had not rained in the interval. Intrigued, he began tunneling through the dampened earth, which turned progressively darker and wetter until he reached mud. A little farther on he struck a leaking pipe. Excited by the discovery, he filled in the digging, smoothed over it, and entered the house.

"Hello," he had said quietly, knocking on the first door inside. "Is anyone there?"

His voice landed at his feet.

"Hello," he said, putting his ear to the door. "Hello."

Cautiously, he rattled the knob. It was loose. He let himself into a dark room.

As soon as his eyes adjusted, Eugen headed for the sink and opened the tap. There was a void, followed by an expulsion of air, a sputtering, and eventually, as he had suspected, a gurgling excretion of sludge. He left it running while he explored the premises, expropriating a meat knife, a butter knife, a fork, a spoon, and a cup. Before long the flow had cleared sufficiently to resemble potable water. He shut it off and departed, satisfied that he had made an important finding.

But the recovery of the gun turned out to be problematic. Certainly it was fortunate that he had decided to reclaim it when he did. It would have been bitter to have conducted himself on the assumption that it was there for the fetching, only to learn at a critical time that it had been ruined. Why then, once it was back at his side, had the Bankart dreams redoubled instead of subsiding? They became ever more persistent, including segments now in which the tiger's head transfigured into a snarling steel muzzle.

Eugen began to reconsider. He had not actually been in any imminent danger in the ghetto. Still, his nerves were so frazzled that if trouble arose he might not even be able to react appropriately. The gun was nothing but a nuisance. It was heavy and rigid and had pounded a black and blue splotch into his leg. He had to dip furtively into his pillow case whenever he needed something, lest someone spot it, and this made him continually aware that he was packing not only the potential for self-defense but also the hazard of destruction. He had saved it from possible corrosion. Should he not now again give thought to hiding it safely?

This time, rather than depositing the gun in the ground, he interred it beneath the floor of the house, replacing the boards in such a way that they would be easily removable in an emergency. Almost immediately the dreams regressed to their previous tone. The tiger remained Bankart, and death was savage, but not cold-blooded.

A draft blew the steam that rose from the pot into Eugen's face. It had a sweet, spicy fragrance. He was sitting on one side of the suitcase, fronting the fire, and the women were on the other side.

"It smells awfully good," Eugen said.

He had watched the harelipped woman sprinkle a few shreds of what he took to be tea into the pot and then, from each of several handkerchiefs, touches of unknown essence.

"It's not really tea," she said.

"I think it's ready," said the pockmarked woman.

She handed the harelipped woman a cup and they both ducked into the pot. Steam swirled before their faces.

"Won't you have a cup?" asked the harelipped woman.

"Yes, of course," Eugen said. "Right here."

He reached into his pillow case and brought out a bone cup with a graceful handle and delicate silver trim.

"My, aren't we fancy," said the pockmarked woman.

Eugen filled his cup and took a sip.

"It's delicious," he said appreciatively.

"We like it," said the pockmarked woman.

"What does it contain?" Eugen asked.

Annoyance soured the pockmarked woman's face.

"Lice," she said.

"A little bit of everything," said the harelipped woman.

Eugen studied the pockmarked woman as she replenished her cup. Her head was almost square and fixed on a squat neck, so that her short hair seemed superfluous. She had a thick torso and manly gestures. He wondered what was responsible for her surliness.

"Do either of you have family?" he asked.

The harelipped woman looked away.

"You're it," said the pockmarked woman.

"I'm sorry," Eugen said. "I was simply curious why you were alone."

"Why are you?" the pockmarked woman demanded.

She glared at Eugen until he averted his eyes.

"I'm going to sleep," she announced. "Why don't you wake me up when you have an answer."

Relinquishing her spot before the fire, she began to unfold the bedroll.

"On second thought," she said, "don't bother."

She flattened the bedding and climbed in.

"Aren't you coming?" she said.

"I haven't quite finished," said the harelipped woman.

The pockmarked woman drew the covers up over her head.

"Do you mind if I share your side of the fire?" asked the harelipped woman.

"It's yours to start with," Eugen said.

The harelipped woman scooted over beside him.

"This way we won't disturb her," she half-whispered.

With her voice lowered, her slurred speech was even more difficult to understand.

"I hope I didn't offend her," Eugen said.

"You didn't," said the harelipped woman. "That's the way she is."

"It's unusual to see two women reporting without parents or husbands or children," Eugen said.

"We've always been together," said the harelipped woman. "As children we were like sisters. Then, at the stage when girls are supposed to be infatuated with boys, we remained inseparable. Our parents tried to break us up, but it only reinforced our relationship."

Eugen noticed that if he focused past the woman as she spoke, concentrating on her words without the distraction of her lip, he could more easily comprehend her.

"We had nothing against boys. In fact, we enjoyed being with them more than with other girls. But we didn't see why we should cast aside so many years of devotion just because we had reached a certain age."

"There must have been a lot of disappointed young men in Warsaw," Eugen said.

"You can say that because you're not looking at me," said the harelipped woman.

Embarrassed, Eugen viewed her face on. Except for the lip, she might have been pretty. She had high curved cheeks and receptive eyes.

"Sincerely," he said. "You appear to be a fine person. Any eligible man would be glad to have you."

"There was one," said the woman.

Eugen fixated on the lip in an effort to disintegrate perception of it.

"It surprises you, doesn't it?" said the woman. "His name was Joab. I loved him very much."

"It seems that everything has been taken from us," Eugen said.

"It wasn't the war," said the woman. "It happened before. I was studying to be a nurse. He was a patient at the hospital. Nothing serious. An appendectomy. We made friends. When he got out, we saw each other often. It became intense. I got to know his parents. We were going to get married. One night he said it was off. Without warning. Without anything. I never saw him again."

She stopped and glimpsed at the pockmarked woman lying on the other side of the fire. Only the top of her head was visible.

"I was truly despondent," she continued. "If not for her, I might have killed myself."

"Did you ever find out why?" Eugen asked.

"I knew all along," said the woman. "It was the lip. In the hospital it didn't matter. But the minute it carried outside, it became a problem. He was ashamed of me. I could feel it. When we were alone he was very loving, very considerate. But whenever we were with friends, he tried to disassociate himself from me. It was a subtle thing, but it began to eat away at him. In the end he couldn't face himself."

Eugen admired her courage for speaking so matter-of-factly about her affliction.

"It's a shame that such an insignificant flaw should make such a big difference." he said.

"You can't decide whether to look at me or not, can you?" said the woman.

Eugen lacked a reply.

"I'm used to it by now," said the woman. "She alone accepts me as I am."

"What about your parents?" Eugen asked.

"They resented the fact that I was defective," said the woman.

"And that you never married?"

"Undoubtedly," said the woman. "It ceased to interest me."

"Where are they now?" Eugen asked.

"Wherever we're going."

"They went without you?" Eugen asked.

"I wanted to stay."

"And she?" Eugen asked.

"Her mother died," said the woman. "Her father's on the Aryan side."

"She's leaving him behind?" Eugen asked.

"He's not Jewish," said the woman.

The wind thinned and sharpened, cutting through Eugen's shirt. He put his cup back in his pillow case and clasped his arms across his chest.

"You must be uncomfortable in that shirt," said the woman.

"It's nippy," Eugen said.

The days were still hot, but the nights were growing cooler. He would not be able to do much longer without a jacket.

"Have you any family?" the woman asked.

"A brother," Eugen said.

"Alive?"

"As with your parents," Eugen said.

"Was he by himself?" the woman asked.

"With a daughter," Eugen said.

"And the mother?"

"There were just he and Tzipora," Eugen said.

"Why didn't you go with them?"

"I had to look for someone," Eugen said.

"Who?" the woman asked.

"A distant relative," Eugen said. "My brother was entrusted with something for him, but he couldn't stay on because of Tzipora, so I took over the responsibility."

"What is it that you would risk your life to deliver?" the woman asked.

"A personal item," Eugen said.

"You can't tell me?"

"Unfortunately not."

"Who was the man?"

"Abrahm Bankart."

The woman's face shifted.

"Do you recognize the name?" Eugen asked.

"Should I?" said the woman.

"You might," Eugen said.

"I don't," said the woman.

"I wouldn't expect you to," Eugen said.

"Did you find any trace of him?" asked the woman.

"None," Eugen said.

"Maybe you'll come across him where we're destined," said the woman.

"Maybe."

The woman stretched her hands over her head and yawned.

"We'd better get some sleep," she said. "Tomorrow will be a strenuous day."

"Would you mind if I just sat here?" Eugen said. "I can stoke the fire."

"Not at all," said the woman. "But take my sweater. I won't need it under the covers."

"Why don't you keep it," Eugen said.

"Please," said the woman.

Reluctantly, Eugen accepted the primrose sweater. He was hardly conscious of the lip.

"See you in the morning," said the woman.

She lifted the covers and slid underneath.

A poignance brushed Eugen as he stuck his arms into the sleeves of her sweater. It was too scant for him to button, but it bore her body heat and would temper the wind. He felt like a voyeur observing the women snuggled abreast. When had he slipped in beside someone so naturally? Never. He had only known whores.

The best part of each day was night, Eugen thought, gazing into the fire. In the morning the anxiety of the search for Bankart would reestablish itself and he would have to cinch his loins for another foray. It had gotten to be worse than rising and going to work in a factory. He could not wait for his shift to end so that he could come back and forget his cares. Not until curfew had fallen and he had found a roost could he allow himself the persuasion that there was nothing more to be done before sunrise.

There was no movement on the street. It was more crowded than ever with the sudden disruption of tranquility by resumed deportations. But it was late, and those awake deferred to those reposing. As he surveyed the bodies arrayed in circular patterns around fires and piles of luggage, Eugen could not avoid the image of soldiers bivouacked on a plain. He had never been to the front, but he had heard so much about the Great War, and now again there were German forces spread throughout Europe. How many places were there this very night where darkness had mercifully suspended action and the troops had withdrawn to repair for tomorrow's fray?

It would be satisfying, he had sometimes reflected, to sit around with a group of men with whom he had gone through the torments of hell, resting after a harrowing day, grateful for an interlude, basking in the fellowship that could only be achieved at the cost of the battle.

If he had been younger, he would have joined the military instead of the SS. Even camped before a fire alone behind enemy lines was preferable to working out of a drab office, poking into people's lives like a dentist probing teeth. And there was no comraderie at the Metropole.

Of course he understood very well that it was anything but romantic to march relentlessly, destroying everything in sight and continually tempting death. It was no laughing matter to be bogged down in mud and snow and ice, hungry, frozen blue. Or to be blown asunder, with or without food in one's stomach, legs flying through the air, arms slithering off on their own like snakes bleeding into the gelid ground. He had seen them after the war, deaf, blind, limbless, returning in protean shipments like mannequins that had been derailed and rived into fragments and then patched back together, mosaically, this nose with those ears, by artists hired to make them resemble the boys who had been sent out to the trenches.

And yet he had heard them later, on the job, in bars, at rallies, avowing that those were the days. He had seen them embrace each other and sing moving songs that brought tears cascading down their faces. Many of them had first been sung somewhere under an open sky. Some were even learned from the enemy. In the depth of winter, Eugen was told, when the going was very tough, the Germans and Russians would cross lines at night and share their fires to give each other courage.

Within the flames Eugen beheld streaks burning the color of Tzipora's hair. Wherever she was, he hoped that she was peacefully asleep, and that her dreams were pleasant.

"Are you still up?"

The voice disengaged Eugen's mind from the flames.

"You must be chilly."

It had grown considerably colder.

"I'm all right," Eugen said.

The harelipped woman had crawled partly out of her covers and was looking at him across the charred spot where the fire had been.

"I shouldn't have let it go out," Eugen said.

His heart jumped as he fumbled around for the matches to start a new fire. At any moment the tiger might spring out of the darkness and puncture his throat.

"Easy," he said to himself.

It would only take a few seconds if he went about it systematically, but he felt himself disordered by the impulse to light all the matches at once.

"Patience."

"What?" said the harelipped woman.

"Nothing," Eugen said.

He struck a match, but the wind extinguished it before it would flower.

"Shit."

"Why don't you come in with us?" said the woman. "There's room."

Eugen hunkered over the fire like a flue.

"There," he said, watching the first sparks ignite.

"You should get some sleep," said the woman.

She squinted up at the sky. Eugen sat back and folded his arms.

"An hour or two will do you good," said the woman.

She raised the covers in invitation. Eugen eyed her absently. Her face grew lighter.

"Don't worry about the fire," she said, wriggling further out of the bedding. "You need the rest."

Her motion activated the pockmarked woman, who stirred and mumbled something. For an instant it sounded as if she were awake. Before Eugen knew it, the harelipped woman had reached out and placed her hand on his forearm. Uncertain whether he was going of his own accord or being drawn, he skirted the fire and passed under the covers.

Awkwardly, he wormed over on his left side, with one hand beneath his head and the other holding his pillow case against his leg. He was back to back with the pockmarked woman, while the harelipped woman's hair smothered his face. Gently, he squirmed up a few inches. His breathing cleared, and a coolness grazed his eyelids. For a minute or so his body felt neutral. Then the animal heat of three people closely sandwiched together began to build up. Soon it became almost oppressive, but then he grew used to it and became so relaxed that he could not muster up the energy to check whether the fire was keeping its vigil.

Immersed in sleep, Eugen felt something skim his stomach. It was a sweet sensation, as if a child were playing on his lap.

The movement halted, then renewed, and he half-realized that his fly was being opened. A warm hand tugged up the hem of his shirt and smoothed a path to his crotch, patting it softly. There was a feathery tickling in his hair, and around his scrotum, and blood began flowing into his genitals.

Dreamily, he was aware that his pants were being lowered over his hips and his penis coaxed with plying fingers that primed it as it sprouted, manipulating it until a purgative was running through him, then guiding its tip downward and positioning it against something that pressed back, resisting briefly before giving ground, yielding, yielding, unctuously, like soil that was sodden beneath its crust.

SHEOL

Olek stepped through the black curtain into the underworld of the Metropole.

The room weltered in semi-darkness. Pungent smoke curled through the spotlight focused on the singer. She wore her standard costume—black stockings, crimson garters, short petticoat, skimpy blouse—and delivered her song dispassionately with her hips. Her voice was hard and scratchy.

"Bravissimo!" a drunk called out.

"Shut up, you boor," said his inebriated tablemate. "The lady's singing."

Olek surveyed the scene and was immediately put on guard. It did not surprise him that there was no sign of Officer Glueck, but his accustomed place was being occupied by someone who was watching the entrance just as Glueck would have done. There were two tables empty. Rejecting an about-face, he walked directly to the closest one and sat down.

A hostess promptly came over. She had sturdy legs and

plump breasts, but her sensuality was marred by a mouth so
bleared with lipstick that it suggested a wound.

"What can I get you?" she asked.

"Coffee and whiskey."

"Something to eat?"

"Not now."

"Anything else?"

"No."

He followed her passage. The bottoms of her buttocks
overlapped the line formed by their juncture with her legs and
jiggled.

As she went by the table where Glueck would have
waited, he took as good a look as he could at the man who was
sitting there. He was of medium height, perhaps slightly
more, with a stocky build tending toward corpulence, a beer-
keg neck, and a broad, unsympathetic face of yellowish-gray
complexion. His hair was clipped short, almost shaved, on the
sides of his head, and bristly on top.

Glueck had always been there before him, Olek thought.
He would wait fifteen minutes, no longer.

The hostess returned with his beverages.

"Are you sure you don't want anything else?" she asked.

He ignored her.

The singer was winding up her number. Olek braced
himself. In a moment the room would brighten and break into
a swirl of activity. He was tired. Very tired. His body ached
with fatigue and the trauma of constant adrenalization. He was
losing his elasticity. Whatever his resilience, there was a limit.

Was the man at Glueck's table eying him?

There was a clatter of applause and the lights went on.
Waiters who had receded into the background became prominent again, brandishing their trays and bottles. The din grew
and filled the room.

Olek took a sip of whiskey, letting it trickle over his
tongue. Then he poured some off into his coffee. All the while
he kept a sideview of Glueck's table.

It was curious about Glueck. Until his disappearance, he

had never known him to miss an appointment or renege on an agreement. It was part of a peculiarity that he had noticed from the start. Glueck did not believe wholeheartedly in what he was doing. He was sincere when he was civil, and relatively honest when provoked. Someone else would have better dissembled his motives. But his enmity seemed not to exceed his instinct for self-preservation to the degree common in other Nazis. He was not an admirable character, but neither was he a fiend.

"Pardon me," said the man who had risen from Glueck's table and strode over, "but are you by chance waiting for Herr Glueck?"

Olek looked up warily. At close range the man's face appeared as if it had been spread with honey and left in the hot sun to the insects.

"Could be," Olek said.

"Permit me to present myself," said the man, moving oppressively near. "Thierbach. Hans Thierbach."

"It means nothing to me," Olek said.

"Herr Glueck is an associate of mine," Thierbach explained. "He was unable to meet you and asked me to take his place."

"A likely story," Olek said.

"May I?" asked Thierbach.

"If it saves us trouble," Olek said.

Stiffly, Thierbach backed off and took a seat opposite Olek. Responding to his signal, a waiter brought over his glass, a pitcher of water, and a newly unsealed bottle of whiskey.

"What do you want?" Olek said testily.

"Are you Olek Vaczek?" Thierbach asked.

"John the Baptist," Olek said.

Thierbach's eyes narrowed to slits. His swart pupils were dull and fuzzy around the edges, like olive pits, and his stubby hands resembled pig's feet.

"Herr Glueck never mentioned that you were such an unfriendly person," he said.

"I'm not a madam," Olek said.

Forcing a brusque smile, Thierbach poured half a glass of whiskey for himself and the same for Olek.

"To our acquaintanceship," he toasted, raising his glass.

Olek left his untouched.

"Getting down to business," Thierbach said, "I believe that you are involved in the case of one Abrahm Bankart. Is that correct?"

"Is it?" Olek said.

Settling his hands across his lap, he observed that Thierbach's suit was well-made but unbecomingly tight, and that his inflated posture was geared to the aggrandizement of a uniform.

"It is my understanding that you are carrying on a profitable trade railroading Jews out of the ghetto, situating them, and providing them with false identities, and that you are being allowed to sustain this activity in exchange for your cooperation in the search for Bankart?"

"So?"

"It is further my understanding that until now you have been of no real assistance whatsoever."

"I've done all I can," Olek said.

"If this is your best, it will not be good enough," Thierbach said. "So far we have not received a single helpful clue from you."

"I reported his presence at Tebbens' factory," Olek said.

"Your generosity is exceeded only by your uselessness," Thierbach said. "You know very well that you have been leading our friend Herr Glueck on a wild goose chase."

"A wild goose-step chase," Olek corrected him.

Anger spread over Thierbach's face like oleo.

"You cannot address me in this manner," he said.

"Why not?" Olek said.

"Because I . . ."

Thierbach's voice rose precipitously, then declined.

"Because I have done nothing to warrant your disrespect," he said.

"Nor my respect," said Olek.

"If you will just hear me out," Thierbach said, "I am confident that we will reach a sympathetic accord."

Olek reserved comment.

"As I was saying," Thierbach resumed, "Herr Glueck has been conducting the investigation of Bankart and you are supposed to have contributed. Thus far you have not. I presume there is a reason for this."

"There is," Olek said.

"What is it?" Thierbach said.

"It's simple," Olek said. "While Herr Glueck has been in pursuit of Bankart, Bankart has been in elusion of Herr Glueck."

"Are you implying that Bankart is aware of Herr Glueck?"

"He certainly knows his head would make a prized trophy," Olek said.

"But what about Herr Glueck?"

"What about him?"

"Do you think Bankart is cognizant of him?"

"It's conceivable."

"Is it likely?"

"Who knows?"

"In your judgment, what would he do if he were?" Thierbach asked.

"Avoid him," Olek said.

"Are you familiar with Felix Erdmann?" Thierbach asked.

"Unfortunately," Olek said.

"What do you mean?"

"Nothing more, nothing less."

"It was through Erdmann that you first established contact with Herr Glueck, is that not right?" Thierbach asked.

"Right."

Thierbach restored his glass to half fullness.

"You haven't touched yours," he said.

Olek continued to stare at him.

"You were using Erdmann to forge identification papers and other documents for your 'clients,' were you not?"

"Right."

"One day you mentioned to him that you thought you knew the whereabouts of a man who you surmised was wanted by the authorities."

"Right."

"He related this to Herr Glueck, and Herr Glueck arranged to interview you. A compact was fashioned, and you divulged to Herr Glueck that Bankart was hiding in the attic of a particular building. A careful inspection was made of the premises, but neither Bankart nor any conclusive indication that he had ever been there was found. After that you met regularly with Herr Glueck, but no advance was made in locating Bankart. A ripple here, a nibble there, but the line always surfaced with the bait gone and the hook empty."

"Fishing is a sport of patience," Olek said.

The overhead lights were dimmed and the spotlight rekindled. Grinding a cigarette under her heel, the singer climbed back onto the round platform. The beam striking her flesh created a momentary excitement akin to the revelation of nakedness that turned with exposure to normalcy. As she began to recite the words of an embittered prostitute, her tinsel voice followed her mouth like the track of a poorly synchronized movie.

"In the meanwhile," Thierbach said, "you have been conducting a highly lucrative enterprise with the knowledge and consent of the authorities."

"It hasn't been as enriching as you may think," Olek said.

"Nevertheless," Thierbach said, "you are hereby notified that if your good offices do not soon produce something of value, your privileges may be revoked."

Thierbach was of a different stripe than Glueck, Olek reflected. He took special pleasure in exercising power, and his language was that of posters and decrees.

"What about your good offices?" Olek said.

"Please clarify yourself," Thierbach said.

"If Herr Glueck and all his associates can't find Bankart, how do you expect me to?"

"We don't," Thierbach said, arching his back. "We would

be grateful if you could. But if you cannot, you are worthless to us. There would then be cause to stop coddling you and to curtail your endeavors."

"It seems unreasonable," Olek said.

"Was it not you who came to us?" Thierbach said.

"Erdmann did."

"But you knew that he was in communication with Herr Glueck," Thierbach said.

"How could I have?"

"You had no idea that he was volunteering his services to the authorities?"

"A lot of people are," Olek said. "I didn't tell him anything in anticipation of his passing it on."

"What did you think he would do with it?" Thierbach asked.

"I didn't consider it," Olek said. "It was shop talk."

"Has Erdmann discussed his work with you?" Thierbach asked.

"Casually."

"What in specific?"

"The cost of ink."

Thierbach raised his left hand beside his ear and snapped his fingers. A waiter scurried over.

"Yes?" he fawned.

"What will you eat?" Thierbach asked.

"Nothing," Olek said.

"Hors d'houevres," Thierbach said with relish. "And for me, a white piece of chicken with potatoes and carrots and a nice plate of broiled skin if the chef has any."

The waiter waggled off like a dog after a bone.

"Surely you can remember a less trivial example of Erdmann's prattle," Thierbach said.

"It was consistently without importance," Olek said.

"And when you enlightened him regarding Bankart, you deemed that unimportant?"

"Absolutely."

"The disposition of a person being sought by the authorities is unimportant?"

"Unless there's a price on his head," Olek said.

"So you offhandedly informed Erdmann that you knew the whereabouts of this man, and he relayed this to Herr Glueck, and as it turned out you didn't know his whereabouts at all."

"As it turned out," Olek said.

"Why did you advise Herr Glueck that you knew his whereabouts if you didn't?"

"I thought I did."

"Why?"

"Because I overheard someone say that he had been sighted."

"And what did you do when you learned that you were mistaken?" Thierbach asked.

"What should I have done?" Olek said.

The waiter reappeared with two place settings. He deposited the plates with a flourish and began to lay down the silverware.

"I won't be needing any," Olek said.

He planted his hand on the tablecloth like the flat of a broom and swept the plate to the edge of the table.

"The gentlemen might change his mind," the waiter said, putting down the rest of the silver.

Olek shoved his aside emphatically. The fork stood on end and flipped over, landing on the plate with a ping.

"Very well," said the waiter.

He snatched the plate up in one hand and the silverware in the other.

"You mustn't be so rude," Thierbach said.

Removing the cloth napkin from beside his plate with two fingers, he undid the second from the top button on his shirt, tucked his tie into the opening, flicked open the napkin, and threaded a corner through the buttonhole.

"Whom did you overhear discussing the whereabouts of Bankart?" Thierbach asked.

"I don't know," Olek said.

"Was it a disembodied voice?" Thierbach said.

"It belonged to someone," Olek said, "but I didn't stick around to find out who."

"And why do you suppose he was being pursued by the authorities?" Thierbach asked.

"It was common knowledge," Olek said.

"What was?"

"That Bankart had rescued a woman from a Jewish police-man who was trying to rape her."

"That's utter rubbish," Thierbach scoffed.

"You asked me," Olek said.

"It is common knowledge," Thierbach said, "that Bankart viciously and without justification murdered an official of his own blood. He is wanted as an enemy of his people."

The waiter arrived with a wicker of bread and an oblong platter packed with ham slices, cold beef, wedges of yellow and orange cheese, olives, pimentos, and sweet gherkins.

"Beer or wine?" asked the waiter.

"A red Bordeaux," Thierbach said. "Medium dry."

His face brightened at the show of food.

"Be my guest," he said munificently.

"No thanks," Olek said.

"Starve if you wish," Thierbach said. "You won't be missed."

"It's mutual," Olek said.

"What else is common knowledge about that murderer?"

"That's it."

"You're omitting something," Thierbach said.

He skewered a pickle between clumps of ham and cheese and stuffed the truss into his mouth.

"Really?"

"Didn't you indicate to Herr Glueck that you had a score to pay off with Bankart?"

"Right."

"And is that not in fact why you broached the subject initially to Erdmann?"

"It's possible."

"You apprised Herr Glueck that your dislike for Bankart derived from an incident in which someone lost his job to a Jew because of him. Who was this victim?"

"I can't recall," Olek said.

"You have an unusually selective memory," Thierbach said.

"It was ten years ago," Olek said.

"Yet you've born a grudge all this time?"

"I'm the spiteful type," Olek said.

"How did you encounter Erdmann?" Thierbach asked.

"I knew his son-in-law before the war," Olek said.

"In what capacity?"

"We were lovers," Olek said.

Thierbach drew back, his face distressed. An oily sweat beaded his pores.

"I don't find that amusing," he said.

"Neither do I," said Olek.

"You are here by virtue of a finite tolerance," Thierbach said.

"At least . . ."

"I forbid you to say another word."

Puffed with anger, Thierbach blotted his face with the end of his napkin and speared a slice of beef and a pimento.

"Answer the questions," Thierbach said, "but gag your wit."

"Fair enough."

"Did you suffer directly as a result of Bankart's influence?" Thierbach asked.

"Indirectly."

"You had nothing private against him?"

"That's right," Olek said.

"But you cared enough to implicate yourself in tracking him down?"

"Apparently."

"You are engaged in illegal commerce and yet you bring yourself to the attention of the authorities in connection with a

Jewish assassin whom you have never met and who has never done you any personal injury?"

"Not exactly," Olek said.

"Then what?" Thierbach demanded.

"Several customers were prevented from crossing over," Olek said.

"By Bankart?"

"Evidently."

"Didn't you require payment in advance?"

"Naturally," Olek said. "But it discouraged others."

"How did he know enough about your transactions to thwart them?" Thierbach queried.

"Why don't you ask him?" Olek said.

"I'm looking forward to the opportunity," Thierbach said.

"Undoubtedly," Olek said, shifting as though to rise. "Now, are we finished?"

"Not quite," Thierbach said.

The waiter removed the decimated hors d'houevres from the table and returned with a steaming plate of chicken breast, roasted brown potatoes, and glazed carrots.

"The skin will be out shortly," he said.

He produced a wine glass for Thierbach and uncorked a bottle of Bordeaux.

"For the last time," Thierbach offered.

Olek spurned his invitation.

"Murder is a serious offense," Thierbach said, "It can transcend economics."

He smoothed his napkin, poised his knife and fork, and attacked the chicken.

"This criminal Bankart is more dangerous than you imagine," he said, assuming an intimate air. "While your incentive for revenge is venal, he is skulking somewhere like a crocodile in a swamp, waiting in ambush for his next prey. We recognize that you have been stringing Herr Glueck along since your original lead came to nought. Perhaps you regret having entangled yourself. But now that you have taken advantage of the authorities, the authorities propose to take advantage of you. You will be called upon to comply unreservedly. If you do not, your immunity will terminate, and you may as well."

A burst of applause and illumination crashed over the room as the singer vacated the platform and sidled into the kitchen.

"Every attempt to flush Bankart out has foundered," Thierbach continued. "We have repeatedly been betrayed."

As he spoke, Olek could see the pumpkin mush being ground in his mouth of the chicken, potatoes, and carrots laced with red wine.

"Did you know, Herr Vaczek, that Abrahm Bankart's granddaughter was actually given asylum in Erdmann's house?"

"Of course I knew," Olek said.

"Hold your impudence," Thierbach said. "It happens to be true."

The waiter intruded with a plate of chicken skin broiled to a crisp and freckled with paprika.

"She was there for a period of months," Thierbach said. "Then she was smuggled into a convent, where she came upon an untimely death."

Thierbach popped a piece of skin onto his tongue and crunched it into a savory mince.

"The best part of the chicken," he said.

He rinsed his palate with a dram of wine and ingested another patch of skin.

"My mother used to fix mouth-watering capon," Olek said.

"Did she really?" Thierbach said.

"With beets and dumplings," Olek said.

"When the girl died," Thierbach said, "we thought that Bankart might risk his cover to attend the burial. It was not the way we preferred to apprehend him, but fortune bestowed on us an opportunity and we were prepared to avail ourselves of it. Our luck miscarried, however."

"That's too bad," Olek said.

"We suspect that someone may have forewarned him," Thierbach said.

"Who?"

"The same person who had been responsible enough to notify us that Erdmann was harboring an illegal," Thierbach said. "Ivan Voytek."

"You're not serious," Olek said.

"Indeed," Thierbach said. "He disappeared after the funeral."

"Disappeared?" Olek said.

"Are you surprised?" Thierbach said.

"Shouldn't I be?" Olek said.

"We have made a material discovery about Bankart's ring," Thierbach said. "Voytek could be the key to cracking it. If you can steer us to him, your own situation will improve immeasurably."

"And if I can't?" Olek said.

"That would depend on what else you did to fulfill your commitment to Bankart's capture."

"I'll do my utmost," Olek said.

"Let us hope so," Thierbach said. "Otherwise you may find yourself being questioned under less congenial circumstances."

"Am I to re-establish liaison with Herr Glueck?" Olek asked.

Thierbach pushed the remnants of his chicken aside and drew the plate of skin nearer to him.

"There's what remains of Herr Glueck," he said.

"You've eaten him?" Olek said.

Thierbach dabbed his lips with his napkin and took a sip of wine.

"Regrettably," he said, "Herr Glueck is no longer with us."

He sighed and patted his lips again.

"How did it happen?"

"Suddenly," Thierbach said, plucking the wishbone from the orts and snapping it.

ASHES

A light eddy swirled over the dead fire and curried Eugen's face. He opened his eyes and raised his head just enough to glimpse the street. A few people were up and around, but for most the night lingered.

The freshness of the wind contrasted with the heat of his body pressed between the two women. Both were with their backs to him. He wanted to kindle a new flame, but he could not extricate himself without waking them. He lay back, facing the neuter moon.

It was about the hour when Thierbach would be returning from the Britannia, Eugen thought. He wondered whether he would have a young officer with him, or a vile Goth like Heinrich, or even a boy seized from a work detail.

More than sitting in a club, Eugen had always enjoyed emerging on the verge of morning, with the world still asleep and its manifold dangers suspended. At that hour the misty air was a cool balm, and the echo of his footsteps on the deserted pavement evoked an invigorating serenity.

There had been one such pre-dawn when Thierbach had

offered to walk him home. It was following a rare visit to the Britannia, the Metropole being his regular haunt. When they reached Eugen's building, Thierbach insisted on accompanying him to the door. Then he suggested a nightcap. Once inside, he declared himself too tired to go out again and asked to stay over. Eugen could not refuse.

They slept together, fully clothed, atop the bedspread. In his slumber, Eugen felt something rubbing against him. A most unpleasant experience ensued. For several weeks thereafter, Thierbach coerced Eugen into attending the Britannia whenever he was not otherwise bindingly committed. Each time he went, Thierbach escorted him back to his apartment. His days became insufferable in anticipation of the oncoming darkness.

Within a month Eugen was afflicted by a painful stomach ailment and a bloody stool. Finally he was able to ward off Thierbach on the strength of a doctor's prescription of a rigorous diet and the restriction of all unessential activities. At this, Thierbach, the cruel master, became solicitous of his health.

"Good morning, Eugen," he took to saying. "How is your stomach faring."

"Not too well," Eugen would answer, screwing up his face.

When weeks passed without apparent improvement, Thierbach's interest waned. He returned briefly to his customary indifference, then began to chide Eugen.

"How's your shit today, Glueck?" he would ask. "Bloody, as usual, I suppose."

Eugen could not entirely fathom Thierbach's new-fledged rancor. He had done nothing reprehensible. His cases were being handled satisfactorily. Certainly his illness was not his fault. It was true that he had not made dramatic progress on Bankart, but he was not to blame. The needle in the haystack had simply not turned up yet.

What exactly had gone wrong then, that led first to his

increasing humiliation and subsequently, without a warning rumble, to the ground collapsing beneath his feet?

Thierbach had walked him home, and he had no resistance, and stayed with him, and he had no resistance, and slept with him, and he had no resistance, and abused him, and he had no resistance, and banished him to the wilderness— and he had no resistance.

He had accepted his sentence as automatically as if he had been sent down to the corner for a tin of cinnamon cakes.

He had not even possessed the strength to compel Erdmann's fealty. Although the girl had been kept from him, he had believed Erdmann, and then he had let the matter slide until it was jerked out from under him. Of course, he had no way of knowing that there was any connection between the girl and Bankart. But why had he assumed that Erdmann was guileless?

Vaczek had not been of much help either. But Eugen had made only a minimal effort to keep him in line. In fact, he had found it rather stimulating to exchange affronts. It was tiresome always to tyrannize, ridicule, rule by fear. And it fostered his most despicable traits. There was pleasure, after all, in liking someone.

Perhaps Vaczek had not been docile, but he had nevertheless been decent. And he was no less informative about Bankart than other sources. The deportations had started again, and still Bankart was at large. They were emptying out the ghetto in earnest now. In a few days there might be no one left but a labor detail. It was a dire prospect. Eugen had no work token, and nothing else was honored at the *umschlagplatz*.

The Metropole had better food than the Britannia. A waiter had told him that the head chef was once in the employ of Smigly-Rydz. He could do with a tender piece of chicken dressed with peas and carrots. That was the one taste he shared with Thierbach. There were fancier foods in the world, but there was nothing so pure and easy to digest as plump spring chicken broiled with garlic, paprika, and butter.

His stomach emitted a labyrinthine rumble.

If he had been at the Metropole, he would have been strolling home just about now. The dewy air would be enlivening after the smoke and noise and congestion, and the trees would glisten as their patterns were unveiled. What had Vaczek thought, Eugen mused, when he had disappeared?

The harelipped woman was awake.

Eugen remained immobile as she boosted herself on her elbow, keeping her back to him. Her movement evoked a mental space around his genitals. His penis stirred, catching against his underpants, and he wondered whether his fly was open or closed. He would wait until she rose to check.

"Good morning," said the harelipped woman.

She had slipped out of the bedding into a sitting position.

"Good morning," Eugen said.

He looked at her. There was no acknowledgement in her eyes of what had gone on during the night.

"Did you sleep?" asked the woman.

"Yes," Eugen said. "And you?"

He slid sideways, severing contiguity with the pockmarked woman, and sat up.

"Like a log," said the harelipped woman.

Eugen felt his body beginning to shed heat. He wanted to reach out and crush the harelipped woman in his arms.

"I'd better start the fire," he said.

"Don't bother," said the harelipped woman. "We'll be going in a while."

The sky was not yet the color of day.

"But she's still asleep," Eugen said.

The pockmarked woman had not moved since Eugen had awakened.

"Sometimes she just lies there," said the harelipped woman.

"It's not worth talking about," Eugen said. "It won't take a minute."

"Have it your way," said the harelipped woman.

As she went to rise, Eugen lunged forward and grabbed her around the waist, pulling her toward him. His action stunned her momentarily. Then she tried to wrench herself away, but Eugen's hold was tenacious. Her head squirmed from side to side, dodging his lips.

"Don't," she said, struggling to free herself.

But Eugen would not desist. He kissed her on the neck, the hand, the ear, wherever he could.

"Stop it!"

The commotion had caused the pockmarked woman to come to life. She struck Eugen in the back with the heel of her fist and gripped his throat from behind.

"Let go," she said, digging her fingers into his Adam's apple.

The pressure brought Eugen to his senses. He released the harelipped woman. She sank onto the bedding. He felt neither relief nor regret.

"Is this your morning exercise?" said the pockmarked woman.

In wrestling with the harelipped woman, Eugen's penis had found its way through the slit of his underpants as it grew erect. Now it bulged against his trousers, with the tip peeking out of his fly, which was agape.

"I'm sorry," he said, reaching down as nonchalantly as he could to extricate himself. "I lost my head."

The harelipped woman straightened herself and stood up. She appeared reconciled to the incident.

"I hope it's the last time," said the pockmarked woman.

A hitch in her voice caused Eugen to turn toward her. In the morning light, her square face was puffy and cragged, as if her skin had been studded with pebbles and scalded with searing fat. He looked away in revulsion, but something drew him back. Confronting her, he saw that her eyelids were swollen, and that her eyes were red and dejected.

"Didn't you sleep well?" Eugen asked.

The pockmarked woman deliberated before responding.

"I didn't sleep at all," she said.

"You heard us talking?"

"Of course."

"But you seemed to be resting so peacefully," Eugen said.

"That could be," she said.

Eugen glanced at the harelipped woman. Her mouth was firmly set, but otherwise her face was impassive.

"I apologize if I kept you up," Eugen said.

"You didn't," said the pockmarked woman.

"But you said you heard the conversation," Eugen stated.

His mind raced ahead, attempting to sort impressions of sleep and waking.

"I was thinking about today," said the pockmarked woman.

The harelipped woman extended her arms sideward at shoulder level, raised them over her head, took a deep breath, and returned them to wing position. She repeated the procedure five or six times and sat down.

"I feel better," she said.

Eugen avoided her gaze. Only now did he wonder whether anyone had witnessed his outburst. If so, it was not apparent in the self-preoccupation of those who were bringing the street gradually to life. A few, as had the harelipped woman, were limbering up, doing calisthenics, walking in place. Others were grooming, or packing. A handful were already making their way toward the selection point. At one fire site, an old man with beautiful white hair was blackening it with cinders to restore a semblance of youth.

"Do you think it's true?" asked the harelipped woman.

"Don't be stupid," said the pockmarked woman.

"I'm asking him," said the harelipped woman.

Both women fixed their eyes on Eugen. He studied their faces futilely for a sign.

"I don't understand," he said finally.

"Where do you think they'll send us?" asked the hare-lipped woman.

"East," Eugen said.

The women held back, awaiting elucidation.

"But they're not shipping everyone out," Eugen said. "We look relatively healthy. They might have a use for us here."

"I wouldn't count on it," said the pockmarked woman.

"If not," said the harelipped woman, "where do you think we'll wind up?"

"I told you," Eugen said.

"East," said the harelipped woman. "But where?"

"Near Kiev, maybe," Eugen said. "Wherever they need hands."

"You're deluding yourself," said the pockmarked woman.

"It's possible," said the harelipped woman.

"Even a fool would have to doubt it," said the pockmarked woman. "The evidence to the contrary is too strong."

"Anyone can be wrong," said the harelipped woman.

"Not about this," said the pockmarked woman.

"More question it than not," said the harelipped woman. She directed herself to Eugen.

"Don't you?"

"What?"

"Do you believe the stories?"

"Which ones?"

"That every person evacuated is being put to death in a secret camp near Treblinka," said the pockmarked woman. "Have you heard the same?"

"No," Eugen said.

"They built a spur that shunts at Sokolow," said the pockmarked woman. "Only cars from the *umschlagplatz* are allowed on this line. No food or necessities have ever gone down it."

"Tell him," said the harelipped woman.

Her voice implied confidence in the absurdity of the rumor.

"When a shipment of Jews arrives, they are ordered to

strip for bathing prior to being assigned quarters and work. They are given bars of soap, led into hermetically sealed chambers, and gassed."

Eugen felt himself growing faint. There had been intimations of these kinds of things, but he had never pursued them.

"What do you think?" asked the harelipped woman.

"It's hard to conceive," Eugen said.

"It's fact," said the pockmarked woman.

"It's propaganda," said the harelipped woman. "They want to terrify us."

She spoke in a sing-song, as if she had rehearsed the conversation.

"Who?" Eugen asked.

"The underground," said the harelipped woman.

"That's nonsense," said the pockmarked woman.

"Why would anyone fabricate such a tale?" Eugen asked.

"To inspire resistance," said the harelipped woman.

"If only that could have done it," said the pockmarked woman.

"Resistance would have given the Germans a perfect excuse," said the harelipped woman.

"They don't need excuses," said the pockmarked woman. "Just cars and showers."

Eugen envisioned a train rolling out of the geometric confines of the city, ticking off ties away from the river, through expansive fields, past aromatic September woods, into the dormant countryside.

"Are you sure?" asked the harelipped woman.

"Yes."

"Then why are we going?"

The pockmarked woman stared intently at her companion. Her pensiveness softened her rough face.

"You know why," she said.

"You see," said the harelipped woman to Eugen. "She really can't believe it either."

AMERICA

Heykel wet his fingertips in the semen that glistened on Sonya's abdomen and rubbed them over her nipples. The strawberry flush of love was still spread across her throat and under her breasts.

"Let's have another child," she said.

Her voice was soft and husky, and her breath was hot as she whispered into his ear.

Leaning down, Heykel licked the tip of each breast with his tongue. Her dilated nipples were smooth and puffy.

"Please," she said, taking her right breast in her hand and holding it for him to suck.

He drew her nipple between his lips, damping it, scraping it with his teeth, flicking it playfully. She moved her body sensuously, pushing her breast farther into his mouth and forcing him to revolve his head in a circular orbit.

Cradling him to her bosom with her left hand, she released her other hand from beneath her breast and ran it down his side. His muscles flinched reflexively as it passed over his stomach, caressingly, through his hair, onto his flaccid penis.

Instinctively, he began sucking harder at her breast, gulping as if to slake a primordial thirst. She stroked the back of his head with one hand, and his penis with the other.

Pliably, the seemingly lifeless penis became animated. Relinquishing it, she reached under and cupped his scrotum, massaging it gently, tickling its roots, feeling the testicles rise in their thickening fluid. Then, quickly, she slipped her hand lower and found his anus with her middle finger.

His body bent like a strained bow as he tried to continue his sucking while shifting to accommodate her finger. Sinking it deeper into his canal, she detached her breast from his mouth and nudged him flat against the mattress.

"Lie still," she said, resting her free hand on his thorax.

He relaxed, closing his eyes, and she kissed his neck, his chest, his ribs, his navel, intensifying her kisses with her finger. His penis flared upright. She clasped it, sliding her palm up and down its shaft, and fitted her lips over its mushroom cap.

First she sucked it as he had sucked her breast, brushing her tongue over the tip, moistening it, gradually admitting it into her mouth. As she stirred his bowels, he arched his back, driving his penis at her. She swallowed it eagerly, clamping her lips over it each time he entered or withdrew, working him into a rhythm that lifted his buttocks from the bed.

Removing her finger from his anus, she switched to a sitting position, fomenting his penis with her hands. He attempted to raise himself, too, but she urged him to remain down. Getting up on her knees, she propped her left hand on the mattress beside his shoulder and swung her right leg over him, straddling his loins. Then she parted her thighs widely, stretched back to locate his penis, and brought her weight to bear on its ascent.

"Oh, Heykel," she whispered, beginning to describe a lyric gyre.

She descended, engorging his penis, and paused before receding, enticing him to buck after her, so that he was half way up when she started down.

As the ballet accelerated, she felt rearward for his testicles. The pressure of her fingers transmitted itself through his motion and he thrust up harder and harder as she rode him with her knees tucking his hips, her sex sheathing his, her jutting breasts joggling, her hands behind her and under his balls, powering him on.

He felt that he was going to spend.

"Easy," he said, placing his hands on her waist in an effort to brake her agitation.

But she would not be checked.

"Don't think about anything, my love," she said.

She nipped her thighs, creating a high friction, and squeezed his testicles until they hurt.

"Sonya," he said.

"Oh," she murmured. "Oh, oh . . ."

"No, Sonya," he said. "Not now."

She ignored him, whipping herself into an impelling frenzy.

"Sonya," he repeated, boosting himself up on his elbows.

There was a trancelike expression on her face as she did everything she could to make him come. Timing her cycle, he caught her pulling up and escaped with a swift twist of his pelvis.

"Oh no, oh, oh Heykel," she gasped.

She kept on plunging and flouncing while her hands frantically sought to retrieve his penis. But he turned sideways to block her, and she was not able to reinsert it. She tugged wildly at it, and soon the quicksilver pumped out of him, splashing her wrist, her breast, her belly, and the inside of her forearm.

Yet she would not abate. Desperately, she wiped his sperm off her skin and stuck her fingers into her vagina. Then she clutched at his hip, straining to sway him over and mold herself onto his shrinking, seeping penis.

"Oh please," she importuned. "Please, Heykel."

She made a final endeavor to repossess him, but he wrenched himself away and sat up.

"What's affecting you?" he asked.

She hesitated, as if seeking her bearings. Her eyes flickered. Emitting a torn cry, she threw herself at him, hitting him with both fists in the stomach.

"Sonya," he said, grabbing her by the shoulders. "What is it?"

"My child," she said. "My child. Oh, Heykel. Please. Please. Please . . ."

Her voice broke, and she collapsed in a tearful paroxysm.

"Calm down," he said quietly. "Whatever it is, it won't do any good."

He tried to tilt her face up, but she buried it tightly in her arms, muffling her racking sobs against the bed.

"We *can* have another child," Sonya insisted.

Her features, swollen with grief, were set in resolution.

"I thought we agreed that it wasn't desirable," Heykel said.

"We didn't know then what we know now," Sonya said.

"If anything, conditions are worse," Heykel said.

He extended his hand to hold hers, but she rejected his gesture.

"That's all the more cause to fight them," Sonya said. "You and Abrahm convinced me that she died for whatever reason she died, we all die, and if she were meant to die so young, there was nothing we could do about it. Nature had its ways, you said. But nature had nothing to do with it. She didn't die of pneumonia or typhus or smallpox. She died of hate. They killed her. *They killed her.*"

Her voice fluttered up and plummeted, like a clipped thrush.

"Shhh," Heykel said.

This time she did not avoid his touch. Her flesh was clammy.

"They had no right to kill her," Sonya said.

Heykel smoothed her hair.

"When a flower dies, you plant another," Sonya said.

She nestled her face against his chest.

"They can't do this to us."

Heykel felt her body tensing.

"Let's see what happens," he said.

"What is there to see?" Sonya asked.

Her voice was clearing, regaining strength.

"We have to be realistic," Heykel said.

"Leora's dead."

"Nothing will bring her back."

"What about us?"

"We've lost her."

"They wrested her from us."

"We sent her out."

"We took a chance."

"It was a mistake."

"Why didn't you stop it?" Sonya asked.

"You wouldn't listen," Heykel said.

"Then it was my fault?"

"I should have been adamant."

"To prevent me from killing her?" Sonya said.

"No," Heykel said. "So that we could all have stayed together."

"And died together," Sonya said.

"It would be better than dying separately," Heykel said.

"There," Sonya said. "You're blaming me."

"I'm not."

"*You are.*"

"I'm blaming myself."

"For permitting me to lead her into a trap?" Sonya said.

"I didn't say that," Heykel said.

Sonya's shoulders stiffened.

"She might have survived."

"But she didn't," Heykel said.

"They didn't allow her to."

"Nor will they us," Heykel said.

"That's just the point," Sonya said.

She shrugged him off and rose.

"We must have another child!"

"So that they can do it to us again?" Heykel said.

Standing before him, Sonya was a different person: not his warm, loving wife, but a cold, abstract arrangement of legs, breasts, pubic hair, and thin, dangling arms.

"So that we can have something to look forward to," she said.

"How about staying alive?" Heykel said.

"There has to be something beyond that," Sonya said.

"If we get that far, there will be," Heykel said. "Otherwise it doesn't matter."

"Life has to have a purpose," Sonya said.

"We can't provide for a child here," Heykel said. "We've proved that."

"We'll forward it for safekeeping." Sonya said.

"Sonya!"

"To America," Sonya said. "And when the war is over, we'll follow her there. It will work, Heykel. We can do it."

Her hands registered her words like signal flags.

"It's day to day now," Heykel said. "We don't have any idea where we'll be in ten months or a year, or whether we'll be anywhere."

"Maybe I'll go with her," Sonya said.

"It's preposterous," Heykel said.

"You'll join us as soon as you can," Sonya said. "We'll have a decent life again."

"And if I don't make it through?" Heykel said.

"You will," Sonya said.

"It's as if we were strangers," Heykel said.

"They're reducing us to animals," Sonya said. "Why can't we at least die human beings?"

"We can," Heykel said. "By resisting. By refusing to be slaughtered. Not by fantasizing about America."

Sonya stepped back. At a remove, she looked unappealingly slight and haggard. Her breasts were slack, and her legs seemed atrophied. Slowly, she brought her hand up and laid it evenly over her stomach.

"We're going to have another child *whether you want one or not,*" she said.

UMSCHLAGPLATZ

Suddenly the time had come, and a headlong madness filled the summer air. The old man with the ashes in his hair broke into a trot, hastening toward the corner where the Lett and Ukrainian soldiers were assembling. He pumped his arms vigorously in a piston movement, but his legs were weak and wobbled disjointedly, like a marionette's. Any second, it seemed, his wires might snap and he would crumple in mid-stride.

His determined rush toward the area that had been designated for registration appeared to galvanize the crowd. Until then the object had been to stay away as long as possible. Now people hurriedly mustered their belongings and began walking toward the station, falling into rows as they went.

Eugen hesitated as the crowd gathered momentum. Originally he had planned to approach the registration area and quickly canvass it for Bankart before retreating to his vantage point to observe the proceedings. But the precipitous decampment made it obvious that his design had been unrealistic. The two women had pulled out by ten or twelve steps when they perceived that he was lagging.

"Come on," said the harelipped woman, doubling back.

Eugen withstood the impulse to bolt.

"Don't wait for me," he said.

"What's the matter?" asked the pockmarked woman.

"Nothing," Eugen said. "I'll be along."

"It's much safer if we go together," said the harelipped woman.

For a moment Eugen's procrastination had not been conspicuous, but now the street was emptying steadily. As people drifted forward they merged, four and six abreast, seeking comfort in numbers. It was as if there were a giant magnet overhead, consolidating the human filings in successive passes until only a few persons remain uncombined. Eugen braced himself against its sway.

"Go ahead," he said more resolutely.

"You're not coming with us?" said the pockmarked woman.

"No," Eugen said.

"Is it goodby, then?" asked the pockmarked woman.

"We'll probably meet later," Eugen said.

The pockmarked woman darted forward and kissed him on the mouth. Her lips were slightly parted, and moist. As she turned aside, he saw that tears were streaking her face. He felt flushed. She took her leave, and the harelipped woman came up and brushed him perfunctorily on the cheek.

"Good luck," she said.

In a wink she had caught up with her companion.

Watching them draw away, Eugen experienced the same urge to run after them that had gripped him as he beheld Tzipora marching off. But now, as then, he did not follow, and the women promptly united with an elderly man and woman and were swallowed up before and behind by others in the drove gravitating toward the provisional yard defined by compulsory formations of wild Ukrainians and Letts.

* * *

The morning sky was a crystalline blue, suggesting flight and the light-hearted pleasures of summer.

Eugen retreated somewhat sideways, keeping an eye on the lines as they stretched in the distance and then, having stopped in front, began to compact and grow shorter. The foursome containing the two women had become obscured, but Eugen marked their approximate position. He would pick them up when he assumed his post.

It was an excellent day for observation. The buildings on either side of the street framed the throng and the soldiers like a two-dimensional stage setting. It was as if someone had constructed facades to be removed after the people had been processed and herded off, so that nothing would be left to testify that anyone had been there or that anything had happened.

The phalanxes of guardsmen were arrayed as human walls of a secondary *umschlagplatz*. Would those who were not granted the right to remain in the ghetto be led directly to the sidecars, Eugen wondered, or would they be paraded over to the primary *umschlagplatz* for final selection?

"Goddamit," he muttered to himself.

He had never quite decided what he would do in the doubtful event that he spotted Bankart. Now he had to admit the fact that once he was ensconced in his lookout, he would not have many options. The only way to ensure finding him, and confronting him, if he were there, would be to continue on the street. He would have to establish himself near the periphery of the selection funnel and monitor the ranks. But he was not anxious to do this. He did not really expect Bankart to show up. It was far too dangerous. And if Bankart were unlikely to appear, what was the sense of exposing himself to such fearful risk?

As he rounded the corner, Eugen lingered to consider the drama that was developing at the end of the street. Several SS cars had arrived bearing the officers who would determine life and death. A murmur combed the press, and it spasmed like a decapitated fish.

"Halt!"

Casting his eyes down, Eugen tried to shuffle out of range of the voice without acknowledging it. A deserted block extended ahead.

"Halt!"

Eugen's heart jumped. He hopped forward, half-skipping, hoping the voice would abandon him.

"For the last time, halt!"

Whoever it was began to approach him. The sound of his soles scraping the pavement sprung Eugen from his shell. He spurred himself into a scamper. As he accelerated, his left shoe slipped off. In the instant he had to choose whether or not to retrieve it, he was aware of urgent footsteps closing in on him and a winded snorting and the dull thwack of a truncheon at the base of his skull.

"You sonofabitch," he heard as he was falling.

He hit the ground with his hands groping to protect his head, so that the ensuing blows smashed his knuckles and wrists and forearms.

"Where the hell do you think you're going?" asked the voice.

Eugen's hat had tumbled off, and a storm of thumps hailed down on him. Instead of resisting, he absorbed the punishment and waited for his assailant to exhaust himself. Finally, he was dragged up by the hair.

"Hold still," said the voice.

Eugen's knees sagged as he rose. Clutching him was a large man, perhaps ten years his senior, with a thick scar along the curve of his throat. He resembled a demented ship captain. His face was red and sweating from exertion, and he wore a black hat with a blue Star of David sewn into the crown.

"Where did you say you were going?" said the policeman.

Where did he think he was going?

"Answer me!" the policeman ordered.

His truncheon was cocked as if it had the will to strike and he was barely restraining it.

"To the bakery," Eugen said.

"What bakery?" the policeman shouted. "There are no bakeries. Everyone reports today."

He paused, calculating his tack. Eugen stood immobile to minimize the tension on his hair.

"What's your name?"

"Ephraim Schloss."

The policeman unhanded Eugen.

"Where were you going?"

"I told you," Eugen said.

He checked himself from stooping for his hat.

"Have you registered?" asked the policeman.

"No," Eugen said.

"Everyone has to register," said the policeman. "Even the police."

Eugen shifted his weight to relieve the pressure of the stones against his stockinged foot. The policeman was establishing control, figuring the angles.

"Do you have a token?"

"No," Eugen said.

"Papers?"

"Yes."

"What kind?"

Eugen felt something creeping through his hair. He raised his hand to scratch the afflicted region. A flare of pain caused it to recoil. There was blood on his fingers.

"What kind of papers?" the policeman repeated.

"Identification."

"But no token?"

"No."

The policeman sized Eugen up carefully.

"A Berliner?" he asked.

"Dresden," Eugen said.

"Why didn't you go with the others?"

"Circumstances," Eugen said.

His scalp prickled, and his right index finger was beginning to ache.

"Have you any money?" asked the policeman.

"No."

"Any jewels?"

"No."

"Put your hands in the air."

Eugen complied. The policeman searched him cursorily, expropriating a butter knife and a strip key.

"Is there a tin with this?"

"No longer."

The policeman pointed the key at the pillow case.

"What do you have in there?"

"Socks, underwear . . ."

"Let's see," said the policeman.

Eugen pictured his gun resting under the floorboards. Irritably, the policeman attempted to snatch the case out from under his belt, almost pulling him over.

"Untie it."

Eugen obeyed.

"Turn it over."

He opened the mouth of the case wide and tipped it toward the policeman.

"On the ground."

Before Eugen could respond, the policeman's truncheon crashed down on his knuckles. The pillow case dropped from his grasp onto the street.

"Do as I tell you," the policeman said.

He directed Eugen to sit down on the sidewalk and unload the pillow case, passing each article up to him for review.

"You have a gypsy fondness for knives," the policeman said.

"They come in handy," Eugen said.

The policeman pocketed Eugen's meat knife, but evinced little interest in anything else.

"Clean it up," he said when he had inspected everything.

Repacking his pillow case, Eugen was relieved that the policeman had overlooked the penknife secreted in his watch pocket.

"Hurry up," said the policeman.

Eugen finished collecting his things. A few feet away, his hat lay baking in the sun. He wanted to recover it, but dared not stir. His scalp was smarting, and his middle and index fingers were swelling like rolls in an oven.

"May I pick up my hat?" he appealed meekly to the policeman.

At ground level his view consisted of scuffed shoes, dark shabby trousers, and past the policeman's legs, the unreal buildings soft against the mural sky.

"You might as well get your shoe, too," said the policeman.

Gaining his feet, Eugen secured the pillow case through his belt, fetched his hat, put it on, and tracked down his shoe. The policeman followed him closely.

"So you have nothing valuable?" he said.

"Just what you see," Eugen said, examining his shoe.

The slit heel had ruptured, yielding a crack-backed slipper. He slid his foot into it, undid his pillow case, brought out a spare sock, and bound it around the breach and across his instep, contriving an Achilles truss.

"How do you eat?" asked the policeman.

"As I can," Eugen said.

"You don't look starved."

"I've been fortunate."

"Until today," said the policeman.

His face tautened, as if he were keeping an inner storm at bay.

"Where are your papers?" he demanded.

Eugen composed himself.

"Hidden," he said.

"Where?"

"Tebbens."

The policeman looked puzzled.

"What good are they there?" he asked.

"I left them for security," Eugen said.

"What if you don't get back?"

"Then I won't need them."

"But without them, you may not be able to return."

"I could be chosen to work."

"What else did you stash in the factory?" the policeman asked.

"That's all," Eugen said.

"Nothing precious?"

"No."

Eugen doffed his hat, exposing his scalp wound to the sun.

"How many are you?" the policeman asked.

"Myself," Eugen said.

"Where do you live?"

"Wherever."

"Then no one will miss you," the policeman said.

His mouth skewed sardonically, nearly paralleling the scar on his neck. He rapped Eugen in the ribs with the butt of his truncheon. Eugen winced, but did not budge. He poked him again, harder this time, wood on bone.

"Get moving," he said.

He waved his truncheon in the direction from which they had come. Eugen set out with the policeman slightly behind him and to the left. They proceeded in silence.

Palpitating sharply, Eugen's hand trembled to retain his hat. He tucked it into his belt, and the quivering partially subsided. His injured fingers had ballooned grotesquely and were the color of spoiled blood sausage.

He wondered what his captor was thinking. Did he hate him more for being German? There was a seven head quota now. Was he number one for the day? The final concession to the police and their families was that they were being allowed to register last.

Eugen balked.

"What's wrong?" said the policeman.

They were almost to the corner.

"Where are we going?" Eugen said.

"Guess," said the policeman.

"I don't know," Eugen said.

"You'll find out," said the policeman.

He poked Eugen in the kidney with his stick.

"Wait a minute," Eugen said.

He whirled around. The policeman half-cocked his truncheon and planted his feet.

"Let's go," he said.

His fingers clenched and unclenched nervously.

"What do you want from me?" Eugen pleaded.

"What would I want from you?" the policeman said. "You have nothing."

"Then why don't you leave me alone?" Eugen said.

"I'm only doing my job," the policeman said.

"Is it your job to split my head?" Eugen said.

"It's my job to make sure that you register," the policeman said.

"But not to cripple me," Eugen said.

"You were fleeing," said the policeman.

Eugen looked back down the street. The mounting registration commotion pervaded his ears like a conch roar. Once they steered the corner, it would be over. The sharks were feasting.

"I was frightened," Eugen said. "Wouldn't you have been in my position?"

"I'm not in your position," the policeman said. "Now move!"

He raised his truncheon against the sky.

"Wait!" Eugen said.

He inched rearward.

"I have some money."

The policeman's hand vacillated.

"I thought you had nothing."

"I have a small sum."

"How much?"

"A thousand zlotys."

"Where is it?"

"Will you release me?" Eugen asked.

"For a thousand zlotys I wouldn't promise anything," said the policeman.

"It's all I have," Eugen said.

"Before you had nothing," said the policeman.

"My head was ringing." Eugen said.

"Then there's hope," said the policeman.

He motioned Eugen away from the corner.

"Let's have it."

"Do I have your word for my freedom?"

"Quit stalling," said the policeman. "Where is it?"

"In the factory," Eugen said.

The policeman eyed him skeptically.

"With the papers, no doubt," he said.

"That's right," Eugen said.

"Maybe someone will stumble across them," said the policeman.

He tapped Eugen on the breastbone with his truncheon.

"About face," he said.

Abruptly, Eugen unloosed his hat from his belt.

"It's in here," he said.

"The factory?"

"The money."

"I'll believe it when I see it," said the policeman.

He clawed the hat away from Eugen.

"A knife is required," Eugen said.

"Meat or butter?" said the policeman.

Handling the hat roughly, he peered into it, rustled it between his fingers, plucked tentatively at the cloth, and ripped it open with an indelicate yank.

"Well, well, well," he said, separating the false layer.

He stuffed the thousand zlotys into his pocket. Assuring himself that there were no other plies in the material, he focused his attention on the papers.

"Ephraim Schloss," he read. "Is that you?"

"Yes."

"You're a machinist?"

"Yes."

"Why didn't you tell me?"

"You didn't ask."

"It doesn't matter," said the policeman.

Folding the outdated work permit in half, and in half again, he tore it into confetti and tossed it in Eugen's face. The paper flakes descended airily, landing about his feet like summer snow.

"Now what have we here?"

The policeman's eyes skimmed the birth certificate and leaped onto the sepia of the boy in the camp shirt with the open collar and the brown tousled hair.

"Who is this?" he asked.

Palming the photograph like a compact mirror, he glanced alternately from it to Eugen, gauging the resemblance. Then he reversed it and studied the inscription.

"Is this you?"

Eugen's mind spurted furiously away from the menacing tumult. The policeman, the buildings, and the street were pastel impressions crayoned over an insidious blue wash.

"Yes."

He was Noah Silver. Born March 11, 1911. Father—Ezra Silver. Mother—Myra (Bronstein) Silver. Jewish Age 12. In the forest.

"Noah Silver?"

"Yes."

"Not Ephraim Schloss?"

"No."

"Then who's Ephraim Schloss?"

"A deceased friend."

"Whose name you were using?"

"Yes."

"How do I know that you're not Ephraim Schloss and that Noah Silver isn't your deceased friend?" asked the policeman.

Eugen pondered the hypothesis. The policeman kicked at the shreds of Ephraim Schloss' work permit.

"I suppose you're Noah Silver now whether you like it or not," he said.

By the angle of the sun to the horizon, Eugen judged that it was not yet nine. Normally there were two deportations a day, early in the morning and in the evening. The gold watch would have read five twenty-six.

"Has your tongue frozen?" said the policeman.

"No."

"Do you have anything else of value?"

"Not with me," Eugen said.

"Then we might as well get on with it," said the policeman.

He jammed the photograph and the birth certificate into the hat and thrust it at Eugen.

"You're making an error," Eugen said.

"Take it," said the policeman.

Eugen accepted the hat. The inset was irreparably damaged. He transferred the papers to his breast pocket.

"What am I to you?" he asked.

"Shake a leg," said the policeman.

"Why?" Eugen said. "You have my money."

He looped his bunched hat through his belt. The policeman nudged him with his truncheon. Eugen began to edge around him, away from the corner.

"Don't get funny," said the policeman.

"Whatever you do with me, you're shit to them," Eugen said.

The policeman sloped to his left, impeding Eugen's drift.

"We're both ciphers," Eugen said.

"You have to report," said the policeman.

"I can report without you," Eugen said.

"Forget it," said the policeman.

"I was going back for my daughter," Eugen said. "I can't forsake her."

"Is that so?"

"It's God's truth," Eugen said. "She's with a cousin. Abrahm Bankart. You may . . ."

Like a branch tilted by a sudden gust of wind, the truncheon reared up in the air and whacked Eugen across the temple. He tottered and slumped onto one knee. The word "fool" buzzed in his ear.

"Left! . . . Right! . . . Left! . . . Left! . . ."

Wielding a riding crop as if it were a magic wand, an SS officer barked out commands that represented a temporary reprieve for some and death for others. With each "Left!" someone was condemned to deportation, arousing a flurry of ululation. "Right!" meant remaining in the ghetto to work. The "Lefts" were thrown to the waiting Ukrainians and Letts, and when a sufficient number had been assembled, they were tramped off to the *umschlagplatz*.

"Left! . . . Left! . . . Right! . . . Left! . . ."

Whips and ropes whistled through the air, goading the lines, lashing the chosen together.

"Left!"

Eugen stood subduedly between two Germans who had just managed to disengage themselves from his clutches. The Jewish policeman had surrendered him to a special officer and disappeared. He had been questioned briefly and then bumped toward a group destined for the *umschlagplatz*. But when a pair of Ukrainians charged forward to receive him, he swerved away from them and barged smack into a nearby coterie of SS men who were milling around like patricians at a livestock exhibition. They tried to expel him from their midst. Beseeching their mercy, he lowered his head, entangled himself in a thicket of legs, and held on for dear life. Something about his performance evoked a tolerance that resulted in the Ukrainians being called off. His bad hand was inadvertently stomped in the melee, but otherwise he was intact.

"Hey, Gustav," one of the SS men proclaimed. "This gentleman says he's not Jewish."

His remark instigated a spate of droll banter.

"He looks as Aryan as Frederick," said Gustav.

"Gustav's right," Conrad said. "Notice his bearing, the fine features, the elegant cloth."

"Appreciate especially the classic aquiline beak," Gustav added.

"It's ideal for catching fish."

A tall, fair-complexioned man with flaxen hair and cold, sky-colored eyes strode over.

"What's going on here?" Officer Spitz asked.

The other SS men straightened up.

"A star-cap brought him in," said Frederick. "He claims he's one of us."

The muscles in Officer Spitz' jaw twitched.

"Name," he asked.

"Eugen Glueck."

"Home?"

"Dresden."

"What are you doing here?"

"I'm with the Jewish Office—Intelligence," Eugen said.

His heels clicked mutedly as his hand fired out in ramrod salute.

"Identification?"

"Hidden."

"Have you searched him?"

Frisking Eugen expeditiously, Frederick found the photograph and the birth certificate and submitted them to Spitz.

"Who is this?" Spitz asked.

He flashed the portrait at Eugen.

"Are you Noah Silver?"

"No."

"Then whose papers are these?"

Suddenly Eugen's eyes bleared and he started crying, noiselessly, the tears rutting his dust-caked cheeks.

"Get rid of him," Spitz said.

Indifferently, he tore the photo of Noah Silver and the birth certificate into sixteen pieces and handed them to Frederick. Then he slapped Eugen contemptuously in the face and stalked off.

"So you're not Jewish?" Frederick said.

"No," Eugen said.

He watched Frederick deposit the scrapped cover documents in his hip pocket.

"Flatten him out," Frederick said.

His cohorts seized Eugen by both arms and forced him to the ground. A rhomboid stone spiked the back of his neck. He closed his eyes to block the light that was blazing on his upturned face. Decrees of "Left!" and "Right!" were audible, but he concentrated away from them, on the white fervor of the sun.

"No! No!"

Eugen began wriggling to prevent his unbuttoned trousers from being drawn down, but his limbs were firmly pinioned and he could not protect himself. He cried out in black anguish as barbed talons wrenched his testicles out of his underpants.

There was a stunned hush.

"Well I'll be a woodpecker's hole."

Eugen was dazed.

"He's not circumcised!"

"I don't believe it."

"There it is."

"Amazing."

"Maybe we ought to do it for him."

"He can get it done in paradise."

The weight melted from Eugen's body, but he stayed motionless, bating his breath.

"On your feet."

The voice was Frederick's. Eugen unlocked his eyes. He was encompassed by faces. Abashedly, he restored his penis to his pants and crawled upright.

"You're a miscreation," Frederick said.

With a peculiar twist of his head, he wheeled away from Eugen and strutted off in pursuit of Spitz.

"On the double," Conrad said.

He and Gustav grabbed Eugen on either flank and spirited him toward the Ukrainians.

"He's yours again," Gustav said, shoving him forward.

The very soldiers from whom Eugen had escaped ramped out of the pack and pounced on him.

"Treat him kindly," Conrad said. "He knows the Pope."

A gray woman with a withered leg hobbled up, appended to a healthy girl of eighteen or twenty.

"Left!" the inspector snapped, flicking his crop at the enfeebled woman. Then, switching it at the girl, "Right!"

The woman leaned to her left, but the girl jerked her to the right. A soldier intervened, hooking her elbow in an effort to detach her from the woman. She bent her knees to countervail his tow. Another soldier latched onto the woman and began tugging her to the left. Still the girl would not relinquish her. Truculently, the first soldier plunged his fist into her groin. Her legs faltered, and she was impetuously routed to the left, along with the woman, into the conflux in which Eugen found himself.

"Right! . . . Left! . . . Left! . . . Left . . ."

The orders recurred incessantly, eliciting commentary wails and plaints like the soughing of a Greek chorus. There were many more "Lefts" than "Rights."

Eugen noted that the buildings which had appeared artfully jerry-built from afar were appallingly substantial at close quarters. The people, conversely, were less distinct, having been reduced to snags in a line that slid forward like a rope splitting on a horseshoe nail, fraying left and right, left and right, without discernment of individual faces, the right track being spooled for reuse, the left snarling into a clump to be stowed on a freight car and shipped out to be processed.

Standing in the area for "Lefts," Eugen's view became increasingly obstructed by ears and necks and hair until he could no longer scan for Bankart. If Bankart were going to retard the dissolution of the ghetto, now was the time for him to act. But things were happening so rapidly, Eugen would probably not have been able to apprehend him under these conditions anyway. Perhaps Bankart had presented himself and was already at the *umschlagplatz*.

Even that rotten policeman would end up there, Eugen thought.

His scalp nettled. He went to scratch it, but the percolation of blood through his fingers pounded his hand against an invisible anvil. It was doltish of him to have tendered his hat. He had forfeited the money and the work permit and had wound up where he would have in the first place.

The only consolation was that his gun was safe. Had he had it with him, he might have lost it too.

As the "Lefts" accumulated around him, Eugen began to quake. His aggrieved arm fluttered against the person to his right. He was not sure whether it was a man or a woman. His nostrils were tinged with the musty odors of the bristly uniforms that had overpowered him: damp wool, lye, sweat, urine, semen, pollen, and from one jacket, the bouquet of soured French perfume.

Where were the pockmarked and the harelipped women? He had hoped to come across them, but not at the *umschlagplatz*. He did not want to meet anyone there. Not even Bankart. The old man with the charcoal in his hair would be there, and several thousand others. Tzipora and her family had gone before. No one who had been there had come back.

His whole body was trembling. He wedged against whoever was behind him. There was a stabbing beneath his shoulder blade, but he stood fast. Soon the space around him shrank until all that could tremble was his neck.

Eugen exhorted himself to think ahead, but was unable. The ghetto was nearly defunct, and yet he had not uncovered Bankart. He pictured himself groveling on the street with his genitals parching in the sun. Franz had counseled him sagely. Without a uniform, virtually anyone could be mistaken for a Jew.

*　*　*

The flock was migrating to the *umschlagplatz*. Eugen's legs functioned autonomously. His mind was a swirl of images as he cast about for a scheme, a projection, anything that would integrate his faculties and permit him to implement a resolution.

Left. Right. Left. Right.

With each step the interval in which to commit himself foreshortened. He had to take advantage of every moment. To formulate a plan. *Now.* But he had never been proficient in doing two things at once. He was padding, one foot after the other.

Left. Right. Left. Right.

The lame woman and the girl were almost abreast of him. They had been farther up, but the pace was too arduous for them. The woman was using the girl as a crutch, hopping on her good leg while the shriveled one scraped the ground.

He had to stop moving forward, but he could not. There were guards all about. The slightest untoward gesture might trigger them. He did not want to be culled out. A design was essential. Then he would make his break.

Something glinted in the corner of his eye. A gun was jutting out from under a soldier's arm. The left.

The walls of the *umschlagplatz* loomed ahead.

In mid-step Eugen raised his left foot inward and removed his shoe with his right hand. Inserting it furtively in his shirt, he divested himself similarly of the other shoe. The lame woman and the girl had lost ground. Eugen lagged until he was beside them and placed the woman's arm around his shoulder complementing the girl's support.

A yellow dust floated up from the stones and the shoes of the people in front of them. They were entering an intersection beyond which the street became a cul-de-sac, terminating in the *umschlagplatz*. The pandemonium of registration faded, giving way to a more somber clamor.

Left. Right. Left. Right.

Deliberately, Eugen missed a count and brought his foot

down slashingly on the lame woman's heel. Her wilted leg snagged and buckled like a snipped stem.

"Oh, my God," she said, caving in as Eugen shed her arm.

The girl managed to keep the lame woman from totally collapsing, but the couple behind stumbled over them, causing a snarl. In the commotion, Eugen ducked to his left and sprinted back into the intersection.

UNTERMENSCHEN

Abrahm stirred sluggishly. He had drugged himself to sleep and now his head was clogged with chemical dreams. But the signal was insistent. He lit the kerosene lamp and implanted the match in the thin crust of grease that had congealed on his plate. Then he reached for his gun and stretched to release the cross-bolt.

The door opened, admitting Nicholas.

"What is it?" Abrahm grumbled.

His voice was thick.

"House guests," Nicholas said.

A pair of feet dangled through the hatch. Nicholas extended his sturdy arms and lowered a woman into the bunker. She was followed by a girl, two suit-cases, and finally Olek.

"Surprise," Olek said, securing the latch.

Abrahm slipped his gun under the covers.

"Welcome," he said.

He rubbed his eyes to disperse the energies that were screening him from greater wakefulness.

"How are you feeling?" Olek asked.

He placed a hand on Abrahm's shoulder.

"Groggy."

Nicholas kindled a lamp at the dark end of the bunker. "There," he said.

He unchained the set of cots farthest from Abrahm and began making them up. Immediately the room felt smaller.

"You're sure you want this?" Olek said under his breath.

Abrahm's eyes flickered. The girl, who was comforting the woman, acknowledged his with a slight smile. She wore a napped orange coat and a sienna beret. Her face was attractively intelligent. The woman appeared to be in shock. She was attired in brown shoes, sheer stockings, a navy coat with a fox collar, and a matching hat. With their double-strapped leather bags beside them, she and the girl resembled tourists waiting to be registered at a resort.

"That should do it," Nicholas said, putting the finishing touches on the bunks.

Olek grabbed the luggage.

"Right this way."

The woman balked.

"Mother," the girl prompted.

She had a smooth, assuring voice.

"No."

"We have to get some rest."

The girl tried to start her mother toward Nicholas, but she refused to budge.

"Where am I?"

"Among friends," the girl said.

The woman surveyed the bunker gropingly.

"Who's he?" she asked.

"How thoughtless of me," Olek said, hastening back. "Esther, this is Comrade Abrahm. He and Emil are quite fast friends. Abrahm, this is Dr. Adler's wife, Esther. Of course you know Ruth."

"How do you do?" Abrahm said.

The woman stared at him strangely.

"We're sorry to barge in on you," Ruth said.

"It's no trouble," Abrahm said.

"What's the matter with him?" asked Mrs. Adler.

"His leg is ailing," Ruth said.

"What's he doing here?"

"Father operated on him," Ruth said. "He's recuperating."

"He looks awful," said Mrs. Adler.

As Nicholas approached, she shuddered and pressed closer against Ruth.

"Don't be frightened," Nicholas said. "It's not home, but you'll have everything you need."

Reluctantly, Mrs. Adler allowed Ruth to guide her the short distance to their quarters.

"These are your beds," Nicholas said. "When you want privacy . . ."

He unfurled the black cloth, shrinking the bunker drastically, and explained the ventilation system, toilet and hygienic procedures, storage, and meals.

Abrahm glanced quizzically at Olek.

"She's in poor shape," Olek whispered. "Emil gave her a heavy tranquilizer. She'll get another if she can't drop off. Ruth will take care of everything. She's a doctor herself these days."

"It's a pity she couldn't have stayed in the hospital," Abrahm said.

"She has instructions for you too," Olek said. "You can trust her completely."

"I'll leave the curtain down," Nicholas said. "Once you've changed, it would be best to put it up. Otherwise it will get stuffy."

"Thanks very much," Ruth said.

"Don't mention it," said Nicholas.

He emerged trailing a shadow.

"I'll be in touch," Olek said.

He clasped Abrahm's hand. Nicholas unstopped the brace. Olek climbed out first. The door descended. Abrahm barred it and extinguished his lamp.

"What was that?" he hear Mrs. Adler ask.

"Abrahm's light," Ruth said.

Their voices were clear despite the curtain.

"I'd rather not undress," Mrs. Adler said. "It's cold."

"Lie down as you are, then," Ruth said. "I'll help you with your shoes."

"I don't like it here," said Mrs. Adler.

"Just relax," Ruth said. "In the morning you'll be fresh and chipper."

She patted her mother and mounted the upper bunk. Their lamp still glimmered. Abrahm shut his eyes and turned his head toward the wall.

"Good night," Ruth said.

Abrahm tossed his head to the left and burrowed for a restful position on the pillow. His neck was tense and his leg ached as if it were day. He considered taking another pill, but resolved to hold off until dawn.

He puckered his nose. The bunker air, normally charged with the medicinal redolence of his wounds, smelled of wool coats and leather and perfume and a sweet body musk that he imagined to be Ruth's.

Were it not for her mother, Abrahm thought, Ruth would yet be in the ghetto, assisting her father. Esther had wanted to leave ever since Isaac had been cared for at her house. But Emil would not go with her. She was free to depart, he said, he would make safe arrangements for her, but he had to remain. As things got worse, she tried to coax Ruth into joining her. But Ruth also wished to stay. Esther was crushed. Notwithstanding, she managed to endure until it became apparent that Emil would never abandon his station. He ceased coming home at all. Gradually, Ruth adopted a similar schedule. Esther was forced to venture to the hospital to see them. She did this several times, despite her squeamishness and nervous frailty, but when Emil rejected an ultimatum to tear himself away, she finally broke down during a visit. She was kept there a few days. After initial improvement, she suffered a relapse. When her condition began to affect other patients, it was decided to transfer her to the Aryan side.

The pressure was building in Abrahm's leg. He eased it laterally. Progress, he thought, grimacing. A week ago he had not been able to move it at all.

"The doctor says you're to start exercising the leg," Nicholas had informed him.

"He must be joking," Abrahm responded.

He could hardly budge without causing vicious pain. It was a major project to slide his heel the least bit edgewise.

"You're to prop up and channel your strength into your hips," Nicholas said. "Lift the shank through your thigh. I'll catch it if you can't bring it down."

He took a stance at the foot of the cot.

"Ready."

Abrahm strained to raise his leg, but it seemed to weigh a thousand pounds. He tightened his buttocks and funneled his will downward. The only result was a searing jag through his knee. No degree of effort sufficed to unite his limb with his desire to elevate it.

"We'll have another go at it later," Nicholas said. "In the meanwhile, you can attempt it yourself if you want. Ultimately, your routine will be five lifts, ten times a day."

"How about ten groans fifty times?" Abrahm said.

For forty-eight hours he had travailed haplessly, with Nicholas in attendance and without. Then one morning the leg suddenly levitated, as if defying gravity.

"Hold it, hold it," Nicholas encouraged him.

Abrahm gritted his teeth and delved within himself for the power to sustain his exertion. His heel was perhaps six inches above the cushion. He struggled to push it higher, but it hovered at that level for ten or twenty seconds, quavering with increasing amplitude, and plummeted into Nicholas' hands.

"Congratulations," Nicholas said.

Abrahm tingled with exhilaration.

"I feel as if I've given birth," he said, grinning broadly.

"I thought you were going to fly out of here," Nicholas said.

The next few take-offs were almost as difficult as the first. After that, Abrahm had progressed rapidly to four or five lifts in succession. But contrary to expectation, the pain did not abate. Instead it was cyclical, surging and ebbing in sharp or steady pulses. The swelling did not subside either. Whenever Nicholas unwrapped the casing, there was the same raw, slippery knee—as fat and as pink and as ugly as a pig's head with its pursed mouth and one eye stitched for roasting.

"Do you suppose it should be this way?" Abrahm would ask Nicholas.

"According to the doctor, it's to be anticipated," Nicholas said.

There was no choice but to accept his word, nor any reason not to. Nicholas had always been honest with him. But maybe now that Ruth was here he would get a better idea of what was what. Anyway, tomorrow would not be such a lonely day.

"Good morning," Ruth said.

Abrahm watched her unfold the lower of the middle bunks. She was dressed in a white smock and a white cotton hair net.

"Good morning," he said.

She had been up for a while, but in the interest of establishing privacy, he had not addressed her.

"Did you sleep well?" Ruth asked.

Her voice was like filtered sunlight.

"Not really," Abrahm said. "But it's no matter."

He had daydreamed something about Job.

"It would have been easier on you if we could have come earlier," Ruth said.

She fetched the smaller of the leather suitcases from behind the curtain and set it on the naked cot.

"Don't worry about it," Abrahm said.

He struck a match and ignited his lamp.

"We've intruded on your peaceful little world," Ruth said.

"More torpid than tranquil," Abrahm said.

"I'm afraid you'll soon miss it," Ruth said.

"How's your mother?" Abrahm asked.

"Fine," Ruth said, putting a finger to her lips.

"And your father?"

"Harried," Ruth said. "But bearing up."

She unbuckled the suitcase and picked out half a dozen prepared bundles. Abrahm boosted himself up so that he was semi-sitting.

"You're pretty spry," Ruth said.

"It's the pleasant company," Abrahm said.

"Don't let your mood be dependent on us," Ruth said. "You might regret it."

The first parcel Ruth husked contained a towel, which she spread over the mattress. The second consisted of four stuffed men's socks. She withdrew a bottle of alcohol from one of these and sponged her hands. Then she uncovered a surgical gown which had been packed with medical instruments.

"You certainly came equipped," Abrahm said.

"Wait till you see what mother brought," Ruth said.

She shook down a thermometer and sterilized it.

"Aaah," Abrahm gasped as she came toward him.

"Lie back," she said.

She began to strip off the blanket, but Abrahm checked her.

"I'll have to do it," he said.

Ruth surrendered the thermometer and turned away. Abrahm slid it under the covers and inserted it in his rectum.

"Have you had much pain?" Ruth asked, arranging her supplies on the makeshift counter.

"I can't complain," Abrahm said.

"Has it decreased?"

"Somewhat."

"Do you use the pills?"

"The large ones."

"How often?"

"Once in the morning and once at night."

"Automatically?"

"Religiously."

"Maybe you should discontinue them," Ruth said.

Abrahm had not yet swallowed the daybreak dose, but he had been contemplating it for several hours.

"Tomorrow I'll turn a new leaf," he said.

Glass and steel tinkled delicately.

"Time," Ruth said.

Abrahm retrieved the thermometer.

"Have you been moving your bowels?" Ruth asked, reading the quicksilver.

"Now and then."

"Your temperature's normal." Ruth said.

Her features were adolescent, Abrahm noted—the frank eyes, the unwrinkled skin, the downy neck—but she had her father's firm and competent manner.

"If you don't mind, I'll have a look at the baby," she said.

"I'd be honored," Abrahm said.

They bared his legs. Ruth posted a crate beside Abrahm's cot, covered it with a linen napkin, and deposited on it the items required to replace his dressing.

"Tell me if I'm hurting you," she said.

Deftly, she scissored through the outer bandage and detached the top layer of batting. It was soiled with discharge. At the point of the principal incision, the knee and the swathe had formed a common scab. She pried up a fringe, gently, and peeled back the gauze as she worked under it with a lanolin-saturated swab.

"That wasn't so bad," Ruth said.

At a glimpse, the shaved leg imparted a fulvous impression of decay. The fibular scar appeared to be healing adequately, but the tinctured knee was gruesome.

"Beautiful, isn't it?" Abrahm said.

Ruth leaned over to inspect it. His left leg, hirsute and sinewy, was gray against her milky frock. The fronts of her thighs tickled his hair.

"You need another drain," Ruth said. "There's too much fluid."

As she washed and repaired his wounds, Abrahm felt himself undergoing a deeper cleansing. Lying in the bunker day after day, he had become more resigned to his condition than he would concede. His progress had been depressingly slow. The ghetto was dying without him.

"How's that?" Ruth said cheerfully when she had finished.

"Professional," Abrahm said.

He was glad that he had not yet taken his morning pill.

Ruth sat on the cube beside Abrahm's cot. Nicholas had come and gone, commenting on Abrahm's spiritedness. Breakfast was a mixture of oats, dried prunes, shredded carrots, and sesame seeds, and a thermos of creamed and sugared coffee.

"It's good," Ruth said, swallowing a spoon of cereal.

"It should be," Abrahm said. "It's what he feeds his animals."

"Does he have a family?" Ruth asked.

"Just a housekeeper."

Something creaked, and there was agitation behind the curtain.

"Ruth," Mrs. Adler said. "It's time to get up. Ruth. Ruth!"

Her voice rasped across the bunker.

"RUTH."

"I'm here, mother."

"Where?" Mrs. Adler screaked, dashing into view, "RUTH. Oh, there you are."

"Good morning, mother," Ruth said, smiling.

Mrs. Adler froze in her tracks. A bewildered expression crossed her face. Shoeless and hatless, she was still swaddled in her coat.

"I . . . excuse me," she said.

She ran her hand nervously through her wiry black hair.

"Why don't you join us?" Ruth said. "We're having breakfast."

Mrs. Adler studied Abrahm as if she were uncertain whether she recognized him.

"I must have overslept," she said. "Let me see . . ."

She pushed up her sleeve, revealing a square silver watch embellished with diamond chips.

"Three-thirty," she said. "It can't be. Ruth, what time is it?"

"Almost seven," Ruth said.

Mrs. Adler raised her wrist to her ear and listened intently.

"What's that noise?" she said.

"Is it broken?" Ruth asked.

"No, the other noise," Mrs. Adler said.

"I don't know what you mean," Ruth said.

"She hears the dogs scratching," Abrahm said.

"Yes, that's it," Mrs. Adler said. "Scratching."

"Would you like to eat now?" Ruth asked, offering her seat.

"I think I'll get dressed first," Mrs. Adler said.

She stroked her fox collar.

"Without your coat you'll be perfectly all right the way you are," Ruth said.

"I am wearing it, aren't I?" Mrs. Adler said uncertainly.

"You were a little cold last night," Ruth said. "I don't think you need it now though."

"No, of course not," Mrs. Adler said.

She sloughed her coat and cradled it in her arms.

"Here, I'll put it on your bed," Ruth said, coaxing it from her. "We'll make a place for it later."

Squinting, Mrs. Adler held her watch directly before her eyes, as if she did not believe the disposition of the hands.

"What time did you say it was?" she asked.

"Breakfast time," Ruth said.

She disposed of the coat and brought over another crate.

"Sit down, mother," she said.

Tentatively, Mrs. Adler took a seat. Ruth fixed her a bowl of oats. She looked into it, and than at Abrahm, who was still eating.

"What is it?" she asked, addressing her first words to him.

"Manna."

Mrs. Adler dipped her nose into the bowl.

"It smells like horses," she said.

"Taste it," Ruth said. "It's very good."

Mrs. Adler watched Ruth consume a mouthful of the cereal with a light crunching sound.

"I don't care for any, thank you," she said, relegating her bowl to the floor.

"Would you enjoy some nice hot coffee?" Abrahm said.

"Yes," she said eagerly. "My head's so fuzzy."

Abrahm rested his bowl on his blanket and removed the thermos from the shelf. A cloud of steam billowed up as he uncapped it. He poured a stream of the caramel colored liquid into a cup.

"This should perk you up," he said, advancing the cup toward Mrs. Adler.

Seemingly preoccupied, she left his hand standing in mid-air.

"Mother," Ruth said, relieving Abrahm.

"Oh, yes, I'm sorry," Mrs. Adler said, accepting the potion from Ruth.

She raised it to her lips and probed it with her tongue, like a bird testing water. Then, approvingly, she drew a sip. Her face brightened. She ventured another. Her eyes bounded off Abrahm's, grazed her watch, and scudded away.

"Rats," she said absently. "We're surrounded by them."

"Where?" Ruth asked solicitously.

"Everywhere," Mrs. Adler said. "Listen to them scraping."

"It's our friends the dogs again," Abrahm said. "They're active in the morning."

"In the walls?" Mrs. Adler said.

"Above us," Abrahm said. "To get here last night, you had to pass through the kennel."

"Dogs?" Mrs. Adler said. "There were no dogs."

Ruth had tacked up the curtain, restoring the bunker to its full length, and was sitting on a cube with her back against the wall, engrossed in a medical textbook.

Mrs. Adler was absorbed in unpacking her belongings. It had taken her nearly an hour to arrange a few skirts and dresses on Ruth's bunk. On her own cot she arrayed stockings, blouses, underwear, and scarfs in quilt-like patterns. Shoes were aligned on the floor, beside her suitcase.

There was enough finery for a state occasion, Abrahm thought. In addition to daily articles, he had already seen displayed a green velvet strolling cape, a silky lynx muff, a pearl felt hat with a stick-pinned tuft of turquoise plumage to one side, and a pair of sequined white evening gloves.

"I can wear this with the green skirt," Mrs. Adler said. "Or with anything, really."

She draped a champagne sweater with a rose embroidered on the left breast across her chest.

"Don't you think so, dear?" she said.

"Yes, mother," Ruth said without looking up from her book.

Mrs. Adler slipped the sweater on over her basic blue dress. As she had for several other garments, she produced her jewelry box from her valise, perched it on a crate, and unlocked it.

"Now, what would be appropriate?" she said, surveying her treasure.

The case had three stepped tiers and was mantled with beaded pink taffeta. Inside, the compartments were brown plush. Ceremoniously, Mrs. Adler selected a beryline grasshopper brooch and positioned it above the rose.

"I don't know," she said, considering it in the inlaid mirror.

Trying to ignore her, Abrahm looked over at Ruth as she sat studying, her hips flared out beyond the edges of the crate and her breasts sloped gracefully inside her smock. She had her mother's body, he thought. Facially, though, she resembled her father, and her cocoa hair was clipped short like a boy's.

Periodically, Abrahm noticed, Ruth's hand embarked for some part of her body, without interrupting her reading, to feel for a bone, a nerve, a protrusion, a juncture, a pulse. She had wanted since childhood to be a doctor. Emil had never prompted her. In fact, he had encouraged her to cultivate alternatives, lest she be disappointed. But she had always identified with him, and would not be dissuaded from her single-mindedness. Now she was undergoing an internship ruefully exceeding her ambition.

What had Leora aspired to, Abrahm mused?

"If only I could stay this svelte after the war," Mrs. Adler said.

She drew a cerise skirt against her waist.

Ruth disregarded her.

"I'm practically done," she said, pursuing Ruth's attention. "But where will I keep everything?"

The cots were laden as if Mrs. Adler had just returned from a shopping spree.

"We could use the other bunks," she said. "He wouldn't mind."

"We'll do nothing of the sort," Ruth said.

"What will we do then?" Mrs. Adler said.

She emphasized her problem with a sweep of her hand.

"It will all have to be repacked," Ruth said.

Mrs. Adler gazed past her at Abrahm.

"I think he's asleep, poor man," she said. "Is he very sick?"

"He's improving," Ruth said. "He'll be all right."

"Why isn't he in the hospital?" Mrs. Adler asked.

"It's safer here," Ruth said.

"My stomach is growling," Mrs. Adler said.

"You'll have to be patient," Ruth said.

"I suppose we'll have oats for dinner," Mrs. Adler said.

"Whatever it is will suffice," Ruth said.

"Hee-haw, hee-haw," Mrs. Adler brayed, cocking her fanned hands above her ears.

"Mother!" Ruth said.

Mrs. Adler stooped down on all fours and wiggled her rump.

Ruth burst into laughter.

Ruth and Abrahm commenced eating. The meal included radishes chopped into wafers and browned potatoes and spinach scrambled together.

"You must accept my apology," Mrs. Adler said, "I was in a daze."

She poked a slice of fried kidney with her fork.

"It's forgotten," Abrahm said.

"I probably drove you crazy with my blather."

"Not at all," Abrahm said.

"It was silly of me to bring all those things," Mrs. Adler went on. "Most of them are absolutely worthless."

Abrahm bridled a smile.

"I'm sure you feel unburdened now that you're settled," he said.

"Immensely," Mrs. Adler said.

She pierced a kidney morsel, pressed the blood out, and gulped it down uneasily.

"You can't imagine how embarrassed I am," she confessed. "How could I not . . . of course, I've never seen you with a beard before. But that's no excuse. Emil would be ashamed of me. He admires you so."

"Coffee?" Abrahm asked.

"Please," Mrs. Adler said.

She crossed her knife and fork and passed her cup.

"Aren't you going to finish?" Ruth asked.

"It's too bloody," Mrs. Adler said, making a face.

"There's a piece of chocolate in the sweet bag," Abrahm said.

"I'll get it," Ruth said.

"It's remarkable . . ." said Mrs. Adler.

She bit into a small dark chunk of chocolate.

"Mother has a habit of hanging sentences," Ruth said.

"That we're sitting here having dinner with Comrade Abrahm."

"Kidney dinner," Abrahm said.

"Your friends certainly know how to keep a secret," said Mrs. Adler.

"What do you mean?" Abrahm said.

"Emil didn't say anything to me about your having been at the hospital," Mrs. Adler explained. "I had no inkling . . ."

Ruth's glare inhibited her.

"Go on," Abrahm said.

"No one would ever dream that you were here," Mrs. Adler said.

"Where would they think I was?"

"I don't know," Mrs. Adler said. "There are so many rumors floating around."

"For instance?"

"Oh, that you're still in the ghetto, that you're not, that you're hidden in Tebbens' or another factory, that you're dead . . ."

"They're all true," Abrahm said.

The ceiling undulated in the darkness. Abrahm lay wide awake. Ruth and Mrs. Adler slept. Their breathing rustled

softly through the bunker, which had been cooler since they
had gone up for air.

"That was marvelous," Mrs. Adler had said. "Can't we do
it once more, quickly?"

"Not until tomorrow," Ruth said.

"I wish you could have seen it," Mrs. Adler said to
Abrahm.

"Shush," Ruth said.

Abrahm peered over the Bible that Nicholas had given
him to read.

"I don't mind," he said.

"The stars were so bright and sparkling," Mrs. Adler said.
"And the grass was so fragrant . . ."

"Why don't we retire?" Ruth said.

"Yes," said Mrs. Adler. "It is rather late. Good night."

"Good night," Abrahm said.

As they undressed, he had heard Ruth suggest that they
sleep with the curtain up. Unexpectedly, Mrs. Adler had
agreed. He reflected on her resilience. The act of quitting the
ghetto had so disoriented her that she had perceived him as a
stranger. Yet in twenty-four hours she had regained a degree
of self-command. She would be all right, he thought, with
tender care.

He had agreed to her transfer, but inwardly he had been
ambivalent about receiving her into the bunker. In his depression, the only solace had been in solitude. Now he understood
that he had become overly dependent on his isolation to mitigate his anguish and anesthetize the urgency of convalescing.
Whatever adjustments Mrs. Adler necessitated, her presence
and Ruth's would be salutary. Already he was infused with a
new-found optimism which he had failed to manufacture on
his own. He had sworn off the pills, yet he was untormented.
There was pain, but it was overridden by the awareness that in
the morning he would not be by himself. He would get well.
And as he did, the shortened days would elapse less gravely.

When Ruth was at the air hole, Abrahm had imagined
that they were in the stomach of a great whale gliding

tirelessly through the silence. Perhaps it was Ahab, not Job, he had dreamed of in the morning—obsessed with the whale, hating it, fearing it, yet drawn to it, pursuing it relentlessly on its soundless course, always encompassed by water. Whatever the dream, he was grateful for Ruth and Esther. If they were to survive, it would be each depending on the other. For there was one earth, and every living thing upon it clung fragilely to its surface as it spun through space on an obscure pilgrimage—the whale navigating its chained seas, and man voyaging through a lifetime.

END
GAME

Victor placed six strips of brown paper on the skirt of the
table and sprinkled them with tobacco. Across from
him, Olek leaned over, hands on knees, to study the
board.

"Why don't you take his side?" Victor said.

He seamed a cigarette with his tongue and tamped it
down with his thumbnail.

"He doesn't stand a chance," Olek said.

"Yes, he does," Victor said. "With a little ingenuity, he
can even win."

"I'm not Abrahm," Olek said.

"What games we used to have," Victor said.

He set two cigarettes down for Olek beside a bishop, a
knight, and three pawns.

"How's Felix?"

"Better," Olek said. "The wound is dry."

"Does he continue to insist that it was an accident?"

"Naturally."

"Do you think he'll attempt it again?"

"Yanina's watching him like a hawk."

Olek craned for a light. The tinder end of the roll flared quickly into the more firmly packed body.

"Anything on Glueck?"

"Zero."

Victor lit his own cigarette, exhaled a puff of smoke from his mouth, and drew it smartly into his nose.

"I've developed a further hypothesis on him."

"Shoot."

"Heinrich arrived at the funeral with one objective: confronting Abrahm. When he didn't find him there, he became nonplussed."

"I still don't understand how he expected to take him singlehandedly," Olek said.

"We have to assume there was help nearby," Victor said. "Perhaps even the wardens. In any case, he was disappointed, and then Theresa stood up to him, forcing him into an uncomfortable position. Also, while the others recoiled, she was able to scrutinize him at close range. That might have disconcerted him. When he reported back, Thierbach became worried about her too. She had been with Leora from the outset and he feared that she had been suspicious of the medical attention accorded her. He upbraided Heinrich for not having retreated immediately upon seeing that Abrahm was absent. Possibly he indicated anxiety about Theresa as well. Humiliated and outraged, Heinrich rushed out to the convent and asked for Theresa. Told that she was not there, he went to the train station and waited for her. Apparently he had at least one accomplice. They ambushed her and then, realizing that he had been imprudent in calling for her, he ordered her head left on the road to intimidate the sisters. If Abrahm is right, Heinrich may not have dirtied his own hands, but his mark is unmistakable. Leora was sacrificed in a sophisticated manner. Theresa was butchered."

Olek was pensive.

"Do you follow me?" Victor said.

"Not entirely," Olek said, suffocating his cigarette. "How did Heinrich get involved in the first place?"

"Through the Britannia ring," Victor said.

"So he backed in," Olek quipped.

"Presumably," Victor said. "But your friend Glueck was not a party. As you've said, he had an underlying decency. That's undoubtedly what did him in. Transacting business with Felix, it's likely he would have known of Leora. But considering her harmless, he disregarded her. The authorities, however, became aware of her through a neighbor or otherwise. Thierbach brought her up to Glueck, who was truthful about why he had been remiss. He was then ordered to investigate. Dutifully, he questioned Felix and accepted the story that the girl was Polish and recently orphaned. But he made no mention of anyone else, whereas Thierbach had come by additional information regarding a strange woman. Without telling Glueck, he put Heinrich on the job."

"Why him?"

"One of his people might have been responsible for the original lead," Victor said. "They're always on the lookout for fleece. Or Thierbach may have smelled a good profit and assigned the extortion to Heinrich. It's also conceivable that Heinrich had once propositioned Glueck and been rebuffed."

"But what would Thierbach have against Glueck?"

"That remains unclear."

"And how does Ivan enter into this?"

"By the time Heinrich had sniffed around, Leora was gone. But in the process he discovered that Ivan, with whom he had been familiar at the Britannia, was Felix' son-in-law. He went to him and asked about the girl. Ivan protested ignorance. Heinrich threatened blackmail. Finally Ivan informed him that she had been sent to a convent, but withheld her identity. When Heinrich inquired concerning the woman who had stayed with her, Ivan was caught by surprise. He maintained that there was no such person. Heinrich disbelieved him, but granted him a period in which to fully ascertain the facts. Ivan lay the matter before Anna. She denied any knowledge of it. The Erdmanns reacted similarly. He pleaded with them to be frank, but he could not confide his desperation. His negative determination failed to satisfy Heinrich. But only under the resulting torture did he divulge his surmise that if the girl was Leora, the woman must have been Sonya."

"He could have let us know," Olek said. "We might have been able to pull it out of the fire."

"Thierbach's very shrewd," Victor said. "He steered Heinrich away from Felix initially in order not to tip anyone off. And later, anticipating the prospect that Ivan might seek assistance, he neither killed him off nor swore him to silence. Instead, he advised him that they were setting him free because his testimony corroborated what Felix had voluntarily deposed. Beyond that, he showed no particular interest in what he had learned. Ivan's dislike for Felix was thereby violently exacerbated, yet he felt compelled to keep his nightmare to himself."

"Shit," Olek said.

"At this point Heinrich approached Felix, identified himself as an SS man, referred to intelligence that an unauthorized woman and girl were quartered with him, and asked what had become of them. When Felix expressed reluctance to talk, Heinrich impugned the purity of his blood and hinted of dire consequences for Yanina and Anna. Curiously, Ivan was exempted. Felix yielded."

"That suggests they were planning to do away with Leora," Olek said.

"Thierbach was," Victor said, "but he did not share his intention with Heinrich. He put him up to examining Felix for two reasons. First, to cover the implication of Ivan and to induce latent guilt in Felix. Second, to structure a trap for Glueck. He imparted only the latter purpose to Heinrich. They would get to the bottom of Glueck's malfeasance. The ramifications of the serendipitous revelation of Abrahm's relatedness, however, were too momentous to be trusted to amateurs. Heinrich, meanwhile, had a motive of his own: to capitalize on the dealings of both Ivan and Felix."

"The horn of plenty," Olek said.

"You know what happened then," Victor said. "Subsequently, Thierbach called Glueck in, stated that the girl had vanished, and raised the subject of the woman. When Glueck still claimed ignorance, Thierbach commanded him to determine the whereabouts of the girl and the woman immediately. But he neglected to mention that Leora had died."

"It's the Devil's work," Olek said, remembering vividly how Sonya had demanded to accompany Leora to her new surroundings. It had been her idea, yet she could not bear to part with her. Eventually they had to drag her back. And Felix, who had bitterly complained that with the two of them under his roof he might as well be in the ghetto, fell poignantly in love with Leora, whom he called Jenny.

"When Theresa and Yanina broke the catastrophe to Felix, he was overcome with guilt because of his confession to Heinrich. Also, he was plagued by the notion that his lineage had something to do with it. Then, in grilling him, Glueck compounded his confusion by speaking of Leora as if she were alive. Felix dared not declare her death, but neither could he tolerate Glueck's discussion of her. So, asserting that she was out of his hands and that he knew nothing more about her or any woman, he drank himself out of his dilemma.

"Glueck must then have gone back to Thierbach and related Felix' story. Since Heinrich had already cracked Felix, Thierbach lost all confidence in Glueck. That might account for his disappearance.

"As for Ivan, his attempt to transfer his culpability onto Felix was fueled less by his obvious resentment of Felix' abusiveness than by the belief that Felix had sold him out to Heinrich. Ivan had stooped to black marketeering primarily, as he rationalized it, to amass enough money to buy his way to America. He was convinced that Europe held no future. His homosexuality may partially have stemmed from the war. He was impotent with Anna but not with men. Thus his deepest grudge against Felix was for saddling him with Heinrich for a partner."

"A tight circle," Olek said.

"Upon hearing of Leora's death, it struck Ivan oddly that Yanina had visited the convent several days before and found her in good health."

"It struck everyone," Olek said.

"Yes, but the extent of his complicity dawned on him only slowly."

"And it might never have if Heinrich hadn't botched Theresa's murder."

"Exactly," Victor said.

He flicked a wisp of tobacco from his lip with his tongue.

"What a mess," Olek said.

"You can withdraw from it now that Abrahm's safe," Victor said.

"Not until the books are balanced," Olek said.

"Glueck may have been rendered permanently inaccessible," Victor said.

"Thierbach and Heinrich deserve the same," Olek said.

"Agreed," Victor said. "But first things first."

He went to the bookshelf and fetched a pad of blank white paper and a thick green pencil with a soft black lead.

"Krecji was apprehended as he was leaving the station," Olek said. "If all went well, he was to have had a disassembled rifle strapped to his person. When he failed to meet Stefan as arranged, Stefan hurried to his house and removed his wife and son. That night two agents came around, questioned the neighbors, and left word that if his wife didn't present herself within forty-eight hours, Krecji would be executed. Stefan advised her against going. She went anyway. They interrogated her exhaustively, but Stefan had counseled her to secrecy about himself, and of course she was unaware of her husband's extracurricular activities in Radom. When they had finished, they said they would let her see him. A guard escorted her to a room with a small, barred window set into a massive steel door. Through it she could look into an interior passageway. In a few minutes Krecji was lugged into view. He was a gruesome sight. They propped him up for thirty or forty seconds, then hauled him away by the arms. He seemed barely conscious. His wife was taken back to the examiners, who said that to deliver him would cost 75,000 zlotys. Any clues to his contacts would reduce the sum accordingly. If she could not produce the ransom within seventy-two hours, her son would also be arrested. She returned hysterical. There's no sign that she was tailed. Probably they want a chance at the money. But time is limited. In Stefan's opinion, it's our obligation to assume responsibility for her and the boy."

"He's right," Victor said. "Morally and practically. It's hard enough already prevailing upon anyone to stick his neck out for us."

"We can situate them with Nicholas," Olek said. "But we have to act promptly."

"Isn't there enough trouble with Esther?" Victor said.

"As a matter of fact, Abrahm's doing much better with her and Ruth in there." Olek said. "He was losing touch."

"Five constitute a much more complicated system than three," Victor said.

"It won't prevent him from recuperating," Olek said. "If anything, it will stimulate him."

"I concede," Victor said.

He tore off a sheet cluttered with geometric doodles. "Now what about Stefan?"

"Undaunted," Olek said.

"Does he want to go into hiding?"

"He wouldn't consider it."

"How do we know he's not hot?"

"He vouches unreservedly for Krecji's toughness."

"Does he have any idea why Krecji was pinched?"

"Unfortunately no."

"What assurance do we have that Mrs. Krecji didn't betray him under duress, or won't?"

"That's another argument for stowing her away," Olek said. "But I'll guarantee you this—if they ever sink their claws into Stefan, the chain will break there . . . unless by some quirk of fate, instead of beating him, they leave a bottle of whiskey in his cell."

"How can you be so sure of him?" Victor said.

"He's been absolutely reliable," Olek said. "And you should see Joseph. Stefan's turned him into a regular demolitions expert."

"A peculiar fellow," Victor said.

"He's not afraid of anything," Olek said.

"When he's drunk," Victor said.

"Or when he's sober."

"How could that be?"

"He's an utter fatalist."

"Then why is he bothering with us?"

"To live up to his father," Olek said.

"So he does have faith."

REASONS
F O R
BEING

Ruth sat on her bed reading. Beneath her, Mrs. Adler played with her jewelry. On the lower of the middle bunks, Marc Krecji comforted his mother, who was crying. A sense of evening resignation ruled the bunker.

Abrahm occupied himself with scoring a bishop. Nicholas had given him a bag of wood scrap and a whittling knife. Thus far he had carved twelve pieces. When he had finished all thirty two, he would paint one set vermilion with the fingernail polish Mrs. Adler had donated for the purpose. Then he would fashion a board out of whatever was available.

He felt good. Ruth had asked Nicholas to measure him for crutches and it appeared that he would soon be up and around. Perhaps even in a week. The first thing he would do is go up for air. Already he could smell the grass and imagine the night fresh and cool against his face.

The Krecjis would fit in nicely, he reflected. Mrs. Adler and Ruth would have company, and after he left, there would be room for a third pair.

Mrs. Krecji was a plain, unassuming woman. He had

noticed earlier that her hands were chapped. She was garbed in a simple cotton house dress, yellow with a blue and green floral pattern, and heavy shoes. Besides her coat and hat, she had brought with her only an overnight bag. She had dark hair combed back into a bun, a narrow-bridged nose, and a brittle, frightened mouth.

Her son, Marc, was a boy of medium height and wiry build with a thin, chiseled face, alert eyes, and a shock of snuff brown hair. He looked to be a year or two older than Ruth. He said nothing to his mother as he held her, nor did he seem embarrassed by her crying. His features, too, expressed sadness over what had befallen.

"Why is she crying?" Mrs. Adler asked.

Her remark was intended to be *sotto voce*, but it was clearly audible to everyone. Ruth leaned down and whispered something in her ear.

"But maybe there's something we can do," Mrs. Adler said, still not realizing how loudly she was speaking.

Before Ruth could stop her, she had risen and traversed the several feet to the Krecjis.

"Would a cup of tea help?" she asked Marc.

"Mother?"

Mrs. Krecji shook her head against her shoulder.

"Thank you," Marc said. "Maybe later."

"It would settle her down," Mrs. Adler said. "An empty stomach heightens grief."

Commanding the situation, she poured a measure of tea and thickened it with an overdose of sugar. Then she pushed a crate over toward Marc.

"Would you like some too?" she asked.

"I can share this," Marc said.

He raised the warm cup and coaxed his mother into taking a sip. Her lips trembled. She wiped her eyes with the back of her hand and took another.

"Do you mind if I join you, just for a minute?" Mrs. Adler said.

"Please," Marc said, unable to refuse.

"How old are you?" she asked him.

"Almost eighteen," he replied.

"What do you do?"

"I'm an engineering student."

"My Ruth is planning to be a doctor," Mrs. Adler said. Marc remained silent.

"Is the tea all right?" Mrs. Adler asked.

"Yes, fine," Mrs. Krecji said.

The effort of responding to Mrs. Adler's kindness motivated her to collect herself. She smoothed her hair back and straightened her shoulders.

"I can understand how you feel," Mrs. Adler said. "You should have seen me at the outset. But I developed sea legs soon enough."

She smiled, eliciting a wan smile from Mrs. Krecji.

"Sometimes talking about things make them easier," Mrs. Adler continued. "They didn't tell us anything about you."

Mrs. Krecji glanced questioningly at Marc.

"Are you from the ghetto?"

"No," Mrs. Krecji said.

"Then from where?"

"We're Christian."

"No one told us," Mrs. Adler said.

Mrs. Krecji pressed her forehead against Marc's shoulder. Mrs. Adler thrust her fingers into her pocket, pulling out an orange candy which she unwrapped and popped into her mouth. It bounced noisily off her teeth like a billiard cue.

"Comrade Abrahm," she said, "were you aware of the background of these people?"

"Yes," Abrahm said, concentrating on the bishop he was sculpting.

"And you didn't say anything?" Mrs. Adler asked.

"What should I have said?"

Mrs. Adler glanced perturbedly at Ruth.

"There's no cause for alarm, mother."

"I'm not alarmed," Mrs. Adler said. "I simply can't fathom why they're here."

"For shelter, as we are," Ruth said, reverting to her loft.

"There's no ghetto on the Aryan side," said Mrs. Adler.

"There is," Marc said, "but of a different kind."

"How dare you?" Mrs. Adler said.

"The danger extends to everyone," Marc said.

"Shut up!"

"That's unfair, mother," Ruth said. "Let him explain."

Quietly, Marc traced the events that had necessitated their flight. As he spoke, he massaged his mother's back soothingly with his fingertips. Gradually, she gained composure, but Mrs. Adler grew visibly distressed.

"WHY?" Mrs. Adler erupted. "What drives them to it?"

Mrs. Krecji reached out for Mrs. Adler's hand.

"Father was approached by an old friend," Marc said.

"But he didn't want to do it," said Mrs. Krecji.

"If he didn't he wouldn't have," Marc said.

"Philip was a peaceful man," Mrs. Krecji said. "He kept his nose out of politics and crossed the street whenever he sniffed trouble. They must have threatened him."

She shuddered and her shoulders sank.

"He wasn't forced," Marc said. "He became despondent, having to pretend each day that nothing was wrong. 'People are dying unjustly,' he fretted, 'and no one is doing anything about it. You should see the faces in the station. Everyone is petrified. One has to be careful, but there must be something I can do. Something . . . ' "

"That was bravado," Mrs. Krecji said. "Late at night he would curl up to me and whisper, 'Xina, I'm so frightened. It gives me goose flesh just to go out in the morning. Who knows what lurks around the corner? It doesn't matter who you are anymore. You can be destroyed in a twinkling for no reason.' He didn't have the nerve for running guns. That no-good Stefan Mierck sucked him into it."

"He may have been afraid," Ruth said, "but that doesn't eliminate the desire or the capacity to act."

"You've been reading too many books," Mrs. Adler said.

"Father and I have been scared silly from the beginning," Ruth said. "Who hasn't?"

"Ruth's father is Dr. Emil Adler, the famous surgeon," Mrs. Adler explained. "He's more terrified of his friends than of the Nazis."

"Mother!"

"Deny it," Mrs. Adler said. "Emil doesn't want to die. They're holding him captive. Comrade Abrahm can vouch for it. He's the one they fear most."

Mrs. Krecji's head pivoted toward Abrahm.

"Emil is invaluable to us," Abrahm said. "But he has always been free to follow his own judgment. The hospital was founded under his guidance. He took it upon himself."

"You're grateful because he saved your life," Mrs. Adler said. "But who's going to save his? Not you."

"We've tried repeatedly to release him," Abrahm said. "He won't budge."

"That's your story," Mrs. Adler said. "But what's the purpose of treating patients who are going to die anyway?"

"How can you prophesy who's going to die?" Ruth said.

"We nursed Isaac back to life," Mrs. Adler said. "What good did it do? He was such a lovely man, but when he left our house, he didn't even recognize me. Everyone in the ghetto is doomed. But Emil has a way out. If only he would admit that his death won't save anyone else."

"It might," Abrahm said.

"It can't," Mrs. Adler said.

"That's exactly the impression the Germans have strived to create," Abrahm said.

"Well, they've succeeded," Mrs. Adler said. "Emil is sacrificing himself for nothing."

"Why is he doing it?" Marc asked.

"Because they've brainwashed him into thinking it's a

noble stand," Mrs. Adler said. "He's ashamed to spare himself now. As if the war was his fault."

"Who's 'they,' mother?" Ruth asked.

"You know better than I," Mrs. Adler said. "I don't have to name them."

"It's unfortunate they're killing people," Mrs. Krecji said, "but it's beyond our control."

"Mother believes that if Jews are being slaughtered, there must be some justification," Marc said.

"Wash you mouth with soap," Mrs. Adler said.

She raised Mrs. Krecji's hand and kissed it.

"May I call you by your given name?"

"Yes, of course," said Mrs. Krecji. "Xina."

"Xina," Mrs. Adler said. "How unusual."

"It's a reduction of Christiana," Mrs. Krecji said. "Philip's parents were Roman Catholic, but mine were Greek Orthodox. Father wore a thick black beard and always addressed me as Christiana. Mother favored Xina."

"It's very appealing," Mrs. Adler said. "Xina and Esther. After all, we're one big family now."

Mrs. Krecji withdrew her hand.

"Why would Philip have risked everything for so little?" she lamented.

"You're twisting it inside out," Marc said.

"Marc is right," Abrahm said. "Resistance is the only alternative to complicity. Your husband behaved as a hero."

"You stay out of this," Mrs. Adler said. "If it were up to you, we'd all commit suicide. That's why Emil is sacrificing himself on his feet while you're puttering in bed. He believes in you. You—a murderer!"

NO MAN'S LAND

It was a raw, oyster gray morning. Eugen edged his way carefully along an empty, desolated street. A bleak gust of wind whorled up and raked his legs. He recoiled against a building, shielding his face with his hand and turning his shoulder to the blast. His skin bristled with goose bumps and smarted.

The wind subsided, leaving behind a haunting silence heightened by creaking windows and the relentless stench of unburied corpses. There was no sign of life anywhere. After the last deportations the ghetto had been reduced to eight or ten acres partitioned into islands. Each remaining factory became a separate ghetto, with the workers billeted at their posts. No one was allowed outside. Those who had permission to inhabit apartments, including employees of the Judenrat, the Jewish police, and the Jewish hospital, were restricted to specified blocks. Between sanctioned residential and occupational quarters lay forbidden zones.

"Bvvv . . ." Eugen shivered as another flurry forced him sideways.

The basement where he had been hiding for some weeks now had grown chilly and dank as autumn encroached, but he would not have minded being tucked away in it this moment. Compared with the God-forsaken street, it was a warm, secure haven.

He would never have subjected himself to such turbulence had it not been a matter of final resolve. The fat had melted off his body entirely, his legs were wobbly from lack of exercise and malnutrition, and he had the dread apprehension that the wind would swirl him off the ground and dash him against a barbed wire fence or drop him into the freezing Wisla.

"Grrr!"

The first few days after his narrow escape from the *umschagplatz* Eugen had been almost paralyzed with fear. A pursuing bullet had creased his temple, nicking it just enough to inflict a burn, and his crushed fingers ached as if the Devil had personally undertaken to torment him. Nursing himself in seclusion, he reviewed everything he had learned about Bankart, piecing and repiecing together every fact, clue, rumor. Things which he had previously regarded as insignificant, or misinterpreted, or forgotten altogether achieved a perspective in seclusion. There was still no direct evidence of Bankart's whereabouts, but every line of reasoning, whether circumstantial or inductive, led to the same place: the bakery. Either Bankart was there, or someone there knew where he was.

Based on this conclusion, Eugen formulated a plan, but when he ventured forth to execute it, he discovered that the ghetto had been rendered virtually impassable. Discouraged, he retreated to rethink his strategy, and promptly sank into an abject depression. He became his own prisoner in the basement, going out only for food, and then at night, since anyone seen where he should not be would draw fire.

Also, it was the rainy season, and he wanted to spare his shoes and keep from contracting pneumonia. Each time it was wet, he promised himself that he would resume his search on the next dry day. But when it came and he had found something to eat and felt slightly revived, he would convince himself that he was better off taking advantage of the first fair days to regain his equilibrium. And while he waited, it would rain again.

Sometimes when he was confined for several days consecutively he was gripped by the deepest hunger. His fantasizing progressed considerably beyond salami, onions, eggs, potatoes, greens, and garlic. He hallucinated about Roquefort and Liederkranz, curried lamb, spiced aspic, baked apples drenched in cinnamon, and creamy chocolate and custard pastries laden with fruit and glazed with buttery icing. Frequently he recalled the menu at the Metropole, savoring the items wistfully and arranging them in numerous combinations. In his desperation, he suffered wide swings of indiscretion in which dogs, cats, rats and even less palatable creatures presented themselves as delicacies. Occasionally he pondered whether Bankart was similarly famished. For some reason, he could not picture Bankart starving. It began to worry him that his adversary was retaining his strength while he was growing weaker.

An even more disturbing thought for Eugen was that the longer he remained in pursuit of Bankart, the stronger his admiration for him grew. But it was not something he liked to dwell on. There seemed to be no way out of the ghetto now. Finding Bankart was his best hope for survival.

During this period Eugen's scalp wound healed and he regained the use of his middle finger, but his index finger obstinately refused to improve. Oversize, inflexible, and agonizingly sore, it jutted crookedly out of his hand like a vestigial claw. Consequently, he was prone to reflexive injury, and often jammed himself awake in the middle of a food dream. At one point he tried to contrive a splint, but the finger was too sensitive. Finally, he fashioned a padded sheath for it out of cloth from a pair of undershorts. It did not deter him from jarring it, but it absorbed some of the shock when he did and provided a measure of insulation from the penetrating dampness.

His hibernation lasted until he realized that winter was fast approaching and that unless he quit clinging to excuses for

inaction he might really freeze to death. He no longer harbored an illusions about mis-identification. Anyone who was
still in the ghetto and had no visible mark of privilege—a
uniform, an insignia, a well fitting coat, or a corpulent midsection—was a Jew.

Eugen proceeded cautiously down the street, walking on
the balls of his feet to prevent his heels from scraping. Under
his shirt, his chest was wrapped in a strip of the house-
painting canvas he had come upon in the basement and converted into a mattress. Instead of protecting his torso, it
seemed to make his arms and legs feel colder. The fingers of
his left hand stung as he trailed them along the front of a
building.

Clip-clop. Clip-clop. Clip-clop. Clip-clop.

Eugen halted. The wind was blowing in spirals and curli-
cues, making it difficult to gauge the direction of the hooves.
Their sound was distant and lonely, like the tugging of a
lighthouse horn or the distant chugging of a train.

As he listened, he clutched his collar tighter around his
throat. There was one horse and it was receding from him, but
he could not determine its precise course. He rotated his head
slowly. The hooves drifted. He envisioned the old man palming the reins, the solemn boy, and between them the beggar,
swaying blindly with the rocky motion of the wagon. Had the
blind man avoided the dragnet, Eugen wondered?

The clip-clop, clip-clopping faded. Then it revived,
faintly. He cocked his ears. Was it an echo from within?

He began moving again, freshly conscious of the stench
that rose constantly beneath the wind. One evening he noticed a foul odor in the basement. He tried to ignore it, but by
morning it was worse, and by nighttime it bothered him
enough that he slept with a piece of cotton over his nose. It
was raining, and the reek pulsated as if it were being driven by
a fan. The following night, when the sky had cleared, he
tracked the scent to a corpse that had been wedged between
the house and a utility bin. It was in such an advanced state of
decomposition that although it was naked he could not focus

on it to ascertain its age and gender. He wanted to absent himself and hope that it would be gone when he returned. But he knew he could not leave it there. The putridity would become absolutely unbearable. So he extricated the body, which had swollen rigidly into its entrapment, and dragged it out to the street by its feet, aligning it with the curb. It was there when he came back a while later, but the next time he went out it was gone.

Still, the smell haunted him even after the rains should have washed it away. More than once he had arisen from his sleep to check whether a new corpse was plaguing him. And now he smelled it as he made his way through no man's land.

Eugen touched his hand to his pillow case. Inside, his gun was reassuringly hard, discharging a sensation of power into his thigh. He had changed his mind about his encounter with the Jewish policeman. It would have been advantageous to be armed. Then he had thought it logical to stow the gun until the confrontation with Bankart. But circumstances had changed. Unless he kept it on his person, it was unlikely he would be able to get to it when the moment arrived.

Out of nowhere, the remote purring of a motor registered. Eugen's heart leapt. Had he been spotted? His eyes flashed the street. The nearest door was padlocked. There was a courtyard on the block, but before he could make a break for it, the grumbling had grown into a malevolent growl.

Panicked, Eugen dove down beside a half-rotten corpse that was sprawled with its legs extended beyond the edge of the sidewalk onto a grate. Instantly, the cloying redolence of decay stuffed his nostrils. But it was too late to switch positions. He heard the soft throbbing of tires on the pavement and then a hot squeal as the car banked the corner. His arms and legs were vibrating, and he imagined them flapping up in the air against his will, provoking a searing spray of machine gun bullets. His back spasmed, but miraculously his limbs stayed put as the car streaked by, its furious roar peaking in a whoosh.

Eugen endured his prostration until the last reverberations had played themselves out in his head. Then he rose and continued along the eerie street. Perhaps the old man relied on snuff, he thought, concentrating on not looking back.

His mind focused on Bankart. What crime could he commit now? Everyone was locked into factories, a few other authorized locations, and an inestimable number of attics and cellars. Yet any notion of abandoning his quest was behind him. If Bankart was still at large, he, Eugen, would have to find him, or he would never be found.

When he was almost to the bakery, Eugen paused to rest. His calves and arches were strained from toe-stepping. Raising each foot, he flexed his ankles and shook out the tension.

He was persuaded that Bankart could be ferreted out through the bakery. Finkel had withheld information from Thierbach, and Eugen suspected the same was true of the man with the narrow face and his muscular comrade. He had analyzed all the particulars. This time he knew exactly how to handle the situation, and would not be deterred.

Emboldened by the coherence of his reflections and the solidity of his gun, Eugen turned onto the street where the bakery was. From a doorway, he observed the circumscribed factory area. Two guards stood conversing at the gate. Were it not for the sludge-black smoke pumping out of the chimneys, they would have appeared to be defending a deserted fortress.

As Eugen surveyed the landscape, something he saw, or rather did not see, unnerved him. He mentally rearranged everything before him as it had been prior to containment. He recalled the yard and the bread line and the fallen woman stretched out with a sheet of paper covering her face. Now there were no corpses on the street, indicating that the wagon was still stopping near the gate. But where he remembered the bakery to have been, there was neither a door, nor a window, nor any trace of an opening—nothing but a solid wall.

PAUNCH
MANURE

All but the final lamp were extinguished and everyone was gathered at the far end of the bunker. From Abrahm's viewpoint, across the length of the room, they conjured up the image of Plato's cave.

"Xina is first tonight," Ruth said.

She climbed onto the crate that was set below the vent and unbolted it.

"Ready."

Marc blew out the last light and Ruth opened the hatch. Quickly she stuck her head through the opening, scanned the night, and cleared the way for Mrs. Krecji, who mounted the box while the others waited patiently. Marc kept time. He tapped his mother in the small of the back to signify that thirty seconds remained.

A finespun breeze was wriggling through the bunker, frailly stimulating circulation as it threaded the stale air. Abrahm drew it slowly into his nostrils. From the refreshing softness of the stir, he judged that it was raining. He felt slight solace that there was still a world outside that had not changed wholly beyond recognition.

The coolness abated and the lamps went on. Ruth patted her mother's hair dry with a cloth and offered to do Mrs. Krecji's.

"You don't have to," Mrs Krecji said, accepting her gesture.

"We don't need any colds," Ruth said.

Marc went over to Abrahm's cot.

"Do you want your light on?" he asked.

"I suppose so," Abrahm said.

Marc struck a match.

"It's raining," he said, blotting his face on his sleeve.

"I can smell it," Abrahm said.

Abrahm's left hand rested on the Bible which Nicholas had given him.

"Are you religious?" Marc asked.

"No."

"You'll be taking your turn soon."

"Not soon enough."

Ruth approached Marc and began toweling his hair.

"Leave him alone," said Mrs. Krecji, combing her tresses.

"He'll catch pneumonia," Ruth said.

"He doesn't require your assistance," Mrs. Krecji said.

Abraham propped the Bible up on his stomach and resumed his excursion into the past.

"There, you're sneeze-proof," Ruth said, finishing her rubdown.

Mrs Krecji and Mrs. Adler unfurled their curtains and prepared for bed.

"Go ahead," Mrs Adler said to Ruth. "I'll watch out for him."

Marc tarried near Abrahm while his mother undressed behind the screen. At his back, Mrs. Adler stood eying him vigilantly.

"It's a bit like Noah's ark," Abrahm said.

Marc smiled bashfully.

"All right, mother," Ruth said.

Mrs. Adler stepped into the enclosed area.

"Whistle when you're set," Ruth said.

"Oh no," Mrs. Adler said. "You stay here with me."

"Don't be silly," Ruth announced.

"Done," Mrs. Krecji announced.

Marc removed everything but his underpants, pinned up the divider, and slipped under the covers.

"What's going on out there?" Mrs. Adler said.

The aroma of a butcher shop floor freshly sprinkled with sawdust lingered in the bunker. Abrahm thought musingly of a late summer afternoon, and then of a torrential storm. According to Olek, there were no more than fifty thousand survivors in the ghetto. One in ten. Characteristically, the Germans had managed it before the weather deteriorated. They had a dark and gloomy Black Forest nature, but they liked to do their opprobrious business on Mediterranean days.

The bunker started out its slumber in a fit of whispers.

"What was that?"

"What?"

"Shhh!"

"Did you hear anything?"

Poof!

Abrahm's light went on.

"Oh, my God, what's he doing?" Mrs Adler said.

"Marc, come over here," Abrahm said.

"Don't go," Mrs. Krecji said.

But Marc had already bolted and was standing beside Abrahm. Although he was in his underpants, his slim, boyish physique appeared nude in the yellow pale of the lamp.

"Don't look," Mrs. Adler said to Ruth.

"Quiet."

"Unbolt it slowly and back off," Abrahm said.

"What time is it?" Mrs. Adler asked.

Ruth rose to silence her. Marc disengaged the bar and withdrew to the Adler's side of the bunker. Something warm touched his flank as he crouched on the floor.

The door opened suspensefully.

"Vaczek."

Two figures lowered themselves through the trap.

"Oh!"

Olek secured the latch.

"It's all right," Abrahm said.

"Who is he?" Mrs Krecji asked.

Marc reared up from his squat at Ruth's feet and sat down beside his mother.

"He has a gun!" Mrs. Adler said.

"Is there anything I can do?" Ruth said.

She came forward, stopping in front of the Krecjis. Marc noticed that her nightdress was too small for her.

"Close the curtains," Olek said.

Ruth turned toward Marc, catching his eyes on her breasts. His penis shifted in his underpants. Embarrassed, he procrastinated rising.

"Ruth," Mrs. Adler called.

"Yes, mother," Ruth said, approaching and untacking their black drape.

Marc followed suit, as did Olek, unfurling the third cloth and drawing up two crates. Victor leaned down and kissed Abrahm on the forehead. His fleecy hair exhaled a hayseed fragrance. Abrahm saw that his face was tallow. He clasped his hand, pressing the cold flesh.

"What happened?"

"Burned."

"Someone ransacked the apartment while he was out."

"Jesus Christ."

"It may have been more than one person."

"Did they take anything?"

"The silver cigarette case from the mantel," Victor said, "the paper and tobacco, some stationery . . ."

"They could have gone to the store for that," Abrahm said.

"The chess set . . ."

"What do you make of it?"

"I don't think they were searching for valuables," Victor said. "At least not exclusively. The bookcase had been thoroughly raked, every volume riffled, but the shelves had been rearranged to appear unrummaged. The dresser, on the other hand, was left in disarray. A few personal effects were missing, but it wasn't a haphazard job."

"Could it have something to do with Krecji?" Abrahm said, mouthing the name.

"I doubt it," Olek said.

"Are we any more enlightened about his arrest?"

Olek shook his head.

"So there could be a connection."

"It's a long shot."

Victor drew a cigarette from his pocket, pinched off an end, laid it in his palm, stripped off the paper, gathered the tobacco with his thumb and forefinger, and inserted it into the fold between gum and cheek.

"Someone might have been followed there," Abrahm said.

"Possibly," Victor said.

"It might even have been Heinrich," Olek said.

"Wouldn't you have known?" Abrahm said.

Olek shrugged.

"It could have been an accident, too," he said. "A routine inquest."

"Was anyone else in the building disturbed?"

"Negative," Victor said.

"Are you certain?"

"I went downstairs to register a complaint," Victor said.

Abrahm smiled.

"He did," Olek said.

In quiet tones they discussed the implications of the raid. The immediate consequence was to dislodge Victor from his seat of operations. Until they could investigate further and re-evaluate his cover, they could not afford to leave him exposed.

"The final say is yours," Victor stated.

"Luckily, we have one berth available," Abrahm said, pointing to the space above him. "The price includes room service and two meals a day."

"I can sleep on the floor," Victor said.

"There's no need to," Abrahm said. "You won't bother me and besides, I'm slated to be up and around shortly."

"I'd better get going," Olek said.

"What's the hurry?"

"I like the rain."

"Be careful," Abrahm said.

"If we play it tight, they'll be back," Victor said. "I guarantee you."

"In the meanwhile, don't step on a mine," Abrahm said.

"I won't," Olek said. "And when they return, will Comrade Mierck have a surprise for them!"

Nicholas froze at the sight of the tiny, elegant man with the white hair and silvery gray mustache.

"How do you do?" Victor said.

Puzzled, Nicholas glanced at Abrahm.

"An emergency," Abrahm said. "Victor, meet Comrade Nicholas, our keeper."

"I've heard so much about you," Victor said.

"I'm afraid I don't understand," Nicholas said.

He stood holding a sack.

"Comrade Victor was forced to go underground immediately," Abrahm said. "Olek brought him here."

A frown darkened Nicholas's face.

"Why didn't he tell me?"

"It was late," Abrahm said, "and there was no chance to warn you."

"I would have preferred to be awakened," Nicholas said.

"Hopefully, it won't happen again," Abrahm said.

Gloomily, Nicholas surveyed the bunker.

"Where's Olek?" he asked.

"Come and gone."

"There were no footprints outside."

"The rain must have erased them."

"Completely?"

"He didn't fly away."

Nicholas' eyes fell.

"How long does Comrade Victor intend to remain here?"

"Indefinitely," Abrahm said.

"There's not enough room," Nicholas said.

"Instead of five children, you now have six," Abrahm said. "You designed for as many."

"But you require special conditions."

"Not any more," Abrahm said. "Just get those sticks ready and I'll be hobbling around like a latter-day Pinnochio."

"You'll have them on time," Nicholas said.

"I'm the only cripple with his own carpenter," Abrahm said.

"You're a blessed man," Victor said.

Abrahm slurped down the bottom of his coffee.

"Let's see how you're doing this morning," Ruth said.

She unswathed his leg.

"It looks good," she said, probing the tenderness. "Much better than last week."

Victor watched as she bathed the wounds and administered clean bandages.

"Are you comfortable?" she asked.

"Perfectly," Abrahm said. "Now bring on the crutches."

"Be patient," Ruth said.

* * *

Victor extended his clenched fists.

"The right one," Abrahm said.

Both hands unlocked.

"You're white," Victor said.

He replaced the pawn atop the crate whose surface had been marked off into sixty-four squares. Every other square contained an X.

Abrahm made the first move.

"Truthfully, how do you feel?" Victor inquired when they were further into the game.

"Anxious," Abrahm said, concentrating on the board.

"You seemed to be wincing earlier," Victor said.

"It's sensitive," Abrahm said, "but that's to be expected."

"Have you thought of summoning a doctor?"

"Why?"

"Consider it," Victor said.

"Your move," Abrahm said.

"I'm not qualified," Victor said, "but my impression is that you're not as well as you might be."

"Ruth," Abrahm summoned. "Could we disturb you a minute?"

"Yes?"

"Victor thinks I'm decomposing. Can you cheer him up a little?"

"What specifically?" Ruth asked.

"He appears to be weak and in continuing pain," Victor said, "though he tries to conceal it."

"The discomfort is natural," Ruth said. "He should start to regain his strength as soon as he gets out of bed. The rest will follow."

"What about the swelling?" Victor asked.

"It has been somewhat slow in subsiding," Ruth said, "but we're doing our best."

"Would you characterize his recuperation as normal?"

"More or less."

"Which?"

"There's no fixed pattern for these things," Ruth said. "He's a tiny bit behind schedule, but recently his progress has been good."

"The wound is still discharging," Victor said.

"The incision is slightly inflamed," Ruth said, "but it's too far healed to tamper with. It will clear up by itself."

"Are you sure?"

"He's in fine condition," Ruth said. "There's no need to worry."

"That's all I wanted him to hear," Abrahm said.

Ruth hesitated a moment, considering another remark, but withheld it. Victor and Abrahm returned to their game— Victor with one hand under his chin, smoothing his goatee, Abrahm braced on an elbow, his tufted eyebrows bunched tensely.

"Satisfied?" he said to Victor.

Ruth and Marc were reading side by side.

"Dear, I'd like a word with you," Mrs. Adler said.

"What is it mother?"

"It's private," Mrs. Adler said.

"Can it wait?"

"That's what I propose to discuss," Mrs. Adler said.

"What do you mean?" Ruth said.

"You'll find out."

Ruth glanced at Marc.

"Never mind him," Mrs. Adler said. "I'm your mother."

Reluctantly, Ruth placed a marker in her book and walked over to her mother, who was perched on a crate, presiding over her valise.

"Here I am."

"Oh, Ruth, I just can't seem to locate the stockings to go with my peach skirt," Mrs. Adler said.

She dug her arms into the mass of goods in the suitcase and fluffed it up like cake batter.

"I'm almost positive they were here the other day," she said. "You haven't seen them, have you?"

Mrs. Krecji, who had been keeping Mrs. Adler company while she fussed with her trousseau, looked on vaguely.

"Have you Xina?"

"No."

"I wonder where they could be?" Mrs. Adler said.

"You didn't call me over to ask me that," Ruth said.

"What?" Mrs. Adler said. "Yes. I plan to wear them."

"You don't even have a peach skirt," Ruth said.

"I always meant to get one," Mrs. Adler said. "Actually, the stockings belong to that apple green skirt your father adored."

"You probably left them both behind," Ruth said.

"And then I thought, Xina's been so kind, attending to me, maybe she'd like a few precious minutes with her son."

"Don't be concerned about me," Mrs. Krecji said. "You have such lovely things. I'm enjoying myself."

"A mother should spend as much time as she can with her child," Mrs. Adler said. "In the past year, I've barely been with Ruth. Isn't that so, dear? I feel as if I hardly know her anymore . . . as if the war took her away from me. And now that we're together, with nowhere to go, she's more of a stranger than ever. She plays doctor and nurse and helps everyone and when her chores are done she buries her head in a book. Our clay heroes huddle over their silly chess game all day and Ruth sits next to your Marc, nice and cozy, as if they were lifetime friends. Can't they read separately, or is that the way they studied where he went to school?"

"I'm very admiring of your daughter," Mrs. Krecji said. "The way she cares for Comrade Abrahm, and her dedication to becoming a doctor. I'll be grateful if Marc is influenced to be as diligent."

"Well, I wish you'd see to it that he keeps to himself," Mrs. Adler said. "Your appreciation seems to be a family disease."

"Surely, you have no cause to insult me," Mrs. Krecji said, standing.

"With your permission, I'd like to confer with my daughter," Mrs. Adler said.

"Don't start anything," Ruth said.

"Dear, what a way to address your mother," Mrs. Adler said. "I see we do need to have a talk."

With unaccustomed vigor, Mrs. Adler jumped up and drew the curtain around their space.

"What are you doing?" Ruth asked.

"It's about time we got this out into the open," Mrs. Adler said.

"Don't shout mother," Ruth said. "It doesn't make sense to enclose ourselves if you do."

"I'm not shouting," Mrs. Adler said, modulating her voice. "But you'd think we could have a conversation without shushing me. No one can hear us through the walls, you know. We're surrounded by worms and dirt, that's all, and the dogs. Maybe some bodies are buried there, too, but they're deaf if they are."

"But we're not alone in the bunker," Ruth said.

"That's the problem," Mrs. Adler said. "One couldn't do anything in the ghetto anymore, and now we're confined to this tomb and I can't even breathe loudly. Why are we here if we can't behave like human beings?"

"We all feel cooped up," Ruth said, "but complaining only makes things worse. Our burden is to pull together."

"You can pull all you want," Mrs. Adler said. "I'd rather pack my bag and check out of here."

"Where would you go?" Ruth asked.

"America."

"Instead of aggravating yourself, why don't you pretend that we're on a pleasure cruise, in a stateroom for six."

"Must I remind you that there's no air on this ship," Mrs. Adler said. "No sun, no wind, no waves, no dawn, no dusk. Just that sourmilk leg of his. I can't sleep because of it. And the gun. Why does he need a gun?"

"Lie down and let me give you a massage." Ruth said.

"And one of those needles?" Mrs. Adler said. "Oh no you don't!"

"Then calm yourself and tell me what's bothering you today."

Mrs. Adler looked around nervously, as if the curtain were animate.

"That boy," she said furtively.

"What about him?"

"He's no good."

"What do you mean?"

"The way he stares at you," Mrs. Adler said. "When you change Comrade Abrahm's bandages, or exercise, whatever you do, he follows you with those beady eyes."

"You're not imagining this?" Ruth said.

"Not on your life," Mrs. Adler said. "He watches you like a peeping Tom. Especially your breasts. It's disgusting how he ogles them. If not for me, he'd break his neck spying on you while you were undressing."

"Mother, your voice is too high," Ruth said.

"The truth never hurt anyone," Mrs. Adler said. "No child pervert is going to feast his eyes on my daughter. Especially a Catholic."

"It's impossible to avoid visual contact in such cramped quarters," Ruth said.

"He doesn't have to leer that way," Mrs. Adler said. "You're not a pot roast."

"For once we agree," Ruth said. "Now, unless I can be of further assistance, I'll go back to my book."

"That's another thing I don't like," Mrs. Adler said.

"I'm listening."

"You two snuggle up as if you were reading," Mrs. Adler said, "but I'm not fooled by what's going on over there."

"What?" Ruth demanded.

"You know very well," Mrs. Adler said, "and I'm warning you, I won't have it. If he so much as lays a finger on you, I'll cut it off, do you understand?"

DEVIL'S LUCK

Huddled at his observation point not far away, Eugen watched the early morning changing of the guard. The sky was still gray, and the factory loomed like a dark beast beneath the white moon.

During the night the wind had died down and given way to a chilling drizzle that gnawed at his bones and set his body trembling. He had not had anything to eat or drink since leaving the basement the day before, and the scraping of rats and the building crackling had rendered his sleep sporadic.

Sometimes he had been able to doze off again immediately after being aroused, but other times there were seemingly interminable spells of wakefulness. Whenever he looked out, he saw only one guard at the gate. He surmised that they were taking turns keeping warm inside the factory. But once, deep in the night, he peered out and found the entrance unattended. He flirted with the idea of going down, but let it pass. The next time he came to, there was one guard again.

Now the new sentries assumed their posts and the old ones shuffled off sleepily, as if they had been flanking the gate at attention all night. In the grayness they appeared powerless and forlorn, their authority transferred onto the men who had replaced them.

Eugen glanced down at his left arm. From up close, the blue lines on his sleeve were abstract scores in a geometric pattern. He did not feel as if he was wearing a star. But from afar, on other people, Eugen was frequently struck by the numbing force of the symbol.

His finger ached with cold. If it came to trouble, he would have to pull the trigger with his left hand. The gun would fire just the same, but his aim . . . no, he had renounced all excuses. He cupped his palms under his mouth and blew into them, but the warmth of his breath dissipated before it could penetrate his skin.

The fresh guards positioned themselves alertly for several minutes. Then one of them produced a coin, flipped it in the air, trapped it on the back of his glove, read it, returned it to his pocket, and marched off into the factory, leaving his partner to stand watch.

With great relief, Eugen viewed the three corpses that had been laid out near the gate sometime during the night. There was no paper over their faces. When he had first noticed them, toward the morning, he felt like a child who had deposited a tooth beneath his pillow and found a shiny gold piece in its place. He had guessed correctly about the wagon.

It was stroke of luck that he had heard the horse's hooves. Had he set out somewhat earlier or later, he would have been at a dead end when he discovered that the bakery was gone. But the clip-clopping had given him an idea. If the old man were still driving the rig, and if, miraculously, the beggar had survived, there might be a way to make contact with the fellow with the narrow face. Another thought presented itself, but he suppressed it. The most he could hope for was a lead. Bankart would not simply be there waiting for him.

There was nothing to do but bide time. Eugen checked the padding he had improvised around both shoes to muffle his steps. The left one, which had been further damaged in trying to escape the policeman, was bound tightly to his foot. He blew into his hands again. It would be nice to have a pair of gloves such as the guards had. Yet, he thought, the man on duty at the moment probably felt as cold as he did, knowing that his partner was warmer and more comfortable inside.

Clip-clop. Clip-clop. Clip-clop. Clip-clop.

The sound was distant, more an echo in the damp air than a stone repercussion, but clarifying. Eugen checked his gun a last time and gathered himself. Quickly, he crept down the stairs to the street and picked his way along to within striking distance of the gate.

The guard seemed to be sleeping on his feet. He appeared as indistinct at short range as he had from afar. The dawn had melded with a fog. Behind the fence, the factory remained shrouded in a grizzling haze. The moon had almost faded, but the dark chimneys were still fuzzy, and the dense atmosphere promptly smothered the pulsating gushes of black smoke.

Clip-clop. Clip-clop. Clip-clop. Clip-clop.

Eugen experienced a roiling in his bowels, and a flock of images swarmed his mind like scattering geese. He forced his eyes to measure the span from where he stood concealed to the corpses, to the gate, and to the factory entrance. Then he calculated the number of seconds it would take to traverse each leg. The wagon would arrive and load and depart and he would have to make an instantaneous judgment, perhaps two.

Clip-clop. Clip-clop. Clip-clop. Clip-clop.

The guard gave no indication that he heard the hooves. Eugene crouched down, ready to dart out and fling himself corpselike onto the sidewalk. The wagon issued from the mist like an apparition—appearing first as a large smudge on the horizon and gradually assuming shape. The horse appeared distorted, its bony form bleared by the gray fog, but as it drew nearer, Eugen saw its feet pistoning, clip-clop, clip-clop, and the bodies swaying on the bench.

He closed one eye to heighten focus, then the other. There were only two persons aboard. Evidently the blind man had not made it. He was about to commit himself when an instinct stayed him. Again, he shut an eye and telescoped the fog. There was something arresting in the motion of the bodies . . . the one on the right was swaying in a tight, stable arc . . . he was sure that it was the old man . . . but the one on the left was lurching from side to side like an unbalanced pendulum. It was not the boy after all, but the beggar.

Someone must have been looking out for him, Eugen reflected. He watched the horse move abreast of him, never quite shedding its blurriness, and pass. One decision had been made.

As the wagon creaked to a halt before the gate, the guard snapped to. Approaching, he addressed the old man, who stood up in the bench well. The beggar did the same. The old man gripped him under the arm pits and lowered him to the guard. Then he resumed his seat. Without the reins being touched, the horse pulled out, hauling its charge toward the three corpses.

The guard let the beggar take his arm and led him across the yard, the knotted loop at the end of his rope trailing them along the wettish ground. Eugen set himself. As they disappeared inside the factory, he sprinted into the open. Racing toward the unguarded entrance, he glanced down the street at the wagon. The driver was stooping over with his back to him. Instead of stopping at the gate, Eugen bolted into the yard, stopping only when he reached the wall near the entrance.

His heart thumped like a kettledrum. What luck! The beggar was still alive. He felt peculiarly sanguine about finally encountering Bankart. Behind him, the old man was scooping up the third corpse. Thus far Eugen had gone unnoticed. But he was completely exposed now, and any moment either of the guards might emerge.

Holding his breath, Eugen edged up beside the doorway and listened in. Silence. He stretched his neck and peeked into a small, drab anteroom that was empty save for a hard chair and a smudge pot. There were doors to the left and right, but they were closed.

Eugen withdrew his head. He would have to make a choice he had not counted on. But there was no delaying. As the wagon groaned and started with a slow initial cadence—clip, clop, clip, clop—Eugen dashed into the vestibule and broached the door to the right.

CYCLOPS

The singer droned on despite a flinty hoarseness that sand-papered her already rough voice. Between lines she blew here nose into a crumpled handkerchief, resuming her song without a break in her distant, mechanical aplomb.

A waiter swooped in and delivered a plate of hors d'oeuvres to the table recently occupied by Olek and Thierbach.

"I hope you've eaten since the last time I saw you," Thierbach said.

Resplendent in a black dress uniform, he tipped his head back and stuffed a piece of pink ham and a green olive into his mouth.

"I've been worried about you."

The bright red swastika on his sleeve glistened as if it had been put on with fresh paint.

"I'm touched," Olek said.

He scrutinized Thierbach's attire, trying to reconcile the impression it made with his civilian appearance.

"I have a sincere concern for your welfare," Thierbach said.

He picked up another morsel of ham, then changed his mind and replaced it in favor of a slice of sausage, popping it into his mouth like a peanut. His walrus neck hardly moved as he swallowed.

Without his uniform, Olek thought, Thierbach had come across as a rather gross but not invulnerable bully—physically robust, perhaps, and overbearing, but degenerately corpulent and ultimately fallible. Now, however, he seemed like a much more formidable man—powerful, cunning, willfully offensive, beyond ordinary danger.

"You haven't lost any weight over it," Olek said.

"I don't intend to tolerate your impudence," Thierbach said. "Quite the contrary, I propose to deal harshly with you."

"As harshly as you dealt with Herr Glueck and Ivan Voytek?" Olek said.

Thierbach's mouth hooked in irony.

"What do you mean?"

"That you were responsible for Voytek's disappearance."

"Surely, you're joking," Thierbach said.

"I'm not."

"Where did you hear this canard?"

"From Erdmann."

"He told you that I disposed of Voytek?"

"He said that you tortured him."

"How would he know such a thing?"

"Voytek confided in him."

"It's preposterous."

"Didn't you?" Olek said.

"He was interrogated," Thierbach said.

"Call it what you will."

"We do not employ torturous methods," Thierbach said.

"For humanitarian reasons."

"Exactly," Thierbach said. "But that's neither here nor there. We obviously had nothing to do with Voytek's disappearance. If we did, why would we be tracking him?"

"I'm unconvinced," Olek said.

"Do you doubt my word?"

"That's beside the point," Olek said. "You may not be fully aware of your implication."

"It's curious," Thierbach said. "For months you don't have any information, and now all of a sudden you know more than I."

"You ordered me to find out as much as I could," Olek said.

"Indeed."

"So I did."

Thierbach glanced around uneasily, as if he perceived something invisible. Then, peering down at the hor d'houevres, he snapped his fingers for a waiter.

"At your service," the waiter said, simultaneously rushing and calm.

"Take this away," Thierbach said. "I can't look at it."

The waiter removed the plate from the table.

"Would you like your chicken now?" he asked.

"No," Thierbach said. "Coffee and cognac."

"And for you?"

"Coffee," Olek said.

He watched Thierbach's eyes follow the waiter back to the kitchen. Several times they digressed, skipping nervously to the curtain.

"Expecting someone?" Olek said.

Thierbach returned his attention to Olek.

"I don't care to be overheard," he said.

"Through the door?"

"It's merely a habit," Thierbach said.

Oil began to break from his skin.

"What was it you were saying about Voytek?"

"We were discussing your involvement in his demise."

"Precisely how did I cause him to vanish?"

"It was through him that you learned that the girl who had stayed with Erdmann had been taken to a convent and was Bankart's granddaughter."

"You certainly have researched the matter," Thierbach said.

"A man can't simply forfeit his business," Olek said.

"Of course not," Thierbach agreed.

The waiter swept in with a sterling coffeepot, matching sugar bowl and cream pitcher, spoons, china, and a jigger of cognac. Poising the cream pitcher in one hand and the coffeepot in the other, he poured adeptly from both at once into each cup, creating a walnut froth.

"But again, I must inquire as to your source."

"Voytek, through Erdmann," Olek said.

"I see," Thierbach said.

He took a lump of sugar and dunked it into the coffee, watching the capillary action turn it brown.

"The magic of physics," Olek said.

Thierbach deposited the beige cube on his tongue and pressed it against the roof of his mouth.

"I interrupted you," he said, sucking the sugar. "You were recounting what Voytek allegedly told Erdmann."

"So I was," Olek said.

He dropped three lumps of sugar into his coffee, stirring them in unhurriedly.

"Then proceed," Thierbach said.

Anxiously, he raised the cognac and sniffed it. Then, dipping a finger into the jigger, he coated his gums.

"When he told you about the girl, Voytek had no idea you were going to kill her," Olek said. "Otherwise . . . "

"I beg your pardon," Thierbach said.

"Had he known what would happen, he would have kept his peace even under pain or death," Olek said. "When he found out, he remained silent in the hope that no one would discover his betrayal."

"You're making a grave charge," Thierbach said.

"Don't blame the messenger," Olek said.

"Fugitives who cannot be cross-examined are hardly reliable," Thierbach said.

"He no longer had motivation to lie," Olek said.

"The world abounds with pathological liars," Thierbach said.

"He would have stayed in the bag had Bankart not suspected foul play and sent someone to investigate."

As Olek spoke, the door opened and closed and a figure stepped through the black curtain. Thierbach's head jerked toward the entrance. Instantly, his grim expression gave way to an unctuousness that reminded Olek of chicken fat smeared on bread. The newcomer approached a nearby table. Before he could sit down, Olek saw that it was Heinrich.

"I'm afraid you're harboring a shameless fantasy," Thierbach said.

He sipped his cognac, perceptibly relieved.

"You might be right," Olek said.

"Still, it is my duty to explore thoroughly," Thierbach said. "Only I don't entirely grasp your scenario. Who contended that the girl was harmed?"

"Bankart's people. They confronted Voytek with their surmise."

"Do you subscribe to it?" Thierbach asked.

"It's Voytek's story."

"So," Thierbach said, "They kindly apprised him that in their opinion the girl had been murdered."

"They accused him of giving her up," Olek said.

"And how did he respond?"

"He denied it emphatically and attempted to shift his culpability onto Erdmann."

"Attempted?"

"Evidently they knew that Erdmann was unaware of the girl's identity."

"The connection eludes me."

Having taken a seat at an angle favorable to his good right eye, Heinrich had requested whiskey and was glaring past Thierbach's shoulder directly at Olek. He was wearing an umber tweed suit and a black and green plaid tie. Neither reciprocating nor avoiding his stare, Olek conducted himself as if Heinrich were not there.

"The girl was used to bait a trap for Bankart," Olek said.

"I must caution you against calumnious hearsay," Thierbach said.

He started to glimpse sideways but caught himself and rolled his eyes up in thought. After a pause, he mixed the balance of his cognac into his coffee.

"They must have paid Erdmann a tidy sum."

"He did it at his own expense," Olek said.

"Why on earth would he?" Thierbach asked.

"Out of the goodness of his heart," Olek said.

"Am I to believe that?" Thierbach said.

"That's up to you," Olek said.

Peripherally, he observed that Heinrich had lit a cigarette and was flashing its fire at him like a second eye.

"If they thought Voytek a traitor, they undoubtedly eliminated him," Thierbach said.

"They didn't lay a hand on him," Olek said.

"Bankart is merciless," Thierbach said. "I assure you he's responsible."

"He would have snuffed him out right away," Olek said. "But once Voytek's guilt was established, he was of no further danger to them. Just the opposite. They reasoned he might prove to be of help."

"You give them considerable credit," Thierbach said.

"I'd be a millionaire if not for them."

"If not for us, you'd be kaput."

"No one is immortal," Olek said.

"That is true," Thierbach said. "But there are many ways to meet one's maker."

"How many?" Olek said.

"Let us not be macabre," Thierbach said. "You hypothesized that Voytek may have been spared. Elucidate."

"It's very simple," Olek said. "They squared with him and enlisted his cooperation. He was scared shitless and stricken with remorse."

"So it was not until they found him useless that they did away with him?"

"They may be hiding him," Olek said.

"Without anyone having been notified?"

"As you know, he was subject to intense pressure from several sides," Olek said. "Having gotten all they could from him, they might be fulfilling their promise of protection."

"And yet before he was spirited off he made a confession to Erdmann?" Thierbach said.

"It appears that way," Olek said.

"What a strange family," Thierbach said.

"Not at all," Olek said.

"Then why would Erdmann have sacrificed himself?"

"He didn't," Olek said.

"You're not going to tell me he's still alive," Thierbach said.

"No," Olek said, shaking his head.

"Well, what are you saying?"

"You frightened him to death."

"That's not funny," Thierbach said.

"It's not meant to be."

"What else did he divulge besides Voytek's perjury?"

"That you met him here under a pretext."

"Yes?"

"And threatened him with prodigious unpleasantness if he didn't provide a lead to Voytek."

"I'll admit I wasn't easy on him," Thierbach said. "But if your account is accurate, he was guiltless."

"Which made the terror worse," Olek said.

"War takes its toll of innocents," Thierbach said.

A wave of nausea rose in Olek. He drew a toothpick from his pocket and lodged it in the corner of his mouth. Heinrich was glowering at him with such intensity that his eye seemed to be growing larger.

"It's unfortunate," Thierbach went on, "But inescapable. As for Voytek, I venture that he has been granted eternal safekeeping."

He cocked his hand, bringing the waiter scurrying.

"We'll eat something now," he declared. "A portion of chicken skin for me, never mind the chicken. And what about you, my friend?"

"Fresh coffee," Olek said.

Thierbach dismissed the waiter, sneaking a view of Heinrich in the process.

"A lot of weird people here," Olek said.

"I must say, you've done your homework," Thierbach allowed, ignoring his remark.

His mien had relaxed, and his voice was uncommonly civil, almost genial.

"I took your ultimatum at face value," Olek said.

"You needn't worry, at least for now," Thierbach said. "I didn't expect you to be so informative."

"I'm doing my utmost to stave off disaster," Olek said.

"What intrigues me particularly is why those assassins would conjecture that the girl had been victimized," Thierbach said. "Was anything mentioned about that?"

"According to Erdmann," Olek said, "his wife had visited the convent a few days before and found the girl fine. Then suddenly she took ill. In the hospital, a Sister who was with her the whole time became suspicious of the care she was receiving—but the administration refused to change the attending physician. In the time between the girl's death and the funeral, the Sister somehow passed word of her misgiving to Bankart. He showed up at the funeral, but . . ."

"What?" Thierbach interrupted.

"Bankart came to the funeral . . ."

"It's impossible!" Thierbach said.

Impulsively, he cast an ill-concealed glance in Heinrich's direction.

" . . . but as a precautionary measure, he waited awhile inside the hospital."

"Erdmann revealed this?"

"Yes," Olek said.

"But he didn't know Bankart."

"The facts were imparted to Voytek by Bankart's people."

"They claimed that he was actually there?" Thierbach asked.

There was a strain of piqued incredulity in his voice.

"He was in the hospital," Olek said, "but he left after the service was disrupted."

"I don't understand," Thierbach said.

For the first time a tinge of color seeped into his pasty visage.

"It seems that a person unknown to anyone in the funeral party intruded upon the ceremony with the excuse that he had been invited to another funeral to be held at that time. The Sister tried to dispose of him, but he insisted on staying. Bankart observed this and got away."

"Was it someone he recognized?"

"Yes."

"Who?" Thierbach demanded.

"They didn't say,"

"That still doesn't substantiate their speculation that the girl had been maltreated."

"It was the Sister's murder that did it."

"How?"

"The girl died neatly," Olek said. "But the Sister was butchered. They figure that the funeral trespasser may have killed her, but not the girl. That would account for his odd behavior. He had manifestly come for Bankart. When he didn't see him, he was baffled. So he stood there until they carried the coffin off to the cemetery."

"Why is that strange?" Thierbach asked.

"If he had known who the girl was and that she had been put to sleep, he wouldn't have walked out into the yard like that. He would have lain in ambush. And if he didn't know, why would he have expected Bankart to be there? Therefore he must have been on assignment. And if he was, why would he have wound up indelicately executing the Sister?"

The color in Thierbach's face shaded from turbid pink to bruised pear yellow.

"They're exceedingly theoretical for a pack of dogs," he said.

"I haven't had an easy time with them," Olek said.

"I can appreciate that," Thierbach said. "Their imaginings are preposterous, but there's formidable streak of cleverness in them."

"Herr Glueck may have contributed something to their insightfulness," Olek said.

"The possibility has occurred to me more than once," Thierbach said.

The waiter slithered up and set a plate of broiled chicken skin, carrots, and potatoes in front of Thierbach.

"Coffee is coming," he said, hurrying off.

Making a concerted effort to keep his eyes on Olek, Thierbach removed the napkin from his lap and tucked it into the collar of his uniform.

"You strike me as a shrewd man yourself," he said.

"I'm a pragmatist," Olek said.

"If this intruder, whoever he was, had not been so bungling, things might have turned out differently," Thierbach said.

He pinched a crisp of browned skin and plumped it into his mouth, crushing it vigorously with his teeth.

"Could be," Olek said.

"They're apt to be plotting retribution," Thierbach said.

"It wouldn't surprise me," Olek said.

The waiter returned with steaming coffee. As he served it, Olek took advantage of his interference with Heinrich's view to sight him slantingly on the blind side. His glass eye was fixed on the singer like a camera.

"But things did not turn out differently," Thierbach said, his manner becoming more aggressive," and we still do not have Bankart in our custody. The problem is begging to be solved."

Thierbach leaned forward, bearing in until he seemed to be supporting the table on his lap.

"Now," he said, "have you found out anything?"

Olek faced him coolly, keeping his arms folded across his stomach.

"Haven't I told you enough?"

"You've been very enlightening," Thierbach conceded. "But your immediate mission was to develop intelligence expressly in regard to Bankart's whereabouts. Have you made any progress?"

"To be perfectly honest, I have," Olek said.

"Don't be facetious, Thierbach warned. "You haven't much room in which to maneuver."

"I'm conscious of that," Olek said.

Thierbach moved even further over the table, gripping its sides and embracing it as if it were a sculptural extension of his uniform. His spoiling features softened into an apprehensive intimation of a smile.

"Do you know where he is?"

"I know where he isn't."

"Yes," Thierbach said impatiently.

"He isn't in the ghetto."

"Then where is he?"

"He's abandoned the city."

"Are you certain?"

"No."

"From whom did you hear it?"

"Various people. Clients. Contacts."

"Rumor!" Thierbach whispered gruffly. "That's what you dished Herr Glueck. I want facts."

"I can't make them up for you." Olek said.

The table slid forward, pressing against his forearms.

"What is his alleged destination?"

"Some say England," Olek stated. "Some say America. Some say he just went into the forest."

"The first two would be entirely out of character," Thierbach said. "The third is conceivable—there has been a puzzling decline in the resistance level recently—but I would be reluctant to accord it serious attention without some sort of corroboration."

"That sounds logical," Olek said.

The toothpick hung from his lips like a loose tusk.

"What is your viewpoint?" Thierbach asked.

"Personally, I would guess he might still be in the ghetto." Olek said. "But wherever he is, I don't think you're going to catch up with him now."

"Why not?"

"You haven't yet," Olek said. "And if you ever had a chance, the Sister's murder choked it. It was done so cruelly, it didn't leave anything unanswered. You might as well throw away your files and save your tricks."

A round of applause accompanied the singer off the platform. The spotlight was extinguished and the overhead lights switched on. In the transition, Heinrich's false eye emitted an elongated sparkle, like a lens reflecting a latent image.

"You're being overly negative," Thierbach said. "With persistence, and your expert help, it's only a matter of time until we snare him."

"I was hoping to wean you from my services." Olek said.

"I sympathize," Thierbach said. "But as admirably as you've done, its premature."

"What if the grapevine's accurate and he has sought refuge?"

"The farther he is from here, the better," Thierbach said, "although it would be disappointing in one respect."

"Are we finished for the evening?" Olek asked.

"Unless you would enjoy a nightcap at the Britannia," Thierbach said.

"No thanks," Olek said.

He pushed himself away from the table.

"Someday I'll have to escort you home," Thierbach said. "Just to see how life proceeds near the river."

Standing, Olek felt an excruciating desire to snatch Thierbach's fork out of the carrots and plunge it, like Ulysses, into Heinrich's unquenched eye. But he restrained himself, having consigned the privilege to Thierbach.

UNDERGROUND

Eugen awoke in a coal black room the size of a large closet. Where was he? His squinting eyes saw nothing. He closed them again. His head ached on the right side, behind his ear. The pain pulsed like a radio signal between his auditory canal and his right eyeball, which felt as if it were being lanced with a long needle. He kept it shut, unsealing his left eye to confront the darkness.

Around him Eugen heard the muffled polyphony of whirring machinery: the hoarse roar of power, the grinding of gears, the screeching and whining of saws and drills, the spinning of lathes, and a composite rhythmic suck and blow.

He touched the wall. It was cool and faintly throbbing. Tentatively, he withdrew his hand and slammed it slowly against the plaster. It produced a dull, solid thwap. He pulled back a second time and smacked the wall hard enough to make his palm smart. Once more, the same flat thud.

Dazedly, he leaned his ear against the wall. The kinetic noises diffused and whitened, as if the room were filling up with water. When he removed his ear, it broadened and grew sharper, as before.

"It's hot as hell," he said to himself, wiping his forehead. It was slightly damp, and his body had broken into a thin sweat that was dribbling from his armpits down his ribs beneath the canvas wrapping.

He wanted to remove his shirt, but dared not. What if the door suddenly swung ajar and he had to scramble out? Door? He had no recollection of having entered the room, and in the darkness there was no indication of a door. Of course, he had only probed one wall. He would have to examine the others. But not until he had established his bearings.

"Impossible," he said, folding his legs so that he was sitting in a lotus position. He closed both his eyes and envisioned himself racing across the street, behind the wagon, through the gate to the building, and into the antechamber. The morning was raw and then the smudge pot sent off a wave of warmth and the next thing he knew he was in a black space whose shape he was frightened to explore.

He reached down blindly to draw a handkerchief out of his pillow case. His hands came up empty, descended again, and bobbed up and down as if it were grasping for a phantom limb. The pillowcase was gone!

Unbelievingly, he groped about for it, careful not to jolt his injured finger. Gone! A horrible realization spun through his mind. Getting onto all fours, he described a creeping circle, sweeping the floor with the palm of his left hand and the heel of his right. It was bare.

Something pricked his arch. He grabbed his foot. A metal sliver had penetrated his sock. His sock. His shoe. His shoe? His other shoe? His shoes were missing too!

They were gone, and the pillowcase, and with it not only his linen and whatever else he owned, but also his gun! It was the one thing he could least afford to lose. Now, as he was closing in on Bankart. He should never have allowed himself to panic into bringing it with him. It was like the question of

life: it made no sense to take it today—one could always take it
tomorrow.

But the option had been eliminated. At any time the
room might open, however it opened, and Bankart would rush
in and attack him and he would be virtually defenseless. He
could not even run.

"Excuse me, Comrade Bankart," he would say. "I regret
to inform you that you are under arrest. Unfortunately, in my
search for you, I've misplaced my gun, but I do hope you'll
cooperate."

He burst out laughing.

If he pounded on the walls, he would probably find the
door. But someone would also hear him. He did not feel like
facing anyone at the moment. It would be better to acclimate
first to being without shoes. Besides, whoever had locked him
up would have to look in on him sooner or later.

Or perhaps there was no door. Perhaps they had built the
room around him. He had no idea what time it was or for what
duration he had been incarcerated. Perhaps he was dead.
Entombed.

Little bubbles began squirting around in his stomach,
forming a gas. The Egyptians had buried their most honored
citizens with a supply of edibles. He had still not eaten since
quitting the basement. Yet had he been asked what food he
most desired, he would not have been able to reply. De-
spairingly, he shoved the back of his hand against his mouth
and started sucking the hairy skin on his wrist.

Licking himself, Eugen pictured the beggar, eyeless,
slurping his soup and rubbing his gums over a bit of potato.
Why had they allotted him enough nourishment to sustain
several healthier persons? There were the lines, "Left! . . .
Left! . . . ," and the final quarantine, and perpetual starvation,
and an ongoing business for the old man, and his wagon, and
no explanation for the bakery. The boy was no longer on the
bench, but the beggar was still there, riding the bumps like a
spectral equestrian. Someone was taking care of him. Not only

on the defunct bread queue. The guard had greeted him and shepherded him into the factory as though he were officially welcome. How could that be?

As if he had transgressed a forbidden divide, a metallic creaking issued an alarm. Eugen jumped. The siren ceased. He angled his head futilely in quest of it. Shortly it resumed. Then the sounds of machinery heightened, and the frailest thread of light prayed into the crypt.

CRUTCHES

A chicory incense spiced the stagnant bunker air. Victor raised his cot and lashed it to the wall, opening up the space above Abrahm. In his long underwear, divested of his elegant suit, he resembled an elderly schoolboy who had gone off to camp for the summer and neglected to shave.

"Would anyone like coffee before breakfast?" asked Mrs. Krecji, who had taken over responsibility for the kitchen.

"I wouldn't mind some," Victor said.

"Wouldn't mind?" Abrahm chaffed. "You couldn't see straight without it."

"That's not so," Victor said.

"I suppose you wouldn't mind a cigarette either," Abrahm said.

"You're a sadist," Victor said.

Ruth came out from behind her curtain, which remained closed to shield Mrs. Adler.

"You're certainly boisterous this morning," she said, smiling at Abrahm.

"Did you hear that?" Abrahm said. "Our Mother Superior thinks the old goat's acting up."

"Let's hope so," Marc said, grinning.

He had put up his set of bunks and was studying a chapter on bridges. Having been assigned maintenance, there was nothing for him to do until later.

"It is a big day," Ruth said, "but you should conserve your energy. You'll need it."

"Don't worry," Abrahm said. "If I don't work off a little now, I may just walk right out of here."

"Coffee?" Victor asked dourly, offering Abrahm the cup that Mrs. Krecji had handed him.

"With that scowl, it must be bitter," Abrahm said.

"It isn't," Mrs. Krecji said. "But no matter. I'm fixing you tea this morning."

"There's an understanding woman," Abrahm said.

To please everyone, it had been decided that tea and coffee would be served on alternate days.

"By what authority is this exception being made?" Victor inquired.

"Divine," Abrahm said.

Ruth arranged her supplies around him and began to strip his bandage. He winced as she removed the last of the wadding.

"How does it feel?" she asked, swabbing the wounds.

"Better than yesterday," Abrahm said.

He was propped nearly upright and beaming.

"It still looks angry," Victor said.

"We've been through this."

Victor continued staring at the knee.

"Is it progressing?" he asked Ruth.

"Gradually," she said.

Deftly, she fashioned a fresh dressing under Victor's observation.

"You won't overdo it," Victor said.

"Go on," Abrahm said. "It hurts you worse than it does me."

He lifted his leg vigorously, lowered it, lifted it, lowered it, five times in all and then, after a pause, another five.

"And another," he said, beginning a third round.

"You really ought to save your strength," Ruth cautioned him. "The first excursion will be more difficult than you might expect."

"So were the first twenty-five years in the slaughter-house," Abrahm said.

His remark prompted a smile from Victor. Ruth viewed him uncertainly.

"I can understand your consternation," Victor said. "You thought him a steady, well-behaved patient and now he's in a state of agitation somewhat beyond what you're accustomed to. But let me assure you, this is innocuous compared with what will manifest itself as he improves. Under normal conditions, he's a wild man."

"Don't ruin the surprise," Abrahm said.

"Rather, I want to spare us the embarrassment," Victor said.

"You're finally admitting that I'm on the upswing?" Abrahm said.

He resumed exercising his leg.

"Do yourself a favor," Victor pleaded.

Mrs. Krecji dropped a few shreds of tea into a glass, put a spoon in, and poured hot water over it.

"What service," Abrahm said.

"Are you all right, mother?" Ruth asked, taking her place beside Marc.

"Fine, just fine," Mrs. Adler said from behind the curtain.

No one seemed to pay attention to Marc and Ruth sitting abutted like Siamese twins.

Nicholas held Abrahm's legs off the mattress as he rotated sideways and inched his buttocks forward until he was perched on the edge of the cot with his feet extended out over the floor.

"After the war we should mount a trapeze act," Abrahm said.

"Who's planning to end it?" Victor asked.

"This has to be done efficiently," Ruth said. "Once we get you up, you're going to walk to the curtain and back. The we'll ease you down in reverse."

"How many trips?" Abrahm asked.

"One," Ruth said.

"That's hardly worth my trouble," Abrahm said.

"We'll see," Ruth said. "Now drop your left leg gradually."

Retaining Abrahm's right leg, Nicholas released the left. It descended slowly until it almost reached the ground. Abrahm grimaced.

"Give me the crutches," Ruth said.

She received them from Marc and directed him to stand on Abrahm's left.

"Nicholas should be on the right," she said. "He'll have all he can do to keep his foot off the ground."

"Let it drag," Abrahm said spiritedly.

Nicholas transferred Abrahm's right heel to Victor.

"Hold it, lightly," he said.

"You'll experience some dizziness upon becoming vertical," Ruth said. "Don't fight it. We'll support you. Just concentrate on controlling your leg. It will quickly grow heavy and start to burn."

"Fortunately, I'm fireproof," Abrahm said.

"As Victor lets go, push off with your hands and up on your good leg. You'll get help from both sides. Are you ready?"

Abrahm drew a long breath and braced himself. Nicholas and Marc held him on either side.

"Ready," he said.

In one movement, Victor relinquished his grasp and Abrahm felt himself gravitating toward the floor and weight piling onto his leg and an equalizing force jerking him upward. Ruth and Victor grabbed him in front and steadied him as Nicholas and Marc adjusted their grips.

"Is it bearable?" Ruth asked, stepping back.

Abrahm grunted. The color was filtering from his face

and his shoulders were straining against a fierce downward tow. Ruth slipped the crutches in under his arms.

"Plant them ahead of yourself, not too far, six or nine inches, sloping . . . wider apart . . . that's it . . . and swing your body through the arc."

The blood pumped into Abrahm's arms as he hopped forward, and his triceps delineated like stone stirrups.

"Now again," Ruth said, retreating before him.

He followed the hem of her smock, clenching this teeth, his head bowed with exertion. A searing pain began flowing into his legs, inflaming his foot. Faltering, he barely managed to snatch himself out of his discomfort by intensifying his commitment to Ruth's skirt.

"And again," he heard her say.

From his bed the curtain had seemed a few effortless paces away, but it appeared to be receding as the floor danced around Ruth's feet.

"Once again."

Two or three more strides would do it, Abrahm thought, but he could not be sure. A liquid fire was raging in his foot, and he was succumbing to vertigo.

"Again."

His forearms twitched.

"Again."

The crutches were transfixing his armpits. If he crumbled, he would try to slump toward Nicholas.

"Yet again."

Abrahm was almost blind when they helped him turn around. It was too torturous to rest. Closing his eyes, he summoned up a reserve of will, advancing his crutches, swagging through, sustaining the elevation of his leg.

"You're doing excellently," Ruth said.

Abrahm sucked in his breath and strained to visualize the curtain, his bed, anything to divert his draining consciousness from the seething flush that was consuming his leg below the knee. He no longer waited for Ruth's commands. Each pendulation generated the momentum for the next.

"We're here."

A white pain shocked Abrahm's system as he was relieved of his crutches and his legs were guided clockwise over the cot. Then his heels touched the mattress and he fell back, drenched in sweat.

A cloying fragrance spread rapidly throughout the bunker.

"Mother, what on earth are you doing?" Ruth asked.

She set her book down and rose from her seat beside Marc just as the curtain billowed and Mrs. Adler emerged wearing a black floor-length evening gown with lace decolletage and slender velvet straps over her otherwise bare shoulders. One gloved hand was muffed in lynx, and her heavily powdered face was harlequin with turquoise and silver eye shadow, a mouth unnaturally wide with fuchsia lipstick, and cheeks penciled with oversized black beauty dots.

"Good morning," she said cheerfully.

"Morning was some time ago," Ruth said.

Her voice expressed annoyance.

"You'd think the sun shone around here," Mrs. Adler said. "I didn't wish to interfere with Comrade Abrahm's acrobatics."

Reeking of perfume, she sidled toward the center of the bunker.

"Congratulations, Comrade Abrahm."

"Shhh! He's sleeping," Victor said.

"No, I'm not," Abrahm said.

"You'll be leaving us soon, won't you Comrade?" Mrs. Adler said.

"I'm afraid so," Abrahm said.

"What would you say if I declared I was going with you?"

"To the ghetto?"

"Of course not."

"Then where?"

"Out of Warsaw. Away from Poland."

"Sorry," Abrahm said. "I'm going back."

"On spider legs?" Mrs. Adler said. "With four attendants providing a safety net wherever you move? The ghetto's no place for cripples."

"I'll make it," Abrahm said.

"In that case, if you have no objection, I'll accompany you as far as the corner," Mrs. Adler said.

"And from there?"

"I'll head West."

"You'll be much safer here," Abrahm said.

"But I've grown so used to the smell of your leg," Mrs. Adler said, "I probably wouldn't like it here without you."

Victor slid his crate even with Abrahm's cot and posted himself facing him closely.

"If only Eleazer could see you poring over the Scriptures by candlelight."

"He'd have an attack," Abrahm said.

"So may I," Victor said.

"Why?"

"You're not the type."

"Who is?"

"I wonder."

"Nicholas?"

"Also not."

"But this is his," Abrahm said, laying down the Bible.

"He's an anomaly," Victor said.

"Aren't we all?"

"Still, I wouldn't have guessed it would infect him," Victor said.

"It's full of animals," Abrahm said.

"Does that explain it?"

"It helps," Abrahm said.

"Nothing helps," Victor said.

"That's untrue," Abrahm said. "Nothing cures."

"There must be more," Victor said.

"There is," Abrahm said. "He believes it word for word."

"Historically?" Victor asked. "Or spiritually?"

"Both," Abrahm said. "And he can quote you chapter and verse."

"Behold," Victor said. "Nicholas, who would not contract with any group, has been converted into a reverent Christian."

"I'm not certain whether that or covertly into a Jew," Abrahm said. "But he's become damned religious."

"And you couldn't mold a socialist of him," Victor said.

"A socialist has to believe in man."

"Doesn't he?"

"Never."

"Then what are you, for whom he risks his life?"

"That's a good question," Abrahm said.

"There must be an answer."

"Whatever I was ten years ago."

"Have you changed?" Victor asked.

"No," Abrahm said. "But he has."

"How?"

"He's acquired faith in himself."

"Success?"

"Partly."

"But that doesn't account for his dedication to you, let alone the hazard to which he's exposing himself on behalf of the rest of us."

"He didn't volunteer, remember."

"Yes," Victor said. "But given the responsibility, he's done a superior job."

"He doesn't know how not to," Abrahm said.

"Neither do you," Victor said.

"I haven't achieved any milestones recently," Abrahm said.

"That's what concerns me," Victor said.

"Pity you," Abrahm said.

Victor moved forward so that his face was intimate with Abrahm's.

"I hope you won't go before you're ready."

"I'm still here, aren't I?" Abrahm said.

"But you're scheming to get out as quickly as you can."

"It's a sign of health," Abrahm said.

"You're not well," Victor said.

"Don't be a washerwoman," Abrahm said.

"You're in no condition to go anywhere," Victor said.

"All I need is a little practice hopping around," Abrahm said.

"How can you navigate the ghetto on crutches?" Victor said.

"It won't wait for me," Abrahm said.

"What will you do in your state?"

"Be there."

"As long as you're hobbled, you're more valuable here."

"The subject bores me," Abrahm said.

"That walk took quite a bit out of you."

"It wasn't so bad."

"You were bleeding perspiration."

"I was hot."

"Melting," Victor said. "And gritting your teeth."

"There was some burning below the knee," Abrahm said. "But it's only a matter of circulation."

"Is it uncomfortable now?"

"It's not too bad," Abrahm said.

Casually, as if in the process of reaching into his pocket for a candy, Victor brushed Abrahm's good leg, jostling it against the sore one and causing him to flinch.

"Hey," Abrahm said, pressing his hands against the mattress to float the pain.

"I'm sorry," Victor said.

"You don't have to kill me to stress your sentiment," Abrahm said.

"You refuse to regard it seriously," Victor said.

"I thought I'd never get out of here," Abrahm said.

"Do you know why you failed to make a socialist out of Nicholas?"

"Why?"

"Because you didn't think he should be one," Victor said.

"I didn't think he could be one," Abrahm said.

"Because he was a loner?"

"Because he was incapable of believing in anything," Abrahm said.

"But you said he had become a believer," Victor said.

"A believer is someone who doesn't believe in anything," Abrahm said, "and so reaches out for something to exercise faith in. It might have been different if he had stayed in the slaughterhouse. But that's ancient history. The question now is, what do we believe in?"

"Resistance," Victor said.

"What about liberty, fraternity, equality?"

"As always," Victor said.

"A new and better world for all?"

"Yes."

"Even if there's no one to live in it?"

"There will be," Victor said.

"There will be *nothing!*" Abrahm said.

The word impacted like a cork jammed into the mouth of a bottle.

"Has Nicholas converted you, when Eleazer couldn't get you to stop fighting on Saturdays, let alone pray?"

"I've learned to appreciate oats," Abrahm said.

"Don't rush off before you're mobile."

"How did you get back on that?"

"There's no sense throwing yourself on the altar," Victor said.

"I don't intend to," Abrahm said.

"If it could do any good, I'd go in your place," Victor said.

"You're not afraid to die?"

"Afraid, but able."

"So am I," Abrahm said.

*   *   *

The bunker was dim. Everyone was assembled near the vent.

"Marc, come over here and give the old man a boost," Abrahm said.

He was sitting crosswise on the cot, as he had prior to being walked before breakfast and dinner.

"You've done enough for today," Victor said.

He extended his arm to check Marc.

"You're neither the doctor nor the patient," Abrahm said.

"I don't have to be to see that you're spent," Victor said.

"All the more reason I need some air," Abrahm said.

"It is too much for you," Ruth said. "Tomorrow you'll be stronger, and soon a new man."

"Tomorrow is fine," Abrahm said, "but first tonight."

"You're not a jack-in-the-box," Victor said.

"Marc, will you do me a favor?" Abrahm said.

Torn, Marc remained immobile.

"Then it'll be done without you," Abrahm said.

He slid arduously toward the wall where the crutches were posted and seized them in his left hand.

"Abrahm!" Victor said.

Resolutely, Abrahm transferred one crutch to his right hand and inched toward a position from which to raise himself.

"Abrahm, please," Victor said, rushing over.

Excitedly, he attempted to wrench the right crutch from Abrahm's grasp.

"Get away," Abrahm snarled.

"You must come to your senses," Victor said, hanging on to the crutch.

"If you won't help, stay clear," Abrahm said.

But Victor refused to yield. Exasperated, Abrahm recoiled his arm and thrust out, crutch and all, slamming his fist into Victor's chest. The blow propelled him several feet backward.

"I'm obviously not going to fight with you," Victor said, "but I implore you to simmer down a minute and reconsider."

His voice was tremulous.

"What is there to deliberate?" Abrahm said. "I've been breathing earth fumes and body rot and belly gases for too long now. I'm entitled to some goddamned air."

"Who would disagree?" Victor said. "If you would only forbear another two or three days."

"I've waited the limit," Abrahm said.

He planted his crutches on the floor and prepared to hoist himself up. Victor ran his tongue over his lips.

"All right," he said. "We'll assist you. But with deep reluctance."

"God forgive you," Abrahm said.

"It would be much safer if Nicholas were here," Victor said.

"But he's not," Abrahm said restively.

With Ruth fronting him and Marc and Victor on either side, Abrahm struggled to his feet. His body quivered under the strain of self-support.

"It would be better to wait until morning," Victor said, as Abrahm ventured a step.

"Get ready down there," Abrahm said between his teeth.

"We'll need more crates," Victor said.

When they reached the vent, Ruth and Victor mounted the cubes which Mrs. Krecji had provided in addition to the ones normally positioned beneath the hole. Stooping down, they enabled Abrahm to place his arms around their shoulders. At Marc's direction, Mrs. Krecji took hold of his left thigh just under the crotch, and Marc interlaced his fingers and slipped them under Abrahm's foot to serve as a lift. Mrs. Adler stood by to extinguish the lamp.

Abrahm channeled his courage into his good leg.

"You can have my time," Marc whispered, crouching to heave.

"Now," Victor said.

* * *

Abrahm experienced an awesome burning in his ailing limb, but it did not matter. The first gasps of fresh grass-perfumed air after so many sunless days and starless nights were like an exhilarating infusion of mountain oxygen. This was how Noah must have felt, he thought, after the diluvial waters subsided. The earth was still there.

Instantly, as though his blood had been regenerated, he was returned to an earlier reality. He had entered the bunker with the expectation that his stay would be short. Thus, Olek's initial visits were purposeful. The news he brought was essential. And he reacted to it vitally. But gradually—with time, pain, and frustration—this consciousness grew abstract. Increasingly, he used Olek's appearances selfishly—to personalize, to small talk, to indulge in the sedative warmth of their friendship. As if a clear detailed photograph had been duplicated through an abused negative, his memory and perception of the ghetto had waned, becoming blurred and grainy. Until finally Olek's presence evolved as an end in itself.

Victor's discussion of resistance had also progressively declined in substantiality. Resistance had been synonymous with existence, but life in the bunker was not existence, it was barely subsistence. The desire to hold out lingered, but the hardened instinct for retribution withered. There was little to withstand underground except the tendency, if not the absolute necessity, to detach completely from any previous actuality in order to render interment endurable.

It was as with his health. For the period that he had been bedridden, he had sunk helplessly into acceptance of his condition. But upon receipt of his crutches, he sprang instantly out of the mire. Now, although he was not yet walking, he was once again capable of resisting.

Without being able to see it, he sensed that the moon was sharply projected against the Prussian sky. Ruth had opened the trap with the hand that was pressed to his abdomen, and there were hands on various parts of his body, as there had been during the operation. The sweet night air was analgesic.

He was on the verge of a new phase. But it was grievously too late in terms of the hundreds of thousands of Jews whose fate had already been sealed. Resistance within that framework had become practically meaningless. Instead, it had assumed a primarily symbolic aspect. It no longer stood for physical survival. It stood rather for courage, integrity, and boundless love for those who had died.

It stood for revenge.

It stood to show the Nazis the tragic hollowness of their victory.

It stood to redeem all those who, for whatever reasons, had not resisted in their time—the millions of Jews and non-Jews who, stunned by the German onslaught, caught unorganized and unarmed, had not done anything until lives as numerous as grains of sand, including their own, had been wasted.

It stood to repay the Jewish police for their cowardice and cruelty.

It stood for defiance toward the beast of the *umschlagplatz*.

And it stood to demonstrate to the world that the Nazis were not invincible—that a handful of besieged Jews, half-famished and unequipped, could oppose them at a disadvantage of five or ten to one, a hundred to one, a thousand, and no matter how powerful and seemingly insuperable a machine-image they had created, they were fundamentally base, demented men encased in steel shells filled with entrails.

Abrahm felt someone tapping him on the kidney. Thirty seconds.

He drew an extended breath, swallowing as much air as he could. His lungs pumped revivingly, absorbing nourishment, expelling accumulated dust and toxin.

Resistance stood for Leora, lying in the same ground through which his head was sticking, not a morning away, and Eleazer, buried within kite-drift of her, and all the others who were there and wherever.

It stood for Heykel and Sonya and Joseph and Isaac and everyone else who was still alive.

It stood for the fighting front, and within it, the Bankart division.

And in the final uprising, in the cluster of a few fragile, honeycombed blocks that had shrunk irrevocably in his absence, resistance would stand for life to come.

Abrahm took a last gulp of air. Soon, in a few days, he would be resurrected. He felt volcanically infused with the motivation to practice furiously on his crutches, to regain his strength quickly and become ambulatory, and to fling himself back into the battle.

The ghetto was so near, and yet so far.

PROTECTIVE CUSTODY

"I was wondering when I'd see you again."

Eugen trained his ears, trying to capture the voice. It was familiar in tone, but elusive. A different tongue had commanded the forces that had entered the darkness where he was imprisoned, blindfolded him, tied his hands behind his back, and led him through a maze to the room in which he was now sitting. It was quite large, as far as he could tell, and sounded like a workshop of some sort. From the footsteps in the foreground, he judged that there were four or five people moving about. They spoke in whispers, and he could not ascertain what they were doing. Above him and slightly to his right, someone stood guard. He held as still as he could, cowed.

"Who are you?"

Little dots and specks of light sparkled before his tightly bandaged eyes. The voice was civil but insistent. Who was he?

"Well?"

The portrait of "Noah/Age 12/In the forest" floated to mind. Ephraim Schloss meant nothing to him.

"Silver," Eugen said. "Noah Silver."

"German?"

"Yes."

"You were shipped here?"

"Yes."

"From where?"

"Dresden."

"Alone?"

"No," Eugen said. "With my wife and child."

Deep in the background he thought he discerned the droning of a bell.

"Where are they?"

"Gone."

"Deceased?"

"Deported."

"Why aren't you with them?"

"My place is here."

"You stayed behind voluntarily?"

"Yes."

"Couldn't they have done the same?"

"They chose to go," Eugen said.

His voice tripped over the image of Tzipora marching to the *umschlagplatz*.

"Do you have a work card?"

"No."

"A billet?"

"No."

"Any identification?"

"No."

"But you did have."

Eugen paused. The voice he could not quite place was cool, low, of medium pitch, not unpleasant, but resolute.

"In your hat," the voice went on. "Someone ripped it out."

"It was a policeman," Eugen said. "He wanted to turn me in."

"What happened?"

"I resisted," Eugen lied.

"How did he get the papers out of your hat?"

"I was momentarily unconscious," Eugen said.

He slunk ahead of himself, straining to anticipate the questions.

"Did you kill him?"

"I might have."

"What have you been doing since?" asked the voice.

"Hiding."

"You parted with your family in order to hide?"

"Not intentionally."

"Be clearer."

"There are a few of us," Eugen said. "We didn't foresee the final partitioning. It locked us in."

"You're a group?"

"Yes."

"How many?"

"Five."

"And you all remained without your families?"

"Yes."

"Why?"

"To fight."

"On your own?"

"If need be."

"Are you in contact with anyone?"

"No."

"Where are you based?"

Eugen pressed his lips together unresponsively. He sensed several pairs of eyes staring at him.

"Speak up."

"Where am I?" Eugen said.

"Don't ask, answer," said the voice. "What brought you here?"

A cold point touched against Eugen's forehead. He stiffened.

"I saw an open gate," he said.

"You were strolling by?"

"I was looking for the bakery."

"What bakery?"

"The one beside the factory."

"There is no bakery there."

"There was a bakery attached to the factory."

"Did you find it?"

"No."

"You were looking for a bakery that isn't there?"

"It used to be there."

"When?"

"Some weeks ago."

"More precisely?"

Eugen squirmed to relieve the pressure of the wood slats crimping his back. He felt as if he were being welded to the chair. The voice was at an angle to the gun, nuzzled hard to his brow.

"I'm not sure," he said. "Six, eight."

"But it's not there any longer?"

"No."

"It just vanished?"

"Apparently."

"Then how do you know it was there?"

"I saw it."

"Perhaps you merely think you saw it?"

"No, I definitely saw it," Eugen maintained. "I even stood in line."

"Six or eight weeks ago?"

"Yes."

"And not more recently?"

"No."

"Why not?"

"It's been too dangerous to venture out."

"But you risked it now?"

"I was ravenous," Eugen said.

"Do you get hungry every six or eight weeks?" asked the voice.

"I became desperate."

"So you traversed a forbidden area and trespassed on factory grounds in quest of a bakery that wasn't there?"

Eugen drew his head back fractionally, disengaging it from the steel.

"You have one minute to explain yourself."

Behind the blindfold, the interior sky sparkled with multicolored stars. Eugen strove to navigate the swirl.

"You're lucky we remembered you," said a second, less sympathetic voice that seemed to belong to the chilling prod that returned to his forehead.

"Your time is up."

There was ratchet sound.

"I was searching for someone."

"Who?"

"A man named Abrahm Bankart."

The cold point left his skin and the room became muted.

"Do you know him?"

"Indirectly."

"How?"

"That must be kept a secret."

"You have our word."

"I can't divulge it."

"What choice have you?"

"Regardless."

"What is it you want with him?"

"Something personal."

"Why did you expect to locate him at the bakery?"

"He was well-known there among the workers."

"On what do you base this?"

"I asked around."

"Where?"

"On the street."

"And everyone directed you to the bakery?"

"Not everyone."

"Anyone?"

"Yes."

"Who, for example?"

"I don't have any names."

"How long have you been poking around?" asked the second, gruffer voice.

"A couple of months," Eugen said.

"You must have questioned a thousand people."

"Quite a number."

"And you don't recall a single name?"

"Obad Finkel," Eugen said.

"Who?"

"Obad Finkel."

"Is this someone you met during the course of your investigation?" asked the first voice.

"No," Eugen said. "A member of our party made the acquaintance."

"And introduced you?"

"No."

"Then why did you mention him?"

"Because he had some connection with the bakery."

"Yes?"

"According to him, I was told, Bankart could be reached through certain individuals there."

"Who?"

"He didn't specify."

"Why didn't you pursue it?"

"I tried to," Eugen said, "but evidently he'd disappeared."

"You must have been disappointed?"

"I was," Eugen said.

He perceived a slackening in the voice of the first interrogator. Perhaps because he was verging on the truth, he thought. But he could not relax. Thierbach would not have shown any softness under similar circumstances.

"Your mission must be very important."

"It is."

"What does it concern?"

"I swore only to reveal it to him."

"To whom did you swear?"

"I can't say any more," Eugen demurred.

Intuitively, he knotted the temporary safety web he had spun of intrigue. He was not prepared to face Bankart, but there was no drawing back.

"There was a gun among your possessions," said the voice. "Where did you get it?"

"I stole it," Eugen said.

"From whom?"

"I . . . I found it . . . I ca . . . "

Where did he acquire a German-manufactured official issue pistol? Stolen? From whom? Hermann, who wore his so casually, like a fob watch? Dieter? Thierbach? Hitler himself? It would not have been impossible to steal one. But where? At the Metropole? Oh, God. It was the wrong speculation. A plate of chicken sprang before his eyes, golden brown and dripping fat.

"I'm so weak, my brain isn't functioning," Eugen said. "Could you spare something to eat?"

"Where did you get the gun?"

"Please," Eugen said. "I'm starving."

"You're certainly thinner than the last time we encountered you," said the voice. "You hadn't really suffered yet. But there's enough of you left to answer the question."

Eugen tore himself away from the chicken.

"I bought it," he said.

"You just claimed you stole it."

"I bought it from someone who stole it."

Where the chicken had been, the old lady appeared—a yellow, wrinkled, ulcer-mouthed dummy that had been moldering too long inside her clothes.

"Where?"

Now the salami and eggs were materializing, the bread, the onions, the greens, the potatoes, the garlic, and Miriam's strawberries and herring.

"At the wall," Eugen said. "From a smuggler. But I beg of you . . ."

There was a brief, whispered conference away from Eugen. He had given up guessing what might be ahead of him. They would grill him exhaustively. His instincts would have to carry him through.

"We'll try to provide you with something as soon as we're finished," said the voice. "Now, about the gun, how much did you pay for it?"

How much was it worth, Eugen wondered? He had no idea. Five years of his life? No. It was like food. One had access to it or one did not.

"You're having difficulty recalling?"

"I traded for it," Eugen finally said. "My wife had a box of heirlooms. It cost me everything. Diamonds, rubies, gold."

"And what were you going to do with it?"

"Nothing," Eugen said.

Couldn't they see that he was harmless?

"You didn't go through the trouble of digging up your wife's treasure and bartering it away in exchange for a gun you weren't going to use."

My wife has a harelip, Eugen found himself wanting to say.

"I purchased it for protection," he said instead. "Isn't that understandable?"

"Yes," said the voice. "But what do you wish with Bankart?"

Eugen's stomach spasmed and sank. Bankart was like a disease, eating away at him, from the inside out.

"It regards his granddaughter."

"What about her?" said the voice, rising sharply.

A granite fist grabbed Eugen's shirt at the neck and was throttling his Adam's apple.

"Out with it!" said the gruff voice.

The fist bore up into his chin and lifted Eugen off the floor by his collar. He wriggled in protest, but his hands were bound, and he was choking.

"Let him down," said the first voice.

Eugen fell back onto his chair. His throat was clogged, as if the fist had left a permanent indentation.

"What do you know about his granddaughter?"

Eugen began coughing, stalling a response. He had piqued their interest and now they would squeeze him until he bled. Why had he gotten himself into such a predicament? Was it better than dying a slow death in the basement? Spittle was spraying onto his chin. He wanted to get to Bankart. But not as he was—shoeless, crooked-fingered, without his gun.

Whoever was surrounding him had backed off while he was hacking and he became aware again of the noise in the room. There was a variety of industrious sounds—as if a class of children were building something—but he could not integrate them. Also, there was a fair amount of movement, and once or twice someone stopped in front of him for a moment before passing on.

He hoped that they would not throw him back in the closet. *They.* Who were they? Why were they being so cautious with him? Would they never peel off his blindfold? It made no sense to keep it on if they were ultimately going to undo it. He would see whatever there was to see. So they were not going to take it off. They were going to leave him in the Stygian blackness until they discovered exactly what it was he wanted. And then what would they do? There would be no reason for them to restore his sight. Or let him live. They would never free him if they knew. He was on a short rope. Whether or not he confessed. But what would he say? Exactly what was it that he wanted?

"If you have a message for Bankart, you will have to transmit it through us," said the voice.

Eugen's chest constricted. They had acknowledged him! He had stumbled onto someone who actually granted his existence. Where was Bankart? In the factory? In the very same room with him? Preposterous. He was overreacting. But one thing was clear: he was nearby.

It was happening so quickly. For months he had not made any headway, and now he was being offered intercession. What would develop? Would they present him to Bankart? Blindfolded? Or would they bring Bankart here? He had the foreboding that he would be forced to confront the situation before he was fully ready. What would he say? "It's an honor, but I have no message?" Would he find words as Bankart strangled him?

"How can I be positive that it will attain its destination?" Eugen asked.

"You can't."

"It involves life and death," Eugen asserted.

"Whose?" asked the gruff voice.

"Most imminently, his," Eugen said, "but ours as well, and that of the resistance."

He said this with such conviction that it startled him.

"If it's that crucial, it will be imparted," said the first voice.

"What assurance have I?" Eugen reiterated.

"None," said the voice. "Nor any alternative."

"I can withhold the information," Eugen said.

"Then it's not a case of life and death."

"It is," Eugen said, "but only in the proper hands."

"Our patience is trickling thin," said the voice.

"The resistance must not be allowed to fail."

"What have you to convey?"

"There is no margin for error," Eugen said. "The sanctity of the message has been pledged, regardless of personal consequences."

"Commit it to paper," said the voice, "and it will be relayed."

A request was issued for writing supplies.

"When will it be delivered?" Eugen asked.

"At the first opportunity."

"There is no time to waste."

"You have nothing but time," the gruff voice said.

Again, Eugen faintly apprehended the vibration of a bell. A chill spiked him. An ethereal vapor seemed to permeate the room and he envisioned himself being borne along winding corridors, quietly, easily, out of the bowels of the factory, across the yard, through the gate, and deposited on the street as softly as a baby laid in its cradle. Then, in a buoyant, peaceful trance, he heard the wagon lumbering up the street—the percussive clip-clopping of the horse's hooves on stone and the ligneous wheels squeaking like good cheese—and when it halted he felt the strong, steady hands of the old man pluck him up off the ground and swing him gently through the air, with the grace of a father raising his child onto the platform for the sweet, painless ride to the cemetery.

G O D ' S
PECULIAR
TREASURE

Marc helped Nicholas tilt Abrahm to the left and then to the right while Ruth slipped the blanket underneath him.

"Ready?" Nicholas asked.

Abrahm nodded. His face was pained and feverish, and his eyes, though alert, were almost luminous.

Don't rush," Victor said anxiously.

Nicholas signaled him to assume his post at the foot of the bed. Ruth stationed herself beside him. Marc leaned over Abrahm's middle. Nicholas gripped the corners of the blanket on either side of his head.

"One, two, three."

Together, the four of them lifted Abrahm on the blanket and carried him gingerly the length of the bunker, setting him down on the bottom cot of the pair vacated by Ruth and Mrs. Adler, who were transferring to the front berths.

"There, you'll be better off now," Ruth said. "The air will be fresher here, and you'll be less affected by the goings on."

She covered Abrahm, except for the leg, which lay

propped on several pillows. It was wrapped more lightly than before, to facilitate treatment. The knee had ballooned since the mishap, and an apparently latent infection had manifested itself. The swelling and discoloration made it seem as if a rotten melon had been grafted onto his thigh.

"How do you feel?" Victor asked.

"It's become litany," Abrahm said.

"Nevertheless."

"Like a maharajah."

"He's delirious," Victor said.

"Don't princes ride on stretchers?" Abrahm said.

"By choice," Victor rejoined.

"And keep harems of nubile maidens?"

"He's in an oriental mood," Ruth said.

She placed the back of her hand on Abrahm's forehead.

"Your temperature is up."

Nicholas hovered attentively. Marc repaired to the other end of the bunker to assist his mother and Mrs. Adler in stripping and refurbishing the beds that had been Victor's and Abrahm's.

"I think your father should have a look at him," Victor said to Ruth.

Then he addressed Abrahm.

"Olek will make arrangements."

"Like hell he will," Abrahm said.

"It would be to your advantage," Nicholas interjected.

"Then keep your nose out of it," Abrahm said.

"What is your opinion?" Victor asked Ruth.

"It requires attention," Ruth said earnestly.

"It's getting attention," Abrahm said. "Very fine attention. There are more than enough people in need of Emil's services. For me, yours will do exceedingly well."

"You're a misguided martyr," Victor said.

"And you?"

"A worried comforter."

"It's your nature," Abrahm said.

"And it's contrary to all nature and common sense for a

conspicuously ill man to go running around in the dead of night on his crutches."

"I wasn't running," Abrahm said.

"Forgive me," Victor said. "Falling."

"I was *practicing*," Abrahm said.

"For what?"

"The Olympic four-hundred meter crutch crawl."

"While everyone else was asleep?"

"So as not to disturb anyone," Abrahm said.

"You certainly succeeded," Victor said.

He could not restrain a grin.

"You see, there is a vein of humor in it," Abrahm said.

"Why couldn't you have waited until morning?" Victor said.

"Practice makes perfect," Abrahm said, "but useless repetition results, at best, in a crashing headache."

"I'm sorry," Victor said. "If only simple prudence had prevailed."

"It's done," Abrahm said.

"I'm afraid it is," Victor said.

"I'll be up again in no time," Abrahm said.

"I hope so," Victor said. "But we're going to bring Emil in just in case."

"No," Abrahm said emphatically.

"It's our collective judgment," Victor said.

Ruth nodded agreement.

"You're all addlebrained," Abrahm said.

"What harm can it do?" Nicholas asked.

"More than good," Abrahm said.

"You're being perverse," Victor said. "It isn't fair to you or to us."

"I'll think it over," Abrahm said.

"Don't let them trick you into it," Mrs. Adler shouted.

Charging across the room, she barged her way past Nicholas and Ruth.

"They'll do to you what they did to me," she warned Abrahm.

"Mother!" Ruth said.

"Don't mother me," Mrs. Adler said. "I heard what's going on here."

"And what about it bothers you?" Ruth asked.

"As if I have to tell you," Mrs. Adler said. "But I won't allow you to fool him. Hold fast, comrade. They won't presume upon you as long as I'm here."

"I'm sure of it," Abrahm said.

"Emil won't cure you," Mrs. Adler blurted. "Most of his patients die."

Ruth grabbed her mother by the shoulder and slapped at her, stinging her ear. Mrs. Adler, normally docile, fought back. Nicholas stepped between them.

"I don't want him in here," Mrs. Adler screamed, scratching at Ruth.

"Tempers," Nicholas said.

"You shut up," Mrs. Adler said, whipping herself into a spit. "You'd be happier if we were all gone. You regret having put your shovel to this hole."

"You don't believe that," Nicholas said, constraining his anger.

"Don't I?" Mrs. Adler said. "Then why are you so eager to turn Emil loose on us? Let him stay where he belongs."

"No one's forcing him on you," Nicholas said. "But Abrahm's condition demands the highest competence."

"You don't live down here," Mrs. Adler said. "You're insensitive to it. I've listened to them whispering. They want Emil to see me. 'He can talk to her,' they say. 'He can best determine what should be done with her.' That's right. They'd make dogfood out of me if they could. You'd like that, wouldn't you? Anything that's good for dogs pleases you. But we're not dogs. We're human beings. We shouldn't be in this hole. But you dug it out and now you hate us for it. It's on your face. It's in the way you bring us our meals. You won't even visit with anyone but Comrade Abrahm. I'm not worthy of you. None of us are. You despise us. Only Comrade Abrahm means something to you, and you're frightened to death he'll jump up on his crutches and hop right out of here. You're glad he took a tumble, aren't you? Yes you are. He was getting ready to leave us. But he was in such a hurry, he pressed his luck. You should have heard him flump. You would have enjoyed it. Because he won't be going anywhere now. Not for a while. And you're not about to sic Emil on us. We can manage without him. We don't want to lay eyes on him. Just remember, Mr. Dogkeeper, he's my husband, and if he comes down here, it'll be over my cold body."

As she reached a conclusion, Mrs. Adler lunged forward and began pummeling Nicholas in the chest with clenched fists.

"You won't do it," she yelled. "You won't!"

Nicholas made no effort to defend himself. Ruth quickly intervened. The instant Mrs. Adler felt her touch, she froze and started drifting into a daze. Ruth led her away.

"You've successfully braved another attack," Abrahm said.

Nicholas wore a solemn, wounded expression.

"You'll have to excuse her," Victor said. "She didn't mean what she was saying."

"Of course she did," Abrahm said wryly.

Nicholas stood rooted to the spot where Mrs. Adler had assailed him.

"Before I go, there's something I must discuss with you," he said to Abrahm.

"Who's to stop you?" Abrahm said.

"I'd prefer it if we were alone," Nicholas said.

"We have no secrets here," Abrahm said.

"It's personal."

Victor looked at Abrahm.

"Pardon me," he said finally, edging away from the bed.

Abrahm waited for Victor to withdraw.

"What is it?" he asked.

He had never seen Nicholas so filled with gloom.

"Would it be all right if I drew the curtain?" Nicholas said.

"For such a formal occasion, why not?" Abrahm said.

The black cloth dropped behind him and curled half way around the cot, screening him off from the rest of the bunker.

"Let me guess," Abrahm said, breaking the ice. "You've come with a communique for Hitler."

He observed that Nicholas' hands were trembling.

"The holidays are rapidly approaching," Nicholas said.

"So I've noticed."

"Katrina wants to spend Christmas underground."

"Where?"

"Here."

"Just like that?"

"I was flabbergasted," Nicholas said apologetically.

"What did you tell her?"

"That it was impossible."

"Then what's the problem?"

"She's determined to do it."

Abrahm tried to raise himself to a sitting position, but the move and the ensuing turmoil had weakened him and it was too painful. He settled instead for rotating toward Nicholas and propping his head up on his palm.

"What are you suggesting?"

"She wants to meet whoever's down here," Nicholas said.

His voice rang hollow, as if he had disassociated himself from his utterance.

"Perhaps Victor should be in on this conversation," Abrahm said.

"I'd rather not," Nicholas said.

"I'd rather."

Reluctantly, Nicholas exited through the curtain and summoned Victor.

"Tell him," Abrahm said.

Nicholas glanced down at Abrahm with a mixture of reticence and humiliation. When there was no reprieve forthcoming, he focused on his hands.

"Katrina wants to celebrate Christmas in the bunker," he said.

Impassively, Victor fetched a berry-colored candy from his pocket, stripped off the cellophane, and planted it on his tongue.

"And you want her to?"

"I said no," Nicholas explained. "But she insists."

"It's obviously impracticable," Victor said.

"But it's not that simple," Nicholas said.

"Why not?"

"For months she's been very cooperative," Nicholas said. "Here I am the proprietor of a mysterious hotel and she's not permitted to know anything about it. I don't even let her see how much food I'm preparing. It's built a wall between us. I'm constantly occupied with the bunker and yet I can't involve her in it. It's as if I were living down here too."

"It's knotty," Abrahm said, "but I wouldn't have come to you for help if I hadn't been sure you would shoulder the burden, whatever its weight. Thus far my faith has been well-placed."

"Then I urge you to consider her desire in this context." Nicholas said.

"Is it un-Christian to say 'no' on Christmas?" Victor said.

"I've said 'no' several times," Nicholas said. "This isn't her first request."

"What's changed except the weather?"

"Her feelings on the subject are quite strong," Nicholas said. "I've always kept to myself. Even on holidays. But for Katrina it's been very trying, existing furtively, steering shy of the neighbors, shifting like a thief's accomplice. Naturally, she looked forward to Christmas. When no dinner invitation had been extended to us and none was prospective, she resolved to have a few people over to the house. I objected. She asked why. I said, 'You know why.' So she said, 'All right then, let's have it in the bunker. No one will be the wiser.' I said, 'We'll have an enjoyable time, just you and I.' But she became angry and absolutely intent upon providing a proper Christmas for 'those poor people down there.'"

"Did you indicate to her that Christmas isn't our favorite holiday?" Abrahm said.

"I repeated that it was out of the question," Nicholas said. "Again she demanded to know why. Why this and why that? I couldn't tell her any more, and that made her blood boil. She was outraged by the notion that I didn't trust her."

"Do you?"

"Certainly."

"And you favor her cause?"

"It's as I've stated."

"But why?" Abrahm stated.

"I've just told you."

"You haven't really."

Nicholas clasped his hands tormentedly.

"It would be best for everyone concerned," he said, wrestling with himself.

Victor flinched, suppressing the reflex to prevent Abrahm from raising himself in evident discomfort.

"Are we being blackmailed?" Abrahm said.

Nicholas' face darkened as if an eclipse were impending.

"She threatened to go to the authorities," he said.

"Would she?"

"It's perplexing."

"You assert confidence in her, yet you display considerable respect for her rancor."

"She was extremely aggravated," Nicholas said.

"Because of Christmas?"

"Because of the whole business."

"But Christmas brought it to a crisis?"

"Yes."

"Do you have a solution?"

"Only what I've already submitted."

"If she's capable of betraying us now unless we accede, how do we know she won't do it anyway at a later date?"

Nicholas' eyes grew cloudy.

"I guarantee it."

"What control would you have then that you don't have now?"

"Her frustration will have been discharged," Nicholas said. "There would be no motive."

"That's scarcely reassuring," Victor said.

"Is the wish to commemorate a holy day with others a sin?" Nicholas asked.

Abrahm reclined once more, sinking into meditation. A silence mushroomed in the bunker.

"What's going on in there?" Mrs. Adler suddenly called out.

"Quiet, mother," Ruth said.

"They're plotting to get rid of us," Mrs. Adler said. "Why else would they hide behind the curtain?"

"Don't be silly," Ruth said. "It has nothing to do with us."

"I'm always wrong," Mrs. Adler said.

Abrahm squeezed his eyes more tightly shut, intensifying the sensation that he was nestled in the innermost chamber of a Chinese puzzle box.

"Nicholas is right," he finally said.

"How?" Victor asked.

"The risk has been inherent from the beginning," Abrahm said. "If we can't depend on Nicholas and Jesus, we might as well give up the ghost."

"Does Katrina definitely know that we are Jewish?" Victor asked.

Nicholas paused to deliberate.

"It's never been explicitly mentioned."

"Then we are presuming her awareness?" Victor asked.

"I don't follow," Nicholas said.

"If she hasn't been told who we are, the character of our festivities will be a dead giveaway," Victor said. "We are not inclined to feign the Christmas spirit."

"No problem," Abrahm said. "We pray to the Father and they to the Son—it's all in the family."

"Splendid," Victor said.

"It wouldn't matter if we adorned ourselves like pine trees and fixed crosses on our heads," Abrahm said. "One glimpse would tell her."

"What?" Victor asked.

"That we're God's peculiar treasure."

SILENT MUSIC

Eugen could not shake the feeling that the blind man was watching him. His eyes were shut, enhancing the grotesque, imbecilic aspect of his countenance, but he seemed to be looking straight ahead, as if he were seeing through closed lids.

Was he really blind, Eugen mused, or was he a trained beggar such as those who had descended on Germany after the first war—sitting on the streets with their eyelids blackened or their sockets patched, their clothing artfully disarrayed, legs folded under, empty sleeves pinned up, their faces set in stupid spittle poses, jangling cups expertly stocked to evoke sympathy and guilt?

Eugen veiled his eyes. When they had first blindfolded him, he was so anxious and disoriented that he actually experienced his skin discharging pulses of measurement and fear. But then he acclimated to the darkness, and in truth regretted lacking the courage to request that they leave him bound. He would have been more comfortable now, detained in a strange, windowless sanctum—half laboratory, half dormitory, sealed by a metal door, solidly barred, and lit alternately by electricity and calcium carbide—were he not laboring to avert his gaze from the blind man. And the boy.

There was something compelling about the boy's wide, rectangular face, his brown thatch of hair, and the hard lines of his body—just as there had been something familiar in the voices that had interrogated him. Eugen felt as if he had been delivered into a *déjà vu* world.

He wiggled his hooked finger. It had not pained him for a while. He was prepared to inform them that he had injured it resisting the policeman, but they had not expressed the slightest curiosity. They had, however, given him back his pillowcase, minus the gun, and his shoes, which unfortunately no longer fit. He could jam them on if he had to, but for the moment he preferred a second pair of socks.

There were six or eight people in the room, some standing, the rest seated on the floor, but his eyes refused to count them. Instead of encompassing the scene, they followed the boy as he took the blind man's pan from the woman who was ladling out of a pot and brought it over to him.

"Suppertime," the boy said.

The blind man lowered his nose toward his ration.

"Aah, it smells good," he said.

Eugen's stomach cramped. The aroma of simmering vegetables and the sight of the boy tearing the beggar's bread were enough to make him bellow. He became conscious of the man and woman situated to his right, a young child between them on the floor, dipping snippets of bread into their rich, hot stew, sucking the goodness out of them, and dunking them again.

The child, a boy of two or three, partook of offerings from both his parents. Streaks of orange stained his lips and the corners of his mouth as he strained the bread held out for him. His face was thin and wasted, and in a puppet fashion he appeared to be the oldest person in the room.

The blind man fumbled for a pinch of dough, plunged it into his pan, and came up with his fingers dripping. He leached the morsel with his gums and licked his hands.

It was notable how the boy had nipped the blind man's bread with the same gentleness that the man with the narrow face had displayed in serving him his special soup. They were huddled now around the home-built stove, conferring with the woman tending the pot. Eugen caught himself focusing on them and turned away.

He had sought the bakery, and it was gone, yet he had hit upon it. Still, it had not revealed itself wholly to him until his blindfold was removed. He should have realized that the gruff voice—"Go poke your eyes out!"—and the large knuckles digging into his throat were Samson's. But who was he? And who were the others? If this was the inside of the bakery, what had happened to the outside? Where was the food coming from? The man with the narrow face was evidently in charge. But what had become of the people in line? Had they expired one by one, slumping in place like a woman that day, to be carted off by the wagon? Or had those who survived reported to the *umschlagplatz*, defying Bankart?

The boy was approaching.

"Here," he said, extending a plate of stew and a chunk of bread.

Peering up, Eugen viewed him closely for the first time. He had a broad forehead, high, flat cheekbones, somewhat knobby ears, and a wedge-shaped nose. His eyes were deeply brown and smoldered with intensity.

Eugen nodded his thanks. He did not want to call attention to himself by speaking. The boy retreated. A quick smile brightened the woman's face. She dished up a portion for the boy, one for the man with the narrow face, and a third for herself. They dined together, curled around the stove.

Inclining toward his bowl, Eugen inhaled its steam. He wanted to indulge himself slowly, privately, savoring each molecule of flavor. But he would not begin immediately. It would be torture, once his appetite had been released, to have finished his repast while those about him were still nursing theirs.

The boy ate gracefully, sopping his uncut bread and nibbling the soaked edge while listening intently to the man with the narrow face. What were they discussing? Despite their proximity, he could not hear them. It was as if they were insulated by a transparent curtain. Was the boy staring at him? Yes, he was. Eugen dropped his eyes self-consciously. Perhaps it was because he was abstaining. The man beside him had polished off his stew and was mopping up the smudges with a last bit of bread.

"Might there be a few allocated drops left in the pot?" asked the man, whose name was Nussbaum.

His head was like a pumpkin gourd with glasses.

"I'm afraid not," Sonya said.

Reaching out, Nussbaum ducked his fingers into his wife's plate and raised them to his mouth. She continued feeding herself and the child without protest.

Eugen tried to ignore Nussbaum's uncomfortable presence as he poised himself, fingered his bread, and tore a soft, crustless wad out of the center. It was fresh. Beyond doubt there was a bakery nearby.

He immersed the squib in the orange liquid. Although meatless, it had been stirred and thickened until it smacked of beef stew. He pressed the bread between the roof of his mouth and his tongue and squeezed the juices out over his taste buds.

"You did quite a good job," Samson said.

Gripping it with both hands, the blind man lapped his pan metal clean.

"Could you manage a little more?"

"Yes, of course," said the blind man. "Excellent."

Samson started to get up but the boy came over and fetched the pan. The woman produced a slab of bread and dropped it in the pot. She scoured the bottom and sides with it, converting it into an orange sponge. Then the boy reduced it to plump bits and set it in front of the blind man.

A flush of warmth welled up in Eugen. He was receiving nourishment from these people who treated the blind man like a child. Several days of torment were ended. He had pursued Bankart, and shortly he would be meeting him—if he had not already. The case was finally verging on resolution.

Eugen was about to drench a tufted crust in stew when Nussbaum's hand suddenly reached out to pull his plate away. Before Eugen realized what was happening, a crashing force drove his hands afly and sent his plate skidding. His reflex was to retrieve it, but as he scrambled forward, a large foot planted itself before him.

"It's not yours," boomed Samson's voice.

Eugen was stunned.

"Don't touch it," Samson warned.

But Nussbaum disregarded him, bending over to fish up the plate.

"Put it down."

"I have more right to it than he."

"We can debate that after you've given it back," Samson said.

Nussbaum looked around for support. When there was none forthcoming, he set the plate down grudgingly.

"Now, what is it?" Samson asked.

"It's difficult enough to abide by a certain one of us regularly receiving a double portion," Nussbaum said. "But to work all day and half the night and then be required to donate a part of our meager resources to a non-contributing stranger is too much. What has he done to earn it? If neither we nor a growing child can have it, I would favor throwing it away."

Eugen crept back to his spot, abandoning his plate.

"The only food you have the option to spill is your own," Heykel said. "And but once at that."

"One-eighth of his award is rightfully mine," Nussbaum said. "One eighth is Gittel's. These, and his own share, three-eighths in sum, we claim for Benyk."

"Comrade Silver is our guest," Heykel said.

"Nonsense," Nussbaum said. "He's a captive."

"At our insistence," Heykel said. "Therefore it's our responsibility to provide him with the necessities."

"He's here because we don't know how to dispose of him," Nussbaum said. "Is that reason for us to starve?"

"For a distinguished advocate, your logic is remarkably like a camel's lip," Heykel said.

"You're not a judge of such matters," Nussbaum said.

"No one else is complaining," Samson said.

"They haven't the strength," Nussbaum said.

"What do you suggest we do with him?" Heykel asked.

Nussbaum removed his glasses and rubbed his eyes fretfully.

"I don't trust him," he said.

"He seems to have come with good will," Mrs. Nussbaum said.

"Packing a German pistol?" Nussbaum said.

He spun around on Eugen.

"What is the message?"

"You needn't shout," Heykel said.

The words "Comrade Silver" wove through Eugen's mind.

"Well, what should we do with him?"

"Let him carry his own weight," Nussbaum said.

"How?"

"We could use additional revolvers."

"If you're going to be so exacting," Samson said, "why don't you snatch Isaac's dish next time?"

"He's our Isaac," Nussbaum said. "Of kindred flesh and blood."

"Crazy Isaac," Samson said.

"No," Nussbaum said. "Isaac Bloodstein."

"He might once have been ours," Samson said, "but now he's Zirka's."

"To me he will always be Rabbi Isaac." Nussbaum said.

"But he's not supplying anything."

"At least God watches over him," Nussbaum said, "and consequently over us."

"Tell me, Julius," Samson said to Nussbaum. "Would

Rabbi Isaac have condoned dragging a half-famished man into our house, teasing him with food, then promptly stealing it back from him?"

Nussbaum recoiled in shame. The boy stooped to retrieve Eugen's plate and stepped toward him. Eugen felt a sourness rise in his stomach. He started to say something, but the ferment rose quickly, surging like acrid lava. His body began to heave and tremble.

"What is it?" the boy said.

His eyes were probing. Eugen moved to ward him off with one hand while slapping the other over his mouth to block the flow of orange slime—but it pumped up urgently, filling his throat and forcing its way out between his lips, squirting through his fingers and onto himself, the plate, the boy, and all over the floor.

The electricity had been switched off and a flame defined the night. Eugen lay stretched out with his pillowcase doubled beneath his head. He did not feel like sleeping. His mind was lucid, and the wall was solid beside him. If only he could stop shivering.

His stomach was void, but sated—as if retching had purged him of his hunger. The boy, whose name he now knew was Joseph, and the woman had cleaned up after him, with an assist from Mrs. Nussbaum. The sole traces of the vomit that had spattered everything were the buttermilk-smelling wet spots where his clothing had been scrubbed. A sourness, too, lingered in his nose and throat.

Everyone in the room had either bedded down or was relaxing. The man with the narrow face had given Joseph a few instructions and departed. His place had been taken some minutes later by the man who was playing cards with Samson. He appeared to be in his late twenties and possessed a military mien focused about his rapier face and terse, slashing mannerisms. Samson addressed him as Gideon.

The quiescent atmosphere was not unlike that on the

street, Eugen ruminated. Only no one was sporting an arm
band—his had been stripped from his sleeve when he was
thrown into the closet and tossed in with his other effects—
and when they awakened in the morning they would not all
trudge over to the *umschlagplatz*. But what would they do?
What was in store for him? And what about the rabbi? Did
they let him in and out as one would a pet? This much was
sure: he was not faking blindness. He wa . . . it was too black to
contemplate.

The room was considerably warmer than the basement
had been and sweltering in comparison with the windraked
building across the street from the factory where Eugen had
spent a freezing night, yet he found himself shivering uncontrollably.

"Are you all right?"

Nussbaum's voice was like castor oil. Eugen pressed
his head against the wall in an effort to stop his trembling.

"Evidently you caught a chill," Nussbaum said.

He freed himself from his blanket and draped it carefully
over Eugen.

"There," he said, stroking him. "That should help."

Eugen did not acknowledge his voice or his gesture, but
he experienced an intimation of sympathy as Nussbaum
wrapped the blanket around him and tucked it in. His quaking
subsided into a gentler motion that in a sense was even comforting, like the self-rocking of a cradle.

"I must apologize for my behavior," Nussbaum said.

He had moved away from his wife and child and positioned himself directly alongside Eugen.

"It was unforgivable," Nussbaum said. "Please believe
me. I have nothing against you. We're under such great
strain."

Eugen felt the pressure of Nussbaum's body through the
blanket and the offensiveness of his food-ridden breath.

"Comrade Silver, I implore you, permit me to make
amends."

Where had the man with the narrow face gone, Eugen wondered? He had heard the woman call him Heykel.

"Comrade Silver . . ."

Eugen eyes opened, and he rotated his head toward Nussbaum.

"Perhaps you would consent to talk for a few minutes," Nussbaum said. "Ill feelings are like good—one cannot contain them overlong."

"It's over," Eugen said.

A raspiness crabbed his throat.

"It's not," Nussbaum said. "There are . . ."

"Truly, its forgotten."

"You're still shaking," Nussbaum said.

Viewing him face on, Eugen was struck by the kindliness of his expression. The war had contracted his skin tightly over his capacious skull, accentuating his enormous brow and soft, intelligent eyes. Magnified by bulging lenses, they were obscurely reminiscent of Eugen's father's.

"You'll have my breakfast in the morning," Nussbaum said.

"It's not necessary," Eugen said.

"But it should be so," Nussbaum said. "You're clearly weak. It will fortify you, and I'll feel better in the bargain."

"It's not necessary," Eugen repeated.

"You needn't accept now," Nussbaum said. "The offer stands."

He withdrew his face from Eugen's and settled against the wall beside him.

"So you're from Dresden?"

"Yes," Eugen nodded.

"Was it difficult there?"

Eugen raised himself aslope.

"Somewhat."

"It must have been hell," Nussbaum said.

"It wasn't really."

"You suffered no anguish?"

"One adapts."

"Are you reconciled now?"

"The nightmare began with Warsaw."

"But earlier, were you not painfully aware of second-class citizenship?"

"No," Eugen said.

"You never had the perception that regardless of how strenuously you applied yourself to carving out a niche, your existence was merely being tolerated?"

"It was equivalent for every worker," Eugen said.

"But you must have been conscious of a special vulnerability," Nussbaum said.

"A person is what he is," Eugen said.

"You were a Jew."

"We were Germans."

"In your eyes," Nussbaum said. "Not in theirs."

Nussbaum eyes floated upward as if they were poring over a memorized scroll. Eugen took advantage of the interlude to glance sideways at Joseph, who was posted against the door. In his hands he held the barrel of Eugen's gun, and Eugen saw that he had disassembled it and methodically arranged its part on the floor beside an assortment of sundry scraps and tools. What was he doing?

"Was your father a religious man?" Nussbaum asked.

"No," Eugen said.

He had the squirming sensation that now Joseph was scrutinizing him.

"What was his profession?"

"He was a printer."

"How long did his job last?"

"Until 1934."

"Was he fired?"

"He set out for Berlin one day and vanished."

"Premeditatedly?"

"We never learned."

"What is your definition of hell?" Nussbaum asked.

"I'm not a scholar."

"What are you?"

"Tired," Eugen said.

"Before the war what were you?"

"We searched for him," Eugen said, "but it was useless."

"One wonders if anything is of avail," Nussbaum said. "Eight years later we still cannot persuade sufficient persons to join us in the only course of action that does not lead inevitably to the *umschlagplatz*."

"I suppose there's always the hope that an alternative will magically spring up."

"Indeed," Nussbaum said. "In the past two years, we ourselves have obstinately striven to sustain the illusion of life as it had been—feeding people, generating work, maintaining schools for the children, promoting programs, concerts, things to do, things to look forward to. That was our error."

"Why?" Eugen asked. "Isn't the will to live a positive force?"

"In this instance it was misdirected," Nussbaum said. "Comrade Abrahm was right from the beginning. Every man, woman, and child should have channeled all his energies into preparing to fight. But annihilation, however imminent, is too abstract for most. Even within the political core, the majority believed that it was suicidal to resist. That the Nazis would punish everyone for the resistance of a few. And now that ninety percent of us have been transported, there are still those who deem it foolhardy to offer active resistance."

Eugen's thoughts scrambled to keep pace. In all the mayhem and confusion, amidst bodies flying, blood streaming, eyes spouting, stomachs splitting, Bankart materialized and dissolved, in waking as in sleep, a figure of strength and powerlessness.

"Noah . . ."

Eugen jerked his hand away from Nussbaum's clasp.

"I'm sorry," Nussbaum said. "I shouldn't have taken the liberty."

"There's no harm done," Eugen said.

"Comrade is such a clumsy formality," Nussbaum said. "I don't want you to . . ."

"I understand," Eugen said.

"If I could just indulge my curiosity a final time," Nussbaum said.

What was he thinking?

"What forged your conversion to the resistance?"

Eugen noticed Samson's head tip slightly toward them. An undertow began to drain Eugen. He did not have the stamina to contend with Noah Silver, Bankart, Franz, his father, the ghosts of his life. It was grueling enough to coexist with Thierbach and Isaac and Joseph and the queasy foreboding that they would kill him when the message was delivered.

"Comrade Silver . . . ?"

Was that why Heykel had sallied forth into the night?

"You've worn him out with your morbid eloquence," Samson said, observing that Eugen had slumped to the floor and lapsed into silence.

Nussbaum had leaned over as if to rouse him, reconsidered, smoothed the blanket perfunctorily around him, and retired, leaving Eugen ensconced in his cocoon.

Though he felt enervated, Eugen's body still rejected sleep. Unburdened of Nussbaum, his weariness was vaguely pleasant, as when he had come home as a boy after school and several hours of soccer and been too exhausted to eat or study or even take a nap. Then he would daydream, drifting into reverie, and when he snapped to he would be miraculously refreshed.

At least, that was how he remembered it having been. But he was not overly sure about those years. He could visualize very little about them, and next to nothing about his mother. He had been worried that Nussbaum would ask him about her and that he would not know what to reply. His *mother*. He could barely recall her. She had a melancholy face—fallow, softly creased, with a dolorous mouth and plaintive cedar eyes—but the rest of her was indistinct. There was no voice, no particular shape, only a kerchief, a blood-warm bulk beneath a nondescript dress, a darkly flowered tea rose apron, and rough spun orange-ocher stockings.

It was a singular memory, private but detached, the color of the blossoms on her apron, long forgotten. He could not enhance it or distill it, and regarded alone, it made him feel nothing.

Dresden corresponded to his mother in that Eugen could scarcely conjure it up either. It was an ink dot on the map, a fleck beside the Elbe, and everything that he had done since quitting it had contributed to the disintegration of his past. Instead of continually gaining substance and significance, his past had particularized like cold ashes, unchronicled, and been scattered by the currents of the earth's rotation.

Every place Eugen had been, and every room he had stayed in, had left him with the image of the inside of an immense incinerator. And every woman he had known reminded him of Ellen. He had shoved his prick into her ass, and Thierbach had done the same to him, and Franz was somewhere in Europe, stalking a city or slithering across a mudbogged field or sprawled contortedly with his blood congealed in bug-encrusted icicles protruding from his wounds.

What if Joseph questioned him about the gun?

A silver needle was spiraling slowly from the back of Eugen's mind to the front. There was a quality about the room and its inhabitants that imparted a desire to belong. In the face of adversity, they were living as people should—closely, cooperatively, with respect. It impressed him as profoundly natural and good, radiating harmony and oneness. Abashedly, he almost wished that he could remain among them. He was as safe from Bankart here as was achievable in combination with such a high possibility of access. Of course, once Bankart was apprised of his presence he might . . . but that was an inescapable hazard.

The needle was feathering through Eugen's brain, parting the tissue of his cortex.

Simultaneously, Eugen sensed a pair of weightless feelers

grazing his forehead. Then they were gone—like the brush of
a fly on its blind dash through a room in quest of blood. Did
Joseph recognize him? Joseph Bloodstein. Son of Menachem.
Eugen knew the eyes. But the other features had changed. He
would not have placed them had it not been for Nussbaum.
Perhaps Eugen's own appearance had mutated sufficiently so
that, similarly, Joseph could not identify him. Apparently that
was the case. Otherwise, the probability was that he would
have said something—to them, if not to him. Conceivably he
had. But why was Joseph peering at him now? Maybe he was
planning to shoot him in his sleep, Eugen thought. Well, what
did it matter? Sleep was sleep.

Joseph had finished whatever he was doing and wedged
himself into the doorway. The pillow at his back indicated that
he was posted there. No vestiges of the pistol were visible.
There was a chess board beside him, and opposite, Samson
was studying it.

"The master taught him too well," Samson said to Isaac,
who was perched to his right with his face trained skew-jawed
on the game.

Joseph glimpsed at his watch.

"Don't be so fidgety," Samson said. "I just sat down."

"He's overdue," Joseph said.

"I should have taken your side and vice versa," Samson
said. "At least you'd know how this predicament developed."

"We can still trade," Joseph said.

Bewilderingly, it dawned on Eugen that Gideon was absent. How could it be? He had seen him playing cards with
Samson. And then? He had not heard anyone go out.

"Let's buy some time," Samson said, making a move.

Joseph eyes surveyed the board and skipped up, catching
Eugen unawares. His gaze was unblinking. Eugen tried to
avert his eyes, but a contrary force held them there. Finally,
he brought his hand up to his mouth and coughed, meanwhile
disengaging.

Eugen's lids fluttered to stay shut. In his mind's eye he

saw Joseph's mother lying on the floor and the rabbi moistening a cloth for the little girl to apply to her bleeding scalp. How impudent he thought it then.

"Isaac, I need a touch of inspiration," Samson said. "Not quite a lullaby, but something sweet."

"Yes," Isaac said. "Very good."

Could the rabbi comprehend Samson's words, Eugen wondered? *Inspiration? Lullaby?*

The first tremulous notes emanated from Isaac's harmonica. Immediately, Eugen envisioned him as he had seen him previously on the street—before a fire, his face ardent with concentration, fondling his instrument in both hands and blowing into it as if he were the wind and the reeds were a responsive forest.

If Isaac could create such an intricate mixture of mathematics and prayer, Eugen thought, then what was madness? Was it being tortured beyond sufferance and bearing it?

It was his fault that Rabbi Bloodstein had been transmogrified into Crazy Isaac. Eugen had pleaded for his life after it had been destroyed. After his body had been burned and broken, after his teeth had been shattered and his nose crushed and his head lay at Thierbach's feet, numb in the ooze of its eyes . . . after all that survived was that dumb vacant look . . . he, Eugen, had gotten him a reprieve. That was madness.

The sighing notes of the harmonica seemed to kindle the room with a spiritual incandescence. Samson began to sing, and the others followed.

> *Childhood years, sweet childhood years,*
> *Rooted in memory so dear,*
> *When I think of your lost glow,*
> *My longing and regret cannot be told;*
> *Oh, how quickly I have grown too old.*

Eugen pursed his eyes tightly so that they would not roll open involuntarily. It sounded as if everyone who was awake was singing now.

Crazy Isaac? Because he herded an imaginary cow? "Please . . . a piece of bread . . . a drink of water." What then of Noah Silver? "Have mercy . . . a message for a plate of stew."

Hitler was bedeviled, and Himmler, and Heydrich, and Thierbach, and Hermann, and whining Erdmann, and rodential Vaczek, and glass-eyed, pederastic Heinrich, and all the others, each with his own dementedness.

Even young Joseph was not altogether sane, welded to the doorstep, protecting the room like a guard at the siege of Masada. Did he truly intend to pit himself against the German Army?

> *Childhood years, sweet youthful flowers,*
> *You will not bloom for me again,*
> *Few leaves on the lorn trees remain,*
> *The summer birds have fled the cold;*
> *Oh, how quickly I have grown too old.*

There was a slender likeness between Joseph and "Noah/ Age 12/In the forest"—the lock of hair tumbling onto the forehead—but Eugen could not picture Noah coping with Joseph's circumstances. Whereas Joseph had a toughness about him, a tensile strength, Noah was a frail plant that fared sickly even in sunlight. Noah could never had withstood the stress and deprivation of the ghetto.

"Whoa," Sonya said suddenly, grabbing her rounded stomach.

"Are you all right?" Samson said.

"She's really kicking up," Sonya said.

"Maybe she's a mule," Samson said.

"That would make Heykel an ass."

"What a thing to say," Samson objected.

"Shhh," Sonya said. "Our guest is dreaming."

The harmonica continued wailing. Sonya would make a good mother, Eugen thought, feigning sleep. She had a pleasant, soothing voice, and when she had helped spruce him up after he had thrown up he felt the gentleness of her hands.

Several times she had inadvertently rubbed against him with the soft, warm, electric bulge of her stomach and he was aroused. Eugen envied Heykel for being able to behold it and caress it and nuzzle his face to it and feel life taking form within.

He had never been a father. There had been occasions when he perceived momentarily that this was how it would feel to have derived from a woman and to have enjoyed a mother's love. He had experienced the love of a woman fleetingly in his dreams, or sometimes when he masturbated to a fantasy, or in the touch of Tzipora's hand on his thigh, or in listening to music, or the hypnotic pulsing of Hitler's voice. But he had never possessed it.

Eugen longed achingly to raise Sonya's dress and see her marvelously delicate ball of love and smooth its silkiness with his fingers and track the bluish-green veins over her milky translucent skin and lay his ear against it and feel the blood throb and perhaps the kicking and pull down her underpants, gingerly, so that he could stroke the underside as well and reach the conduit through which she had been inseminated and would give birth.

He would kiss the entrance, humbly, and insert his tongue, and sample the pre-natal liquor, and then he would introduce his penis and ease it into her as far as it would go, and by concentrating on transmitting his repressed sensitivities through this extension of himself, he would try to experience directly, physically, less delusively what he was capable of feeling when he was moved not only by the red fire and the yellow sun, the clip-clop of the horse's hooves, and the plaint of the harmonica, but also the vision of the rabbi's eyes dispersing like a sanguine nightfall or the crowning child, severed from its placenta, dripping clay fluids and emitting the airless scream of light, the scream of darkness.

CHRISTMAS

Abrahm sucked the robust perfume of the dying sapling into his nostrils. There was snow on the ground, he had heard Katrina say, and he pictured a stand of dark green needle trees set on the white powdered earth. It would be peaceful in the forest now.

He lay on his cot with the light out and the black curtain wrapped around him like a shroud. In the darkness, the snow was bright, the drape smelled of pine, and the plumes of the melting candlewax rose wispily, like jinn.

On the other side of the curtain, behind him, the bunker was festive. His eyes were closed, but he saw everything: the tree, greener than emerald grass, hung with multi-colored stars and patchwork streamers cut and pasted by Mrs. Krecji with all the care accorded a pontiff's robe; the Channukah candles, softly orange, burning with goldenwheat flames; the table, covered for the occasion with a beige cloth embroidered in orange and green; and the redolent food—pork, plums, sweet potatoes, spinach, cinnamon bread and butter, almonds, raisins, coffee, milk, and a heady wine pudding.

"And now," said Nicholas, when dinner was done, "let it be as we agreed. First Channukah."

There was a bustling, a tinkling of plates, a shifting of seats, and a settling into attentiveness. The Metropole was undoubtedly surging with merriment, Abrahm mused.

"The history of the Jews," Victor began, "is the age-old struggle to maintain a cultural and spiritual identity in the face of hostile forces of superior physical and economic strength."

Abrahm's mind flashed to Leora, laughing at Isaac's comic faces, spinning the dreidel, crashing playfully into Joseph.

"Two centuries before Christ, the Jewish territory of Judea fell under the Hellenistic influence of the Seleucid rule. Jewish Hellenists arose, casting their lot with the Seleucids. The orthodox Jews resisted secularization, but as history usually has it, they were of the poorer classes and had no power . . ."

It had always been thus, Abrahm thought, just as Joseph would always be Leora's.

"When Antiochus IV Epiphanus followed his brother to the throne, he led a large army against the Jews, slaughtering thousands, defiling the Temple, instituting a barbaric reign of terror, and outlawing the most sacred prescriptions of the Jewish law, including the reading of holy books, and circumcision . . ."

Leora would touch Joseph's hand and blush, as Sonya had touched Heykel's and Sonya's mother had touched his.

"For all they had suffered until then, the Jews had never before been denied the right to observe their faith. Now Antiochus sent envoys throughout the country to harness them to the pagan yoke . . ."

Marc and Ruth were sitting hand in hand, self-conscious, cheeks flushed.

"When they came to the village of Modin, south of Jerusalem, they requested that Mattathias, a priest of high standing, render the first sacrifice. Mattathias refused, denouncing the King and pledging himself to his land and his religion. Just then another Jew came forward and tendered oblation. Enraged, Mattathias rushed up with his five sons and slew the offender and also the general who had come in the name of the King and a few of his soldiers. Then he made a speech petitioning support and fled into the desert. Others responded to his example, evacuating with their families, and they lived in caves . . ."

It had been one of Eleazer's favorite episodes, Abrahm remembered. He was fascinated by the lore of grottoes and legendary rebels.

"When the King's generals in Jerusalem learned of this, they pursued the Jews into the desert. The Jews resisted. In retaliation, the generals took advantage of the Sabbath, on which day the Jews declined to engage in combat, and burned them alive in their sanctuaries. More than a thousand died this way. But a number survived and joined Mattathias, whom they now accepted as their new ruler. He trained them to fight concertedly, even on the Sabbath. Under his guidance, they waged continual war against the generals. Then, after one year, Mattathias died, leaving his mission to his sons, under the leadership of Judah, called Maccabee, the Hammer . . ."

Was it on a Saturday that Heykel's apartment had been raided?

"Judah Maccabee was the greatest warrior in Jewish history. Soon he had established control of the region, winning important battles, outsmarting the enemy generals, and exhorting his own troops with stirring speeches of life and death . . . "

There had been no one to urge Eleazer on as he held his breath in the blackness of his secret closet.

"One year, smarting from a previous defeat, the regent Lysius amassed sixty thousand soldiers and made provisions to scourge the region. But Judah beat him to the punch, launching an offensive with ten thousand men and inflicting such a serious defeat that Lysius evacuated the area. He was frightened by the Jews' desperate manner of fighting, noting that they were ready to die rather than surrender their liberty . . . "

Eleazer, the father of Olek and Heykel, had sprung out of the closet primed with the courage of those who had preceded him.

"Now, having compiled a string of victories, Judah led his adherents to Jerusalem to purify the Temple. When they arrived, they found it abandoned and in ruins. They refurbished it exactly three years from the date of its desecration by Antiochus. Sacrifice was made upon the new altar, and then, for eight days, they celebrated the restoration. Some attribute the eight days duration to a can of oil that was chanced upon in the Temple and placed lit upon the altar, where it burned that long. In memory of the occasion, an annual festival was promulgated, which was named Lights, or Channukah . . . "

Abrahm envisioned Judah—lean, muscular, sunbronzed, fierce but reverent, with a fire in his eyes—raising his knife to the throat of a white lamb, spurting its bright red blood over the unhewn stones of the altar.

He curled his nose to fix a whiff of his putrescence. Underlying the other smells of the bunker, his leg was like an exotic incense. He wondered whether it carried to the table. Victor had stationed the tree and the candles in front of the curtain to mask the malodor. The less Katrina knew the better.

"That was beautiful," Katrina said.

Through the screen her voice was not unpleasant. Abrahm imagined her to be a fairly attractive woman in her thirties who had been a menial and become a mistress. Her hands would be rough, her hair short and thick, her complexion brunette, her eyes weary, and her figure toughened by work, with strong arms and legs, yet appealing.

"It's history," Victor said.

"Yes, but its more than that," Katrina said. "It's so inspiring."

"What did you expect?" Mrs. Adler said.

She was clad in a burgundy silk evening gown with short puffed sleeves and a low neckline exposing her breasts almost to the nipples. A brilliantine tiara was perched atop her head, and a matching choker encircled her throat. Below her sleeves, her arms and wrists were ringed with bracelets, like those of the Egyptian queens carved into the limestone walls of pyramids.

"Well, what did you expect?"

"I'm not sure," Katrina said defensively.

"I'll tell you what," Mrs. Adler said. "Defeat. You saw candles and you expected humiliation. But there were no pigs served when Maccabee had anything to say about it."

Katrina strained to ignore Mrs. Adler's remark. There had been tension building since Mrs. Adler had pointedly abstained from eating the pork loin which Katrina had prepared.

"Admit it," Mrs. Adler continued. "You thought the candles were in mourning. Well, they're not. They're in jubilation. Jerusalem was liberated, they routed the swine, and they reveled for eight days around the clock. And that's just what I'm going to do, starting tonight."

"God help us," Victor said.

He was posted at the foot of the table, with his back to Abrahm's curtain. To his left were Mrs. Adler, Ruth and Marc, and to his right, Mrs. Krecji and Katrina. At the head, facing him, sat Nicholas.

"A lot of fun you are," Mrs. Adler said.

She leaned over and kissed Victor zestfully on the neck.

"That's the way to rejoice," she said.

"Watch your step, young lady," Victor said.

"Watch your eyes," Mrs. Adler replied, covering her breasts coyly with her hands and striking a coquettish pose.

Everyone laughed.

"Am I so amusing?" Mrs. Adler said.

Abrahm smiled at the notion of her flirtation with Victor.

"What became of the priest's sons?" Katrina asked.

"It ended regrettably," Victor said.

"Did they lose the Temple?"

"No," Victor said. "They held it, won Jerusalem and

established a long rule. Unfortunately, the protracted exercise of power usually results in corruption, no matter who wields the scepter."

"That was Christ's point," Nicholas said.

"What was his point?" Mrs. Adler said.

"That without a transformation of the human spiritual character, all rulers and all institutions will continue to be oppressive."

"I thought his business was loving his neighbor and turning the other cheek," Mrs. Adler said.

"That too," Nicholas said.

"You might as well begin at the beginning," Victor said.

"Yes," Mrs. Adler said. "But not until we've sung a few songs."

"That's all right," Ruth said. "We can all sing later."

"We can all sing later!" Mrs. Adler exploded. "You're all going to throw up later. First you devour a pig on Channukah, than you want to mix songs . . . the next thing you'll be mingling blood."

"Mother, please control yourself," Ruth said.

"I'm not the one who needs to be restrained," Mrs. Adler said emphatically.

"Please don't aim your finger at my son," Mrs. Krecji said.

"I'll do whatever I want with it," Mrs. Adler said.

She shook her finger at Marc, at Mrs. Krecji, at Marc again, then at Katrina.

"Please, mother," Ruth said.

" 'You'll have to excuse her,' " Mrs. Adler said, mimicking Ruth. " 'She's a little tired. Why don't you lie down and rest, mother?' Because I'm not tired, daughter dear. I'm not drunk. I'm not sick. I've gone crazy, that's all. There's nothing to be done about that."

"As long as you're pointing, can you conduct a song?" Victor said.

Mrs. Adler poised her hands and with a flourish commenced to sing and lead, joined by Ruth and Victor:

Eight small brothers
Of a large flame,
Sing silent songs
In Maccabee's name.

Sing of days of fighters
Armed with bravery;
Sing of mighty victors
Over slavery.

Eight silent witness,
Your kindred flames replay
The courage of forefathers
Born another day.

As he listened to their voices—he had forgotten how poorly Victor sang—Abrahm heard Isaac's harmonica accompanying them, lyrical, eloquent, recounting stories without end, wonders of ago.

"Bravo!" Marc said.

A sweet, poignant air filled the bunker.

"Is there something wrong?" Mrs. Adler said, noticing Katrina wiping her eyes.

The sharpness in her voice was tempered, and Abrahm wondered whether she was thinking of Emil.

"It must be the candles," Katrina said.

"Now tell us your tale," Victor said to Nicholas.

"With your indulgence," Nicholas said, picking his Bible up off the floor.

Again there was a flurry of adjustment. Abrahm thought of all the meetings he had attended at Bronis' house, when Nicholas was still a hired hand.

"The story of Christianity is a Christian one," Nicholas said, "but the life of Christ is the last great story of the Jews."

It was not true, Abrahm thought. There had been others, and Warsaw could have been, and yet might be.

"Before the Maccabees and after," Nicholas said, it was believed among Jews that the Roman domination would end

with the arrival of the Messiah. The prophet Isaiah had fore-
told that he would come as an earthling under the roof of the
house of David:

"*And the spirit of the Lord shall rest upon him, the spirit
of wisdom and understanding, the spirit of counsel and might,
the spirit of knowledge and of the fear of the Lord . . .*

"*And the wolf shall dwell with the lamb, and the leopard
shall lie down with the kid; and the calf and the young lion and
the fatling together; and a small child shall lead them . . .*

"And Isaiah prophesied that he would be a man despised
and rejected by other men; a man of grief and sorrow, who
would suffer for other men, and through his wisdom and
agony, redeem them. But a long time passed without his
appearance. There were worthy leaders, like Judah, and there
were impostors, but there was no Messiah."

The bunker had become very quiet, as if the vision of
Isaiah had cast a trance.

"Jesus Christ was born in Bethlehem, a short distance
south of Jerusalem. His parents were Jewish, and his Jewish
name was Joshua, or Yeshu—our Joshua, the help of Yahveh.

"His father was a simple carpenter. His mother was Mary.
When he was eight days old, Jesus was circumcised.

"During his childhood, his family moved to Nazareth, in
Galilee. There he grew up among the craftsmen of the village.
The valley where they lived was green and abundant, and the
sea was shimmering and stocked with fish. Jesus loved
the glory of nature, the shapes and colors of the flowers, and
the life-giving cycle of the fruit trees. He also attended the
Synagogue, heard the Scriptures, and became familiar with
the Prophets and the Psalms.

"His passionate calling to religion seems to have been
aroused by the teachings of John the Baptist. John condemned
hypocrisy and sinful living, warned everyone to ready themselves for the Last Judgment, and proclaimed that if all Judeah
would cleanse and prepare itself, the Messiah and God's Kingdom would come at once.

"When he was late in his twenties, Jesus went down and

was baptized by John. Shortly thereafter, John was imprisoned by Herod. Jesus took up his work.

"Jesus' outward features are unrecorded. The dress of the time was a tunic under a cloak, sandals for the feet, and a woven headdress to shield the face and shoulders from the sun.

"He was a magnetic person. Wherever he went, his following grew. It is not known precisely why. Presumably it was not how he looked, but rather his style of speaking, and the power of his vision.

"Like Caesar, Jesus allied himself fundamentally with the lower classes. But whereas Caesar sought to change man through modifications in laws and institutions, Jesus strove to alter them from within.

"Twelve Apostles attached themselves to Jesus. In addition, he appointed seventy-two Disciples, who spread his Gospel. Jesus believed that the Kingdom of Heaven was at hand, and he urged upon his adherents the Jewish prayer:

"Thy Kingdom come, thy will be done on earth as it is in heaven.

"But whatever man might do to please God and speed deliverance, Jesus also preached, the human heart needed to be cleansed before the world would rise above violence, misery, and greed.

"Thus was Christ the supreme revolutionary of the spirit.

"For a long while, Jesus regarded himself only as a Jew. Yet among Jews, only the Essenes did not oppose him. The majority were shocked and disturbed by his strange behavior, his fervor, and the growing assumption that he could speak for God. The most vehement objections were advanced by those privileged Jews who feared—on behalf of the Roman Authorities and their own interests—that he was pursuing political upheaval under the guise of religious reformation.

"In the year 30 or thereabouts, Jesus, in a burst of wrath, provoked a commotion in the Temple of Jerusalem. The Jewish authorities worried that in the emotional climate of Passover, he might fan a revolt against the Roman power. The

Sanhedrin was convoked, and the high priest declared 'that one man should die for the people, instead of the whole nation being destroyed.'

"Jesus learned of the order that he be taken into custody, but made no attempt to flee. On the fourteenth day of Nisan, he partook of Passover supper at the home of friends in Jerusalem. The humble meal of good and devout Jews—commemorating the escape of Moses and his people from Egyptian bondage—was to become honored as the Last Supper.

"That night Jesus and his company hid in the Garden of Gethsemane, on the outskirts of Jerusalem. There Temple police discovered and arrested him.

"Crucifixion was a Roman punishment. People followed Jesus in great numbers up the hill of Golgotha, wailing and beating their breasts. There he was pinned naked upon a wooden cross, as were two other men said to be thieves, and subjected to a cruel death."

Abrahm envisaged Jesus suspended on the cross, his flesh scourged, his face uniting anguish and resignation, unable to ease his weight or flick away the insects that were banqueting on him.

"I thought you were never going to finish," Mrs. Adler said.

Nicholas sat solemnly, spellbound by his own narrative.

"It's not over," Mrs. Krecji said.

What could he see from atop Golgotha, Abrahm mused?

"I'm sorry," Mrs. Adler said. "He seemed to be done."

"He didn't die," Mrs. Krecji said. "He came back."

"Yes, he did," Katrina added.

"Dead is dead," Mrs. Adler said.

"That's not so," Mrs. Krecji said. "He did come back, didn't he?"

With a vengeance, Abrahm considered. Here they were, two thousand years later, buried alive in a hole, talking about him.

"It is reported," Nicholas said, "that two days after his interment, Mary Magdalene, who loved him, went to his tomb, along with Mary, his mother, and Salome, and that they found it empty. Both frightened and overjoyed, they set forth to tell the Disciples. On the way they met a man whom they recognized as Jesus. They fell down and clasped his feet. Later he was seen by two Disciples on the road to Emmaus. They conversed and dined with him, and then they encountered him again in Galilee, and soon after were blessed with a bounteous haul of fish."

"There!" Mrs. Krecji said, tilting her face triumphantly at Mrs. Adler.

It was an enduring dream because it was hopeful, and the longer it went unfulfilled, the more exquisite and compelling it became.

"They were probably drunk," Mrs. Adler said.

"They were perfectly sober," Mrs. Krecji said. "He was there."

"What happened then?" Mrs. Adler asked.

"Tell them," Mrs. Krecji said.

"Forty days after he was beheld by Mary Magdalene," Nicholas said, "he ascended physically to Heaven."

"It sounds as if he was a bird," Mrs. Adler said.

"He was the greatest man who ever lived," Mrs. Krecji said.

It was conceivable, Abrahm reflected, experiencing a surge of admiration. Maccabee had not risen, and Moses, though rightfully exalted, did not compare. He had delivered the Jews from bondage, and received a new set of laws. But they were pragmatic, uninspired guidelines that had changed nothing. As it had been in Pharaoh's time, so it was still with Hitler.

"If Jesus was the father of Christianity," Mrs. Adler said, "that means we're all Jewish."

"We're not," Mrs. Krecji protested.

"You heard him," Mrs. Adler said. "Christ was born a Jew, he practiced Judaism, his cohorts were Jewish, even his prostitutes were kosher."

"It's a Jewish lie!" Mrs. Krecji said.

It was always the Jews, Abrahm thought.

"What's a lie, mother?" Marc said.

"We're not Jewish," she said.

"But historically we're of Jewish descent," Marc said.

"We're not," Mrs. Krecji insisted.

"Then what are we?" Marc asked.

Mrs. Krecji's eyes dilated, than narrowed, and her head twitched from side to side with a rapid, birdlike motion. She began to cry softly.

"Now, now, we're fretting needlessly," Victor said. "On with the ceremony."

"Yes," Katrina said. "Why don't we sing a carol and then we can exchange gifts."

"What gifts?" Mrs. Adler said.

"The ones we prepared," Ruth said.

"I didn't prepare any," Mrs. Adler said.

"It doesn't matter," Katrina said. "We'll all share whatever there is."

"I don't want anything from you," Mrs. Adler said.

> *It came upon the midnight clear,*
>   *That glorious song of old,*
> *From angels bending near the earth,*
>   *To touch their harps of gold.*
> *Peace on earth, good will to men,*
>   *From Heaven's all gracious King,*
> *The world in solemn stillness lay,*
>   *To hear the angels sing.*

It was awesome, Abrahm contemplated, that this man, who never authored a book or composed a song or painted an icon or constructed a temple, had inspired more literature and music and portraits and magnificent edifices than any man who had ever lived. And that although he was not a militarist, more blood had been spilled in his name than in any other.

> *Still thru the cloven skies they come,*
>   *With peaceful wings unfurled,*

And still their heavenly music floats
  Over all the weary world.
Above its sad and lowly plains
  They bend on hovering wing,
And ever over its Babel sounds,
  The blessed angels sing.

His vision was inspiring—the love, the sharing—but the Kingdom would never come because there was continually oppression to combat, and whoever failed to fight it with the vehemence of the Maccabees might go on cherishing the dream, but would never realize its fruition.

Taking revenge on a few apostates along with their Nazi debauchers would not promote love or brotherhood or socialism or peace. But their obscene deeds could not go unrequited.

O ye, beneath life's crushing head,
  Where forms are bending low,
Who toil along the climbing way
  With painful steps and slow.
Look now, for glad and golden hours
  Come swiftly on the wing,
O rest beside the weary road
  And hear the angels sing.

Now was the perfect time to strike, Abrahm thought. This very minute. While they were exulting at the Metropole and the Britannia, wassailing in Christ's honor, and in the brothels, where a premium was paid for Jewish girls.

Now would have been the time. If Krecji and others had been able to smuggle in enough weapons to sustain at least one round of fighting; if the long-awaited transport from the Polish Home Army had arrived; if finally all the dwindling factions could have discarded their parochial reservations—they should have been mounting an attack. If . . .

Now: as he reposed feebly on his cot, his bedpan beside him, the black curtain sheathing his helplessness, and his body constricting with futile rage, driving cold splinters of pain through his decomposing leg like barbed glass slivers.

> *For lo! the days are hastening on,*
>   *By prophets seen of old,*
> *When with the ever circling years*
>   *Shall come the time foretold.*
> *When the new heaven and earth shall own*
>   *The Prince of Peace their King,*
> *And the whole world send back the song,*
>   *Which now the angels sing.*

"That was nice," Mrs. Krecji said, having recovered from her crying.

"I must admit," Katrina said, "it is turning out to be a heart-warming Christmas."

"We must not forget what brings us together," Nicholas said.

"Naturally, dear," Katrina said. "But it's a holiday, after all, and there's no profit in being gloomy."

"I'd rather you were enjoying it without me," Mrs. Adler said.

"Think what you'd be missing," Victor said.

"I know," Mrs. Adler said, frowning at Ruth's and Marc's hands intertwined. "Jews and Christians congregating like wolves and lambs."

"No, Esther," Victor said. "Like innocent children."

"It's silly to squabble," Katrina said, "when we have presents to open."

"I can't wait," Mrs. Adler said.

Abrahm heard the rustling of paper and floss.

"Who'll go first?" Katrina said.

On the table before her was a pool of gaily decorated parcels, each topped with a brightly colored ribbon tied in an exaggerated bow. Two of the knots were larger than the packages they adorned. Ruth and Mrs. Krecji also had several gifts in front of them. Marc had one, which he wordlessly deposited on Ruth's lap.

"Why don't you start?" Mrs. Krecji said.

"If it's all right with everyone else," Katrina said.

"We'd be delighted," Victor said.

"Well, here's yours," Katrina said, extending a slim packet the size of a cigarette case with a flowering ribbon embracing it like an octopus. "I hope you like it."

"Whatever it is will be sincerely appreciated," Victor said. "Thank you."

Katrina distributed her store amidst a flutter of pleasantry.

"What shall I do with this?" she said, holding up the last present.

"Give it to yourself," Mrs. Adler said.

"It's for him," Katrina said, looking vaguely at Victor.

"Who?" Mrs. Adler said.

"I'll take it," Victor said.

Suddenly the badinage dried up. The sound "him" seemed to buzz through the bunker like a trapped bee. Abraham felt the blood drumming his temples.

"I hope it's suitable," Katrina said. "It's difficult to gauge a sick man's disposition."

She passed Victor an oblong book-shape swathed in gold paper and bound with a shamrock green ribbon.

"Who said there was anyone ill?" Mrs. Adler asked.

Katrina shunted her eyes.

"Who?"

"No one," Katrina said.

Her face blotched.

"Then where did you get the idea?"

"I made up six presents and one for Nicholas," Katrina said.

"But what made you think there was someone sick back there?" Mrs. Adler demanded.

Victor nipped his underlip and sniffed nervously.

"Isn't is obvious?" Nicholas said, intervening on Katrina's behalf.

"Is it?" Victor asked.

"The curtain's drawn, the light's off," Katrina said. "What else could it be?"

"But you appear to have entertained this assumption in advance," Victor said.

"That's not so," Katrina said.

"Then why did you say you didn't know what to give a sick man?" Mrs. Adler said glaringly.

"I was matching as I went along," Katrina said.

"You expect us to believe that?" Mrs. Adler said.

Katrina's shoulders braced.

"It reeks horribly down here," she said.

"You're not so sweet smelling yourself," Mrs. Adler said.

"What do you mean?"

"Here we are," Mrs. Adler exclaimed, "a covey of dung-hill chickens, merrily clucking away, praising God and pretending there's no fox in our coop, when actually we're all aware that you threatened to disclose us to the Gestapo. Well go ahead. Turn us in. But remember to warn them to pinch their noses before they come after us. Otherwise the stench might paralyze them, and that would be most unfortunate, for them and you."

NO MORE ILLUSIONS

Dear Comrade Silver:

I am moved by your message.

It is painful to lose family and friends. It is agonizing to reject that which might be secure for that which is unmistakably jeopardous. And it is difficult to risk one's own life for another. I am deeply grateful.

We have known from the beginning that Leora was destroyed, and we have identified the murderers. Their act can never be redressed, but still it must be punished. Death to everyone who has brought death upon us in this fashion.

As much as I would like to meet with you, it is at present impossible. There is too much to be done. If necessary, you can communicate with me again through the same channel. Regarding personal things, be assured that your confidence will be respected.

I am assigning you to the battle group with which you currently find yourself. You will be given work preparing munitions. Heykel will direct you.

There was a time when everyone was obsessed with self-

preservation. But most of us have since been dragged away, and those who remain have breath, but no inspiration. Now we must undertake alone what earlier should have been dared collectively: RESISTANCE!!

"Life for life!"

Let there be no more illusions. Our lives are wasted. We must RESIST so that when we die, hope may at least survive.

My heartfelt love to all our brothers and sisters. Keep faith.

I will be there when the fighting starts.

Comrade Abrahm.

FAREWELL

T he lamp shone glancingly across Abrahm's forehead and struck the curtain. As he lay with his eyes closed and his beard rankly covering his chin and throat, he seemed to be asleep. But he was not. He had heard Olek place a crate beside his cot and take a seat, and he was conscious of Emil's presence at the other end of the bunker. He had been feeling anguish, trembling like custard, but now a warm bathwater sensation soothed his quaking. Blindly, he pushed his hand over the blanket toward Olek.

"Happy New Year," Olek said.

Abrahm opened his eyes. The face above him was stretched drum-tautly over its frame. Eleazer had worn a beard all his adult life. He could not recall at this point whether it was Olek or Heykel who had inherited his mask.

"How's she doing?" Abrahm asked, referring to Mrs. Adler.

"She'll survive," Olek said.

He squeezed Abrahm's hand gently.

"Have I become appalling to contemplate?" Abrahm asked.

His forehead felt as if it could be peeled away with little effort, and his eyes weighed in their sockets like agate slugs.

"You're starting to resemble a nocturnal monster," Olek said.

"A Darwinian adaptation," Abrahm said.

"Did anyone suspect what was coming?" Olek asked.

"She'd threatened to do it on a number of occasions," Abrahm said, "but no one quite took her seriously."

"What then?"

"Apparently the holidays sparked her tinder."

"It's too bad she didn't make it."

"Did you hear anything?" Olek said.

"Dogs."

"Nothing before?"

"Not a swish," Abrahm said. "I was dreaming of geese and the next thing they were yelping like fox hounds."

"What did you think?"

"I didn't know what the hell to think," Abrahm said. "One of the dogs fell through and began dashing around as if he were rabid. It was pandemonium. Marc finally had to brain him."

"You're lucky a few more didn't drop in," Olek said.

"Evidently the dogs got to her before she could shut the door," Abrahm said.

"So did Nicholas," Olek said.

Abrahm's eyes rotated stonily toward the light.

"What do you make of it?"

"He probably saved her life," Abrahm said.

"But how did he get there so quickly?" Olek asked.

"He was sleeping in the barn," Abrahm said, "and the instant he heard the commotion he ran over."

"So he explained," Olek said.

"It's possible," Abrahm said.

"Isn't the house good enough for him?" Olek said.

"Ask him," Abrahm said.

"I did," Olek said. "He claims that since Christmas he's been waking up in the middle of the night in a cold sweat, often accompanied by the compulsion to go out there."

"That's conceivable," Abrahm said.

"But not convincing," Olek said.

"What's your hypothesis?" Abrahm asked.

"Either he's been forsaking Katrina's comfort and freezing his ass instead in order to protect us from her," Olek said, "or he's lying for some other reason. Heads or tails, we could be in trouble."

"I feel better already," Abrahm said.

"Do you have a more reassuring view?" Olek asked.

"He might have been around the kennel itself," Abrahm said.

"How do you figure?"

"It was almost morning," Abrahm said. "He's always been an early bird."

"Then why wouldn't he have said just that?" Olek asked.

"It's puzzling," Abrahm said.

His mind zeroed in on the gift Katrina had given him: a well studied volume of Oriental erotica. Would Bronis have left such a prize behind? It was a thoughtful choice for an invalid.

"Did she scream for help?" Olek asked.

Abrahm reflected a moment longer. The women were all graceful, voluptuous, seductive, but the men were grotesque, with Siamese projections, distorted limbs, distended organs, bizarre claws, and wicked, draconic faces.

"No."

"At least he was telling the truth about that," Olek said.

"What did he say?"

"That she didn't utter a sound while the dogs were working her over."

"Confirmed," Abrahm said.

"And that she bled considerably less than the wounds might have justified," Olek said.

"She must have hypnotized herself," Abrahm suggested.

"Leave it to Esther," Olek said.

"The power of determination is a transcendent force," Abrahm said.

"She'll be holding seances soon," Olek said.

"An interesting prospect," Abrahm said.

The curtain rippled, and Victor entered.

"Emil's finishing up," he said, setting a hand on Olek's shoulder.

"Why is it so quiet?" Abrahm said.

"He has her sedated," Victor said.

"Did he find many teeth?" Abrahm said.

"Don't worry," Victor said. "She'll be attempting another break before we know it."

"I have a premonition that this time she'll succeed," Abrahm said.

"The dogs will certainly recognize her," Olek said. "That's a plus."

"Where do you suppose she was going?" Victor asked.

"America," Abrahm said, smiling weakly.

"Try again."

"The barn?" Olek said.

"The ghetto!" Victor said.

"Who couldn't use a vacation?" Abrahm said.

"The humor eludes me," Olek said.

"As long as Herr Thierbach doesn't," Abrahm said.

Olek released Abrahm's hand as though a shock had repelled him. Then he realized that it was good. Abrahm could still hold the sweet and the bitter together. He returned his hand, resting it on Abrahm's forearm.

"She had decided to go back and assist Emil," Victor said.

"I don't believe it," Olek said.

"Why not?" Victor said.

"She's not that crazy," Olek said.

The three men pondered the depths of Mrs. Adler's psyche.

"Whatever her motivation, she wound up doing us an immense favor," Victor said.

"How?" Abrahm said.

"By bringing Emil in," Victor said.

"I don't agree," Abrahm said.

"That was her objective all along," Olek said.

"On what do you base your assertion?" Victor asked.

"She felt sorry for him," Olek said. "She resolved to do something about it, and that was her only option."

"The queen of fools," Abrahm said.

"Let Emil be the judge," Victor said.

Abrahm shifted his head on the pillow, squinting up darkly.

"What about the guns?" he asked, referring to the shipment which had recently been received from the Polish Home Army.

"Mierck made contact Tuesday," Olek said. "We're awaiting an answer."

"Ten pistols after all these months," Abrahm said.

"It's a seller's market," Olek said.

"I don't care what it is," Abrahm said. "They fucked us."

"Mierck told them that we were unhappy and that time was running out," Olek said. "I instructed him to be emphatic."

"They're hoarding for their own fight," Abrahm said. "Only by then it will be over for everyone."

"Perhaps someone else should have gone," Victor said.

"He's doing a tremendous job," Olek said. "Thursday he brought in five hundred liters of gasoline."

"It's a lucky thing we're not smuggling whiskey," Abrahm said. "We'd have to order double to allow for inventory shrinkage."

"But our supply would be assured," Olek said.

"What a character to entrust with such a delicate mission," Victor said.

"You can't imagine the half of it," Olek said.

"I'm afraid I can," Victor said.

"He's blown up his uncle," Olek said.

"I don't doubt he's capable of it," Victor said.

"It's done," Olek said.

"Are you serious?" Abrahm asked.

"Perfectly."

"Why haven't you said anything?"

"There's been no chance."

"We're listening."

"The week after Stefan rigged Victor's apartment," Olek said, "the front window was shattered, signaling, as we had hoped, that whoever had previously rifled the premises had come back and walked into our trap. But who it was, and how much damage had been inflicted, we had no way of ascertaining. Our only tangible satisfaction derived from Stefan's boast that he had planted enough explosives to splatter an elephant.

"Shortly thereafter, our hero was passing through the fountain district and spotted his distinguished uncle, whom he hadn't seen since his mother's funeral, sitting in a cafe with his arm wrapped like a pipe and his head swaddled in a turban bandage. Instinctively, he flashed to the apartment, made a quick-about face, and disappeared unnoticed."

"Several days later, he showed up unexpectedly at his uncle's residence, three-fifths pickled, on the pretext of needing money. He had a brown bag with him. 'What do you have there?' Stracho asked, and Stefan said, 'Oh, a little whiskey. The way things are, it's best to keep it handy.' And Stracho said, 'if you're so hard up, save it, drink mine. I have a few drams to spare.' 'A few warehouses full,' Stefan said, and Stracho said, 'Enough to drown you in.' He put a bottle and two glasses on the table and Stefan deposited his bag on the floor. Drinks were poured. 'To your beloved mother,' Stracho said. They quaffed their shots and he dispensed another round. 'To my beloved father,' Stefan said. When they had toasted Pilsudski, Marlene Dietrich, Smigly-Rydz, Churchill, Stalin, and Joe Louis—this is how he related it—Stefan excused himself to go to the bathroom. The second he was out of sight he climbed out a rearward window and watched from the street as the brown bag he had abandoned at the foot of his chair blasted what remained of his family to Kingdom Come. 'Hallelujah!' he thought to himself, strolling home on air."

"When I asked Stefan whether it had occurred to him that he was drawing an inferential connection between Stracho and the apartment, he said, 'However you look at it, he was a rotten sonofabitch.' 'But what if he was innocent?' I said, and he answered, 'Then the stuff wouldn't have gone off.'"

"What a morale booster," Abrahm said. "We have a mad bomber on our side."

"Don't laugh," Olek said. "Now he wants to come into the ghetto."

"For what reason?" Victor asked.

"He craves the action and sympathizes with the odds," Olek said.

"Jew envy," Abrahm said.

"He belongs where he is," Victor said.

"Perhaps," Olek said. "But he may not wish to stay there."

"See what's taking Emil so long," Abrahm said to Victor.

Victor exited around the curtain. Present, shutter, absent, Abrahm thought. There, not there. Two cot lengths behind him Mrs. Adler lay chewed up by dogs.

"Spit it out," Abrahm said.

Olek renewed the pressure on his hand.

"I'm not clairvoyant," Abrahm said.

They viewed one another with love, their eyes slightly missing.

"Alas, I am that ugly," Abrahm said.

Olek wavered on the verge of speaking.

"En route," Victor said, reappearing.

The shutter clicked. Beyond the cave and the curtain and Esther and the kennel were the barn and the house and the city and the ghetto and the Nazis and the cemetery and God knew what else. There, not there.

"Is the date set?" Abrahm asked.

Olek swallowed.

"Set."

"Any hitches?"

"Not yet."

"How did you deal with Mierck's request?" Victor asked.

"I promised to accommodate him," Olek said.

"On January 22?"

"No," Olek said. "Prior to the general resistance."

"So, Stefan Mierck will make victory ours," Victor said.

"We could do with more like him," Olek said.

"What's bothering you?" Abrahm said.

Olek remained uncommunicative, but a change came over him. His jaws slackened, and a softening tremor caterpillared down his face.

"Is something wrong with Sonya?" Abrahm asked.

He though he detected a flinch. But what could it be? There was no indication that Victor was privy to the problem. He yanked his hand away from Olek.

"Unburden yourself or get out of here," Abrahm said.

Olek's neck quivered, and an odd white spot surfaced high on his forehead. His eyes cleared to a pale crystal blue focus.

"Victor and Henryk are dead," he said.

Abrahm struggled to keep his eyes from clamping tight, but his vision faded anyway and the room grew black. He heard Olek's voice tapping out the obituary, tormenting his ears. His cot began to spin. They had been negotiating with the Russians for their release, but the process had been derailed. No one knew how or why. The announcement had come over the underground radio. They had withheld the news from him for verification, but they could no longer withhold it. The two greatest leaders of the Polish Jewry had been executed by the Russians for "*conspiring with the German enemy.*"

A tusk was puncturing Abrahm's chest, crumpling his lungs. Victor Alter. Henryk Ehrlich. Expired. He felt his hand being squeezed, but he was numb. Leora's visage sped toward him phantasmagorically and vanished. Brave Victor. Brave Henryk. They had devoted their lives unstintingly to democracy, justice, decency. Yet it was as if they had never been.

Contrary impulses contested for Abrahm's will: the desire to spring regenerated from his sickbed and inhale the snow-crisped winter air; and the siren urge to abandon himself to the swirling darkness.

He clutched his blanket and pushed himself up on his forearms.

"You should have told me sooner," he said.

Victor was crying, blotting his face with a patch of curtain.

"The upshot is the same," Olek said.

His face had regained its tenseness, but his eyes were bleared.

"Herald the cobbler," Emil said, stepping into view.

He was followed by Ruth.

"Welcome, doctor," Abrahm said.

Olek stood and took Victor by the arm.

"If you'll excuse us," Emil said, "we'll examine the shoe tree."

Emil Adler was a short, compact man, once somewhat fleshy, now lean, with compassionate eyes, an intelligent face, and unusually large, sensitive hands. His manner was gracious but firm.

"How's Esther?" Abrahm asked.

"Resting peacefully," Emil said.

"Isn't anyone going to inform me of her condition?" Abrahm said.

Ruth spread a towel over the crate which Olek had been occupying and proceeded to set out alcohol, swabs, and other accessories.

"Her left arm may be permanently impaired," Emil said. "The bicep is lacerated. Otherwise she should heal fairly routinely. If there are any complications, Ruth will know what to do."

Emil unclasped his satchel and arrayed a selection of instruments on the shelf Ruth had prepared.

"Lie back," Ruth said, stripping Abrahm of his bedding.

As his head sank onto his pillow, Abrahm strained to focus his eyes on the section of the vent that was visible like a quarter-moon beyond the edge of the curtain.

"How have you been feeling?" Emil asked.

"Fair."

"Specifically?"

"Weak. Moderate pain. But shivers, and a persistent festering."

Abrahm heard himself replying to an efficient succession of questions, and he was aware of his mouth yawning, "Aaaah," the cold touch of steel in his nose, his ears, the flat metallic chill of the stethoscope sounding his breast, transmitting his heart-thump, and then his body yielding to Emil's long, percipient fingers—probing like extraterrestrial sensors for clues to his nature, systematically approaching his leg.

"Esther pledged us to relay a message," Emil said. "She implores you not to be pressured or inveigled into reverting to the ghetto."

Breathe in. Breathe out. Contract. There. Not there. There. There. The fingers conducting their complex search. The instruments silently surveying his landscape.

Abrahm tried to concentrate on each contact, drawing himself away from the gravity of Ehrlich and Alter, the numbness, the darkness, the dungeon, toward the moon.

Fingers of flesh, fingers of steel.

"This is going to be painful," Emil said, holding up a large needle. "Tell me if it becomes intolerable."

Ice and fire slipped into his leg, the sterile spike gimleting the fragile bonds between cell and cell.

There, not there.

"We'll have to operate without delay," Emil announced.

Abrahm disengaged his mind from the moon and peered over his beard. Emil was supporting his leg aloft while Ruth was padding the mattress with towels. Then she was bathing his decomposition with alcohol and coating it with a rich emollient lotion which she smeared generously over his skin without rubbing it in. Over this she draped a long white band of linen that settled over him like a light snowdrift.

"Don't bite your lip off," Ruth said. "You may still need it."

"For what?" Abrahm said.

There was pain, but Abrahm had no emotion for it. Ruth

patted him affectionately on the left foot and departed. A smile lingered where her face had been.

"I should have insisted on visiting you earlier," Emil said.

Having wiped his instruments, he rolled them into a towel which he set beside his satchel. Heinrich would have appreciated such a fine assortment of probes and talons, Abrahm mused.

Perhaps he should have summoned Emil after the fall, as Victor had urged. But he had been loathe to dispirit Sonya and Heykel and all the comrades who were expecting him back in the ghetto. Despite the reversal, Abrahm had retained every intention of insuring that Thierbach, Heinrich, and certain of their ill-starred accomplices were duly paid their deserved, though inadequate, retribution.

Ruth had reappeared with Olek and Victor.

"What's the verdict?"

"The deterioration is dangerously advanced," Emil said. "Surgery is imperative."

"Where?" Olek said.

"It will have to be in the house," Emil said.

"That's a ticklish proposition," Victor said.

"Given our requirements, there is no alternative," Emil stated. "And not an hour to squander."

"All right," Olek said. "What happens first?"

"Ruth and I will attend to the technical preliminaries," Emil said. "Your responsibilities will be enlisting the necessary cooperation, security, and Abrahm's transfer. There must be effective coordination between . . ."

"With or without the patient's consent?" Abrahm asked.

"With your consent, of course," Emil said.

"How serious will the procedure be, in terms of convalescence time?" Abrahm asked.

"It's difficult to predict," Emil said.

"I have an appointment on the twenty-second," Abrahm said. "Three weeks."

"Naturally we'll do our utmost to have you up as quickly

as possible," Emil said. "But let's not be unrealistic. Your condition is precarious. Hesitation is a luxury if we're to save the leg."

Abrahm felt the back of his skull being sawed away and his eyes and the cotton lobes of his brain being detached from their architecture and sucked out of his head by the pull of a night-filled vortex peopled with nameless stars.

Which of them had resisted? Where was Eleazer, flushed from his closet, and Leora, cloistered in her wooden box? She had dreamed of being married on the First Feast of Passover. History was the morning prayer and the evening prayer. One minute life was there, then it was not.

"You have my permission," Abrahm said.

LIFE
FOR
LIFE

Eugen dug his fingers into his beard, pursuing an itch that had lodged in the underbrush of his cheek. He scratched it vigorously, scraping loose pieces of dead skin.

He was sitting on the floor in a circle with Heykel, Samson, Gideon, Joseph, and Nussbaum. Their faces were harsh in the yellowish cast of an indirect light. Samson's resolute features resembled a large, unscoured potato freshly uprooted from the earth. Nussbaum's suggested a minced carrot pudding baked with brown sugar. Behind him, Nussbaum's wife, Benyk, Sonya, and Isaac had formed a ring.

"The time has come to rid the ghetto of all Jewish agents of the Gestapo," Heykel said.

He spoke with his lips contracted as though he were spitting nails.

"So, we finally have at the bastards," Samson said.

Eugen removed his fingers from his beard. Something in Samson's voice frightened him. He had heard rumblings of an imminent "action," but he had not related personally to them

and was careful not to evince curiosity. Now Heykel's eyes
were cold with passion.

"We have three distinct assignments," Heykel said. "Gideon will develop the operative details. Simultaneity of attack
will be the sole thread between our missions and those of the
other groups. In all other respects, we'll be on our own. This
will maximize our chances for success and isolate failure."

Gideon fidgeted with his cuffs during Heykel's remarks,
but when he was called on, his composure firmed. He began
by discussing, in a clipped military cadence, certain strategic
requirements of the general uprising that was being projected
to take place in several months. Pre-positioned arms storage
would have to be worked out, so that if any unit fell en route to
a combat station, its weapons would remain intact. A signal
code would have to be perfected. As for "hot" support from
the outside, none could be expected. The Polish underground
might respond once the hostilities were in progress, but thus
far its repeated declarations of sympathy and solidarity had
been yoked to a plea of "unpreparedness" for confrontation.
With regard to the Home Army shipment of arms, this would
prove immediately useful in the forthcoming assault on specified German and Polish Nazis and, principally, Jewish collaborators.

Eugen listened intently. Ten pistols. Thierbach would
laugh. Although faced with such an easily crushable chal-
lenge, he would also allow himself to become genuinely in-
censed. He could envision Thierbach sneering to Dieter:
"Issue an alert. A gang of Jewish criminals have organized a
'self-defense' force. Their plan is to assassinate their own
police, then turn on us. These felons will be heavily armed,
possessing handkerchiefs and firecrackers. Oh yes, and ten
pistols."

"We must conserve ammunition," Gideon was saying, "to
a degree consistent with our high level of risk acceptance."

Any of these people would have opposed the Jewish policeman who had collared him near the *umschlagplatz*, Eugen
reflected. But he had let himself be bullied. He felt shame and

regret. It was up to those who could defend themselves to do so—not only to save their own necks, but for the common good. He wished that he could lay his hands on that cannibal now. He would teach him to value compassion.

But it was water under the bridge. The man had probably been transferred to the East and sprinkled with quicklime.

It seemed too late to worry about starcaps, Eugen thought. Or even the Thierbachs and, worse, the Hermanns and Dieters who were waiting in basements and antechambers to replace them. Why hadn't the Jews acted when what were now irreversible developments might still have been prevented? Thierbach would not have mocked them in the early days. He was as apprehensive of them, in a peculiar, personal sense, as they were of him. It was not until after it became apparent that the ghetto would be relatively untroublesome, and that the deportations could be carried out expeditiously, that he found humor in the situation. Ten pistols!

"Julius will pair with Samson," Heykel said.

For Eugen himself, however, there would be a capital advantage even now in a change of personnel. He could emerge from the ghetto and report back that Bankart was dead. Charge discharged. They would not question his word. Thierbach was the one who had it in for him.

"Joseph," Gideon said. "You'll team with me."

Eugen observed Joseph's face as he received his orders. It was spare, severe, impassive.

Evidently Gideon was coupling him with Heykel, Eugen thought. He was glad. No doubt Gideon was as effective in executing tactics as he was in conceiving them, but he struck Eugen as having a perverse streak of absolutism—absolute honor, absolute courage. He would rather be with Heykel, whom he estimated to be equally brave but more pragmatic. There were times when it was suicidal to go straight ahead.

Thierbach was still there, daring Eugen to return. Scoffing him. But he had ceased to care about Thierbach's coarseness. Thierbach could jeer himself to distraction. Eugen had been given an assignment, and he was pursuing it. He would persist until he could reach out and grip Bankart's arm as readily as he could Joseph's. All the better that Heykel would be his partner. He was the direct intermediary to Bankart.

"Heykel will work alone," Gideon said, "linking up with Olek."

"What about me?" Eugen mumbled.

"You're to stay here and keep guard," Gideon said.

Eugen felt as though he had been spat on. They were leaving him behind with the women.

"I would prefer active duty," he said.

"You'll contribute most by following instructions," Gideon said.

"Why can't I participate in the field?" Eugen asked.

"One of us has to stay back," Gideon said.

"Comrade Abrahm appointed me to a battle squad," Eugen said. "I insist on fulfilling my responsibility."

He enunciated the last sentence with a boldness that startled him.

"You've forgotten how inhospitable it is out there," Nussbaum said.

"It's irrelevant," Eugen said.

"We're the only 'fiver' with six men." Samson said. "Seven, counting Isaac."

They were ridiculing him too, Eugen fretted. He was growing angry.

"You may not use my gun unless you also use me," he asserted. "I too have debts to repay."

There was a stranger within him, struggling to break out.

Eugen directed his gaze at Heykel. Their eyes met. Then he realized that Heykel was not there. The orbs were uninhabited. He was off somewhere in meditation.

"I'll take him," Heykel said.

His voice was flat, atonal, like a robot's. Eugen was shocked. He looked away and back. The eyes were still remote.

"Are you certain?" Gideon said.

Heykel nodded gravely.

"Thus commences the adventure of Noah Silver at the Metropole," Samson said.

"What?" Eugen said.

"The Metropole," Samson said. "It's a nightclub. A very nice place, I hear. I've never had the pleasure of visiting there myself, but it has a considerable reputation."

Eugen's heart twinged. Was he going to be taken to the Metropole? Why? It was impossible.

"I don't understand," he said.

"It will all become clear," Heykel said.

Slowly, his eyes resumed an outward bearing.

"Prime yourself for a rich experience," Samson said. "The fare includes every variety of game, roast goose, sugarplums, champagne, music, and a singer who'll pop your eyes out."

"Stop it," Heykel said.

"Then it's decided," Gideon said. "Samson and Nussbaum, Joseph and Zadok, Heykel and Silver. Are there any questions?"

Gideon glanced from man to man. The remoteness in Heykel's eyes had evolved into a glare of fierce determination that was spreading over his face as if it had been stained and glazed and were being fired in a kiln. His mouth pursed, but would not open. Then his cheeks started to quaver, and his jaw.

"We have lost everything," he said. "We have suffered too much. Victor and Henryk are dead. Eleazer is dead. Leora is dead under a Christian name. Only one prospect is yet ours! *REVENGE!!*"

Heykel's fists shot into the air and his voice peaked, then plummeted. A live-wire stillness filled the room, like the sudden electric drop in the atmosphere before a storm. Eugen felt himself tightening. Heykel was on the verge of fulmination—the flame that had stolen out of his heart was consuming him—and his combustion would be contagious.

But instead of detonating, Heykel simply rose, moved over to where Sonya was reclining, laid his hand on her convex abdomen, and kissed her on the forehead.

And then, undemonstratively, the cloud that was lowering overhead gave off a gentle dew, slacking the tension, and everyone stood, subduedly, and went about his business.

Eugen stretched, trying to flex the stress out of his limbs, and sat down again, this time beside the door. He had been sentry for three nights and had two to go in the rotation. He would not have objected to more. It afforded him satisfaction that the group was willing to sleep under his watch. He had not yet been entrusted with his gun or any hardware, but that might come shortly.

The group's attitude toward him had steadily improved. Samson and Nussbaum had been sharp this evening, but that was the result of anxiety. On the whole, Samson had been quite helpful—to the point of bringing in a doctor who had rebroken his finger and straightened it. The pain had been acute, despite their plying him with vile, peppermint-flavored alcohol, but now the bone was healing well. Wearing a splint, he was able to assist Joseph in formulating and stockpiling incendiary mixtures and devices. He had not wanted to be treated as a prisoner, nor like Isaac, and it was rewarding to have won respect for his diligence.

Bankart had been wise in postulating that every man, woman and child should be engrossed in the resistance. It was the key to enduring. There was no equilibrium in the ghetto. A person lived or died. And food itself was not sufficient for sustenance. The psyche also needed to be maintained.

Eugen had gotten into a rhythm, putting in the night watch and then, after a morning nap, helping Joseph just as he had before drawing guard duty. Eugen had viewed it as a therapeutic regimen, but now that he was going to the Metropole with Heykel, he felt like a gladiator training for combat.

What had he gotten himself into?

His stomach began a deep, compressive churning, as if to cope with a clump of fermenting dough which he had swallowed inadvertently and, refusing to be digested, was swelling within him.

The Metropole. Was he still in command of his faculties?

He had never finally arrived at Thierbach's motives—events had ensnared him so quickly, then and since—and now, when his connection with him had nearly withered, he had discovered that he was in the presence of the father of Bankart's granddaughter. He had been there all along, but he had not made the association explicitly until Heykel's outburst. Yes, and he had found the mother too, who was Bankart's daughter. He was sure of it, for Bankart had a daughter whose name was Sonya, and Heykel, mourning Leora, had cried out for revenge and kissed Sonya on the mouth. No. It had been on the brow. And she was pregnant, which meant that Bankart would have another grandchild to replace the child Thierbach had murdered.

But Thierbach would not kill this one. Eugen would defend it against harm until he had apprehended Bankart and acquitted himself of the obligations and accusations that had turned his life into a nightmare.

Eugen's stomach constricted further, laboring to contain the expanding mass inside it. Why had he been so gullible as to believe that Felix Erdmann had not known about the girl? He pictured Erdmann steeping his guilt in wine. Was that why they were going to the Metropole?

Eugen was confounded. Gideon had mentioned an Olek. Was it the same Olek with whom he was acquainted? Vaczek? Mouse-face? Yes, it had to be. They were planning to use him to set up Erdmann. But what was their relationship with him?

If he had known the facts in advance, he might not have jumped into the pot, Eugen thought. Heykel had refused to explain what it was that he had volunteered for. It was inconceivable that he would continue to keep him in the dark. But if he did, Eugen would have to spear an advantageous moment in which to pin him down. No matter what. There would be several weeks of preparation. The value of his unconfessed familiarity with the Metropole might be appreciable. It was a perilous den to wander into unwelcome.

What if the foray had nothing to do with Erdmann?

Under no circumstances would Eugen enter the Metropole. He would appeal to Bankart if necessary. They were due to strike on January twenty-second. Why then? What was their strategic design? Would they cross onto the Aryan side? Or were all their targets in the ghetto? And when would he meet Bankart?

"I will be there when the fighting starts."

Did they hope to trigger a wider rebellion then and there?

"I will be there when the fighting starts."

The sentence had been revolving in his mind like a trussed fowl on a spit.

"RESIST."

The loaf in Eugen's stomach was rising insuppressibly, causing him to cramp. He felt himself succumbing to a force akin to the writhing, bending agony of a waterless diver.

Inexorably, the pressure ascended, impinging upon his thoughts. He strove to insulate them, but he could not. They began skittering away from him, reacting to an influence that was beyond his jurisdiction. Thoughts of Dresden. Thoughts of Berlin. Thoughts of Franz. Thoughts of Thierbach. Thoughts of Isaac. Thoughts of Erdmann. Thoughts of Vaczek. Thoughts of the Metropole. Thoughts of Bankart. Thoughts of Ellen. Thoughts of the Britannia. Other thoughts. Sensations. Stampeding: dashing this way and that, jostling one another, flailing, flitting, colliding with mental barriers like moths against glass, dropping, picking themselves up, and crashing again.

Eugen felt himself being overwhelmed, but the harder he wrestled for control, the more unruly his thoughts became: assuming strange, elastic shapes, snapping themselves inside out, hurtling about helter-skelter, bumping, leapfrogging, ricocheting off the contours of his skull with increasing energy until they had routed his resistance.

Suddenly they were corporalizing into harlequined, bow-legged dwarfs with black, evil-favored faces and gnarled extremities, turning cartwheels and somersaults and hugging and shoving and jabbing each other with long, jagged knives.

He envisioned them invading the Metropole like a swarm of locusts, storming in over the tables, upsetting them, sending their contents—food, bottles, china, silverware—smashing onto the floor. A brawl erupted, and before the situation could be checked, everyone had become involved. Chairs flew, tables careened, glass shattered. Only the spotlight was on. Dark shrieks and curses of retaliation quailed through the air as the dwarfs scurried among the kelp-like tangles of flesh that were strewn about, wading into them with malice, piercing, punching, pinking, gouging.

The singer had been knocked to her knees and clawed and was clinging to the platform while several dwarfs scuffled to drag her off. A blade perforated her chest, and blood began to trickle out of her mouth, but she went on uttering her lyrics with decelerating speed, like a cranked victrola running down.

Some of the dwarfs had gotten behind the bar and glugged massive, undiluted doses of vodka, whiskey, rum, whatever poured, and now they were scuttling about the room like drunken maggots, circulating liquor and exploring the carcass of a living beast undergoing mutilation, biting, sticking, broaching, stoking the madness.

In the bedlam, it was every person for himself, lashing out left and right, scotching and maiming indiscriminately. To exacerbate the mayhem, the diabolic dwarfs issued a spate of threats and imprecations in the perfectly imitated voices of the patrons.

"You son-of-a-bitch, I'll split your ass like a pomegranate."

"I'll have you drinking your liver first."

"You whining coward."

"Look out!"

"Screw you and your fathers both."

"Have that."

"Hail Mary for your gonads."

"Aye!!"

A peal of gunfire provoked a wail of distress and precipitated a spray of bullets that zipped into the mangle like blowtorches carving snow, crunching into bones and embedding there for future archaeologists to treasure. The tumult grew more frenzied, like a savage rite of spring winding toward a sacrificial climax.

"Murderer!" the dwarfs trumpeted in the blackthorn pandemonium.

"Nazi!"

"Pimp!"

"*Schmalzovnik!*"

"Smuggler!"

"Wheedler!"

"Eel!"

"Stoolie!"

"Butcher!"

"Whore!"

"Cocksucker!"

"Ass-licker!"

"Pederast!"

"Torturer!"

"Profiteer!"

"Motherfucker!"

"Jew!"

"Where!"

"Over there."

"There's a Jew in here!" a frantic voice screamed out.

The rumor descended upon the melee like a bombshell, raising howls of anguish.

"Oh my God, there's a Jew in the room."

"Where?"

"WHERE?"

"Over there!"

"Quick."

The room exploded in a violent orgy of venery. Wings, breasts, ribs, onions, beets, cabbage, natural juices, gravy, waiters, guests, hostesses, wines, fondue, peanuts, chutney, mocha, cream and pastries all came together on the floor, squirming and flouncing furiously. And a stench more noxious than camel-dung cigars and regurgitated swill began to permeate the room—a fetid exudation of fear, incontinence, and urine sizzling on a radiator.

"Jew!" a dwarf mimicked hysterically.

"I've got him."

"No, here he is."

"By the bar."

"There, you devil-bastard."

The air reeked like the inside of an abattoir, and the floor was thickly covered with a squealing, paroxysmic mass of antagonists tearing each other apart with hands, teeth, knives, forks, corkscrews, anything which cleaved or augured, and muttering oaths and execrations.

"Jew!"

"Blood guzzler!"

"Child killer!"

"Fairy!"

"Christ slayer!"

"God hater!"

"Judas!"

"Zhides!"

"Jew!"

"Lousy Jew!"

The epithetal barrage abated as the Metropole became reduced to a heap of oozing, twitching pulp. But the dwarfs, their depravity unquenched, dug their way through the morass of crowbait, shards, turds, spindles, viscera, ureal sauterne, blood-tawney port, sweetbreads, and sausage, trampling, spiking, poking, gnawing, roiling the last putrid ounces of vitality.

"Jew!" a dwarf resumed.

"Where?"

"Over here," said a voice pitched with necrophilic excitement. "I've got him! I've got him!"

Under the spotlight, the strident-lunged exclaimer—who had been the most vociferous instigator throughout the affray—had climbed the platform and mounted the life-drained body of the singer, which was sprawled with its head dangling over the edge like a wrung-necked emu.

"Jew!" he blared feverishly, humping her and stabbing at her throat with a triangular dagger. "Jew! Jew! Jew! Jew! Jew! Jew! Jew! Jew! Jew! Jew! Jew! Jew! Jew!"

As he reiterated the word like an exorcism, it shed its literal significance and became a tone, a mantra, mesmerizing him and attracting the other dwarfs from their feast.

"Look!"

"Up there!"

"In the light."

They crawled and wallowed through the fecal pudding toward the platform, and one of them scrambled up, ripped the chief dwarf's pants from his buttocks, and pounced on him from behind.

"Don't!" bellowed the darkest dwarf. "Get off!"

But the singer's vulva had locked around his penis and he could not extricate himself in order to unhorse the dwarf who was cramming his black rapier cock into his anus with unlubricated ferocity.

"Jew!" screeched the second dwarf, ramming him. "Jew! Jew!"

"Let go!" the first dwarf implored. "I can't get out."

"Uh!" the second dwarf grunted as a third dwarf straddled him, and a fourth the third, and so on until there was a catena of dwarfs writhing in the mire like a miscreated serpent, poising itself and thrusting forward convulsively, impacting the first dwarf into the singer.

"JEW!" the serpent chanted. "JEW! JEW! JEW! JEW! JEW! JEW! JEW! JEW! JEW! JEW! JEW! JEW! JEW! JEW! JEW! JEW! JEW! JEW! JEW!"

"Help!" the first dwarf croaked. "I'm being devoured."

The singer's corpse had begun to wriggle, its legs twitching, its hips and pelvis twisting and jerking, and its vagina contracting spasmodically, as though to ingest him into its womb.

"HELP!"

In gruesome ecstasy, the dwarf's black face began to glisten like a chunk of coal. Then his features started to melt away, transforming into the face of Franz: and the face of Franz became the face of Ellen; and there followed in bewildering protean succession the faces of Thierbach and the vegetable crone with the cankered gums and a crude metalworker encountered in a beer hall in Berlin and the harelipped and the pockmarked woman and Rabbi Bloodstein and Crazy Isaac and the flushed, choleric policeman and other faces—young, old, some androgynous or gorgonian or inexplicably smiling—and the foliage-brown face of Noah/Age 12/In the forest and the blond, orient face of Tzipora and a grim face that he could not identify . . . a green, brooding countenance that said, *"NO!"*

A PRAYER FOR THE DEAD

There was no sign of Abrahm's grave.

Nicholas inhaled deeply, raising his chest against the weariness that had worked into his arms and shoulders. He had toiled methodically in the darkness, straining not to disturb the silence. Tomorrow his muscles would be stiff and sore. Now he felt relieved that it was over.

Thank God, he thought, drawing another breath.

He had taken meticulous pains to camouflage his labor. In the morning he would double-check for traces. If there were none, it would be as if the ground had never opened.

The cold, lightless barn was rhythmic with sleep. Outside a snow was falling. Softly and steadily, its whiteness tranquilized the night—damping noise, absorbing odors, cushioning the solitude.

Nicholas resisted the temptation to lie down and catch a few winks before sunrise. It might only becloud his mind and weight his legs, and he anticipated a trying day. He would be better off getting his thoughts in order, paying his final respects to Abrahm, and keeping vigil until it was time to make his rounds.

With a growing feeling of alleviation, he sat down on a mound of fodder. It was accommodatingly firm beneath his buttocks, and the earth was solid beneath his feet. He had remained dry while he was digging the grave, but now a cool, thin wash of perspiration broke over his upper body. He unbuttoned the front of his jacket and the collar of his shirt and posted his hands on his thighs, with his elbows akimbo, to let the crisp air sting his chest and circulate under his armpits.

The first thing he had to resolve was whether to withhold the news of Abrahm's death from those in the bunker until Olek was advised. He could pretend that nothing was wrong. There had been sufficient practice with Katrina. But did he have the right to assume such responsibility in this case? Would Olek approve? And how would they regard his action when they found out?

He would be less reluctant to inform them immediately if he felt they possessed some fundamental source of solace. But as far as he could perceive, their reality was absolutely stripped of comfort. God was the only inspiration that could by itself sustain people in such dire, isolated circumstances. Yet all but Mrs. Krecji stubbornly resisted religious sentiment.

Ironically, he was grateful that he had been ignorant of the Divine Presence in the slaughterhouse. Otherwise he might have persevered there. Of course, whatever became of him then would not have been as bad as if he had stayed without attaining faith. He was fortunate to have been rescued by a man before coming to God. And now, in a cataclysmic triumph of evil, that person, who was good, had been consumed.

He would tell Olek and let him handle the bunker. If they had to know, it would not be from him. How would it avail them? Were it solely his decision, he would . . . no, they had as much title to survive as anyone, despite their misery. But it was true that he would probably not have helped them to begin with had it not been for the one man to whom he was unable to say no.

Although he could not altogether justify it, Nicholas

would rather have gone through the war avoiding any involvement. It was not his conflict. He would not profit from its being won or lost. No one would, except perhaps munitions manufacturers and black marketeers. The first great war had taught him that it mattered relatively little whether there was a president, a premier, a dictator, or a king—as long as there was peace. Only then could the other ingredients necessary for a decent life be cultivated. He preferred that the Germans be defeated, but whatever happened, Poland, which had managed to be independent for twenty years, would revert to thralldom.

Poland: such a tiny plot viewed from the moon. What were they fighting for?

Olek would ask his questions.

Nicholas would tell him how Abrahm had risen from his deathbed, feverish, without crutches, and dragged himself to the front door of the house.

"Where do you think you're going?" Nicholas had asked him.

"To the ghetto," Abrahm said.

"You're not going to get very far in your condition," Nicholas said.

"Life is gone," Abrahm said. "Only resistance remains."

Nicholas did not exactly struggle with Abrahm, but he did forcefully help him back to his bed and give him a pill to ease him down.

The next morning, when he went in to bring Abrahm his tea, Nicholas found the bed empty. He rushed around the house looking for him. Then out back. Then in front. Abrahm had almost made it to the sidewalk—his body sprawled lifelessly in the snow.

Nicholas expected that Olek would want to arrange for a new tenant to fill the empty cot. But he would not agree to it. He had already done his part. There was no indication when the war would end. He would not go on accepting one ward after the next. It could continue indefinitely.

Those who survived the war in the bunker would be living proof of his Christian virtue. But even so he wished they were not there. He had not bargained for them, and they had cost him dearly.

Were it not for Olek . . . Nicholas shook his head vigorously, trying to clear it. He would have to unbosom himself about Katrina. Since her leave-taking, he had gone back to his old room overlooking the yard—the one Bronis had originally assigned to him. Almost mystically, it soothed him in his forlornness.

Nicholas had not mentioned her departure to anyone. She had reached the point where she could no longer bear the intrusion that had taken over their lives, or the tension. But she had come to know too much. He had loved her and needed her, but he had loved Abrahm above all. And it was with the strength of that love that he had tracked her down and strangled her.

The first gray filaments of dawn filtered in through the rafters. Nicholas stood and laced his hands around the nape of his neck, with his elbows protruding from behind his ears like misplanted horns. He stretched dynamically, arching his neck, tensing his muscles and ligaments in opposition, flexing his joints. Then he sucked in an extended draught of air, expelled it with a bellows sigh, and repeated the process, his thick chest rising and flumping like quartered beef dancing on a pulley.

He had best finish up, Nicholas thought, before the sun unhooded the barn and everything around him stirred to life. Then he would walk backwards to the house, reversing his trail, cleanse himself thoroughly, change clothes, prepare breakfast, and attend to his routine chores.

Pacing over to the doors, he peered out through an aperture. The snow had slackened and was descending in a morphine drizzle. Against the pearlescent sky, the elaborately antlered trees were delineated with woodcut sharpness: stark, glistening lines of bark gloved in white.

The winterscape accentuated his fatigue and yet refreshed him. He returned to the spot where he had been resting. In the half-light, the grave was undetectable. Raking a few wisps of hay aside with his shoe, he knelt facing East.

He rejoiced in the spirit of Jerusalem, but he also grieved.

For that which befalleth the sons of men befalleth beasts; even one thing befalls them; as the one dies, so dies the other; yea, they have all one breath; so that a man has no preeminence above a beast; for all his vanity.

All go unto one place; all are of the dust, and all turn to dust again.

Once more alone.

HALYCON
DAYS

Ruth and Marc perched on Abrahm's cot. Above them, though it was vacant, Victor's bunk was down, effecting a low canopy. All the lamps were snuffed. Beyond the curtain, waves of slumberous breathing confirmed the quietude.

"She's asleep now," Ruth whispered.

In the darkness, their eyes had been first to emerge: Ruth's hazel, languid, candid; Marc's darker, busier, more defensive. Their forms were less distinct. Ruth was robed in a cornflower-blue cotton nightgown, with her hair draped frontally, like a shawl. Marc wore underpants and an undershirt with narrow straps. Both were barefoot.

Ruth reached out for Marc's hand, drawing it to her mouth and kissing it. Then she folded it to her chest. Her gesture sent a nervous current through his body. He leaned forward and with the other hand stroked the top of her head. A pleasurable sensation spread downwards from his arms.

Tickling the hair on his thigh, Ruth's fingers arrived at the edge of his underpants and slid into the gap where his genitals were separating the cloth from his loin. As they crawled under his scrotum, his face grew hot and his penis, tingling, dilated and reared up impetuously.

For a moment he remained stock-still. Then he brought his hand down from her head, so that both his palms were placed against her chest, and began to caress it hesitantly. In reaction, Ruth dropped her hands to the hem of her night-dress and started to pull it up—over her legs, maneuvering her buttocks to extricate it from beneath herself, and her hips, to the level of her breasts, which hung heavily against the fabric.

Awkwardly, Marc's fingers accepted the partially furled cotton as Ruth relinquished it, thrusting her arms overhead. He raised the gown over her breasts, glimpsing them re-vealed, and her chest, and her throat, and her face, eclipsing and reappearing, and her hair splashing brownly over her white skin.

Ruth's hands fell into her lap as she sat naked on the cot, one foot on the floor, the other tucked beneath her.

Marc did not attempt to touch her, but backed off, as if better to focus on what was before him. Shortly he would be fondling and embracing her. But now he only wanted to be-hold her beatifically, imprinting her upon his memory.

Ruth was exposed to him as she had never been and might never be again. Soon she would be gone, back to the ghetto, and he would be left to tend to their mothers. It was not a happy prospect. Mrs. Adler had sworn to prevent Ruth's departure. Why should others be granted egress, she protes-ted vehemently, while she was denied it? Had she become a leper? But the decision had been made. What would happen subsequently, he did not know.

The atmosphere was charged with intrigue and sadness.

Marc became aware of Ruth tugging at the bottom of his undershirt. As he peeled it off, she hooked the band of his underpants, slipped them down over his hips, disengaged them from his erection, and removed them entirely.

Now Marc too was naked, modestly.

Ruth's breasts tapered conically as she inclined toward him, placing one hand beneath his balls and the other around his penis—clasping it, tilting it toward her, examining it, rubbing its tip, squeezing it, feeling the blood swell, releasing it, watching it spring away, and recapturing it.

With a combination of embarrassment and curiosity, Marc found himself wondering whether his mother was dreaming or listening to their rustling. She had received the news that Mrs. Adler was to remain with them with remarkable calm. Although she had no real alternative in the matter, he was glad that rather than complain she had displayed compassion.

Bringing her foot up from the floor, Ruth moved laterally to the inside half of the mattress and stretched out flush with the wall. Her breasts settled on her chest like muffins.

She extended her left hand liltingly, as though she were holding a wand, and tapped Marc lightly on the knee, beckoning him to lie down with her. And he did, so that they were flank to flank, as they had studied, dined, conversed, only nude, belly-up, wedged together on the narrow cot.

Their fingers brushed below their hips, glancing, groping, sticking and unsticking like magnetic rods, and crossed onto each other's thighs, tentatively, instinctively.

Then, in an unrehearsed ballet, they began to rotate toward one another: Marc and Ruth, unclothed, unencumbered, her breasts nestling against his chest, her stomach sandwiching his penis between them, face to face, ribs to ribs, their feet tickling and intertwining.

They did not kiss or speak, but only lay there, consolidating their nearness, transcending the confining shelter of the bunks, becoming suspended in the darkness and the silence like two mythic stars mating in a remote corner of the galaxy.

TIMELESS MOMENTS

Eugen stood with his hands raised above his head.

The sun was out, and the air resounded with a cacophony of wrenching noises: sharp cries, harsh commands, desperate pleas, shrill oaths, brutal retorts; trucks whining, horns blaring, the piercing sputter of motorcycles; bursts of shots intersecting the turbulence like shuttlecocks; explosions—PRRCHHHH!—followed by collapse . . . brick crumbling, wood crepitating, steel snapping; the counter-rush of wheels and feet over the cobblestones; people dashing for cover, pitching headlong, or suddenly flouncing off stride, spasmodically, like sailfish contesting a shortening line; and, amidst shouts of incitement and shrieks of pain and horror, wrathful exclamations of surprise.

The Jews were resisting!

The morning had broken so quickly that Eugen had neglected to take his pillowcase. The first thing he knew there was a pounding at the door and the word "Germans" was being repeated urgently. The SS and their Latvian hounds had entered the ghetto at dawn and started blocking off buildings and dragging everyone into the streets. Apparently, without a call for registration or any other notice, the final liquidation had begun. And equally without warning, several Jewish battle groups had opened fire.

There was no time for Eugen to collect himself. Isaac was turning in frantic circles like an animal trapped in a blaze and Gideon was barking orders and Samson was pushing Eugen over the threshold and the five of them—Heykel, Samson, Gideon, Eugen, and Joseph—were running through an extended gray corridor, up stairs, along successive passageways and up more stairs, past closed portals, causing Eugen to wonder fleetingly where he had been incarcerated, around machinery, boilers, tanks, trellises of pipes and ladders and cable vines, Gideon in the lead, pistol drawn, then Samson, then Eugen, then Joseph, then Heykel, running, running, on the balls of their feet, almost on their toes, wordlessly, not encountering anyone, as if the route were known only to them, and it seemed to Eugen that they were hedging him in, two before him, two behind, but he could not dwell on it, they were moving swiftly and he was straining to keep pace, pumping, veering, slowing, ascending, curving, accelerating, instinctively becoming a section of a five-link train, and then, as though they were emerging from an underwater tunnel, they surged through a doorway into the very vestibule to which Eugen had originally gained access, and the muted hum and roar that was in his ears ceased, and there on the floor near the smudge pot a guard lay tangled in his chair, his forehead seeping blood, and then the twilight smacked them coldly in the face and they were scampering through the yard toward the gate, sighting no indication of the second guard, and across the street, already hearing pops of gunfire in the distance, retracing the course that Eugen had previously navigated.

Eugen's familiarity with the terrain quickened his adrenalin, making it easier for him to pursue Samson, and it occurred to him that at last he would actually be confronting Bankart, but the thought vanished, and he was struggling again, scaling a barbed wire fence, snagging a pant leg, tearing free, gashing his ankle, jumping clear, running, exhaling cloudlets, rounding a corner, and feeling his heart drop as the sirens and the motors that had been waxing louder erupted with elephantine plangency and the hollow shooting became fuller and more immediate, reverberating startlingly, and rubble sprayed and windows shattered and some of the people who were being delivered to the *umschlagplatz* and had bolted, seeking to take advantage of the confusion, were scrambling furiously to shake the soldiers who were giving chase, cutting them down at medium range, or point blank, or both, and reinforcements stormed in, and a home-packed bomb flew down from a rooftop and detonated beside a motorcycle that had deliberately rammed into an elderly woman who had fallen to her knees to pray for mercy and flipped over, pinning its rider, and blew both him and his mechanical boar off the ground, spewing them up like a high-powered thresher mutilating the leaves and branches and fruit and petals of a preternatural organism—green and black and red and gray and white . . . steel, flesh, blood, leather, bone—and a heavy truck lumbered up the street, crunching the felled woman, and four machine-gunners dismounted and started strafing the building from which the projectile might have been lobbed, three raking the eaves and the upper floors, one the lower, and presently people began staggering out the front, hands aloft, a few of them wounded, and the reapers leveled them—brrrrp! brrrrp!—and in this commotion Eugen was still running behind Samson when a German policeman singled them out with a potshot—*ptzew!*—and enlisting several soldiers, set out after them.

As they were sprinting Gideon whirled and returned their salvo, firing once, and then he curled to his left, yelling something behind him, while Samson persisted in the direction they had been going, pulling Eugen with him—he was not certain whether Samson had grabbed his arm or whether he had reacted automatically—and they were racing away, leaving Gideon and Heykel and Joseph in the area where the hostilities seemed to be the heaviest, and soon it appeared that they had lost their tail, and then they negotiated a corner and found that the tempest had spread and they were on another tumultuous street, and up ahead a group of five men was being led away by three soldiers who were poking them maliciously, and then a shot whizzed by Eugen's neck and blood squirted out the back of Samson's shoulder and Samson stumbled, starting to crumple, but regained his balance with Eugen's assistance and began to charge forward again, angling for the courtyard of a building to their right, just as another shot slammed into him and Eugen felt a jolt in his lumbar region.

"Halt!"

He lurched forward, then stopped abruptly.

"Hands up!"

As they were being escorted to the *umschlagplatz*, together with the convoy that had briefly anteceded them and another party of four men and two women, Eugen had experienced a severe twinge between his shoulder blades each time an individual shot sounded. Volleys were not as harrowing. In turmoil, the zone in which they had been captured was virtually alien, though he had traversed it a number of times, both when it was desolate and when it was populated with families waiting out the moon. If there had been an opportunity to gather his wits, he would have secured his pillowcase. But would he also have demanded his revolver? No, it would have been up to Heykel to restore it to him. His throat was parched from having swallowed so much dust.

"Form a row at arm's length! Hands overhead! No movement!"

The officer who had assumed command of them was a short, wiry, fair-skinned German with a sinewy, boyishly handsome face narrowing to a Doberman jaw. His voice was reedy but authoritative. In his left hand he carried a swagger stick which he held like a baton and flicked into his right palm with metronome regularity.

Under different circumstances he might still have been a student, Eugen reflected as the officer strutted away, aban-

doning them to a squad of guards who were posted fore and
rear with spring-loaded eyes and weapons at-the-ready. He
pictured him in civilian dress, swinging a satchel of books to
school or masturbating. His arms were already beginning to
waiver slightly.At this stage it was more nervousness than
fatigue, but what if they grew too weary to support? He did
not want to let his sight wander, but he could not avoid
noticing that other batches of prisoners were not being made
to keep their hands in the air. The young officer had disappeared from view.

He would have to relax and maintain complete self-
control if he was to have any chance of salvation, Eugen
thought. Presently the mandate to march forward would be
issued, and they would be prodded toward the boxcars, merg-
ing with other prisoners into a herd that would be loaded,
sealed in, and shipped off to the East. Or perhaps they would
be stampeded.

Treblinka.

They would not really be transported toward Kiev or
Moscow to work, nor back to Germany. Instead, they were
slated for . . . could such a place exist? *Treblinka.* The name
was strong but lyrical.

Eugen had heard all the details from Nussbaum and the
others. But he had been reluctant to believe them. They
seemed to be reciting memorized propaganda as they related
the testimony of several comrades who had been there, or
almost, and managed to escape. It was incredible. Apocry-
phal. He had seen what the Germans were capable of doing,
yet he had never been exposed to what was claimed to be
transpiring at Treblinka. How could more of this be known in
the factory than at headquarters?

His skepticism had especially exasperated Heykel and
Gideon. Hotly, they had barraged him with numbers, dates,
names, insistent facts. And always there was the refrain: "How
could we be fabricating this? How could anyone?"

But nothing they had said had wholly convinced Eugen.
He had been aware from the beginning that a dark purpose

was being served. But exactly what it was had eluded him. An unenviable fate awaited every Jew who wound up at the *umschlagplatz*. He had not wanted to know more than that. And now, with his destiny taking shape around him, he still preferred not to comprehend it.

Eugen knitted his forehead to squeeze off his unproductive thoughts and screen the kindling sun. His right eye had started to ache in a tiny, intensifying spot, as though light were being trained on it through a magnifying glass. He had not been outside in more than a month. Nearly two. Like a woman marking pregnancy, Eugen had counted the days toward January 22, when he was due to accompany Heykel to the Metropole. But he was at the *umschlagplatz* instead, and it was only January 18.

Although he was uninjured, Eugen's arms were becoming distressingly heavy. How could Samson bear it? He had raised his hands and walked to the *umschlagplatz* with blood streaming from his shoulder. Eugen's mind skittered. Was that why they were being punished?

He would have to determine how Samson was faring. It would require subtle maneuver. The soldier closest to him was stationed with his gun welded to his side, tensely braced, his lips zippered, and his eyes riveted on an unseen cross-hatch. Deliberately, Eugen altered his facial expression in an effort to establish contact. But the guard's eyes stayed fixed. Was it antipathy, Eugen pondered, or apathy? He hoped the former. A dispassionate guard might pounce on him unpredictably, without having telegraphed annoyance. But a hostile one could be tested. If he switched his eyes instantly to the left, he would likely get away with it. But he lacked the courage. He would have to slide them over gradually.

As he began to do so, Eugen was distracted by something beyond the guard. He expanded his field of view. The *umschlagplatz* presented a less forbidding scene than it had during the principal deportations, when there had been inducements, first aid facilities, tokens of privilege, and physical evaluation. Now there was less pandemonium within its

confines than without. The atmosphere was more like that
attendant upon a sporting event.

Motion. An umber dust was rising from the ground,
stirred by shuffling feet. People were starting to move toward
the cars. Eugen's mind clarified, as though he had been unconscious without realizing it. The herders were driving their
wards firmly but not irascibly. It was going to be a low key
proceeding, defused by the irregular flow of prisoners being
brought in from the battle.

There was a flicker. Eugen had caught the guard's eye.
So, he was not altogether disinterested. Cautiously, Eugen
rotated his head leftward just enough to sight Samson peripherally. There he was, four persons down, his arms still above
his head but quivering so deeply that it appeared they would
wrench themselves out of their sockets. His jacket was saturated with blood. In contrast, his face was chalk white.

Eugen winced, looking away from Samson and once again
staring ahead. Could anyone fail to perceive that he was in
need of immediate medical attention? He would not last long
under such torture or crammed aboard a boxcar. And Eugen
was five spans removed and could not help.

His eyes hitched Several officers had congregated across
the way, among them the lean-hipped blond and a swarthier,
stockier man to whom the others were deferring and who was
pointing in the vicinity of Eugen's group. Toward Eugen himself, it seemed. Or was it toward Samson? Eugen tried to
bring the conference into focus. The man resembled a pros-
perous grocer. He felt disappointed and relieved. For a minute he had thought that it was Thierbach.

The schoolboy nodded emphatically and took leave of his
cohorts. Sensing his approach, the guard's eyes re-soldered.

"Hands down."

Eugen lowered his hands slowly to his sides. The officer
glared up and down the line, then slanted forward, to Eugen's
left and out of range. His arms felt uncomfortable in their new
position, disoriented by their relative weightlessness.

What was the officer doing?

The guard was watching him sideways, as though anticipating a signal. Behind him, the man whom Eugen had mistaken for Thierbach was blowing his nose into a green
handkerchief. Then, dismissing the meeting, he strode off.

"Are you all right?" Eugen heard the officer inquire.

There was a garbled response.

"Speak up!"

The guard's hands tightened.

"Yes," Samson said.

"Yes what?" the officer demanded.

"I'm all right."

Eugen shivered. Samson's normally assertive voice was
quavery and barely intelligible. He diverted his concentration
to his fingers, which were needling with resumed circulation,
and also the chilliness that had not bothered him when he was
flushed with exertion but was beginning to get a grip on him
now. He was grateful for the jacket Nussbaum had furnished
him, but it only had two buttons and did not adequately
protect his chest. His nipples were starting to burn.

What was there about the grocer that had given him
goose flesh? A figure stepped in front of Eugen. He projected
his eyes straight ahead, withdrawing behind them as he had
learned to do when someone was reprimanding him. His face
was undergoing scrutiny. Had he been recognized? No. He
was becoming paranoid. Why would Thierbach . . . ?

The officer snatched Eugen's beard and yanked his chin
up, as if in the prospect of uncovering a nest. Then he jerked
his head to the left and to the right, examining each profile.
Nothing was said. When he unhanded him and backed off,
there was a hint of mockery on his lips. What could he have
seen, Eugen wondered? Or been seeking?

Before he could formulate a surmise, he was pivoting and
trudging forward—single file, four men preceding him, six
men and two women coming after. In retrospect, it dawned on
him that one of the women was pregnant. He had noticed her
melon-form earlier, but it had simply not registered.

As the boxcars rose like clay buttes, Eugen began to

experience more urgently the necessity to make a move. But his sense of futility mounted concomitantly. He was not on the street, progressing toward the *umschlagplatz*; he was at the *umschlagplatz*, verging on doom.

The schoolboy guided them over to a larger confluence of prisoners, perhaps fifty or sixty, and went into consultation with the officer in authority. Eugen felt himself being jostled as the row in which he had marched over was ingested by the waiting assemblage. There was no alignment now, only an amorphous huddling that afforded anonymity and a buffer against the guards, but also confined him and threatened to sweep him away.

A surge of dread energized him. Unless he could think of something promptly, while the officers were chatting, he would be finished. He craned his neck in search of Samson, stretching one way and another, not caring who observed him at this juncture. Finally, he located Samson several strata to the rear. His blood-drenched shoulder had dropped and was hanging like a partially severed wing. He tried to catch his attention, but Samson's eyes were unresponsive. Raising his index finger, Eugen described a pendulum arc. To and fro, to and fro . . . in vain. Samson's face was drained of animation. In a few hours, he had aged ten years. More. Twenty. Thirty. He was dying on his feet.

Eugen was jostled from behind. He set himself, but was prodded forward nonetheless. The herd was budging.

Instantly, he began squeezing to his left and back, slicing against the flow, striving to gain a position from which he could bolt.

"No you don't!"

Someone was doggedly impeding his retreat. Eugen shifted tack, squirming obliquely to his right. Again he bumped into an obstacle.

"One for all," said a thick voice.

The herd was compacting, plodding forward, shrinking the span to the siding. Forty paces. Thirty-five. Perhaps fewer. Eugen's mind whirred into high gear. He would not be able to get to the fringe. And if he could, where would he flee? There were no unobstructed exists, no sanctuaries, no one he knew other than Samson.

As he was borne along, Eugen reached down and unfastened his fly. He might have two or three seconds in which to show them their error. It had not exempted him on a prior occasion, but even the briefest delay might spare him from being jammed onto a car. He was uncircumcised and disguised in connection with a special assignment. His superior was Hans Thierbach. Thierbach's adjutant was Dieter. He had been dispatched in quest of a Jew named Bankart. Abrahm Bankart. There was a possibility that he was here among the prisoners. He suggested that they detain him until they could verify his story.

"Halt!"

The herd came to a standstill. Before it an empty boxcar loomed yawning. A glimpse of sky emphasized its abysmal murkishness. When the door shut, Eugen contemplated, there would be stifingly little life sustenance. He pricked his ears toward the sounds of the unrelenting battle in the distance. The Jews were not capitulating.

There was a suspenseful delay. Then, without apparent provocation or behest, a special detachment of soldiers materialized and starting whipping and battering the crowd. Their assault elicited a wretched chorus of squealing and bleating.

"*Shussst!*"

Razor-snakes slashed and basted scalps, shoulders, faces, and the herd began to shamble toward the ramp, lunging, slogging, no one wishing to be first or last.

"Wait!"

Eugen had inflated his lungs and was on the brink of shouting something when a pre-emptive voice roared out with diesel stridence.

"WAIT!"

The appeal plowed through the herd, paralyzing it. Eugen, his mouth agape, turned toward the refractory Jew who had bounded from the press and interposed himself in its path.

"Brothers and sisters," he beseeched. "They are driving us to the slaughter. But do not go. As long as life is yours— RESIST!"

Thus having spoken, the man darted back into the herd and was swallowed up before the astonished guards could nab him. Embarrassed and enraged, they unleashed a wood and leather hail, grunting and cursing, seemingly bent on beating the crowd to death. But no one moved.

In his initial shock, Eugen had flashed that it must be Bankart. Who else possessed such audacity? But reviewing the moment, he established that the man had been twenty-five or so, of undistinguished physique, with pale blond hair and glinting, hypnotic eyes. That was wrong. He had not seen the eyes. But his voice had been bold.

"Brothers and sisters . . . RESIST!"

Despite the unremitting rain of blows, the herd steadfastly refused to regurgitate the transgressor. He might be as old as thirty-two or three, Eugen reconsidered, pondering his curiously Aryan features.

Locked elbow in elbow with the persons on either side of him, Eugen was infected with an unfamiliar elation. Whatever his age, the man was right. It was suicide to ascend the ramp. A steer or a hog might know nothing of sledgehammers, saw-knives, and roasting pits, but he did. A whistling lash nicked him above the left eye. If anyone leapt out again, he would do the same. He felt an erection developing. Hundreds of thousands of people had gone before them, but they were not going. Could the others have been spared the trip if someone had arisen to embolden them?

"As long as life is yours . . ."

The whips went limp and the torrent of flogging and cudgeling subsided. Where the blond Jew had held sway, there now appeared the officer whom Eugen had mistaken for Thierbach. All heads swung toward his presence. He was olive-complected, Eugen saw, shorter than Thierbach, and of greater self-importance. Flanking him were six officers, including the schoolboy. He surveyed the crowd severely.

"Will the orator come forward?"

Stone.

"Then en masse."

Still, no one moved.

"String them out."

Several phalanxes wedged into the passive herd, quickly dividing it into four sausages. Eugen scanned about for Samson, spotting him in the grouping to his right. One hand was still in the air, but the other was dangling uselessly and his head was drooping toward his ruptured shoulder. It was evident that he was able to remain standing only through the sheer distillation of his will.

Eugen had a passing regret that he could not apprise the others of Samson's plight. Were they prevailing in combat, or were they strewn amidst the queerly floral wreckage of the ghetto?

"There he is!"

Like vultures, three soldiers swooped down on Eugen's clump, almost knocking him over, and plucked out the rebellious Jew, who had been half-hiding behind a woman and, to Eugen's amazement, himself. He had no inkling that he was being utilized as a shield. Might he also have been linking arms with him?

Plunked roughly before the grocer, the Jew bore himself stalwartly, his demeanor reaffirming his conviction. But Eugen's sense of unquailing inspiration had faded. Once more he rehearsed his recitation: "Sir, I beg to address you. Lieutenant Eugen Glueck at your disposal. R.H.S.a. Amt IVA 4b. On undercover mission. Objective—the apprehension of Abrahm Bankart."

He could do it now, while there was an interlude. But he would not. If he was not to be heroic, neither would he prostrate himself.

The grocer was glowering mercilessly at the Jew, trying to unnerve him. But the Jew, denying him his pleasure, spat defiantly in his face. A pair of officers plunged in to avenge him, but he waved them off. Then, casually, like a gentlemen sitting down to Sunday breakfast and a leisurely perusal of the paper, he dislodged his revolver from its sleek leather holster, inspected it fondlingly, rubbing its polished handle, and aimed its muzzle, skin to metal, between the Jew's eyes.

Overhead, the sun had burned away a layer of haze and was shining a crisp winter yellow.

CRACK!

In one precise sequence, the finger squeezed, the hammer cocked and tripped, the barrel discharged, and the Jew, who had not flinched, hesitated and slumped to the ground.

The scene had a dreamlike quality imbued with terror but surpassing it: the body lying lifeless on the stones, its brown eyes soft and liquid like those of a deer that had been shot while grazing on the fringe of a salt lick and hauled into town to be dressed out on a bed of ice in a butcher shop window wreathed with Christmas sprig and holly.

Assuming the herd would come forward now, the soldiers arrayed themselves in a channel. But everyone held. A gesture by the grocer sent the schoolboy swaggering over to Samson's group.

"Forward march!"

If they had maimed the blond Jew, Eugen thought, and thrown him into the boxcar two-fifths alive, the spell might have been shattered. But in its neatness and efficiency, the bullet had insured his legacy.

"Lest there be any misunderstanding," the schoolboy enunciated, "this is not a social invitation."

No one moved.

"So," said the schoolboy. "There is a disc . . . uuuuugh-uuh . . ."

Before he could complete his sentence, Samson had hooked his left arm around the schoolboy's throat and hoisted him off his feet, throttling and flapping him violently, as if to wrest his head from its base. The impetus of the posse hastening to the rescue and the momentum of Samson's violent agitation hurled him to the ground, but the soldiers could not emancipate the schoolboy from his strangle-hold until he had

snapped his neck. Even after they had clubbed the fury from
Samson, a bayonet had to be employed to pry the schoolboy
loose.

When both carcasses had been carted off—the schoolboy's with his head awry, floated on eight hands, and Samson's
trailed over the stones like a bull's—there was a solemn consultation between the grocer and his underlings. Upon its
conclusion, the soldiers began pounding the sausages into one
continuous flat strip of prisoners, side to side, with everyone
facing the ramp.

As though the collective resistance was being conserved
against the imperative to advance toward the ramp, no one
balked at being marshalled laterally. Eugen gazed past the
deer's eyes into the boxcar, but his eyes rebounded. While
promptly evacuating Samson and the schoolboy, they had for
some reason left the blond Jew lying. A queasiness dispelled
the impression of a sleepless dreamer. Eugen had to act! But
he would not involve the others in what had become a matter
solely between himself and Bankart. If he stepped forward
now, it would be for deportation. Heykel had told him that
several comrades had survived. The risk was preferable to
public repose with his eyes glued painlessly to the sun.

CRACK!

The grocer had stalked up to the man farthest to Eugen's
left, reviewed him haughtily, trained his revolver, and drilled
him behind the ear.

Eugen shuddered. The first incident had been glazed by
surprise. But this time a sickening realism roiled his bowels.

Hardly pausing, the grocer sidled up to the next man in
line and saturninely skewered his temple.

CRACK!

Eugen blinked just as the gun went off.

CRACK!

The third shot compelled him to glance back. A woman
sagged to the ground. He looked away.

CRACK!

Closing his eyes, Eugen envisioned himself surrealistically as an hour glass, with the sand rising from the bottom chamber to the top, traveling all alone in a hurtling boxcar. It would not be too bad a ride. He could recline comfortably, and once there he would declare himself to the authorities, certify his credentials, and inquire after Tzipora and the harelip. Even if things were as Heykel had portrayed them, he would get by. Yes, he did have characteristically Semitic features. That was why he had been selected for such sensitive service. Would headquarters have dispatched a boxcar bearing a solitary Jew?

CRACK!

Eugen would find the harelip, and she would orientate him, and they would tryst, and he would spend as many hours as possible with Tzipora, teaching her to draw and etch and if the materials were available, to block engrave. His incipient erection burgeoned against the aperture of his undone fly. To soften his arousal, he conjured up a printing press: ptchkyck . . . ptchkyck . . . ptchkyck . . . the sheeted platen thwacking the plate with a rhythmic clatter.

His ears were resonating, presuming the next retort, but instead there was a prolonged, disquieting lull. Had the grocer vented his spleen?

Eugen's nausea simmered upward.

CRACK!

The percussion silenced the interior din, then amplified it.

CRACK!

Peeking out, Eugen saw the pregnant woman sag to the ground, childless. Her hair was cut like a boy's. Then it came to him.

CRACK!

He veiled his eyes again.

CRACK!

And reopened them.

CRACK!

Jesus Christ . . .

CRACK!

. . . He's killing every damned one of us.

The officers and soldiers were witnessing the grisly ceremony as impassively as the blond Jew wilted on the stones.
Was it his will or the grocer's that by rejecting one end, the
herd was succumbing to another?

Thierbach could never have perpetrated such carnage,
Eugen ruminated. But simultaneously he thought the opposite. It was easier than picking people's bones. The grocer was
not tormenting flesh. He was merely dispensing bullets.

There had been twelve shots thus far, Eugen tallied, noting that a second intermission had commenced. He could not
fathom the grocer's obsession with performing the entire job
himself. Was his unloathness the secret to his power?

Fortunately, Eugen had not troubled before to determine
what number he was in line. Now he would prudently avoid
looking to either side.

CRACK!

Thirteen.

CRACK!

It would be more work to dispose of the victims than it
had been to destroy them.

CRACK!

As familiar as he was with the mechanism of firearms, it
remained partially mysterious to Eugen that a lead cartridge
smaller than a pinkie, charged with powder and propelled into
the body, could instantaneously terminate or irreparably dis-
rupt a complex, multi-dimensional life, while other vicious
and extreme abuses were more readily survived.

CRACK!

There seemed to be an element of suggestibility involved, beyond the physical factors, akin to voodoo.

CRACK!

No one had yet ascertained whether the various modes of
death were manifestations of the same phenomenon, or
whether there were infinite ways of causing or attaining non-
existence.

CRACK!

As a youth, his brother Franz had once come across a cat feasting on a still warm robin, and in a fit of umbrage he had stomped it, pulping its brain. The exhilaration Franz experienced led to a nasty habit of squashing kittens under his heel, and sometimes burning them alive. Their father was aghast when he discovered Franz's proclivity. But his reprimand and warning never to do such things again were ineffective. He could not hide the fact that he was intimidated as well as repulsed by Franz' confession that he enjoyed his perversion and had more than two dozen killings to his credit.

CRACK!

How many semblances of death had the old man on the wagon catalogued?

CRACK!

Eugen stiffened. The woman to his left had clutched his forearm and was pinching it. He restrained himself from turning toward her, preferring not to behold the grocer's handiwork.

CRACK!

Twenty-odd Jews sprawled like aborted fantasies.

CRACK!

Eugen desired to see Tzipora's hair shining in the sunlight between the trees as they sat together, sketching, and when it was night, to cushion her head on his lap as they lounged around a fire with the harelip and Heykel and Sonya and Joseph and Gideon and the Nussbaums, yes, they too had become his family, and listen to Isaac charm nocturnal goblins with his melodic recollections of golden dreams.

CRACK!

CRACK!

Eugen heeded the echoes from beyond the *umschlagplatz*. The clash was still in progress! There might be greater firepower in one column of German tanks then in all the assiduously fabricated fortifications and stockpiles in the ghetto, but the stubborn spirit of everyone who had been interrogated in the quest for Bankart and the tenacious resolve and hunger for revenge that Eugen had been exposed to in the factory were nevertheless fusing in revolt. He would like to have seen the look on Thierbach's face.

CRACK!

"I will be there when the fighting starts."

CRACK!

Bankart was keeping his promise. Eugen had always known that he would never allow himself to be seized. It was Eugen who would fail to fulfill his commitment. They had mobilized with just two pistols, consigned to Gideon and Heykel, unaided by their store of laboriously concocted devices. Eugen had not wittingly blundered or shied away. On the contrary, he had gripped the bit in his teeth. But he would not be at the Metropole.

CRACK!

His system was in turmoil. He could feel the fear percolating through his entrails. But it would not do to defecate.

CRACK!

The sun was flashing as though in anger. Would it discharge a fiery bolt of indignation, rendering the earth a ball of flames?

CRACK!

Or was it winking?

CRACK!

Was there anyone watching, Eugen wondered, besides the official personnel on hand? A lookout ensconced in a nearby nest? An eagle gliding by? Was any being outside the *umschlagplatz* aware that he was about to die?

CRACK!

He wanted to feel that Bankart knew.

CRACK!

Like the moments of his life, Eugen had lost track of the shots . . . each one counting, whether or not accounted for.

CRACK!

But they were coming inevitably closer, vibrating his juices.

CRACK!

The woman's fingernails sank into Eugen's flesh like a crazed dog's fangs.

CRACK!

In his rags, he was Noah/Age/12/In the forest.

CRACK!

No! He was Eugen Glueck. *Resisting.*

CRACK!

His ears were ringing.

PZING!

The searing heat of the revolver intensified, its sulfurous fumes reminding Eugen of the whispers of stale air and melting tallow leaking out from under the door of the closet to which his mother and father had sternly denied the boys admission. He had never been inside, but Franz had breached the prohibition once, shortly before their father disappeared. They had always gone in on Friday nights. First his mother, in her shawl. Then his father, his black silk yarmulke hidden in his pocket.

T H E
FOREST

The sky was a pure seamless blue and the forest sparkled in the cheerful, airy, citron light of spring. Crowned by sun, the sap-filled trees glistened freshly. Birds stirred and bustled in the branches and hopped along the ground, bobbing for worms and seeds and chirping sprightly trills. Squirrels streaked up trunks and scampered down, bounding over the soft, glossy patches of carpeting moss. The swollen earth, brown and green, gave off a strong, sweet, blossoming perfume, and brightly colored wildflowers transformed the shrubbery into spray peacocks.

"Aah, it smells tantalizing," Isaac said, chafing his hands.

"It should," Heykel said, stirring the pot. "There's meat in here."

He was squatting in the center of a clearing set behind a rain swamp and encompassed by a dense covert. The pot over which he presided was suspended above a fire at the bottom of a pit which had been dug with four flues to disperse the smoke.

"Meat," Isaac said, savoring the word.

Hunkered beside Heykel, he placed his hand before his upturned face, then removed it, feeling the sun's glow disappear and appear.

"You're eclipsing the sun," Heykel said.

"Yes, naturally," Isaac said.

Close about, ten or twelve persons occupied themselves with various tasks: building, mending, fashioning increments of security and comfort. Others dozed, or simply idled. Two men were ill—Nussbaum with pneumonia, the second with a bullet wound in his hip. The prevailing tempo was slow and relatively relaxed. It had been more urgent while the site was being established, a process which included the construction of two camouflaged, straw-lined bunkers that served both as sleeping facilities and as shelters in case of inclement weather or a raid.

"I need an opinion," Heykel said, extending the tip of the mixing rod toward Isaac.

Interrupting his experimentation, Isaac reached out for the stick and guided it to his mouth.

"Mmmm . . . exquisite," Isaac said, licking his lips.

"Who doesn't appreciate the aromatic touch of our master chef?" rasped Nussbaum, who was stretched out next to the pit swathed in a blackish-green wool blanket.

"Sshhh," said the woman who was attending to him. "You must conserve your energy."

"It's obvious he's malingering in order to be first in line," Heykel said.

Suddenly a voice groaned in discomfort.

"Oh . . ."

Heykel jumped up, leaving the stick in the pot, and hurried over to Sonya, who was lying in a patch of sun that was beginning to succumb to shadow.

"Are you all right?" he asked, kneeling beside her.

Biting her lips, Sonya looked up at him plaintively. She began to nod yes, but the pain broke through.

"Mmmch . . ."

From the other side of the clearing, where he had been

basking against a tree for several hours, Joseph watched Sonya grab Heykel's arm and push against him as the pain hit. Her body arched, trying to ward off the pressure.

Was it the real thing? Joseph wondered. Sonya had earlier experienced false intimations of labor. Her abdomen was enormous now, like a plasmic satellite that had attached itself to her. She had let Joseph rest his ear on it, and he had heard and felt the child within.

"What do you think we should call it?" Sonya had asked.

"Simcha," Joseph suggested after mulling it over.

"And if it's a boy?"

"You said it wouldn't be," Joseph replied.

He too had come to regard it as Leora's sister. If it turned out otherwise, they would have to re-orient themselves.

Heykel had abstained from any speculation or expression of preference. His and Sonya's estrangement had been evolving by degrees, but it was only within the past week or two that she had begun to behave in an extremely forlorn and alienated manner. In the same period, the flush of motherhood that the forest had revived swiftly faded, her vitality drained, and in contrast with her abdomen, the rest of her body appeared to be wasting away. Emil had stated that there was no cause for alarm, but her conduct left Heykel unreassured, and Isaac alone seemed to have any rapport with her.

Lately, Joseph had felt his own hostility toward Sonya gathering brew. It had been suppressed in the ghetto, but now it was uncapped, like his craving for sleep, and manifesting itself through the obsessive question: What if Leora had not been sent away?

Sonya had been responsible. He did not believe Heykel would have done it. Once he had asked his mother about it, but his father was in the house and she avoided the topic. When he inquired again, privately, she said: "They decided between them, as husband and wife."

Did Sonya know of his and Leora's marriage, Joseph wondered? Leora, his dearly beloved. He had always thought not, but when Sonya invited him to sound her womb, he had revised his judgment. Maybe she did. His compassion for her heightened ambivalently. She had suffered too. As much as anyone. Perhaps more if she was to blame.

Joseph would have raised the subject with her were it not for her condition. As a precaution against complications, there had been talk of transporting Sonya to a location where she could have a bed and more hygienic conditions. But she had refused to budge. Emil was sufficient surety for her, she insisted. The most important thing was to be with the others.

Accordingly, a third bunker had been dug and equipped, to the degree possible, to Emil's specifications. A separate supply of water was kept in readiness, and a special team had been formed to scour the countryside for needed supplies.

Joseph had gone on several forays himself, bringing back sheets, towels, sponges and other items.

Now he experienced a nervous feathering in his belly. After the bedlam of the ghetto, the sense of peacefulness that reigned much of the time over their site belied the hazards that lurked everywhere. In addition to the fundamental difficulties of surviving in the wilderness, there was the overriding problem that they were not alone. Besides other Jews, the forest also contained a Polish Home Army detachment and a contingent of Russian guerrillas. Each of these corps depended on appropriating by persuasion or force from neighboring peasants and villages what they could not buy. While they generally observed an implicit code of live and let live, there were mounting conflicts of interest. On top of this, and most perilous of all—whether by betrayal or discovery—there were recurrent attacks by German troops hunting partisans.

Recently, the corpse of an unidentified young woman—dressed in male peasant clothing and with a blue and white arm band ringing her left arm—had been found in the vicinity of the camp. The body, which was still fairly well preserved, had six bullet holes in its back, placed like the points of a star. Yet no one had heard any shooting.

The discovery caused great consternation. How had the

body gotten there? And why? Were they under surveillance? Was it a warning? Had the woman been trying to reach them?

That was the worst fear. They had been anxiously awaiting a reaction from Warsaw to their SOS regarding the pressures that were being applied to them by their forest co-tenants. Perhaps this woman had been bringing a message.

The SOS had been sent with Olek. Concern arose for his welfare, as well as their own. The suggestion was made to pick up stakes immediately and find a new site. But it was voted down. Olek had yet to fail them. They were well entrenched where they were. For the time being at least, it was best to stay put.

Security measures were reviewed and tightened. By agreement among all the groups represented in camp, Gideon was in command of their defense. He had fought fiercely in the ghetto, strengthening everyone. More than once they had been in death's embrace and struggled free due to his steely nerves and steep courage. Now he increased the number of patrols watching over the surrounding area. The net was broadened, with two-man details positioned further from camp, and singles guarding the inner perimeter.

Joseph had agreed with the decision not to move. It would have been pointless. If they could be found where they were, they could be found anywhere. Olek's mission represented their best chance for relief. If anyone could be relied on, it was he. Joseph admired his icy efficiency, which he viewed as harnessed anger.

He had never really seen Olek's emotions released until his initial visit to their encampment. Communications had floundered during the fighting, and there had been agonizing uncertainties about individual fates. Upon sighting Heykel, Olek had rushed forward and thrown his arms around him, hugging and kissing him and pounding him on the back, and Heykel reciprocated, and tears of joy and relief streamed down their faces. Then they held one another at arm's length, beaming wetly, attempting conversation, but promptly relapsed into squeezing and back-clapping and reassuring them-

selves by repeating their names that they were indeed re-
united.

But their gladness was weighted with sorrow. Olek reported that the battle had run its course. There were a few
comrades persevering in trapped pockets here and there, but
mainly the ghetto was a burial field of smoldering rubble.
Also, he accounted for some of the victimized, Ruth among
them—a devastating blow to Emil, though she had died heroically, jamming herself into the mouth of an escape tunnel,
saving four other lives—and related that neither he nor Victor
had come across any trace of Gittel and Benyk or the sympathetic factory guard to whom Nussbaum had entrusted them
at the last opportunity for transference to the Aryan side.

Business was conducted through the night, with Olek, as
always, sober and steady, and when it was almost sunup, he
had bidden everyone goodbye, and again clasped Heykel,
both of them weeping.

Several persons had gathered around Sonya now—
Heykel, Emil, and the woman who had been attending
Nussbaum. Her name was Rachel and she had been a teacher
before the war. She knelt beside Sonya, holding her hand,
while Emil examined her.

The complexion of the day was changing rapidly. That
part of the sky from which the sun had been shining in on
Joseph had diffused from vivid bluishness to a mauve tone,
while westerly it was becoming orangish. The sun, meantime,
was swelling as it dropped, as though recovering the warmth it
had expended.

Joseph shifted against the tree, seeking a new accommodation with its grainy-barked contours. Now was the hour
when the clearing was pervaded by a twilight serenity that
made him achingly nervous—a hovering quiescence too reminiscent of the shattering calm on the dawn of April 19, the date
of the Warsaw ghetto uprising.

They had been sleeping when notification came that at
two in the morning the Germans had begun to encircle the
ghetto with heavily armed troops, panzer cars, and tanks. By

five o'clock, it had been entirely sealed off. At six, soldiers and machinery started filing through the gates, geared to completing the liquidation that had been stymied on January 18.

But whereas the spontaneous resistance launched by several isolated units of Jewish fighters on January 18th had precipitated an abortive flurry of street skirmishing in which they had been hopelessly disadvantaged and incurred disproportionately high losses, this time they were ready with a comprehensive strategy designed to maximize their limited resources and sustain a memorable rebellion. For three months, during which revenge was finally exacted against designated Gestapo agents and collaborators, the heartened ghetto had been feverish with preparations. And as a German column advanced toward the intersection of Zamenhof and Mila, it was greeted with a fusillade of flaming cocktails and grenades.

The ensuing conflict, which actually began the next day, after the stunned Germans had retreated, reorganized, and disconnected the utilities to the ghetto, raged from block to block, house to house, cellar to cellar, and roof to roof. Fires blazed everywhere, and the air was bitter with toxic gas. By the conclusion of the third week of fighting, when they contrived their desperate exit through the Warsaw sewer system, their ranks had been decimated and their frail bastions mostly destroyed—but not before Nazi blood, too, had flowed profusely in the gutters.

The uprising had begun on Sunday, April 19, the date of the First Feast of Passover. It was hard to grasp that not even a year had passed since the night when he had carved his leather tag:

> *Joseph Bloodstein 14*
> *references in America*
> *Itzchok Meyer/New York*
> *Schmuel Katzin/New York*

Heykel had left Sonya in the care of Emil and come back to check on the stew. Upon his return, Isaac, who had continued with his eclipses, stood and made his way toward Sonya, stopping on route to cup his hand to his ear. Was he listening for Sonya's voice, or heeding the birds, Joseph pondered, or tuning in an interior signal? Whatever, Isaac had an uncanny instinct for where Sonya was, and each day he seemed to gravitate towards her with greater magnetism. That was one of his more recent peculiarities. His beard had sprouted back to fullness since the uprising, suddenly, just as bits and snatches of his previous vocabulary had started popping up inexplicably. Instead of being thick and dark, the beard was now a flossy white threaded with orange wisps. But despite this mutation, there were increasing occasions when his profile or a phrase or gesture poignantly recalled the Isaac of old.

Although Isaac's pan remained slung around his neck, there was no more Zirka. She had fallen casualty during their arduous escape. Some of their party had advocated abandoning Isaac as well, but Joseph and Nussbaum had taken him in tow and even carried him when necessary. It was not until they arrived in the forest that Isaac realized Zirka was gone. Then he sat down and sobbed bereavedly. Fortunately, his harmonica had not been lost, and after having the slime washed out of it and being dried in the sun, it was better than new.

Having exchanged amenities with Sonya and Emil, Isaac tried to lie down in his favorite position—perpendicular to Sonya with his head on her belly.

"I'm sorry, Isaac, not today," Emil said, gently holding him back.

A look of bewilderment crossed Isaac's face. In the mornings he was given to stroking and fondling Sonya's stomach, Joseph reflected, whereas in the afternoons he tended to use it as a pillow. Heykel had tried to discourage him from at least the latter, but Sonya had rejected his intervention. Now Emil was restraining him.

"It's all right," Sonya said weakly.

"It's not," Emil said.

Isaac turned toward the sun. He clamped his hand over his face, then removed it.

"I know," Emil said. "You haven't had your nap today. But it can't be helped. Sonya's not feeling well."

"Don't worry him," Sonya said. "Here, you can lie down beside me."

Joseph watched Isaac curl up parallel to Sonya, facing her, with his head nestled in the crook of her outstretched arm. In the pulsing descent of the sun, their figures were dappled, along with the moss, and Isaac's beard was catching topaz sparks.

"The younger Bloodstein to the kitchen please," Heykel called out.

A crowd had begun to collect around the pit.

"Back off," Heykel said, "before someone winds up in the pot."

The directive produced a casual queue. Joseph uprooted himself and shuffled into the center of the clearing. His legs felt stiff. At Heykel's instruction, he divided up the bread which they had obtained—along with most of the ingredients for the stew and quite a few other things—in a raid on a rich peasant's larder the night before.

This would be by far the best meal they had enjoyed in the forest, Joseph noted, although but a fraction of their haul would be consumed. Their foray had yielded not only such basics as salt, pepper, pork, onions, dried beans, several loaves of white cheese and a wheel of yellow, but also a jar of comfits stuffed with almonds, a box of chocolate bars, and a store of rich Turkish candy for which the proprietor apparently had a weakness. They had even added enough utensils to their inventory to eliminate much of the inconvenience that had accompanied their eating. One batch of plates, in fact, was crystal, and there had been a jocular competition to determine the assignees.

"The Rothschilds petitioned to dine with us," Nussbaum said, receiving his dish, "but I had to inform them, regretfully, that there was no room at the table."

When he had finished apportioning the bread and quartering the potatoes that had been baked on the perimeter of the fire, Heykel handed Joseph a bowl for Sonya.

"In case she wants anything," Heykel said. "And while you're over there, corral your uncle. Wait, you needn't bother."

Busily sniffing the air, Isaac was shambling toward them like a bizarre animal that had wandered into camp. While Heykel removed the pan from around Isaac's neck for filling, Joseph went over to deliver Sonya's allotment. As he approached, he saw that Sonya's face was parchment white, and that her body was in the grip of a powerful tension.

"How do you feel?" he asked, setting her bowl down beside her.

She looked up at him. Her eyes were dilated, and seemed to be speaking to him.

"I think we'd better heat up the water," Emil said.

Joseph hurried back to tell Heykel. With the help of the comrades who were dishing up the plates, the pot of stew was removed from the fire. In its place, they suspended the cauldron of water which they had been keeping specifically for this purpose. Then, the pan in one hand and bread and potato in the other, Joseph led Isaac over to his station.

"It's getting cool," Joseph said, donning his jacket, which he had hung from a horn on the tree.

"Indeed," Isaac said, shivering in agreement.

Having splotched the sky with deepening yellow and reddish-orange pools, the sun had begun to recede behind a fusing liquid screen of hectic gold.

Joseph studied Isaac lifting his pan to his nose, evaluating its odor, and diving in with gusto, staining his beard.

"Very piquant," he said smackingly. "Excellent."

"Have another sip," Joseph said, "and I'll cut the meat up for you."

Isaac's fingers trailed phantoms through the air while Joseph fished out the morsels of pork and stranded them with his penknife, crumbled in the potato, and tore the bread apart, depositing it on the surface of the stew in fluffy wads.

"Here's a repast suitable for the Emperor of Japan," Joseph said.

"By all means," Isaac said. "Nightingales' tongues."

Dipping his hands into the pan, he submerged several puffs of bread, saturating them, and plucked one out, pressing it against his gums.

"Aay . . ."

Sonya's voice pierced the clearing.

"Aaay, aagh, God help me, ooh, oooh . . ."

Joseph had never heard such elemental screams—urgent, forceful, pushing their way up from deep within, tearing out of her throat.

"Agh, ooh, oh God . . ."

Sonya's body was arching with each spasm of pain, and the cries were louder and more frequent than before. This was it, Joseph thought. At the same time that he recognized the urgency of the situation, he felt a sense of detachment, as though he were watching the scene through a window. Before he could gather himself, Isaac suddenly jumped up, spilling his stew, and scrambled across the clearing as fast as his legs would take him, tripping once over a root, knocking over a comrade who tried to slow him down, picking himself up, and arriving at Sonya's side. There he began to circle her, wringing his hands, chanting a garbled prayer.

By this time, Joseph had risen and was making his way back to Sonya. Her cries and grunts were in the air, and the clearing had become a beehive of motion. Gideon was commanding several comrades to uncover the special bunker.

"Get him away from here," Heykel said to Joseph, pushing Isaac towards him. "He's your responsibility."

As he led Isaac away, it struck Joseph that he had not heard him pray since before the arrest.

There was a crackling of leaves and twigs to the left of them. Two comrades emerged from the woods, breathless. One was armed with a pistol.

"What's going on?" he said.

"Sonya," Joseph said.

Just then Gideon ran over to greet them.

"What are you doing here?" he demanded.

"We heard screaming," said the armed comrade.

A disturbed look crossed Gideon's face. He surveyed the clearing, noting the various preparations taking place. Then he seemed to hone his attention to the forest, as though trying to peer into it.

"We'll ask Isaac to play for us," Heykel said.

Then he addressed the sentries.

"Get back to your posts."

They turned and almost immediately disappeared back into the woods. Gideon strode off in the other direction, toward the Zionist corner of the glade, where he stopped to confer with several comrades. Joseph pointed Isaac toward the center of the clearing.

"Rabbi Isaac, how about a song tonight?" one of the Zionists spoke up.

Isaac turned toward Joseph, questioningly. The sun had dipped below the horizon, leaving behind only a halo edge.

"It's all right," Joseph said. "The rules are being suspended for the occasion."

Leaving Isaac by the fire, Joseph retreated back to his tree. Lying down on his side with his head propped up, he watched Isaac draw forth his harmonica, plant himself in a semi-crouch, and raise a tremulous melody, the notes quavering about his head like wafting leaves. As he swayed and breathed his fervor through the reeds, comrades began subduedly to sing in accompaniment.

Across the way, Sonya, in growing agony, was being transferred onto a blanket and carried into the bunker, accompanied by Emil and Rachel. Gideon also entered the bunker, emerging with a large pot which he dipped into the cauldron of heating water, filling it, and carried back to the bunker. He repeated the process with a second pot.

Joseph closed his eyes and tried to tune out his surroundings. He did not want to see or hear what was going on, and he was not in the mood for a stifled concert. Some of the comrades, he knew, were crying as they chanted. But it would not help him to hum or whisper his sorrow. He wanted to scream out at the top of his lungs, like Sonya, to bellow ragingly until he had vented all his anguish.

"What ails you?"

Joseph looked up to see Heykel standing over him.

"Nothing."

"It's always nothing," Heykel said, putting a plate of stew and a chunk of bread in front of Joseph and taking a seat.

Leaning away from him, Joseph tore the bread apart and stuck half of it in his jacket to feed the birds with in the morning.

"Why don't you unburden yourself?"

"Leave me alone," Joseph said sharply.

He felt Heykel regard him searchingly before departing. A tremor of guilt struck him. Heykel had only been acting out of kindness. His antagonism was unjustified. But Joseph had not been himself since about the time Sonya had experienced her first spurious birth throes and Isaac had taken ill in sympathy.

He was not sure exactly what had upset him more— Isaac's behavior or a dream he had dreamed, the specifics of which he could not recall. He had since thought that it might have had something to do with Isaac's being the father of Sonya's child. But Joseph could not bring himself to believe that he had dreamed this.

His mind had still been in an edgy ghetto after-haze when Gideon had dispatched Joseph one afternoon to relay a message to a patrol. As he was strolling back, stopping now and then to glean wild berries, his eye was attracted by a sunstruck plot of flowers. They were somewhat off his path, but so enticing that he ambled over to them.

There seemed to be several hundred blossoms in the patch, delicately cupped like the smooth hollows of babies' throats and palms. Some were cream brown, others were yellow ecru, or champagne white, and all were variegated with combinations of ivory, apricot, cocoa, violet, carmine and ultramarine. Gently, Joseph picked a tan posey, blotting the milk from its broken stalk on his trousers, and admired its velvety texture and vibrant mottle. Oddly, the posey had no fragrance. Yet the longer Joseph scrutinized it, the more it began to assume a personality. It was as fragile and graceful and beautifully patterned as a butterfly. He regretted having picked it.

Parking himself on the ground, Joseph examined the other flowers and perceived that each one was a butterfly on a stem and that together they were not just a random bed but a unique perfumeless lepidopteral garden.

He relinquished the idea—which until that moment he had not been wholly aware of entertaining—of harvesting a bouquet for Leora and putting it in a secret place where he could come to meditate. Instead, he dibbled up a finger-depth of earth, installed the detached posey, packed it in, and reclining beside it, his head on his arm, he fell asleep.

When Joseph awoke, it was utterly dark and a wind had risen. The posey had fallen on its side. He scratched out another hole for it amidst a clump of grass that would prop it upright. As he inserted the stem into the ground, he noticed that while the flower had become partially shrivelled, it had begun to exude an overripe scent.

Joseph was conscious of having had a powerful dream, but he could not recall it. Also, he realized with trepidation that the nap and the nightfall had scrambled his bearings. Calculating that the clearing was in the direction of the moon, he set out accordingly, enveloped by a living silence—the shrill screaking of cicadas, wild animal cries, and the incessant rustling of nocturnal elves.

Navigating celestially, his knife unsheathed, nerves and muscles tensed, Joseph was just achieving a measure of momentum and confidence when he was startled by a loud snap, followed by scuttling. Defensively, he backed against a tree.

There was a needly pause. Then he heard a whistle. He pursed his lips to respond, but his mouth was dry and he emitted a corky squeak.

"Halt."

The injunction had come from overhead.

"Who goes there?"

He thought he recognized the voice.

"Joseph," he said nervously.

A comrade sprang out of obscurity, pistol poised.

"Step away from the tree."

Joseph obeyed, and the partner who had spoken first climbed down from his perch. The pair was pleased to have met up with him, but simultaneously bothered. There was grave perturbation in camp over his disappearance. Patrols had been increased, and everyone was on the alert. He would have some explaining to do.

They escorted him back to the clearing. Heykel and Gideon pounced on him agitatedly. Was he all right? Where had he been? Why had he given them such an ungodly scare? Apologizing, Joseph claimed that he had become nauseated and faint and had therefore stopped to rest, whereupon he had blacked out. But he omitted mention of Leora and the flowers.

Heykel grabbed him by the shoulders and flapped him vigorously.

"There has to be more to it," he said. "Pull out of your trance and tell us exactly what happened."

But Joseph could only repeat his story, begging Heykel to unhand him.

"What are those stains around your lips?" Gideon asked.

"I ate a few berries," Joseph said.

"He probably poisoned himself," Gideon said.

That was the beginning, and he had been increasingly distracted and mopish since. There were periods when a clogging melancholy so overwhelmed him that he could barely function, and others when he was suddenly possessed by rancorous fantasies of vengeance. And there was nothing he could do to clear his mind. He was unable to summon up to consciousness whatever it was that had been revealed to him in his sleep. Yet it perversely refused to have its influence dispelled.

Joseph snapped to. The music had suddenly stopped, and Heykel was standing beside Isaac. In the dim light cast by the fire, his face was streaked with tears.

"Comrades," he said, "we have lost our beloved Sonya. But her love and courage will always be with us. She has given birth to a healthy boy. We shall call him Abrahm . . . "

His voice broke, and he buried his face in his hands. A comrade came forward and led him away.

As though he had understood everything, Isaac resumed playing with an inspiration greater than before. Joseph found himself softly singing along.

> *Oh strike, little hammer, oh strike,*
> *Keep driving in nail after nail,*
> *There's no piece of bread in the house,*
> *Just hunger and endless travail.*

> *Oh strike, little hammer, oh strike,*
> *The clock will be soon sounding twelve,*
> *My eyes are beginning to close,*
> *Give me your strength, God, please help . . .*

Joseph gazed up at the sky. The sun's embers had dwindled away, and the moon had taken on a shine. In the early darkness, he could already distinguish Scorpius dragging its venomous tail. A dreadful excitement fluttered his heart. While the Aryan side abided, the ghetto was extinct, and with it the life that he had known. He was in a new existence: a different person in a different world. Yet, shortly, as ever, the firmament would become midnight blue and brilliantly clustered, and he was aware from Uncle Isaac's teaching that what he could behold constituted but a minute fraction of what there was. How many partisans, he wondered, were scattered throughout the universe, in other forests, singing kindred songs?

As Isaac played his heart out, Joseph scanned the clearing, discerning not only silhouetted comrades and sylvan forms, but also illusory configurations—dancing sylphs, mobile objects, and chimerical beasts drawn to the fringes of camp by the haunting calls of the curious creature with the white-haired face and lightless eyes.

Soon he and Isaac would repose together, back to back, and he would dream about the flowers that bloomed on distant stars.

The text of this book is set in Caledonia 12/14; the chapter titles are set in Eurostile 42/48. This book was designed by Erika Rothenberg, Los Angeles, California; produced by Ripinsky & Company, Newtown, Connecticut; typeset by Pagesetters, Inc., Brattleboro, Vermont; and manufactured by Maple-Vail, Binghamton, New York.